MARK ATHERTON is Senior College Lecturer in English Language and Literature at Regent's Park College, Oxford. At present he is also Visiting Professor in English Medieval Literature at the Heinrich-Heine-Universität Düsseldorf. He is the author of *There and Back Again: J.R.R. Tolkien and the Origins of The Hobbit* (I.B.Tauris, 2012, paperback 2014). His other publications include *(Teach Yourself) Complete Old English (Anglo-Saxon)* (2010) and *Hildegard of Bingen: Selected Writings* (2001).

'This pithily written book elegantly combines the literary, historical and archaeological evidence for that most energetic and energising period of the Anglo-Saxon past, as King Alfred and his successors struggled to create a coherent England. Mark Atherton offers a fresh and refreshing perspective, full of insight, on these teetering times – where success was far from certain and disaster ever close.'

Andy Orchard, Rawlinson and Bosworth Professor of
Anglo-Saxon, University of Oxford

'The language of the Anglo-Saxons, long beloved by a succession of notable poets, has for the rest of us too often been afforded the status of a vulgar tongue. In Mark Atherton it has found a new and exciting champion. Atherton provides a rich geographical context that gives not only a sense of how the Anglo-Saxons thought of their local, closely observed, landscapes but also of how they conceived their place within a largely uncharted and perilous world. Over the whole book looms, rightly, the figure of King Alfred and his court to whom, even when all the legends have been dispelled, is undoubtedly owed the remarkable efflorescence of vernacular writings in later Anglo-Saxon England. Interspersed between chapters, the author has provided what he calls "Interludes", texts in Anglo-Saxon, with a translation in English and a short commentary. The selections are deeply illuminating, providing as they do an introduction both to the language and the "thought-world" of the Anglo-Saxon age, from the time of the migration until the reign of King Edgar and his second coronation at Bath in 973 – an occasion which, in Atherton's words, "marks the theological and political highpoint of the tenth century." Vulnerable though Edgar's kingdom was yet to prove, when faced with the returning Vikings of the eleventh century, its legacy nonetheless endured. The great corpus of Anglo-Saxon literature compiled during the reign provides an unrivalled testimony to the vitality of vernacular culture before the Conquest. Mark Atherton's illumination of this culture and its roots is both arresting and enlightening. It deserves to attract a wide readership.'

Henrietta Leyser, Emeritus Fellow and former Lecturer in Medieval History, St Peter's College, Oxford; author of *Beda: A Journey Through the Seven Kingdoms in the Age of Bede* and *A Short History of the Anglo-Saxons* (I.B.Tauris, 2017)

'Mark Atherton tells the story of the "making" of the kingdom of the English in an original, often diverting and always instructive way. He covers the period from the accession of King Alfred the Great in 871 to the death of King Edgar in 975, and in the process has to traverse some difficult ground. The leading characters play their usual parts; but they are supported here by a cast of lesser-known figures, who appear out of dark corners and then disappear again into the shadows. It is all very skilfully done, and one emerges after reading Atherton's fine book with a good impression of the reasons why knowledge of the Old English and Latin literature of the period is so central to historical understanding.'

Simon Keynes, Elrington and Bosworth Professor of Anglo-Saxon, University of Cambridge

MARK ATHERTON

The
MAKING
of
England

A NEW HISTORY OF
THE ANGLO-SAXON WORLD

BLOOMSBURY ACADEMIC
LONDON • NEW YORK • OXFORD • NEW DELHI • SYDNEY

BLOOMSBURY ACADEMIC
Bloomsbury Publishing Plc
50 Bedford Square, London, WC1B 3DP, UK
1385 Broadway, New York, NY 10018, USA

BLOOMSBURY, BLOOMSBURY ACADEMIC and the Diana logo are
trademarks of Bloomsbury Publishing Plc

First published 2017 by I.B. Tauris & Co. Ltd.
Paperback edition first published 2020 by Bloomsbury Academic

ISBN: HB: 978-1-7845-3005-1
PB: 978-1-8386-0403-5
ePDF: 978-1-7867-3154-8
ePub: 978-1-7867-2154-9

Series: Library of Medieval Studies 2

Typeset by OKS Prepress Services, Chennai, India

To find out more about our authors and books visit
www.bloomsbury.com and sign up for our newsletters.

Contents

List of Illustrations

Acknowledgements

I would like to thank the following colleagues and friends for help at different stages in the composition of this book. In particular, Francis Leneghan, Andy Orchard and Daniel Thomas read through the book and provided useful and perceptive criticism. Henrietta Leyser kindly read the whole work and gave useful feedback. Others have read sections: Andrew Moore read Part I, Greg Waite advised in detail on Chapter 5, Helen Appleton and Oliver Bock advised on parts of Chapter 1. Any errors are mine and not theirs. Julie Dyson read a very early draft and gave wise counsel; I am very grateful for her constant support.

The material has been tested at various seminars and conferences, at Cambridge, Leeds, Oxford and Winchester, and I have received useful questions or individual comments from many people, in fact too many to name, but they include: Debbie Banham, Richard Dance, Carolin Esser-Miles, Paul Fiddes, Vincent Gillespie, Tony Harris, Alison Hudson, Simon Keynes, Ryan Lavelle, Heather O'Donoghue, Daniel Orton, Winfried Rudolf, Barbara Yorke. Teaching undergraduates and post-graduates in recent years at Oxford University and at Sarum College, Salisbury, has also helped me to formulate my ideas.

The foundation for this book was laid on an MA course in the 1990s at the University of York, where I had the privilege of being taught by S.A.J. Bradley, Martin Carver and Edward James, before I went on to doctoral work in other areas. The later inspiration was the Centre of Anglo-Saxon Studies at Manchester University, where I worked for two years for the research project *Fontes Anglo-Saxonici*. I would mention in particular Gale Owen-Crocker and Donald Scragg, as well as Alex Rumble, Nick Higham and the late David Hill, who organised the many exciting inter-disciplinary conferences at Manchester on various aspects of Anglo-Saxon culture, history and literature.

Thanks are due to Susannah Jayes for her research on the illustrations, and to Bill Prosser, artist in residence at Regent's Park College, Oxford, who helped in the selection of the images. I am grateful to Alex Wright at I.B.Tauris for his ideas, encouragement and editorial advice.

A Note on Modernised Spellings

For quotations from Latin, I will follow the model of Latin dictionaries and textbooks and distinguish consonant 'v' from the vowel 'u'; so whatever edition or text I follow, I will write *via* 'road, highway' rather than *uia*. For quotations from Old English (Anglo-Saxon) I will sometimes modernise and sometimes quote the original spellings.

When the Old English language was first written down on parchment by churchmen in the seventh century, they used the Roman alphabet. However, they also had a problem, because some Old English sounds did not occur in Latin, and the spelling system had to be adapted for their purpose. So, for example, in order to represent the consonant sounds of the nouns *edge* and *ship*, which do not occur in the Latin language, Old English writers wrote *ecg* and *scip*, using the letter combinations *cg* and *sc* to render the same values as modern English *dge* and *sh*. A similar problem was met with 'th', the second consonant in words like *bath*. Sometimes 'th' was actually used, but very early in the Anglo-Saxon period two new letters were devised:

Þ / þ, a letter deriving from the rune called 'thorn';

Ð / ð, called 'eth', an adaptation of the Roman letter 'd'.

At the same time, a unique vowel sound was also given a new symbol. Æ/æ is a high open sound, like the vowel heard in southern British

English 'cat'. Here are some examples of these letters used to form familiar words, with their modern equivalents:

æsc, bliðe, broðor, cræft, fisc, forð, græs, hrycg, hwæðer, pæð, scyld, swaðu, þegn, þenceð, þing, þritig

[ash, blithe, brother, craft, fish, forth, grass, ridge, whether, path, shield, swathe, thegn, thinketh, thing, thirty]

To make some words and concepts more instantly recognisable, therefore, I will occasionally modernise the *thorn* and *eth* by writing 'th', as in present-day English.

The same *ad hoc* approach will be used for personal names. Sometimes we will dwell on the meaning, for instance of the names of the West Saxon royal family beginning with *Ead-*, meaning 'blessedness, prosperity', a singularly positive notion for a king and 'blessed guardian' of the nation such as *Eadweard*. Other examples include the names of the two royal brothers *Eadwig*, 'blessed battle', and *Eadgar*, 'blessed spear', or the name of their grandmother *Eadgifu*, 'blessed gift'. Sometimes, however, it makes more sense to modernise the name: this is already common practice for names still in use such as Edward and Edgar, but I will also modernise *Eadwig* as Edwy and *Eadgifu* as Ediva, since these are closer to how the names sounded on the tongues of tenth-century speakers of English.

In short, by modernising Old English names, important words, and some of the shorter quotations, and by periodically reminding readers of pronunciations, my aim is to make the texts more accessible to a wider audience, whether or not they have any familiarity with the language. Since I envisage some readers using this book selectively, choosing a chapter or section to read more closely, I will draw attention to these various points again, at appropriate places in the book.

INTRODUCTION

Helmet and crown

The Sutton Hoo helmet depicted on the cover of the present book was found in East Anglia, in a large seventh-century ship in a burial mound, among an assemblage of weapons and treasure. The ship had been moved up the river Deben and then dragged across country, to be placed in a barrow on high ground overlooking the estuary not far from Woodbridge. Among the other finds were spears, a princely sword, a great gold belt buckle, jewel-inlaid shoulder clasps, an iron byrnie or mailcoat, and a shield decorated with gold images. These were the trappings and equipment of a military leader, and there are Scandinavian connections reminiscent of the celebrated Anglo-Saxon poem *Beowulf*. The helmet was clearly meant to be worn by a great lord or prince. This is more than a simple round helmet; it has a hole on top to sport a tall plume, a heavy band of iron plating to protect the neck, with cheek guards and a mask to cover the face. And it is decorated with all manner of protective images. Across the mask is a bird flying up to meet face-to-face with a dragon that forms the crest of the helmet; at the tip of each wing is a boar's head; panels on the helmet depict a horseman riding down a fallen foe, and warriors dancing.[1] When the large mound at Sutton Hoo was excavated in the 1930s, it was a revelation, for suddenly the world described in *Beowulf* was seen to have a palpable reality.[2] There is a passage in the poem where the hero arms himself for the fight with just such a helmet; almost as if the poet had been at the royal court, and seen his lord wearing it (lines 1448–54).[3]

In the various early Anglo-Saxon kingdoms of post-Roman southern Britain in the seventh century, lordly masked helmets such as this were most likely the personal property of the king, no doubt used for king-making ceremonies.[4] But princely burials went out of fashion in the eighth century with the spread of Christianity. No such helmets have been found for the later Anglo-Saxon period.[5] They are, however, mentioned in literature. The kind of helmet pictured in *Beowulf* is described in other Anglo-Saxon poems; it is mentioned for instance in the writings of the poet Cynewulf, and all these poems have survived in manuscripts copied in the tenth century. By that time the fierce masked helmet was probably seen as archaic and poetic, for a new kind of royal headgear was replacing it.

A passage in the famous tenth-century anthology of religious literature known as the Vercelli Book provides a hint as to what was to come. The Old English writer of the first item in the collection, a sermon now known as Vercelli I, is seeking to explain the crown of thorns as described in John's Gospel, Chapter 19. He even uses the Latin word *corona* in his English text, then adds as an explanation that 'it was the customs of kings and emperors that they often had a golden head-band'.[6] At first sight the remark seems rather curious: surely everyone knows what a crown is? In fact, however, the ninth-century kings in southern Britain (notably the kings of the West Saxons and the kings of the Mercians) did not wear crowns. As a symbol of office, the crown first appears on English coins in the time of King Æthelstan, who, as we will see in Chapter 8 of this book, was to become the first king of a much-enlarged English kingdom from the year 927 onwards. Thereafter the rulers of England regularly depicted crowned kings on their coinage. From the time of King Æthelstan's expedition to Northumbria and Scotland in the 930s, drawings and painted portraits of crowned kings appear in Old English and Anglo-Latin manuscripts.[7] Figure 1a provides one such portrait, of Edgar, king of England from 959 to 975, crowned and sitting between his monastic supporters.

The images in literature and art correspond to actual events. Æthelstan was also the first king actually to be crowned, in a new coronation ceremony that was introduced under Continental influence. This took place at the appropriate location of Kingston-upon-Thames in the year 925.[8] At first he was 'King of the Angles and Saxons'; later the Northumbrians became a third nation and region to be ruled by this monarch. A fourth ethnic group to be ruled by the West Saxon kings of England were the Danes, descendants of farmers who had settled in the so-called Danelaw of eastern England in the wake of the Viking invasions of the ninth century. By the reign of Æthelstan's nephew Edgar, 'King of the English' from 959 to 975, the English emperor (as he sometimes saw himself) probably wore his crown at special 'crown-wearings' that took place at the festivals of Christmas, Easter and Pentecost, and it is clear that this custom was later adopted with enthusiasm by the Norman kings of England.

The transition from ceremonial helmet to royal crown epitomises the theme of this book: culturally, it moves from the 'heroic' times of Bede and the *Beowulf* poet to the 'golden age' of Dunstan and Æthelwold; politically, it charts the coming into existence of the English kingdom in the period from Alfred the Great to Edgar the Peacemaker, that is from 871 to 975. This is a narrative that begins in diversity, like Germany before Bismarck, or Italy before Garibaldi, and it ends in unity with an organised, prosperous 'nation state': with a standard written language and a rich literature, with a tightly controlled administration, an efficient system of taxation and trade, a connected patchwork of shires, and a network of towns. This story has been told before, reign by reign, though it is questionable whether it has ever reached a level of popular consciousness or general knowledge. There is still a need for this narrative to be heard, for this is the time when England became a 'united kingdom' for the first time in its history. And even in well-informed specialist studies, a consciousness of English identity is often assumed to have developed much later in history.[9] But this is contrary to the evidence of ninth- and tenth-century writings.

Where possible, the present book seeks to relate the political history of the English kingdom to the literature that was produced or read in the period; in other words, it aims to present the voices of the participants as well as their actions. What these sources reveal is the affective factor that James Campbell has referred to as the 'emotions and traditions which formed the climate of power'.[10] If they are studied closely and carefully, the documents of the period also offer glimpses of the inner thoughts and feelings of their authors and subjects, and their ideals and aspirations. These insights should also be included in a history of the Anglo-Saxon world.

***

I have written for the interested general reader, but I also have had very much in mind the student of history and the student of literature. For readers of history this book presents the story of the making of England from Alfred the Great to Edgar the Peaceable, with retrospectives and flashbacks where necessary to earlier events and earlier writers, such as Bede. We begin with the journey to Rome of Alfred's father Æthelwulf in the year 855 and that of Archbishop Sigeric in the year 990; there are many similarities, but the two journeys also cast a good deal of light on contemporary culture and ways of thinking. The aim here is to delineate the Anglo-Saxon world in terms of its geography, its world-view, its leading figures. In the early chapters, Alfred and his son Edward will take centre stage, with some attention given to powerful women such as Alfred's daughter Æthelflaed. Once we reach the time of King Æthelstan and his successors, the book will shift its emphasis to the role of the churchmen: Æthelwold – monk, bishop and reformer, and above all Dunstan – scholar, poet, artist as well as monk, abbot, bishop and archbishop, 'the ablest and best-loved figure that tenth-century England produced'.[11] As the near-contemporary illustration in Figure 1a from a book of monastic writings demonstrates very clearly, these two Benedictine reformers were very closely involved with royal power and the governance of the country in the years of Edgar the Peaceable. The picture shows Edgar wearing his crown, seated between the two churchmen; below them a monk unrolls a copy of the Benedictine Rule, which all four figures are holding, in token of their unity and cooperation.[12] The present book will end its narrative in the reign of Edgar, arguably the most successful of the tenth-century kings, whose reign consolidated the successes of his predecessors.

For readers interested in the history of English literature, this book aims to provide a frame for reading the 'makers' of English prose and poetry during a significant period in the tenth century. Some of these writers are identifiable figures: men like Alfred, who encouraged the translation of Latin works into English, or Dunstan who headed a literary school at Glastonbury, or Æthelwold the reformer, and it makes sense to study their life and work together. Others are anonymous: it should be remembered that the Exeter Book and the Vercelli Book, two of the major surviving collections of Old English poetry, were compiled in the reign of King Edgar. In fact, a whole monograph could be written on literature in the reign of that king. This book will not aim so high: it will point to the main developments and look at some case studies in more detail. It will consider what literature was produced in this period, whether in traditional verse (like *The Battle of Brunanburh*) or in modern prose (as in the writings of Æthelwold); whether in English, as in the writings associated with King Alfred, or in Latin, for example in the story of St Swithun as told by the writer Lantfred. In addition we will also take into account what was being read and studied and copied at the

Figure 1a King Edgar, crowned, sitting between Bishop Æthelwold and Archbishop Dunstan

time – texts that range from the anonymous *Beowulf* to Ovid's *The Art of Love* – for these can also reveal the thoughts and feelings and preoccupations of the period. In a relatively short book, the texts covered will be selective, but I hope also representative.

The book is divided more or less chronologically into five parts, in each case with a short introduction to the main themes and events. After each part there is a one-page timeline, and then an interlude in which a relevant text is printed with a translation. For the full story, *The Making of England* can be read from cover to cover, but some readers may prefer to focus on a particular period or personality in which they are interested, or dip into an appropriate chapter or section. For convenience, various texts, including passages from the Vercelli Book, are printed in the appendices at the end of this book. In short, this book is offered as a history of politics and literature in the long tenth century, a formative period in the history of England.

CHRONOLOGY FOR INTRODUCTION

410	Official withdrawal of Roman troops from Britain
from 450	Establishment of Anglo-Saxon kingdoms in southern Britain
500s	The time period in which the story of *Beowulf* is set
597	Italian missionaries arrive in Kent
early 600s	Sutton Hoo ship burial, East Anglia
840s	Rise of Wessex (the West Saxons) as the most important Anglo-Saxon kingdom
871–99	Reign of Alfred the Great, king of Wessex
800s	Danish Viking invasions and settlement
870s	Establishment of the Danelaw (East Anglia, eastern Midlands and Yorkshire)
890s	The Old English *Pastoral Care* and other Alfredian writings
early 900s	The expansion of Wessex into the Danelaw regions
925	Coronation of Æthelstan, king of the English
from the 920s	Use of crowned image on coins
937	Æthelstan's victory at the Battle of Brunanburh, celebrated in a heroic poem
940s and 950s	School of Glastonbury under Dunstan
959–75	Edgar, king of England
970s	Copying of the Exeter Book and the Vercelli Book
973	Edgar's second ('imperial') coronation at Bath
***c.*973**	Æthelwold writes the Latin *Regularis Concordia* (*The Monastic Agreement*)
***c.*975**	Lantfred writes his *Translation and Miracles of St Swithun*, set in the city of Winchester
***c.*1000**	Two scribes make the only extant copy of the poem *Beowulf*

Figure 1b   Map of Anglo-Saxon England

PART I

Mapping a journey through the Anglo-Saxon world

In the year 855, Æthelwulf, ruler of Wessex, a kingdom in southern Britain, set out on pilgrimage to Rome. In a series of pious acts, recorded in a number of remarkable documents that survive today in the archives of cathedrals and former monasteries, the king gave away a tenth of his lands and possessions before he departed. Leaving Wessex in the hands of his elder son Æthelbald – rather unwisely as it turned out – the king stayed away for a year, visiting the holy places in Rome and praying at the shrines and churches. Then, unexpectedly, he returned. The account of his travel home through Frankland (France) is told by Bishop Asser, the biographer of Alfred the Great (Æthelwulf's youngest son), and a few details of the journey are noted in the Anglo-Saxon Chronicle, a contemporary record. That story will be revisited later. It is a tale of unexpected marriage alliances, of desire for royal power, of rivalry and affection between fathers and sons.

In the year 990, Sigeric, newly appointed archbishop of Canterbury in the now much enlarged kingdom of England, also set out on a journey to Rome. He too was on a pilgrimage to pray at the shrines and churches of the great city, but he had the further and very specific duty that all archbishops of Canterbury had to fulfil; his purpose was to meet the Pope and receive a blessing and confirmation of his appointment. This had become normal practice for any new archbishop, and in setting out on his journey Sigeric was merely following in the footsteps of famous predecessors such as Archbishop Dunstan, who had held the see of Canterbury from 959 to 988. We know something of Sigeric's journey, as a short itinerary exists, listing the places that the archbishop saw on his travels. The text was copied in an eleventh-century manuscript, which for convenience will be referred to as the Tiberius Miscellany, after its shelfmark in the British Library where the book is now kept. The Miscellany has an added interest, as we shall see, for it also happens to contain the first English map of the world, along with a variety of texts concerned with the then-known world, the cities and their inhabitants, the flora and fauna, the weather and seasons of the turning year.

Many other people undertook this early medieval equivalent of the Italian journey. On the route to Rome, one such traveller left a book at Vercelli in northern Italy. It was a kind of commonplace book, written in Old English (i.e. Anglo-Saxon), and rather surprisingly it has survived the centuries in the cathedral library at Vercelli. Its contents – examples of which are printed in Appendix II of this book – are varied, but they include the text of *The Dream of the Rood*, a marvellous sample of the religious dream poetry of the period. It is a fortunate deposit. Had the book stayed in England it might well have been lost, for the extant manuscripts of this kind can be counted on the fingers of one hand; we know that others once existed, and some must have perished in fire or flood, while some disappeared at the Norman Conquest or the Dissolution of the Monasteries. Like its sister the Exeter Book, a similar contemporary manuscript, this anthology, now known as the Vercelli Book, provides another kind of window on the English culture of the

Figure 1c The *Via Appia Antica*, Roman road

times: the world of vernacular literature. Unlike much of Europe in the tenth century, where Latin dominated the written record, England promoted the use of the mother tongue in all spheres of life: it was used in religious and secular writings, in administration and in literature.

Travel and the culture of the Anglo-Saxon world, then, and the literature related to it, are the themes of Part I of this book. We will see that many English people in the tenth century were both literate and mobile, that they read books in their own language, that they moved about surprisingly frequently, at least if they were members of the elite. They travelled the old Roman roads, and as they did so they glimpsed the walled cities that stood out prominently in the landscape. These travellers – kings and archbishops, merchants and pilgrims – took similar routes and saw similar sights, returning to England with new experiences in order to fulfil their differing roles. In Chapters 1 and 2 we will follow in their footsteps, exploring the history and literature of the period and mapping out its geography: the contours and horizons of the Anglo-Saxon world as the people at the time knew it.

CHRONOLOGY FOR PART I

CHAPTER 1

'The Italian journey'

THE STARTING POINT

> Now there was in Heorstan's neighbourhood an island belonging to the
> royal court, which the English called by the old name of Glæstonia, with its
> curving shores spread wide, surrounded by waters filled with fish, and by
> rivers and swamps; it was suited to the many requirements of human need,
> and, more importantly, dedicated to the holy service of God.
>
> (B., *Life of St Dunstan*)

Glastonbury in Somerset, Glæstingabyri in the Old English language,
was one of the chief centres of literature and the arts in tenth-
century England. Dominated by its mysterious steep-sided tor, looking
like an island surrounded by the marshy water of the Somerset Levels,
it was a place of ancient roots, and the site of the oldest monastic
house in Britain. This monastery was the alma mater and spiritual
home of Dunstan, who was to serve as archbishop of Canterbury from
959 to 988, a key statesman and man of letters in the long tenth
century that forms the subject of this book. Dunstan, acerbic, poetic,
and musical, is an appropriate personality to emerge from Glastonbury, and later chapters in Parts IV and V will be dedicated to his life
and work. As a politician he had many supporters, and one of these
protégés is the lesser-known but interesting figure of Sigeric, also a
Glastonbury monk, who became archbishop of Canterbury in 990, and
left an account of his journey to Rome that same year to meet the pope
and receive his blessing. We will consider the itinerary of his journey
shortly. But first we will consider what can be discovered of the
characters of this particular archbishop and his more famous
predecessor.

MONK OF GLASTONBURY AND ARCHBISHOP OF CANTERBURY

Like many personal names in the period, the names of our two archbishops had specific meanings in Old English, the language spoken at the time. Dun-stan signifies literally 'hill stone' or 'mountain rock', while Sige-ric (a two-part name pronounced broadly as 'Seeyuh-rich') means 'victory kingdom'. The meanings were felt to be appropriate. Names, for example, had significance in the epic poem *Beowulf*, where the royal ancestor of the Danes is Scyld, because metaphorically he is the 'Shield' of the nation. And the hero himself appears to be named 'bee wolf', perhaps a riddle or kenning for a bear, a man with bear-like strength, perhaps an echo of a lost folk tale of a 'bear's son'.[1] Such 'literary onomastics' was used in the study of the Bible, and is still found in names such as Josiah Bounderby or Mr Bumble in Dickens and other modern novelists.[2] In tenth-century England, the same principle held for contemporary names as well as those of historical tradition and poetry. The Anglo-Saxon ruling elite named their children according to longstanding family traditions, but these 'speaking names' were often commented on by contemporary biographers, particularly if their subjects fulfilled the promise latent in the name. Two of Dunstan's biographers commented on the name as a symbol of immovability and persistence.[3] Another example is Dunstan's colleague and fellow reformer, Æthelwold, later the bishop of Winchester, an equally important political figure in the history of tenth-century England. According to his contemporary biographer Wulfstan Cantor, writing in Winchester itself, Æthelwold's name meant 'noble will' or 'good will' in the sense of *benevolence*, and Wulfstan considered it highly appropriate to his subject's character.[4] The contemporary Anglo-Saxon Chronicle, which incidentally was also written at Winchester in this period, followed suit, describing the bishop as *se welwillenda* literally 'the well-willing', the man of good will, the benevolent bishop.

Did Sigeric also live up to the promise of his name? The sources for Sigeric's life lack detail, but such as they are they allow us some insights into the kind of man that he was. If we do not apprehend his personality, we can at least view the various dynamic roles that he played in the cultural and political life of the kingdom. He began as a monk at Glastonbury, and his last will and testament provides evidence of the affection that he felt for the place where he started his career; on his death in 994 he left to his former monastery a set of seven wall-hangings depicting white lions. Every year on the anniversary of Sigeric's death the

Old Church at Glastonbury was decorated with these hangings in his memory. Evidently he was well regarded in his former home monastery. It is that likely that Sigeric also received his education at Glastonbury – he may have attended the flourishing school, one that had been so invigorated by the teaching of Dunstan (for some accounts of the curriculum and life of the monastery, see Chapters 10 and 11).

Dunstan left Glastonbury in the year 956, after falling out with King Edwy, and he spent a period in exile before his triumphal recall by King Edgar in 958 and then his appointment as archbishop of Canterbury in 959 (see Chapters 12–14). Sigeric was just about old enough to have benefited personally from Dunstan's teaching before the great scholar departed for the Continent.

Whatever his actual age when he became an oblate or monk at Glastonbury, Sigeric certainly knew of Dunstan as a scholar and as a practitioner of the arts, for this was Dunstan's lasting legacy in Glastonbury. The anonymous cleric 'B.', who was completing his biography of Dunstan in the early 990s at the time when Sigeric served as archbishop, praises the achievements of Dunstan's school. It was like a vine, he says, bearing wholesome fruit (B., *Life of Dunstan*, ch. 15.2–15.3).[5] Although B. does not name the many Glastonbury *alumni* fostered by Dunstan, he emphasises that they went on to high positions in the kingdom, and it is possible to identify some of these figures from the records. B. also takes especial care to emphasise the quality of Dunstan's literary activities at Glastonbury through various stories and

Figure 1d   Glastonbury Tor in the present day

anecdotes. He highlights, for instance, Dunstan's youthful promise, and the envy as well as admiration that the young Dunstan provoked. Sigeric had perhaps heard some of these stories concerning the youthful exploits of the most famous *alumnus* of their monastery.

We will consider these narratives again in their appropriate place in this book, but one anecdote is worth relating at this point. As a young man, according to B., Dunstan studied at Glastonbury, and then became associated with King Æthelstan's court (which was not fixed in one location but moved around various centres in Wessex, including Dorset, Somerset and Devon). Dunstan soon gained a reputation for being a wide reader in an age when very few people were wide readers; this in itself was unusual and made Dunstan stand out as different or exceptional. And then as a pupil, Dunstan had met and studied with Irish pilgrims who came to Glastonbury because of its associations with St Patrick. Ireland at this time had a reputation for theology and scholarship, and B. reports that these Irishmen brought books with them. Such visitors certainly brought their language with them too, since some of the English medical texts and charms copied in the tenth century contain snippets of Irish.[6] But to be of use to English readers their writings were almost certainly in Latin, and they were perhaps composed in the characteristic 'Hiberno-Latin' used by Irish writers of the time. These books not only stimulated genuine intellectual inquiry in the young Dunstan, they were also the means, according to B.'s account, by which Dunstan could contemplate and commune with God. But members of Dunstan's kindred at the royal court found all this suspicious. B. speaks of tales going around that Dunstan was dealing in suspect books, learning the 'songs of ancestral paganism' or, worse still, the 'incantations of magicians'.

One wonders what these esoteric texts were that Dunstan was reading. Was Dunstan reading the classics of ancient Rome? There is an intriguing ninth-century school book associated with Dunstan that contains the text of Book I of the Roman poet Ovid's *Art of Love*; the handwriting of a contemporary annotator (known for convenience as 'Hand D') is still visible in the manuscript. This scribe, who is likely to be Dunstan himself, copied the final passage of Book I of Ovid's work which he found was missing from the manuscript (see Chapter 11). Alternatively, do the 'songs of ancestral paganism' also include the native Old English poetry, poems in the style of the epic *Beowulf*? Were they copies of Old English verse such as the rather effusive debate between a Christian and a pagan known today as the poem *Solomon and Saturn*? Or perhaps the Old English *Metres of Boethius* translated and adapted from the *Consolation of Philosophy* by the late Roman philosopher Boethius? Whatever Dunstan actually was reading and copying, the charge of paganism was unfair, the product of envy of the young scholar's success.[7]

The lies, or 'barking of dogs', as the anonymous B. calls it (the motif of dogs is a recurrent theme), soon reached the ears of King Æthelstan, who had Dunstan banished from court. This was the moment that Dunstan's hostile kinsmen were waiting for – they now had the pretext they needed to express their envy in violence. Their motivations are not completely clear, but these assailants were presumably young men too, and the account reads like one of youthful rivalry turned sour. As B. tells it, they ambushed Dunstan on the road and overpowered him, tying his hands and feet before hurling him into the muddy marshes at the edge of the river. (This was after all the Somerset Levels, and before the extensive drainage schemes of later centuries there were plenty of waterways and marshy swamps for their purposes). They kicked and trampled on the hapless Dunstan, leaving him humiliated, and covered in the black mud of the marsh. Here is the continuation of the story as told by B. (ch. 6.6):

> When they had gone away, he somehow managed to get out of the mire of the river, looking as though he had been coated in pitch, and went to a friend's house a mile away, hoping to wash there. But as he approached, his friend's fierce dogs met him, and, thinking him in this state more monster than man, attacked him with hostile barks. However, when they heard him coaxing them, they recognised him from his voice alone, and fell silent.

A theme of metamorphosis runs through this passage. His kinsmen have become dogs, and Dunstan himself even reminds us of Grendel in the epic *Beowulf*, for he has been transformed into a creature of the fen, *magis monstrum quam hominem* ('more of a monster than a man'), barely recognisable to the real dogs that he knows so well from previous visits to his friend's farmhouse. As illustrations in tenth- or eleventh-century manuscripts demonstrate, dogs in this period were not small and cute: big wolfhounds seem to be the norm in the pictures of the Harley Psalter, or indeed in the rural scenes of the work calendar in the Tiberius Miscellany (see Chapter 2). Eventually of course Dunstan managed to pacify these dogs, of both kinds, and the biographer B. reports Dunstan's ironic comment on the paradoxes of this incident:

> He drew a deep sigh, and said to himself with a groan: 'O the fierce madness of my kinsmen that changed from human affection to such a doglike

savagery! For dogs, irrational by nature, have by their wagging tales shown me a human affection; but my kin, their humanity forgotten, took on the aggression of troublesome dogs.

The question of whether or not the *cynocephali* (the monstrous human creatures with dog-like heads which were believed to exist in remote regions of the world) had human souls may lie behind this passage.[8] This kind of interest is very evident in the Tiberius Miscellany, as we shall see in Chapter 2. What the 'monster episode' also demonstrates is both the energy and the irascibility of the young Dunstan. But this shining new light, who made many enemies, eventually became a successful archbishop of Canterbury and, as we will see, a powerful administrator and chancellor-like figure in the reign of Edgar, who became king of England in 959.

We cannot be sure whether Sigeric as the protégé of St Dunstan resembled his spiritual father in character. But Dunstan was evidently impressed with Sigeric's abilities both as a monk and as an administrator. In 980 Sigeric was elected as abbot of the monastery of St Augustine's at Canterbury; this – alongside Glastonbury – was another ancient monastic house, already centuries old by the time Sigeric took up his post. And he was consecrated abbot by no less a person than Dunstan himself, who now had an ally in the neighbouring house, for as archbishop of Canterbury, Dunstan was based at Christ Church, the actual cathedral just inside the urban walls, while St Augustine's was a short walk away outside the city. But Dunstan had further promotions in mind for his younger colleague, and he was instrumental in securing for Sigeric an episcopal appointment. In 985 Dunstan presided at the consecration of Sigeric as bishop of Ramsbury, a position that he held until he in turn became archbishop in 990. The first significant action that Sigeric carried out as archbishop was to travel to Rome to receive from the Pope his pallium, his insignia of office. And, exceptionally, the record of his journey has survived.

AN ANGLO-SAXON MAP OF THE WORLD

What did the world look like to people in tenth-century England? A collection of texts in an eleventh-century manuscript, a miscellany of geography, cosmography and historical fact, illustrated in full colour, offers its contemporary perspectives on the Anglo-Saxon world. Now held in the Cotton collection of the British Library, at shelf-mark Tiberius B. v, it contains the earliest English *mappa mundi*, an attractively coloured but schematically structured map of the whole world. When this Tiberius Miscellany was first compiled, the map perhaps served as a kind of visual summary of the geographical lore and historical information contained within it.[9]

In outline, the map resembles the better-known and much larger Hereford *mappa mundi* of the thirteenth century.[10] In both these medieval maps, and unlike the orientation of most modern ones, the east is located at the top and the north to the left. In the middle and a little to the right is Jerusalem, the Holy City, just above the Mediterranean, or Middle Sea; further up is the ancient city of Babylon. Across the sea and down the page, towards the west at the bottom of the map, there is a rather bulky Italy, without the recognisable boot-like shape that it has on modern projections or satellite pictures. Here Rome stands prominent, once the centre of an empire but now the seat of the most famous bishop of Christendom, the spiritual heir of St Peter. In the bottom left-hand corner may be found the islands, afloat, as it were, in the Great Ocean that encircles the known world. Three are named: Tyleni (Thule, probably Iceland), Hibernia (Ireland), and their larger neighbour Britannia or, as spelled here, Brittannia.

At first sight this Britain is barely recognisable, if only because it appears too big in relation to the rest of the world as shown on the map. But once the left-to-right orientation is taken into account, it will be seen that the basic shape of the country is accurately depicted. The large size betrays an Anglocentric bias.[11] It suggests that the artists were more familiar with Britain and the lands of the north than they were with Italy or Spain or the rest of continental Europe, let alone Asia and the exotic wild places towards the top and right of the map, where dwelt the marvellous creatures and the monsters. Certain details, however, are a little inaccurate in the representation of Britain and its neighbours. Thule or Iceland is a small island very close, in fact rather too close, to Scotland, and the archipelago of the Orkney Islands is vast.

Despite the use of earlier models, however, this is an eleventh-century map, which reflects the late Anglo-Saxon political situation. As far as southern England is concerned, only three towns are marked: London, originally Roman *Londinium*, the most important port in the country; *Cantia*, once a Roman city but now Canterbury, the centre of the English church since the time of the Italian Augustine's mission to Kent in the year 597; and *Wintonia*, i.e. Winchester, originally the lesser city of *Venta Belgarum* but now – five centuries later – the centre of power of the West Saxon dynasty that ruled the country. The older

Figure 1e   Anglo-Saxon *mappa mundi*

origin of these three English cities is significant, for Europe was not a
new society at this time. It stood, often literally, among the ruins of a
far more ancient, and in many respects more technically advanced,
predecessor, imperial Rome. In general, within England itself and in
parts of Europe, the main towns were connected by the old Roman
roads, built on solid foundations and designed to drain off the excess
water and the clogging mud. This is the country as depicted in the
Tiberius *mappa mundi*.

A map such as this is rare in the period, and its purpose is to convey knowledge rather than practical advice for travel.[12] If the latter was needed, travellers eschewed maps and instead conceived of journeys as narratives. Sea voyages required nameable ports, havens, and prominent landmarks along the coast. A famous report made to King Alfred at the West Saxon court narrates the voyages along the coast of Norway and Lapland of two traders and seamen Ohthere and Wulfstan. Their voyages are marked by features of the coastline that they see and by the names of the tribes of Lapplanders that they meet (see Chapter 7). Similarly, land journeys needed an itinerary, a list of destinations on the road you travelled, so that you knew what to aim for each day.[13] Such information was normally acquired through experience and passed on by seasoned wayfarers; it seems that the old routes and pathways were learned by heart and rarely written down.

Exceptionally, however, our Tiberius Miscellany with its world map offers two examples of written itineraries, for it contains the lists of places visited by Archbishop Sigeric on his visit to Rome in the year 990. This famous churchman also features in the historical section of the manuscript; his name is the last to be entered in an episcopal list, a catalogue of names of the archbishops of Canterbury, from Augustine to the then-present day. Evidently Sigeric was in office as archbishop of Canterbury at the time when the text was originally written. What we have in the Tiberius Miscellany therefore is an eleventh-century copy of texts written or anthologised in the 990s, perhaps shortly after Sigeric's return from Rome.

THE TWO ITINERARIES

Of the two itineraries or travel guides, if that is not too grand a title for such brief texts, the first enumerates the sacred sites that Sigeric visited in the city of Rome, where he could spend time in prayer and meditation as befitted a bishop or archbishop on pilgrimage. At Rome itself, on the Vatican Hill, was the establishment known in Latin as the *Schola Saxonum*, or Saxon School, and in Old English as *Angelcynnes scole*, the School of the English. Originally intended to house Anglo-Saxons serving in the militia of Rome, it offered accommodation and special provision for travellers from Anglia (the Latin name for England that was used in the texts). For example, when Burgred, ruler of the English kingdom of Mercia from 852 to 874, was driven out by the Vikings, he spent the rest of his life in exile at the

English School, and after his death he was laid to rest at the church significantly named St Mary-in-Saxia. Here is the Anglo-Saxon Chronicle's brief report on his *obit* as it appears in the Old English:

> he for to Rome ond thær gesæt ond his lic lith on Sancta Marian ciricean on Angelcynnes scole
>
> [he travelled to Rome and settled there, and his body lies at the Church of Saint Mary in the English School.][14]

Angelcynnes scole was known also by the Old English word *burh* or *burg* meaning 'stronghold' (a word surviving in present-day place-names and in the modern word *borough*), and this alternative name for the English School has persisted down the many centuries, so that even the present-day street recalls this distant aspect of Anglo-Italian relations. As Wilhelm Levison, author of a classic account of the connections between Britain and the continent in the eighth century, reminds us:

> How many Englishmen who pass the Borgo Santo Spirito, walking from the Ponte Sant'Angelo to St Peter's, are aware that they are crossing a district which was originally an English 'borough'?[15]

In the ninth century King Alfred negotiated with Pope Marinus (882–4) to free the English School from taxation. As a *burh*, the English School was a safe place to stay, fortified and well-guarded, and Sigeric is likely to have stayed here.

After the audience with the Pope, and after visiting the sacred sites, Sigeric's eyes turned northwards for home. His journey back again across Italy, the Alps, Francia or Frankland (i.e. France), and so to the Channel is the subject of the second itinerary in the Tiberius Miscellany:

> Rome ... Sutri ... Bolsena ... Siena ... San Gimignano ... Lucca ... Pavia ... Vercelli ...

These are some of the eighty stations on his route, and he perhaps covered twenty to twenty-five miles per day.[16] As he crossed the Alps he went through Aosta, Bourg St Pierre, Vevey, Lausanne, and then into France, passing through Besançon, Grenant, Brienne, Fontaine, Châlons sur Marne, Rheims, Laon, Arras, Guisnes and finally Sombre, which is near Wissant in northern France. There, a ship – no doubt similar to those dragon ships depicted in the eleventh-century Bayeux Tapestry – brought the travellers back across the Channel to England.

The road was well travelled. It seems that the stations along the route were accustomed to dealing with English travellers, as well as other pilgrims from the north, and catered for them deliberately. As Sigeric made his long way home he received hospitality at each stage of the journey. Furcari, for instance, now the ruined Forum Casii, had a hospice for pilgrims to stay known as Santa Maria de Forcassi. For Christian pilgrims there was also opportunity to commemorate the holy men and women of Christian history as the journey progressed. At Bolsena was the church of St Christina, a popular saint; the relics of St Margaret, another saint venerated in England from the tenth century, were also present in the region. Two stops later was the famous hospice attached to the monastery of St Peter in Campo di Val d'Orcia, at Abricula, or present-day Bricola. Sigeric's homeward journey evidently took him north-westwards, heading through Lombardy for Pavia, where there was the hospice or lodging house of S. Maria Britonum, which, to judge by its name, was a popular inn for travellers from Britain. And so to Vercelli, home of the famous Vercelli Book (more of which below). Next came the steep-sided Aosta valley flanked by high mountains, the small medieval town of Aosta being the birthplace of Anselm, a later archbishop of Canterbury, famous for his theology and philosophy in the Norman period. Then up through the Great St Bernard Pass and over the Alps into Burgundy and France, the land of the Franks.

Almost literally following his famous predecessor Dunstan's footsteps on the route to and from Rome, Sigeric fostered political and ecclesiastical links as he passed through Flanders, an independent region ruled by counts and the last stopover on the journey back to England from the Continent. A letter from Abbot Falrad of Saint-Vaast in Arras (now in Artois, the French part of Flanders) to Æthelgar (who succeeded Dunstan as archbishop from 988 to 990) shows how this reforming abbot claimed close friendship with Dunstan. Falrad had perhaps met Dunstan during his exile in 956–7; the letter shows him seeking to foster good relations with his successor.[17] This was border country, disputed between Flanders and France, and Abbot Falrad, supported by the ruler of Flanders, Count Baldwin IV (988–1035), was in the middle of a hostile struggle for independence from the local bishop, Rothard of Cambrai (in office c.976–95). Such disputes between abbot and bishop over local power were common in the Middle Ages, but this one was particularly acrimonious; at one stage the abbot's men even set fire to the bishop's fields. Being Æthelgar's successor, Sigeric evidently became involved, one indication being his itinerary of 990–1, which shows that he stayed at the Abbey of Saint-Vaast shortly before he returned to England.

OTHER ROADS FROM ROME

Some pilgrims will have taken the northern route past Lake Como and over the Septimer Pass in the central Alps and so into Germany. Brescia to the east of Milan was clearly a stopping-off place for such travellers; the nunnery of San Salvatore (later Santa Giulia) was founded back in 753 by Desiderius, the last king of the Lombards before they were conquered by Charlemagne. The Lombard church still stands, with its fine wall-paintings and crypt, its stocky stone pillars and rounded arches; it forms part of a larger monastic complex that has received many architectural additions over the centuries. Situated in narrow streets near the old Roman amphitheatre, Santa Giulia is now a museum rich in Roman, Lombard and medieval archaeology. In the ninth century its elaborate architecture must have made a strong impression on visitors from the north.

Prominent Anglo-Saxons visited the monastery at Brescia. The historian Simon Keynes has highlighted the importance of some interesting entries in a manuscript from the library of San Salvatore. Inscribed in the *Liber Vitae* or *Book of Life* – basically, a list of friends of the monastery to remember in prayer – are two sets of English names commemorating men and women who had stayed there on a similar journey to that of Sigeric.[18] These are no ordinary people, for the first set of names includes 'Ædæluulf rex Anglorum', while the second includes 'Burgureth rex' and 'Adelsuith regina'. These names have already been mentioned. 'Ædæluulf' is a continental spelling of Æthelwulf, while *rex Anglorum* means 'king of the English'; this must be the very Æthelwulf who was king of the West Saxons and the father of Alfred the Great. It is likely that he stayed at the monastery on his way to and from Rome in 855.

Beneath Æthelwulf's name in the list entered in the Brescia *Book of Life* is the name and title 'Marcoardus abbas'. Abbot Marcward had formerly been a monk of Ferrières before taking up the abbacy of Prüm in the Ardennes in 829. He had retired in 853; but because of his connection with Carolingian royalty, and because of his knowledge of the route to Rome, he may have been sent to accompany the royal visitors on their Italian journey.[19] With some effort, Marcward's dialect may have been vaguely understandable to the English travellers, for Old English and Old High German are non-identical twins, offspring of the same parent language, Primitive Germanic. Perhaps Marcward also knew some English, but no doubt the guests chatted to their amiable hosts in colloquial Latin, for English was by no means the lingua franca that it has since become for travellers in the modern world.

Figure 1f   Monastery of Santa Giulia, Brescia, Italy

The other royal names from the second set of entries in the *Liber Vitae* at Brescia are those of Burgred, King of the Mercians, who fled Mercia for Rome in 874, and his queen, Æthelswith, who so happened to be the daughter of Æthelwulf and therefore King Alfred's sister. Burgred, as we have seen, departed this life in Rome; his wife is recorded as ending her days in Pavia in the year 888. The presence in Brescia of such royal pilgrims from England is noteworthy. In fact there are political reasons for their visit, since San Salvatore at Brescia was a nunnery with strong connections to the Carolingian royal family, with female members of that dynasty being placed in charge of the house. In addition, Brescia also had links with the dependent monastic house in Pavia known as Sancta Maria Britonum, which, as we have seen, took a special interest in caring for pilgrims from Britain.

THE VERCELLI BOOK

The small town of Vercelli in the north of Italy just south of the Alps was another refuge for Anglo-Saxon travellers journeying to and from Rome. Archbishop Sigeric probably stayed there, for Vercelli is the forty-third item in the itinerary of his journey back to England; he perhaps lodged at the *Hospitale Scottorum*, a pilgrims' hospice (i.e. a lodging house) with Irish connections, the name Scotti originally referring to the Irish.[20]

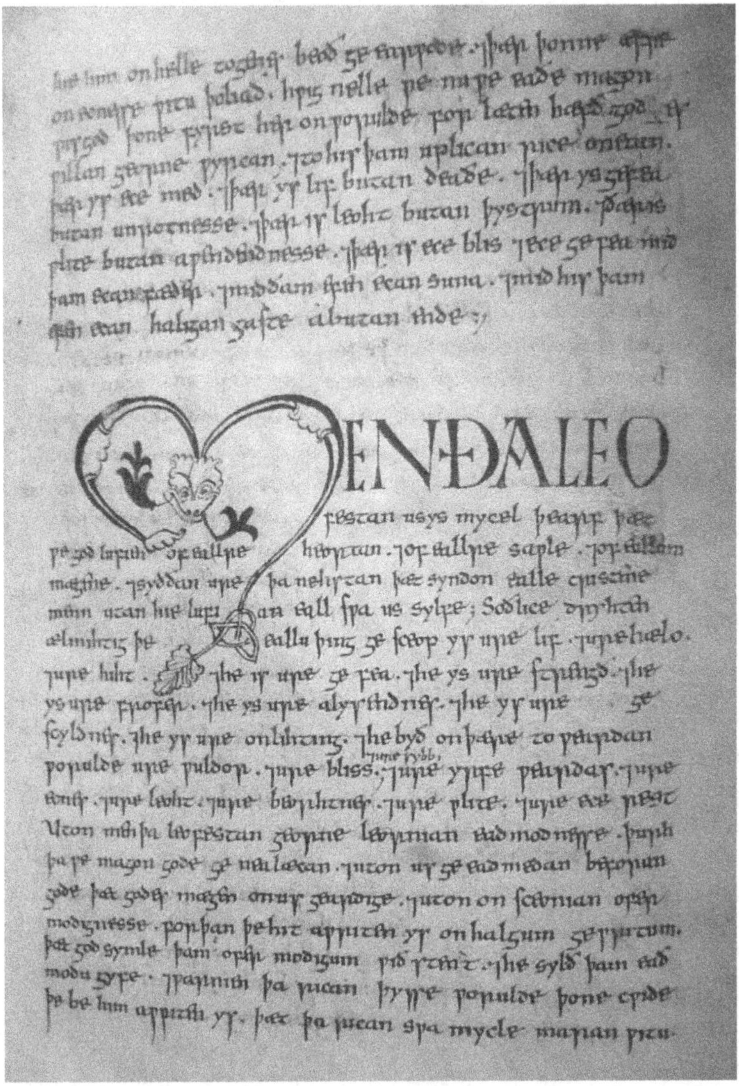

Figure 1g   Homily XXI: Folio 112r from the Vercelli Book

Here in Vercelli, at some time around the year 1000, someone –
presumably an Anglo-Saxon pilgrim – deposited a book of English
religious poems, sermons and saints' lives in the cathedral library. The
book in question is now known formally by its shelf mark as Vercelli,

Biblioteca Capitolare C. xvii, but more usually and informally as the Vercelli Book. Like the Tiberius Miscellany, it is yet another anthology put together from various sources in the libraries of tenth-century Kent.[21]

The book is still kept in the special collections of the cathedral library, housed in the archive building on the Piazza Alessandro D'Angennes near the city square on which the cathedral stands. For the present-day specialist or wandering scholar of Old English, the book is a great draw, although at first sight its appearance is somewhat plain. As is widely appreciated, some of the surviving manuscripts of the Anglo-Saxon age are magnificent works of art, the lavishly illuminated Lindisfarne Gospels in the British Library in London being a prime example, with their elaborate 'carpet pages' decorated in full colour with delicate swirls, stepwork, interlace and animal imagery. By contrast the Vercelli Book is a more practical and workaday document and does not belong in this class of rich *de luxe* manuscripts. Nevertheless, it has great literary value, being one of four so-called 'poetic codices', anthologies of literature that have survived from the period, without which our knowledge of Old English poetry would be considerably poorer. And as a physical object seen in the light of day the Vercelli Book has its attractions: a clear, neat insular script with plenty of room in the margins, and – despite the high cost of parchment – with spaces marking the end of one piece and the beginning of the next. The various poems, sermons and saints' legends are all written by one scribe, probably working at intervals over a longer period. New items are marked by a large capital letter, usually monochrome, but here and there are examples of skilled artistry in the draughtsmanship and colouring of the initials. And when you turn the page the daylight shines through it so that you can see your fingers clearly behind the fine, translucent parchment.

Broadly speaking, we can describe the Vercelli Book as a set of religious writings of various kinds. The nature of its contents can be gleaned from leafing through the opening items, all homilies or sermons (see Appendix II for some extracts). After its opening item, the collection continues with a fiery thumping sermon on Judgement Day (Vercelli II), then a calm exposition of the benefits of charity, almsgiving and fasting (Vercelli III). The fourth homily, inspired by Irish spirituality, offers stirring dialogues between the soul and the body; it is an English version of the kind of Hiberno-Latin literature that Archbishop Dunstan may have obtained from his Irish pilgrims at Glastonbury (see also Chapter 10 below). The fifth homily is concerned with kingship and tells the story of Christ's Nativity from Luke's Gospel. There follows the first of the poetic pieces included in the selection. Famously the volume contains the poem *Andreas*, composed by an anonymous writer who was perhaps influenced by *Beowulf*. Copied immediately after *Andreas* is another poem, *The Fates of the Apostles*, which pictures Christ's apostles as heroic figures in history, and towards the end of the codex, *Elene*, the story of the noblewoman Helen and her finding of the cross during the reign of her son, the Roman emperor Constantine (who ruled 306–37). Both *Fates* and *Elene* were written by Cynewulf, a technically very gifted poet, who is known also from his poems in the Exeter Book, another Old English verse anthology from the same period, now preserved in the library at Exeter cathedral.[22] But the highlight of the Vercelli Book, as far as the modern canon of Anglo-Saxon literature is concerned, is *The Dream of the Rood*, sometimes known as *The Vision of the Cross*, a meditation on Christ's death which pictures the Saviour as a warrior hero mounting the cross in triumph.

The sermons and homilies in the Vercelli Book are not as well known as the poems, but they deserve a wider readership, for they are rich in literary, cultural and even political allusions. We have already seen how comments in Vercelli Homily I can be used to illuminate aspects of tenth-century ideas of kingship (see Introduction). Vercelli Homily IX, to give another example, is another sermon of fiery rhetoric based on Hiberno-Latin models. It contains an extraordinary passage on the delights of kingship, comparing it rhetorically to the delights of heaven. These are expressed in a kind of exemplum, i.e. a short explanatory story, in this case the description of a king at the height of his powers. This monarch, with all the glory and wisdom of Solomon, sits on a golden mountain; he has in his possession all the gold and silver and rich gemstones that the world can offer, and each night the most beautiful of brides comes to him, with all the beauty of Juno, daughter of Saturn; the stones of this king's realm are all gold, the rivers flow with honey, and it is endless summer. But the joy of heaven is greater than all this.[23]

It is possible to imagine an important churchman travelling with a miscellany such as the Vercelli Book. There is in its pages plenty of other reading matter on which he could meditate, with a regularly recurring emphasis on the penitential and ascetic. A favourite theme is Rogationtide, the three-day festival of the Church calendar before Ascension Day, when people did penance in public and processed barefoot through the fields, petitioning the Lord for a plentiful harvest. Perhaps such a book suited a traveller or penitent pilgrim heading for

Figure 1h   The present-day Cathedral of St Eusebius in Vercelli

Rome. But why would he or she leave this book at Vercelli? The magnificent ancient cathedral offers a clue; it displays on its main altar a huge crucifix on which Christ figures as a crowned king triumphant; this cross was constructed during the episcopate of Leo the Great in the years from 999 to 1002/3. There are many possible coincidences here, but perhaps devotion to the cross played a role in the book's eventual appearance at Vercelli.[24]

One of the findings to emerge from the intensive research that has been done on the contents and sources of the Vercelli Book in the last thirty years is a clear association with Kent, probably with the centre at Canterbury where there were two major churches, as we have seen. Another scriptorium that could have produced this book was located at the Cathedral Church of Christ and the Blessed Virgin Mary at Rochester in western Kent. The most recent editor of the homilies favours St Augustine's Canterbury as the most likely location for the making of this book.[25] It looks like the compiler of the manuscript gathered his material over a number of years, touring the libraries of south-east England or borrowing from them, copying a poem here, a set of sermons there, and interspersing other material. He was making a personal *florilegium*, a 'plucking of flowers' from many sources, for his own personal reading. Such commonplace books were popular in the Middle Ages, for books were made of vellum or parchment processed from animal skins; even ordinary books were rare and hard to obtain. Rather than filling your library with expensive volumes, it was expedient to borrow books and write out suitable passages into your florilegium. The process is described in the *Life of King Alfred* by the king's clerical courtier and adviser Asser, the Welshman who later became bishop of Sherborne. Here Alfred asks Asser for assistance in order to make his own florilegium, moving like a honeybee from flower to flower, picking and selecting the passages for his book (see Chapter 3 below).

The Kentish connections of the Vercelli Book make it tempting to wonder whether this particular florilegium was owned by Archbishop Sigeric, who had been abbot of St Augustine's in the time of Dunstan. Perhaps he took the book with him to Rome. The suspicion cannot be proved, however, for there were many English pilgrims who travelled the road to Rome. Perhaps our pilgrim left it as a gift, or maybe by an oversight, but here at Vercelli the manuscript stayed, with only occasional signs of use by Italian readers in the twelfth century. And no wonder it was little used, for apart from a few Latin titles and rubrics, the whole of the book is written in Old English, a language that very few locals will have known (there are perhaps more Italians today who know Old English than there were in the eleventh century). The book remained at Vercelli for eight long centuries; at one point when the manuscript was rebound it was noted in Latin on the spine of the new cover that this was 'a book of sermons in an unknown language', but that, apparently, is all the attention that was paid to it.

In 1822 the Vercelli Book was rediscovered. Tales of mysterious lost manuscripts found by travellers are the tropes of modern thrillers like Umberto Eco's *The Name of the Rose*, but this is the real thing.[26] The German scholar Friedrich Bluhme came across the manuscript on his Italian journey in search of legal materials in 1822 and wrote to his historian colleagues; rumours of his discovery reached the ears of Charles Purton Cooper of the English Record Commission, who commissioned a man called C. Maier of the University of Tübingen to make a transcript. As a specialist in the history of law, Johann Caspar Maier had worked not only with Bluhme but also with Eduard Schrader, professor of law at Tübingen, visiting Italian libraries in the 1820s. Though he did not know Old English in any detail, he was clearly familiar with medieval manuscripts and evidently had a good reputation. In the end he carried out his task on a visit to Vercelli in the winter of 1833–4. His work was swift and accurate, although he damaged the manuscript with his use of a chemical reagent that he

Figure 1i   Roman road in English countryside

applied selectively to a few of the pages to make passages easier to read.[27]

Meanwhile back in England, Benjamin Thorpe, an early pioneer of Anglo-Saxon studies in the Victorian period, attempted to make the journey to Vercelli but was prevented by adverse circumstances.[28] Thorpe was just at the start of what was to be a successful career as an editor of Old English texts, but the academic study of philology was still in its infancy.[29] It was not until much later that editions of the Vercelli Book poems finally appeared, based primarily on Maier's transcript, since it seems to have been difficult in those early days of scholarship to find suitable experts willing to travel and study the actual manuscript.[30] Such is the rather indirect route by which the sources of the Anglo-Saxon world have been transmitted to the modern age.

CHAPTER 2

'On the road'

THE DANGERS OF TRAVEL

If European travel was difficult in the nineteenth century, it was decidedly treacherous in the early Middle Ages, when roads were few, and sometimes dangerous. As if to underline the danger, the Tiberius Miscellany devotes a whole section to the *Wonders of the East* (*Marvels of the East*), a description of a tour through the perilous eastern regions located in the upper part of the Tiberius *mappa mundi*. Here at the top of the page the drawing of a fierce rampant lion is perhaps all that is needed to indicate the perils of this region of the world. As for *The Wonders of the East* itself, this appears in the Tiberius Miscellany as an illustrated prose treatise in Latin and Old English. The text is divided into short sections, each describing a location and its strange, marvellous or uncouth inhabitants, and each accompanied by a picture in pen and ink, as though it is a kind of illustrated itinerary.

The content, by modern standards, is totally fabulous, but the dual-language text suggests a pedagogical aim to inform the reader about the geography and fauna of a remote part of the world, in its correct Latin terminology.[1] At first the text is innocuous enough, for the pictures show images of sheep and hens, but they are perhaps deliberately intended to lull the reader or viewer into a false sense of security.[2] In fact the four sheep are rams of a giant species, and the hens are magical and deadly, for anyone who touches them is consumed by fire.[3] In general, then, the text deals with the horrors that might lie in wait for the unwary traveller, if he or she ventures into the dangerous territory at the top of the *mappa mundi*, the eastern quarter of the then-known world.

Even in the west, in the lower part of the map, a journey to Rome was fraught with danger. There was the Channel crossing, with bad weather to contend with. Then there was the Alpine passage. Archbishop Dunstan's immediate predecessor, Ælfsige of Winchester, died of hypothermia in 958 while crossing the Alps in order to visit Rome and receive his pallium. Travellers also had to feed themselves on the journey, and a lively dispute in the *Life of St Dunstan* illustrates the difficulties. The argument breaks out between Dunstan, the acknowledged leader of the party of travellers, and the *procurator* – the Latin word refers to a steward or reeve responsible, like a quartermaster, for the rationing of their supplies. By this stage of their journey they appear to have crossed the Alps and are lodging on a monastic estate, perhaps in northern Italy, but Dunstan in his charity and generosity has used up or given away all their food, much to the exasperation of the steward:

> ... he said to his steward: 'What do you have to serve us for our food tonight?'
> He answered angrily: 'Nothing at all, since you didn't take care to hold back anything for your own use. Whatever food we thought we had you have been distributing lavishly to all and sundry!'
> The bishop said to him: 'Please don't worry unduly on this account. Christ our God is rich enough and generous to all who have faith in him.'[4]

But the worldly-wise steward is not convinced; 'it will soon be seen,' he declares, 'what your Christ will provide tonight,' and he starts his grumbles again when Dunstan goes off to pray at the hour of Vespers. But his complaints prove pointless, for soon servants arrive from the local abbot bearing gifts of food, and the archbishop's persistence is seen to be justified.

Another hazard on the road was robbery, particularly at the hands of Saracen pirates operating from a base near St Tropez, who attacked pilgrims in the Alps.[5] It is easy to see why a journey charm, which survives in another manuscript written at about the same time as the Tiberius anthology, calls on God and the saints to protect the speaker on his journey. Furnished with the charm, this intrepid traveller rides out with confidence on his chosen way, carrying a rod or staff, probably an echo of the famous verse from Psalm 23 (Vulgate, Psalm 22) 'thy rod and staff they comfort me', or a reference to a cross that the traveller holds in his hand or wears round his neck on a chain. The text ends as follows:

> Forth I go, may I meet with friends, with all the inspiration of the angels and the counsel of the blessed. Now I invoke the God of overcoming, the

grace of God for a good journey and mild and light winds upon the coasts. I have heard of the winds rolling back the water, of men constantly preserved from all their foes. May I meet with friends, so that I may dwell in the safe-keeping of the Almighty ...[6]

Perhaps the charm was chanted at intervals or stages on the journey.

Relevant here is an episode in *The Life of Edward the Confessor*, written perhaps ten years after the Tiberius Miscellany was copied. Though, strictly speaking, the incident lies outside the period covered in this book, it illustrates very well the dangers of attack on such journeys.[7] On this particular occasion in 1061 it was Ealdred – the bishop of Worcester that King Edward the Confessor had appointed archbishop of York – who was travelling to Rome to receive the pallium. But he found papal approval hard to obtain, for 'he was examined on how he had come to sacred orders' by Pope Nicholas II (in office in the years 1059–61). Nicholas was the first of several reforming popes in this period, who had ousted his predecessor Benedict X and introduced papal election by the assembly of cardinals rather than by the Italian nobles, as had previously been the case. The effects of such reforms were soon to hit England. Traditionally many bishops of Worcester had also served as archbishops of York, and these ecclesiastical positions were also important politically. The West Saxon kings of England, based in the south, liked to keep their own men in power in the north. But Pope Nicholas was averse to Ealdred holding two posts at the same time, since it was a blatant breach of canon law. Ealdred's appointment was not ratified, and he was summarily dismissed.

Accompanying the party as it set out on the return journey was an important member of the English nobility, Tostig Godwinson (*recte* Godwineson), brother of the more famous Harold who was to become king of England for less than a year in 1066. Tostig in fact was to come to a bad end after rebelling against his own brother and fighting on the Norwegian side at the Battle of Stamford Bridge in the autumn of 1066. In the previous generation, their father Godwin (Godwine) had been one of King Cnut's right-hand men, and now the Godwinsons were the most important family in the England of King Edward the Confessor. Effectively they were royalty, for many of Godwin's sons held large earldoms in England, and their sister was married to no less a person than the king himself.[8] In the group of travellers leaving Rome in 1061, then, the English king's brother-in-law Tostig was a significant figure, and he no doubt attracted much attention. With the party were two leading English churchmen: Giso, Bishop of Wells, and Walter of Lorraine, the bishop-elect of Hereford; with them too was Gospatric, an important thegn, i.e. a member of the Anglo-Saxon nobility, whose family also had royal connections. As the anonymous author of the Latin *Life* tells the story, the party set off from Rome and almost immediately 'fell among thieves', the biblical allusion to the Parable of the Good Samaritan being no doubt deliberate, and significant for the point of the story. Robbed of all their valuables and possessions, with some of the travellers even stripped of all their clothing, they retreated back to Rome. According to the anonymous author, the Pope now received them with a contrite heart, paid them compensation and undertook to grant Ealdred his pallium, on condition that he now gave up the bishopric of Worcester. This was duly agreed, and the party returned safely to England.

There is more to add to the significance of this story. As prefaces to historical works written in the middle ages often reiterate – in this respect the preface to Bede's *Ecclesiastical History* would be a good example – the genres of history and biography were considered to have moral value as guides to behaviour, providing examples to follow and pitfalls to avoid (see the preface to the Old English *Bede* in Interlude II). Our author here is no exception. We have already noted the allusion to the story of the Good Samaritan, who helps the robbed and destitute traveller. The story also shows how the Pope came to recognise the qualities of a good man like Ealdred. But the anonymous author has other messages to convey. He turns the anecdote into an exemplum of loyalty, for he tells us that when the robbers were on the point of releasing the travellers and sending them back to Rome they also demanded to know which of the richly dressed riders in the party was to be identified as Tostig, the great English nobleman. The implication is

Figure 2a   Harold Godwineson on a journey (Bayeux Tapestry)

that Tostig as a hostage would have generated a large ransom. But the thegn Gospatric, quietly signalling to the earl to ride away, claimed very loudly that he was their man. When the robbers discovered their mistake, the real Tostig was long gone, and Gospatric found himself in considerable danger, but eventually their captain decided that Gospatric's action was worthy of respect, and they released him on honourable terms.

ROMAN ROADS, ESTATE BOUNDARIES, AND WALLED CITIES

The captain of the robbers was no ordinary criminal, as the historian Frank Barlow has pointed out in his notes to the edition of the *Life of King Edward*.[9] Other documentation shows that the perpetrator of the robbery was the Tuscan nobleman Gerard, Count of Galeria, who had supported Benedict X, the deposed pope. Gerard had given refuge to Benedict when he was ousted by his opponents and thus had good reason for wanting to curb the increasing powers of Pope Nicholas. Since Galeria is situated fifteen miles north of Rome on the River Arrone, Gerard and his knights had probably ridden down the Via Clodia, the ancient high-road that was built in the days of the Roman Empire, in order to intercept the English travellers as they journeyed from Rome up the Via Cassia.

The word *via* of course means 'way', but it denotes here a Roman highway. In Anglo-Saxon England, by contrast, the word for a Roman road was *street*. The old highroads had names like Watling Street, Akeman Street, Icknield Street, names reflecting the meaning of the Latin *strata*, or *strata via*, 'paved road' or 'highway', an expression that was borrowed into Old English as *stræt*, hence modern English 'street'. In actual fact these roads are still in use: Watling Street, for instance, Old English *Waclinga stræt*, which became a significant boundary-marker between King Alfred's Wessex and the Viking-controlled Danelaw, is also known today by the more prosaic name of the A5.

Connecting Kent westwards to London, Watling Street then shoots straight as an arrow cross-country to Tamworth, the old seat of King Offa and the Mercian royal overlords of the eighth century.[10] The Roman road of Icknield Street starts at Bourton-on-the-Water in Gloucestershire and heads northwards through Bidford-on-Avon, Alcester, Studley, King's Norton, Birmingham, Lichfield, Derby and Chesterfield. The Fosse Way (named after Latin *fossa* meaning a ditch or dike, but which was also known as a *stræt* in Old English) was an impressive construction,

Figure 2b   Roman road in mountain region

starting at Exeter in the south-west and proceeding in a notably straight line north-eastwards through Bath, Cirencester, Bourton-on-the-Water, Stow-on-the Wold and then directly from Moreton-in-Marsh up to Lincoln. It is remarkable to see how place-names on the latter section of the route (now the minor road B4455 east of Coventry) contain the element 'street' or 'stret': Stretton-on-Dunsmore, Stretton under Fosse, and Street Ashton. Such settlements have their roots in the Old English period, for they were named after the *stræt* on which they were located, and places like these 'may have offered some facilities to people using the roads'.[11]

The Roman roads are mentioned relatively frequently in charters, the official documents recording land transactions in Anglo-Saxon England. In a typical charter the main text is drawn up in Latin but the bounds or shape of the estate are given in Old English so as to facilitate general comprehension: all interested parties could follow the instructions, perambulate the estate and so mark its boundaries in their memory. A fine example is the boundary clause for an estate at Alveston and Tiddington in Warwickshire from a charter issued by Archbishop Oswald in the year 985.[12] (It should be mentioned in passing that, by contrast with his later successor Ealdred, Oswald in the tenth century had no legal problem with retaining simultaneously both the bishop's see at Worcester along with the archbishopric of York.) The estate in question is very close to

Stratford-upon-Avon, a town so named because it is situated at a ford on
the river on a minor Roman road that connects the Fosse Way (which
passes through Bidford-on-Avon to the west) and Icknield Street to the
east, the major Roman route from Exeter to Lincoln.[13]

The boundary clause is printed with a modern English translation in
Interlude I. Full of topographical interest, its Old English place-names
are worth exploring for the details they provide on the estate. The word
tun, meaning 'farm, estate' (modern English 'town'), derives from a
word signifying an enclosure. The cognate word in German is *Zaun*,
with an initial 'z' (pronounced 'ts') deriving from an earlier 't', means
'fence', with an obvious connection to the idea of an enclosure. The
two estates, Eanulfestun and Tiddantun, now Alveston and Tiddington,
are based on personal names: Eanulf's estate and Tidda's estate, perhaps
the earlier owners or tenants. Otherwise the various parts of the estate
named in the boundary clause are literal descriptions of features in the
local landscape; some of these seem to be in the process of becoming
toponyms – names that derive from the topography – but it is hard to
distinguish them from descriptions. Is Claybrook, for instance a name
or a description, or more likely both at the same time? There are, for
instance, two places named Claybrooke Magna and Claybrooke Parva
between Coventry and Leicester.

In the translation I have erred on the radical side in interpreting as
many of the descriptive words as possible as toponyms. Like symbols on
a map, the names represent directly the features of the landscape.
Following the description of the route, the owners could name the parts
of the estate as they walked round its boundary. Most of these are
naturally occurring, a ford, a brook, a stream, a salt-pond (presumably
the water was brackish); other features are the results of human activity,
recent or ancient: a *dic* or ditch, a *hlæw* or old burial mound, a *hrycgweg*
or ancient ridgeway, a *stræt* or 'street', that is, the old Roman road itself.

In the Anglo-Saxon heroic poem *Beowulf* it is a surprise to find the
word *stræt* occurring as part of the description of the hero's arrival at
Heorot, the seat of the Danish king's royal hall or palace. As the
protagonist arrives in Denmark he is greeted warily by the coastguard
and tested cautiously as to his intentions. Beowulf passes muster, for his
credentials are good, and the party of splendidly attired and heavily
armed men are allowed to pass on towards the royal home of Heorot,
where they can declare their errand to the king (lines 320–4). As noted in
the Introduction, the two letters 'eth' (ð) and 'thorn' (þ) have the same
value as the 'th' sound in present-day English:

Stræt wæs stanfah,   stig wisode
gumum ætgædere.   Guðbyrne scan
heard hondlocen,   hringiren scir
song in searwum,   þa hie to sele furðum
in hyra gryregeatwum   gangan cwomon.[14]

[The highway was paved with stones, the road led
the men together. The mailcoat shone,
hard wrought by hand, the bright iron ring
sang in its armour, when towards the hall
in their fierce trappings they made their way.]

The surprise in this passage is occasioned by the idea of a stone-paved
Roman road running through the meadows of the large island of
Zealand, since the Roman legions never penetrated Scandinavia. It is one
of the features of *Beowulf* that it is set in Denmark and Sweden and
depicts a society in a distant pagan past which nevertheless has affinities
with Anglo-Saxon England. The cultural similarities range from the
central position of the hall (as a place of assembly, parley and feasting) to
the role of the king (and his relationship to his sworn men and retainers).
The original story behind *Beowulf* probably went through several oral
performances and rewritings before it became the poem as we now have
it. In the process the cultural world depicted in the poem became to a
certain degree anglicised. It is highly likely that the stone-paved road
leading to Heorot was not seen literally as a Roman road but rather as a
highway of equivalent strength and durability. The poet-author wears
his learning lightly, and he surely knew that the Roman Empire did not
reach as far as Lejre or anywhere else in Danish territory.[15]

Despite this caveat, the Old English word *stræt* literally means a Roman
road in many contexts. An example is a text in the tenth-century
anthology the Blickling Homilies. In the anonymous *Story of St Peter and
St Paul*, in a scene which takes place in the streets of Rome itself, there
occurs the phrase 'be þære stænenan stræte þe is haten Sacra uia', which
may be translated 'by the stone-paved street that is called the Sacra Via'.[16]
Similarly in the poem *Andreas* in the Vercelli Book, the *stræt* is also stone-
paved, a city street, and associated with the poetic formula *eald enta
geweorc*, the 'ancient work of giants' (line 1495),[17] the giants being of
course those who went before us, on whose shoulders we stand, to adapt
the metaphor as commonly found in twelfth-century writings. The giants,
in this sense, are the Romans. The same phrase *enta geweorc* is used a
number of times in Old English poetry, often to signify what is called a

ceaster, pronounced roughly as 'chaster' or 'chester' in the West Saxon form of Old English.

A *chester* is a Roman city, the name deriving from the Latin *castra*, meaning literally 'camp' and by extension 'settlement'. The word occurs of course in the name Chester, and turns up as the second element – *chester* in the place-names *Dorchester*, *Winchester* and *Manchester*, and as the differently spelled later medieval form -*cester* in *Worcester*, *Gloucester* and *Leicester*. It is a reminder that many of the walled towns of southern Britain are built on the foundations of Roman cities. The difference between the time of King Æthelwulf in the mid-ninth and that of Archbishop Sigeric in the late-tenth century was significant: in the intervening period the old cities had been revived, they were no longer ruins, and people were moving from the country to the city.

The new urban streets of tenth-century England, however, were to their citizens decidedly modern; they followed new grid patterns that did not correspond to the old Roman streets now buried under the dust of centuries. It was only the walls that surrounded the cities and the highways that connected the cities which were still in more or less the same state as when the Romans had built them. By the time Sigeric took up office, the process of medieval urbanisation was underway, a process that is hinted at in the image of Winchester that appears on the *mappa mundi* in the Tiberius Miscellany. The theme of Anglo-Saxon urbanisation and its significance for the making of England will be discussed further in the course of this book.

THE SEA CROSSING

It was very rare in the medieval period for any writer to attempt an autobiography, and few people, if any, kept a diary or journal. The bare record of the itinerary of Archbishop Sigeric's journey home is all that we have in the Tiberius Miscellany. It will be clear that his book (if it is indeed *his* compilation, and that cannot be proved) reads at times like a kind of concise encyclopedia, heavy on facts about the world but less forthcoming on thoughts, feelings, and impressions.

For emotional and experiential content, then, we must turn to the literature of the period. Here the classic is the unique poem *Beowulf*, the only surviving text of which was copied at the end of the tenth century from an older manuscript.[18] This tenth-century copy of *Beowulf* forms part of another anthology, which has variously been characterised as 'a book of monsters' or a study of 'pride and prodigies'.[19] The texts in this

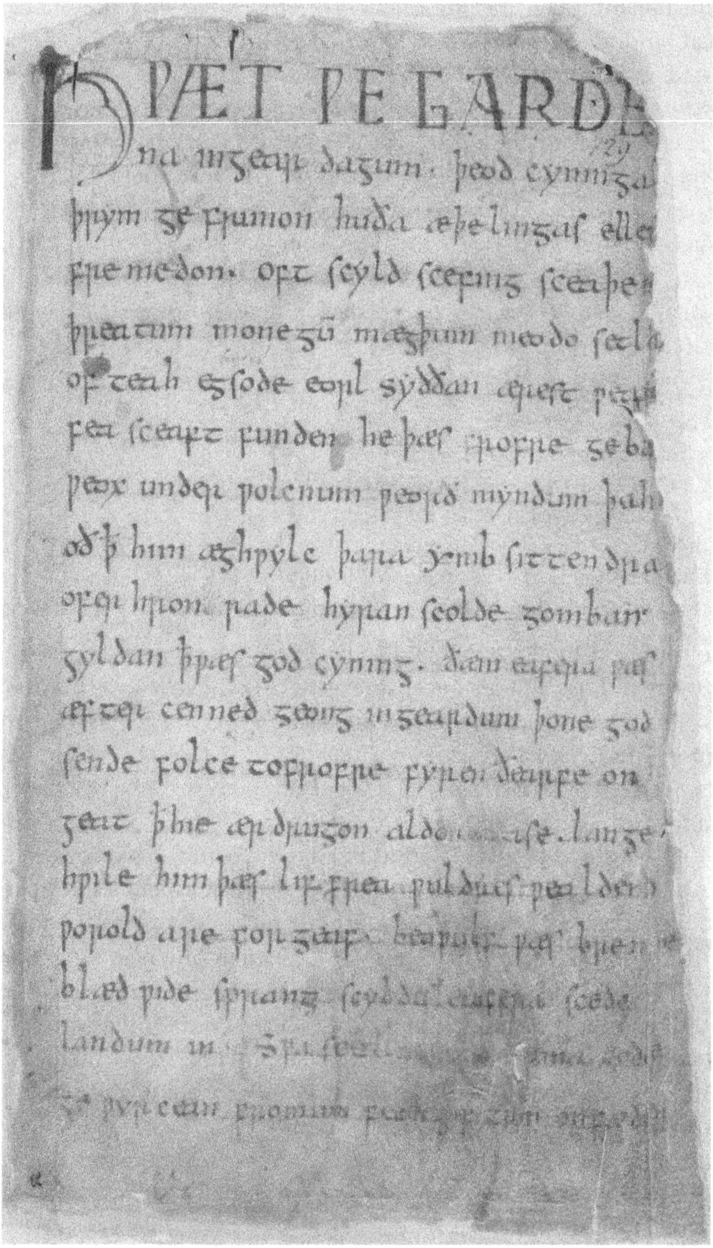

Figure 2c   The opening page of *Beowulf*

particular anthology include a story of another great king, Alexander the Great, and another illustrated version of *The Wonders of the East*; this shared text connects the *Beowulf* manuscript with the Tiberius Miscellany.

Travel, movement, and sea-voyages feature prominently in *Beowulf.* There is a momentous passage of the sea, moving the hero from his home in Geatland, probably the region north-east of Gothenburg (Göteborg) in modern-day Sweden, south to Zealand in Denmark, to take up the challenge of cleansing the hall of Heorot of its monstrous assailants. Here is a section from that voyage, in Michael Alexander's spirited version:[20]

> Away she went over a wavy ocean,
> boat like a bird, breaking seas,
> wind-whetted, white-throated,
> till the curved prow had ploughed so far
> – the sun standing right on the second day –
> that they might see land loom on the skyline,
> then the shimmer of cliff, sheer fells behind,
> reaching capes. The crossing was at an end.

The four-beat line marked by a central hiatus or caesura, the shifting rhythms and rise and fall of the line: generally the music of this passage has struck commentators over the last two centuries as peculiarly appropriate. The sea-crossing was a favourite of the scholar and writer J.R.R. Tolkien, who was a great authority on the poem, and poets such as Seamus Heaney have admired it.[21]

I have already speculated that Sigeric could have known the Vercelli Book. The dates fit well, and Sigeric in fact spent a short period as abbot of St Augustine's in Canterbury, where the Vercelli Book was probably compiled. It is likely also that he knew and read other copies of the Vercelli texts in the libraries of Kent from which they had been anthologised. These poems and prose pieces contain many accounts of journeys and sea voyages, often employing stock themes and motifs, which nevertheless can evoke the atmosphere and sensations involved. For example, in Vercelli Homily XIX retelling the story of the biblical Jonah, there is 'the great rain and strong wind and grim tempest' that arises on the sea so that Jonah's boat could move 'neither forward nor backwards'.[22] Another evocative passage is the sea-voyage from the poet Cynewulf's *Elene* (ll. 225 ff.), on folios 121a–133b of the Vercelli Book:

A throng of men, then, hastened down to the sea. Ships, the horses of ocean, lay ready along the seashore, sea-steeds moored afloat upon the sound ... eagerly along the coast-roads advanced one troop after another, and then loaded the ships, wave-horses, with battle-coats, with shields and with spears, with armoured soldiers, with men and with women. Then they let the tall ships slip spuming over the ocean wave. Many times in the surging of the sea the ship's side caught the waves' buffets; the sea resounded. Neither before nor since have I heard of a woman leading a finer looking force on the ocean tide on the sea-road. There he who watched the voyage could have seen, scudding over the waterway, the timbered vessel sweeping along under swelling sails, the sea-steed racing, the wave-skimming ship surging onwards.[23]

The passage has similarities to the sea-crossing in *Beowulf*; there is the same sense of the force and fury of the sea, even if in *Elene* the passage focusses heavily on the horse-racing imagery; and once the voyage is over the warriors step onto the beach in a scene that pictures, item by item, 'the linked corslet ... the proved sword, the magnificent battle dress, many a masked helmet and the matchless boar-effigy'. The description matches well the equipment of the high-status warrior interred in the large mound at Sutton Hoo, including the fierce masked helmet (as seen on the cover of this book). In *Beowulf* the similar moment of arrival evokes the shining cliffs, and the gratitude of the seafarers for their safe arrival, when they give thanks to God that their passage over the waves has been easy (ll. 224–8).

Among other texts, the Tiberius Miscellany contains some literature, though most of it is functional and practical, and not well known to the modern reader. There is a Latin metrical calendar, followed by astronomical information from Bede and Isidore in Latin prose, and then (on folios 24r–28v) the treatise with a Latin title *De temporibus anni*, a study of the times and seasons in Old English prose by Ælfric, the great master of Old English prose in the England of the 990s, who dedicated his Catholic Homilies to Archbishop Sigeric. His work here contains practical knowledge of the movement of sun, moon and stars and information on wind, clouds and rain; potentially this was a useful compendium for the traveller. Next in this anthology of literary works comes the astronomical poem *Aratea* by the Roman author Cicero, each constellation described in Latin hexameters and pictured on the page with a rather loosely drawn image of the pattern of the stars, juxtaposed over the image of the intended creature or object. Examples are Syrius the dog, Lepus the hare, Argo the ship or, rather, in this particular instance, a clinker-built dragon ship, in which the classical ship is given a distinctly northern European appearance (folio 40v). Following *Aratea*, after extracts from Latin writers Pliny and Macrobius, we have the *Periegesis* by Priscian, a guide to Rome that Sigeric might have found of special interest.[24] Time and the stars, wind and rain, geography and topography: these are the main topics.

THE LABOURS OF THE MONTHS

Especially striking on the opening pages (folios 3r–8v) is the illustrated metrical calendar: each page covers the period of one month and presents an image of the appropriate labour for that month, usually an agricultural task such as ploughing the fields.[25] The illustrated labours of the months provide a window on the Anglo-Saxon country year in the late tenth century: from January and February we see first ploughing and sowing, then the pruning of vines; March shows digging, raking and sowing, while April comes with feasting. From May to August there is the tending of sheep, reaping, woodcutting, and mowing, while from September to December we see pigs or wild boar feeding in the woods, falconry, smithying, and threshing. The pictures attached to these texts allow us to gauge the responses of at least one Anglo-Saxon artist to the world around him. Almost certainly these monastic artists copied their pictures not from life but from earlier models, but they drew extra details and changed certain features.

The best example of added detail is the image of the wheeled plough for the month of January; this probably represents the heavy plough that came into use in the Germanic countries.[26] It has a wheel and a coulter blade and is drawn by four oxen; a man holds the plough and guides its course while a young man in a cloak with a stick or goad encourages the oxen (see Figure 2d). The image corresponds neatly to a passage in the *Colloquy on the Occupations* by the writer Ælfric, the author of the *De temporibus anni*, the treatise in Old English on the times and seasons mentioned above. This question-and-answer dialogue between a plough-man and a schoolmaster forms part of Ælfric's Latin textbook, in use at the schools of Winchester and Canterbury around the year 1000:

> Q: What do you say ploughman? How do you do your work?
> A: I work hard, my lord. I go out at dawn driving my oxen to the field, and I yoke them to the plough. For fear of my master there is no winter so harsh that I dare linger at home, but having yoked the oxen and fastened the blade and coulter to the plough I must plough a whole field or more.

Q: Do you have any companions?

A: I have a lad who drives the oxen with a goad till he is hoarse with cold from all the shouting.[27]

The realism in this Latin conversation manual is striking; it must have considerably enlivened the teaching of Latin grammar and vocabulary in the alcoves of the cloister.

In some of the Tiberius illustrations of the labours of the months, a distinction is made between the labourers, who wear short tunics, and the thegn or nobleman who stands watching, dressed in a tunic and a fine long cloak fixed at the shoulder with a round brooch. An example is the pastoral scene for May, where the shepherd tends the sheep as he speaks to his lord, while other thegns to the right stand and watch. Such lordly figures are seen drinking from horns and wine cups in the feast scene for April while cloakless servile figures wait on their needs. In the scene for September we see a boar hunt: with two large and fierce hunting dogs (reminiscent of the scene from the *Life of St Dunstan*) and a servant blowing his horn. Here the cloaked thegn, armed with a long spear, strides into the trees where the wild boar can be seen feeding on the beechmast on the woodland floor. For October a thegn rides out to hunt with his falcon for a variety of waterfowl, including ducks and a heron. For November we see a smithy: a labourer feeds the central fire with logs while the smith places pieces of metal in the fire using a large pair of tongs; to the right, two thegns and their servant warm their hands by the fire. Winter is approaching and the end of the year, when all travel stopped because of the adverse weather conditions, which prevented any undue movement of men and horses before the onset of spring.

THE HOMECOMING OF ÆTHELWULF

As was noted above, Archbishop Sigeric's journey followed a tried and tested route that had been covered by many others before him, including members of the West Saxon royal family. Strikingly there had been King Æthelwulf, who as we saw earlier gave away a tenth of his property in a series of land grants made over a period of several months that were recorded in the charters and documents of the period. Then, in the year 855, he relinquished the West Saxon throne in order to make his last pilgrimage to Rome, leaving the kingdom in the charge of his son Æthelberht. On his journey he stayed at Brescia, where, notably, his name was recorded in the *Book of Life* of the monastery of San Salvatore.

Once at Rome he remained for about a year, then set off for home. Unlike Sigeric in the 990s, who passed through Wissant to join his ship to England, Æthelwulf was probably on the route for Quentavic at the mouth of the Canche, a traditional 'correct' route to Rome since the days of the lordly bishop St Wilfrid in the seventh century.[28] But other more exceptional events were in store, for Æthelwulf had other business before he embarked on his voyage home. The urgent matter in hand was to secure alliances by means of marriage: Æthelwulf had already been involved in such an arrangement, as we have seen, for he had married his

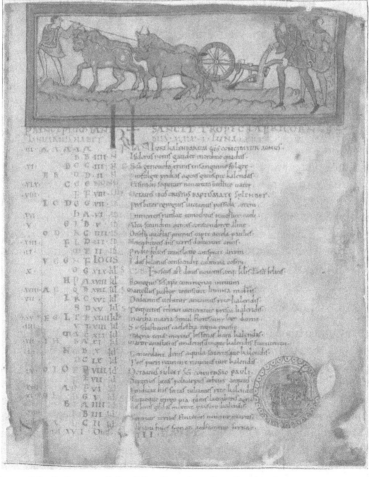

Figure 2d   Labours of the Months: the ploughman

daughter to Burgred King of the Mercians, and Burgred, subsequently deposed by the Vikings in the year 851, had ended his days in Rome.

It was now the summer of 856 and Æthelwulf broke his homeward journey in Francia. The reigning king of the Franks was Charles the Bald, who was experiencing an *annus horribilis*, a year of many troubles in his kingdom: chiefly an attack by Vikings up the valley of the Seine, and a revolt in Aquitaine in favour of his brother Louis the German. In order to secure an alliance Charles had arranged the marriage of his son Louis the Stammerer to the daughter of Count Erispoë of Britanny.[29] In July 856 he betrothed his daughter Judith to the visiting West Saxon king Æthelwulf. He had the same motive: to promote a military alliance with a dynasty successful in war. The Anglo-Saxon Chronicle, preoccupied with kings and bishops and their doings, nevertheless mentions the marriage; the notable fact was that Judith was given to Æthelwulf *to cuene* 'as a queen', rather than simply as 'the king's wife'. The title *cuen* (also spelt *cwen*) was significant for it gave the woman involved more power and status, and most royal wives in Wessex were not granted that privilege (although the situation was different further north in the English midlands, in the kingdom of Mercia). Judith, whatever her personal qualities, had other qualities to recommend her to the West Saxons. She came from an 'imperial' family descended from Charlemagne, ruler of the Carolingian Franks and Holy Roman Emperor, who was anointed and crowned by Pope Leo III at a great ceremony on Christmas Day in the year 800.[30]

From the continental perspective, the Carolingian chronicle now known as the Annals of St-Bertin provides the best account of the wedding ceremony, which took place in Verberie on the River Oise in northern France in 856:

> In July Æthelwulf king of the western English, on his way back from Rome, was betrothed to King Charles's daughter Judith. On 1 October, in the palace of Verberie, he received her in marriage. After Hincmar, bishop of Rheims, had consecrated her and placed a diadem on her head, Æthelwulf formally conferred on her the title of queen, which was something not customary before then to him or to his people. When the marriage had been sealed by mutual exchange of royal gear and gifts, Æthelwulf sailed with Judith to Britain where his kingdom lay.[31]

The Frankish chronicler's account tallies well with the report in the Anglo-Saxon Chronicle. The placing of a diadem on Judith's head was unusual and the anointing by Hincmar of Rheims was unprecedented. As a West Saxon royal wedding, this was exceptional.

But the new royal couple were in for a surprise. When Æthelwulf arrived home in England later in the year he found himself without a kingdom, for Wessex had been taken over in a *coup* supported by a prominent bishop and an ealdorman, and, worse still, it was led by his own elder son, now King Æthelbald. Asser, the biographer of King Alfred, conveys some of the shock that the returning king must have felt:

> However, while King Æthelwulf was lingering overseas, even for so short a time, a disgraceful episode – contrary to the practice of all Christian men – occurred in the western part of Selwood. For King Æthelbald and Ealhstan, bishop of Sherborne, along with Eanwulf, ealdorman of Somerset, are reported to have plotted that King Æthelwulf should never again be received in the kingdom on his return from Rome. A great many people ascribe this wretched incident, unheard of in all previous ages, to the bishop and the ealdorman alone, at whose instigation it is said to have taken place. There are also many who attribute it solely to arrogance on the part of King Æthelbald, because he was grasping in this affair and in many other wrongdoings, as I have heard from the report of certain men ...[32]

As for the son, Æthelbald, he must also have experienced a kind of shock. He had acted as regent in his father's prolonged absence, and he had perhaps imagined that the pilgrimage to Rome was an equivalent to abdication in his favour.[33] But now Æthelwulf had returned with a young bride, and unlike earlier royal marriages, this wife was a consecrated queen. And according to the Anglo-Saxon Chronicle, the people rejoiced at Æthelwulf's homecoming. The position of Æthelbald as heir apparent and acting regent was potentially under threat, for his father's marriage might produce further heirs to the throne.

But a compromise was brokered. Father and son, so Asser reports, now reached an agreement: the son would keep the western part of Wessex, while the father, with his new queen beside him, would rule in the eastern region, including Kent. In this way, according to Asser, civil war was avoided. More sensationally, on his father's death Æthelbald decided to marry his father's widow Judith (who was evidently a strong and decisive personality; later, after her second husband's death, she even returned to Europe and married into the Frankish aristocracy). The story illustrates the delicacy of the balance of power within the royal family, and it anticipates the problems that various West Saxon monarchs had to face in keeping their kingdom together, in the long tenth century that lay ahead.

THE LINEAGE OF ÆTHELWULF

Æthelwulf's journey to Rome and his return in the year 855 is recorded with characteristic brevity in the Winchester manuscript of the Anglo-Saxon Chronicle. In four sentences we are told of the generous tithing of his property, his stay in Rome, his marriage to the daughter of the King of the Franks, and his return home, to the joy of his people. (There is no mention here of his son Æthelbald's rebellion.) The chronicler now reports in sequence that Æthelwulf lived for two years and then died, that his body lies at Winchester, that he had ruled for eighteen and a half years. There follows an extraordinary passage, much longer than the five-sentence narrative just summarised, in which the chronicler lists the ancestors of Æthelwulf in a long genealogy. The list begins as follows, using the heroic and rather archaic suffix -*ing* on the end of the names to mean 'son of', so that *Æthelwulf Ecgberhting* means 'Æthelwulf son of Ecgberht' (note again the use of the letter þ to represent the 'th' sound in words like *broþur* 'brother'):

> Ond se Eþelwulf wæs Ecgbrehting, Ecgbryht Ealhmunding, Ealhmund Eafing, Eafa Eopping, Eoppa Ingilding; Ingild wæs Ines broþur Westseaxna cyninges, þæs þe eft ferde to Sancte Petre ond þær eft his feorh gesealde.[34]

> [And this Æthelwulf was Egbert's son, Egbert Ealhmund's son, Ealhmund, Eafa's son, Eafa Eoppa's son, Eoppa Ingeld's son; Ingeld was the brother of Ine, king of Wessex, who afterwards travelled to St Peter's and afterwards gave up his life there.[35]]

The word *feorh* 'life' in the above passage is markedly high register – it could be translated 'gave up his spirit there', to capture a sense of the high style. There is clearly something poetic about the language of this list of ancestors. One important message it conveys is that Æthelwulf was following in a family tradition in going to Rome, for his ancestor Ine (pronounced Ina) had also travelled to Rome at the end of his reign in Wessex. It is a reminder also that two years before, in the year 953, Æthelwulf had even sent his very young son Alfred to Rome, where he seems to have undergone a ceremony of anointing or blessing by the Pope Leo IV, which was later seen as a royal consecration.[36]

This is not the end of the ancestral list, for it goes back down the generations to Cerdic and Cynric, the names of a father and son who (according to an earlier annal) first came to the island of Britain in the year 495. It now continues through a list of legendary and mythological ancestor-figures, then further to Noah's ark and so back to Adam the first man. Of pressing interest here is the section in which the chronicler lists as the king's ancestors Bældæg and Woden, two figures from Northern European mythology, and then later in the passage the apparently Scandinavian ancestors Geat, Tætwa, Beaw, Sceldwa, Heremod, Itermon, and Hrathra, and – in versions B and C of the Chronicle – Hwala, Bedwig, and Scef. The mythical figure Scef, meaning 'Sheaf', is the key, for he is the man born in the ark, the remote ancestor of Alfred the Great.[37] Along with Beaw, Sceldwa and Heremod, this particular name is intriguing, for its occurrence in the ancestral list has a clear analogue in the Anglo-Saxon epic poem *Beowulf*. Evidently drawing on the same traditions and genealogies as did the *Beowulf* poet, the Chronicler here alludes to myths and stories that are no longer current in his own day, a story of mythical figures named after a 'sheaf' (*scef*) of 'barley' (*beaw*), a 'shield' (*scyld*) of the nation.

The inclusion of the pagan gods such as Woden among the ancestors comes as a surprise. But the gods mentioned in the Chronicle are no longer gods – they have been 'euhemerised' – a term going back to the mythographer of the late fourth century BC, Euhemerus, originator of the theory that the gods were originally outstanding men and women. Similarly in the Anglo-Saxon Chronicle, the gods have been made human, brought down a level from divine status to heroic. And as we have seen, the genealogy for Alfred's father in the Chronicle takes this process of Christianisation further, for the Chronicler was writing in the late ninth century, and the Anglo-Saxon world by then was well and truly part of Christendom, and had been for more than two hundred years.

INTERLUDE I

The charter bounds of Alveston and Tiddington

A 'map' or boundary description of an estate at Alveston and Tiddington near Stratford-on-Avon in Warwickshire (Sawyer catalogue no. 1350). In the year 985, Oswald, bishop of Worcester and archbishop of York, leased an estate measuring five hides (a hide being a unit of land necessary to support one household) to Eadric, one of his thegns. The transaction was recorded in a Latin charter, with the bounds of the estate inserted into the text in Old English.

ðis synd þa landgemæru into eanulfestune, and into tidantune, þonne fehð hit ærest on dondanforda. of doddanforda on cyngces broc. andlang broces on þa dic. of þære dic on þone hlaw. of þæm hlawe on þone weg. of þæm wege on locsetena gemære. of þæm gemærum on þone hrygcweg. of þæm hrygcwege innan westbroc. of þæm broce on saltmære. of saltmere on clægbroc. andlang broces on þa stræt. ondlang stræte on strætford. up andlang streames þæt hit cymð eft on doddanford.

[These are the bounds of the land at Eanulf's estate and Tidda's estate, when it first begins at Doddanford. From Doddanford to King's Brook, from the brook to the ditch. From the ditch to the Mound. From the Mound to the path. From the path to the *locsetena* boundary. From the boundary to the Ridgeway. From the Ridgeway to West Brook. From the brook to Saltpond. From Saltpond to Claybrook. Along the brook to the Street. Along the Street to Streetford [Stratford-upon-Avon]. Along the stream so that it returns back to Doddanford.]

PART II

The reign of King Alfred

The reign of Alfred, king of Greater Wessex, the 'country south of the Thames', from 871 to 899, is a remarkable one for a number of reasons, both political and literary. Faced at the beginning of his reign with seemingly endless war with the Danish Vikings, Alfred devised a double plan: to reorganise the military defences of his country and to revive education and literacy. In the first of these aims he was singularly successful, as history and archaeology show in equal measure. His second policy is more difficult to measure or evaluate, though its by-product is certainly visible in the manuscript record. The means to the end, the literacy programme he implemented, was based on the use of the mother tongue, and this was to have radical and long-lasting effects. Alfred's policy set a precedent, and it led eventually, as will be seen in later chapters, to the widespread use of the vernacular in the governance of the country, and with it a renaissance of literature and the arts in the later tenth century.

As a youth, Alfred witnessed first-hand the effects of the *micel here*, the 'great raiding-army' of Vikings that first reached English shores from Denmark in 865 and then overran the kingdom of East Anglia in 869–70, killing their ruler (later commemorated as St Edmund, king and martyr, after whom Bury St Edmunds is named). In 873 the Vikings ousted King Burgred from Mercia and replaced him with a more compliant ruler, Ceolwulf II. By 876 the Danes had begun to plough and support themselves, i.e. permanently *settle*, in Northumbria, and the same happened the following year in parts of eastern Mercia. Further invasions of Wessex, the veritable 'last kingdom', took place from 875, and by the winter of 877–8 many West Saxons had capitulated, and the king himself was hiding away in the Somerset marshes.

But in May of 878 came the mustering at Ecgberht's Stone and the resounding victory at Edington, and with it a precipitous change in Alfred's fortunes. The following is the account in the Anglo-Saxon Chronicle of the battle:

> And the Easter after, King Alfred with a small troop built a fortification at Athelney, and from that fortification, with that part of Somerset-men nearest to it, was making war against the raiding-army. Then in the seventh week after Easter he rode to Ecgberht's stone to the east of Selwood, and there came to join him all Somerset and Wiltshire and that part of Hampshire which was on this side of the sea – and were glad of him. And one day later he went from those camps to Island Wood, and one day later to Edington, and there fought against the whole raiding-army, and put it to flight, and rode after it as far as the fortification, and stayed there fourteen days; and then the raiding-army granted him prime hostages and great oaths that they would leave his kingdom, and also promised him that their king would receive baptism; and they fulfilled it thus.[1]

Typical for the Chronicle is the objective style, a factual reportage, with only occasional hints at attitudes and feelings in its employment of the *mot juste*, the well-chosen word or phrase to sum up or evaluate the action as it tells its story. The words 'they were glad of him', for example, encapsulate the Chronicler's perspective on the action.[2] There is also the emphasis on the mustering of the local English forces, which took place at a landmark known as Ecgberht's stone, perhaps to be located in Selwood, south of Warminster in Somerset, about half way between Alfred's stronghold at Athelney and the battlefield of Edington.[3] This was perhaps an ancient standing stone renamed in honour of Alfred's heroic grandfather Ecgberht (the name is spelled also Ecgbert or Egbert), the builder of the Greater Wessex that Alfred had inherited when he became king. If the location of the meeting place was significant, so was the date, as Ryan Lavelle has suggested, for the seventh week after Easter coincides with Ascension Day in the Christian calendar, 'connected with the restoration to the people of Israel of their kingdom'.[4]

Three weeks later, the Chronicle tells us that the Danish leader Guthrum was baptised, with Alfred as sponsor, and a further meeting took place at the royal estate of Wedmore, near Glastonbury; the Danes then withdrew to Chippenham and later to East Anglia, where they settled. A Viking hoard of silver arm-rings, ingots and coins deposited at Watlington, in Oxfordshire, suggests that one Danish warrior fled from

Wessex along the ancient Icknield Way, leaving his wealth hidden at an opportune moment.[5] A peace settlement was later agreed; the border between Wessex and the Danelaw was established along the old Roman highway of Watling Street, and legal measures were taken to ensure that law and order was kept in the two regions, especially in those parts where people from the two nations co-existed. The eastern Midlands became an Anglo-Danish region, and the Scandinavian influence was long-lasting. It even came to affect the subsequent development of the English language, which contains a fair number of Norse words in its core vocabulary, words such as *law, skill, anger* and *sky*. Anglo-Saxon England now had a distinctly Norse element in its demography.[6]

Generally, then, what Alfred called 'the many and various troubles of this kingdom' had turned out well, and the king enjoyed a much needed space for recovery and rebuilding. In the event it was a long respite, for Danish invaders did not return in force until 892. In the intervening period, Alfred was active both politically and culturally. He secured his realm, which comprised the ancient kingdoms of Wessex, Sussex and Kent, with a series of fortified towns, usually referred to by the Old English term *burh*, 'citadel, town, borough', and he consolidated the system of territorial militia known as the *fyrd*, 'army, military expedition, standing army'. When the Danes came back, his forces were ready for them. During this period he also arranged a marriage alliance of his daughter Æthelflæd with Æthelred, who seems to have replaced Ceolwulf as the leader of the western Mercians. Alfred gained the allegiance of other English regions, and took over London from the Danish settlers. Written English – which had an obvious advantage for reaching a wider audience – became increasingly important for administration and government. The foundation was being laid for expansion under his successors.

Not content only with political reform, Alfred also reorganised the state of education in the kingdom. As a boy Alfred had travelled on the continent, even visiting Rome, and he made use of various foreign contacts in order to import scholarly assistance from outside the kingdom, not only from elsewhere in Britain but also from the Continent: Plegmund of Mercia (later archbishop of Canterbury), Bishop Asser of Wales (who was to write a Latin biography of the king), Grimbald of St Bertin in Flanders and John the Old Saxon from Germany. Scholars from Ireland also visited Alfred's court, and their learning may also have contributed to the educational renewal. The new policy is outlined in the preface to the *Pastoral Care*, one of several writing projects apparently instigated by the king, and this rationale for his reforms will be examined in Chapter 3. The nature of the *Pastoral Care* itself will be explored in Chapter 4, for it is a neglected text (unlike its more famous preface) although it offers many insights into Alfred's interests and preoccupations.

Alfred's final achievement is very evident in the differences between the beginning and end of his reign. In the year 871, when Alfred succeeded to the throne of the West Saxons after the reign of his brother Æthelred, his Wessex was a kingdom limited in size, corresponding largely to what the poet and travel writer Edward Thomas affectionately evoked in 1909 as 'the South Country', a mild region of chalk hills and market towns, dominated by the South Downs and the English Channel:

> Roughly speaking it is the country south of the Thames and the Severn and east of Exmoor and includes, therefore, the counties of Kent, Sussex, Surrey, Hampshire, Berkshire, Wiltshire, Dorset and part of Somerset. [7]

In his nostalgic exploration of that country Edward Thomas found an imaginative unity in the lie of the land, the direction of the rivers and old roads, 'the study of hill and valley and stream, the positions of houses, mills and villages' (pp. 145–6). In some cases at least the positions of houses, mills and villages go back a long way. As scholars have shown, the Old English description of an estate in an Anglo-Saxon charter can still be used to walk the bounds of a modern property, field or parish.[8] In short, then, though contemporary writers do not remark on it as such, Alfred's kingdom at first had some sense of topographical unity as 'the country south of the Thames and the Severn', a Greater Wessex, as historians call it.

However, by the end of the reign, the situation had radically changed. We know that Alfred had by then taken possession of the port of London on the north side of the Thames, and according to the Anglo-Saxon Chronicle, a document much influenced by royal policy, Alfred's land, power and influence now reached much further:

> Se wæs cyning ofer eall Ongelcyn butan ðæm dæle þe under Dena onwalde wæs.

> [He was king over all the English nation except for the part that was under Danish authority.]

Two words of explanation are required. First, the term for 'rule' here is *onwald*, otherwise spelt *onweald*, which means 'power, rule, dominion, authority'; the same term will recur in various contexts in literary texts associated with the reign of Alfred's son, Edward the Elder. Secondly, the Chronicle tells us that Alfred ruled the *Ongelcynn*, otherwise spelled *Angelcynn*, which may be translated as either 'the Angle-kindred' or the 'English nation'. The meaning of that word is linked to and influenced by the Latin notion of the *gens anglorum* the 'people of the English', which Bede had derived from Pope Gregory the Great and promoted in his *Ecclesiastical History of the English Nation*.[9] As Chapter 5 will show, Bede's eighth-century historical work was enormously influential, and this influence received a further boost when it was adapted and translated into English in the late ninth century.

This was the measure of Alfred's ambition; he devised policies of urbanisation and fortress-building and established a standing army, all of which ensured his success against the massive Danish attacks. He also devised new policies of literacy and learning in the vernacular, with translations and paraphrases issued in his name. What he bequeathed in 899 to his son and heir Edward the Elder was a new entity, the 'Kingdom of the Angles and the Saxons'.[10]

597	Pope Gregory the Great sends Augustine and his fellow missionaries to Kent
	Æthelberht, king of Kent, presents the former Roman city of Canterbury to the missionaries for their use as an ecclesiastical centre
c.600	Augustine Gospels brought to Canterbury
626	Edwin, king of Northumbria, converts to Christianity
731	The Northumbrian scholar Bede writes, in Latin, the *Ecclesiastical History of the English Nation*
850s	Lady Ealhburg's donations to the Church in Canterbury
865	Arrival of the Great Army of Vikings from Denmark
869–70	Great Army conquers East Anglia, killing Edmund their king
871	Accession of Alfred, king of Wessex
873	The Danes depose Burgred of Mercia
876–7	Danes settle in Northumbria and eastern Mercia
878	Alfred defeats the Danes at the Battle of Edington
880s onwards	Building and rebuilding of fortified towns in Wessex
886	Alfred takes control of London
890s	Anglo-Saxon Chronicle first composed and circulated at Alfred's court
	The Old English version of Gregory's *Pastoral Care*
893	Asser writes *Life of King Alfred*
892–6	West Saxon alliance with Mercians foils a renewed Danish invasion
850–930?	The writing of the Old English *Bede*

CHAPTER 3

Literacy and the use of English: Alfred's reforms

In the preface to the Old English *Pastoral Care*, the metaphor of a hunter or deerstalker is used to represent Alfred's quest for learning, literacy and political stability:

> When I remembered all this, then I remembered also how I saw, before they were all plundered and burned, how the churches throughout the English nation stood filled with treasures and books, and also a great multitude of God's servants; and these knew very little of the benefit of the books, for they could not understand any of them because they were not written in their own language. It is as if they had said: 'Our ancestors who held these places loved wisdom, and through it they acquired wealth and bequeathed it to us. Here one can still see their footprints, but we cannot track them. We have lost both the wealth and the wisdom, because we would not bend down to the tracks with our minds.[1]

Composed in the first person, the preface speaks here of a complacent clergy unable to appreciate the Latin books they owned, and then of the catastrophic Viking wars and the ruined churches, despoiled of their treasures and books. To remedy the lack of education in England Alfred proposes – on the basis of historical precedents such as the translation of the 'law', i.e. the scriptures, from Greek into the vernacular of the Roman empire (i.e. Latin) – to introduce a new curriculum based on books translated from Latin into English.

The same policy informs the making of Alfred's Lawcode, his Book of Laws, which also includes a royal preface and a discussion of the history of law-making which sets his laws in the context of the Old Testament.[2] There is an imperial element here, for he gathers together the laws of his ancestors alongside those of the Kentish and Mercian kings, whose legislation he now draws together under West Saxon authority. The ultimate aim, as both the preface to the Lawcode and the preface to the *Pastoral Care* make clear, is to introduce a programme of literacy teaching in the vernacular. This interpretation is supported by Bishop Asser's biography of the king. On Alfred's plan, members of the leading families would educate their children through the medium of English, and only sons aiming for higher clerical careers would proceed to the study of Latin.[3]

'THE CHURCHES THROUGHOUT THE ENGLISH NATION STOOD FILLED WITH TREASURES AND BOOKS'

Famously, Alfred decried the decline in literacy in the years before he began his policy of educational reform in the 890s. At first sight there seems little cause to doubt his assessment of the situation. But there are problems, for Alfred may be guilty of exaggerating the problem.[4] After all, he imported scholars from the central kingdom of Mercia to help with his reforms in the south, which suggests that the situation there was not quite as dire as he implies in his preface. In fact, rather the contrary; Mercian culture was probably in good shape, to judge by its translation of the Old English *Bede* (see Chapter 5), or the literary quality of its land charters. Indeed the Mercian literary influence on charter writing was later felt strongly, both in Kent and in Wessex.[5] But by presenting himself as a rebuilder, Alfred could appear as the saviour of the Angelcynn, and the 'Angle-kindred' or English nation would, under his guidance, recover the levels of culture and learning that it had once had in the days of Bede and the golden age of Northumbria, to which Alfred seems to allude in his preface to the *Pastoral Care*.

In the context of mid-ninth-century Kent, however, Alfred's claim is more easily understandable. The study of literary production here supports Alfred's assertions, showing for instance a decline in literacy at Canterbury, the ecclesiastical centre of southern Britain, whose influence crossed the borders between the various kingdoms of Wessex, Mercia and Northumbria. In the seventh century there had been the great school under Archbishop Theodore, who had trained the likes of the poet Aldhelm (whose legacy and influence will be considered in Chapter 11 below), but the influence of that school had long since evaporated.[6] In addition, the library books that we assume were kept in the city may well have been destroyed in the various attacks on Canterbury by the Vikings in the middle of the ninth century. What was left by Alfred's day were the altar books, written in Latin and lavishly decorated, which survived because they were high status religious texts that were guarded and protected in case of fire or invasion. Altar books were precious, but they remained in constant if careful use. And probably because of their durability, they became also a kind of archive or refuge, where important documents could be copied, on suitable blank pages.

Among the books located in Canterbury is an illustrated copy of the four gospels written in Latin. This ancient manuscript, now known by its present-day library shelf-mark as Cambridge, Corpus Christi College, 286 – or more popularly as the St Augustine Gospels – has some claim to being the first English book. It is not however native in style. Its foreignness is immediately apparent in its script (early uncial), and the text is written in a form of *scripta continua*, that is, in blocks of letters without separation of words. The text is laid out in two columns per page, with indented verses and plenty of space and wide margins. Though the quality of the vellum pages varies (there are a few holes, for instance), this is otherwise a high-status book, expensive to produce, and this fact is reflected in the style of its art and decoration, particularly the evangelist portrait. The usual custom in high-quality early medieval gospel books was to provide each of the four evangelists with a frontispiece, a picture of the author, and probably this book originally had four such portraits, though now only that of Luke survives. A one-page set of narrative illustrations also survives in Luke's Gospel and this may also have been a feature of the whole volume.[7]

To modern eyes the surviving evangelist portrait shows a white-bearded Roman senator in a white toga seated on a kind of elaborate throne under an arched architectural feature held up by pillars, two on each side (see Figure 3a). This is Luke, with piercing dark eyes, his head slightly tilted to one side, shown in contemplation as he displays an open book outwards, towards the reader or viewer. The artist's technique is naturalistic, although without much sense of perspective, and he gives Luke clear and distinctive facial features, as though the gospel writer is an individual rather than a type. Above Luke in the arched frame is the figure of a bull, the usual symbol for that evangelist, and a further hint that the three other evangelist portraits and their symbols (Matthew the man, Mark the lion, John the eagle) are now missing from the codex. On either side of the evangelist in the Luke miniature there is a set of five small panels each depicting, again in naturalistic style, some scenes from the life of Christ.[8] At the bottom of the right-hand column, for example, is a lively, almost humorous illustration of Zacchaeus in a rather spindly tree looking down at Jesus and an apostle.

The style of the Augustine Gospels contrasts strongly with that of native English art, found originally in metalwork and stone sculpture, with its abstract patterning and flat symbolic figures; such a style was to be transferred in the seventh century to numerous Northumbrian gospel books, examples being the Book of Durrow or the famous Lindisfarne Gospels with their elaborate interlacing, swirls and step patterns. Their symbolic art is impressive in its own right but very different from the rather more representational narrative illustrations of this gospel book.

The script and decoration help to date the book.[9] It is likely that it was made in Italy, probably in Rome in the late sixth or early seventh century, and it must have arrived in Kent with the Italian missionaries. Clearly, the Augustine Gospels should be seen as a high quality *de luxe* codex, intended for formal display on the altar or lectern; it most likely had ceremonial use, for the swearing of oaths, for special services and feasts. Possibly it was even used by the Italian missionary bishop Augustine himself, who became the first ever archbishop of Canterbury after his arrival in Kent in the year 597. Appropriately, although Augustine's ownership is not proven, this very gospel book is still used for swearing of oaths at the installation of archbishops of Canterbury, providing a tangible link between the present day and the distant past.

To a certain extent, the history of this book can be traced because of the practice of adding further texts to it. Blank pages at various places in the manuscript of the Gospels of St Augustine were filled with writing in Old English and Latin, and it is these texts and their palaeography (in other words their datable styles of handwriting) which help us to locate the medieval provenance of the manuscript at St Augustine's Canterbury. The earliest addition to the book appears at the end of the Gospel of Matthew and is written in Old English: a copy made in the early tenth century of a ninth-century document, an example of the lay literacy of the period, composed by or for a certain Kentish lady called Ealhburg.[10] (It is a testimony to the persistence of old traditional naming patterns that this Christian lady's name means 'pagan shrine citadel'.)

'EALHBURG HAS ESTABLISHED, WITH THE ADVICE
OF HER FRIENDS ...'

Ealhburg's vernacular text forms a striking contrast to the preceding Latin gospel text both in its language and layout. As a

Figure 3a   St Luke, from the Augustine Gospels

glance at the reproduction of the manuscript on the website or at a photograph of the page will show, the closing section of the gospel text is beautifully laid out, the calligraphy is a neat, fine half-uncial script which changes to Roman capitals to signal the end of this gospel and the beginning of the next.[11] However, for all its attractiveness, most modern readers, including even many classicists, would initially find the text hard to read on the manuscript page, since there are no spaces between words, and there are many abbreviations. This is a book designed to look beautiful on the page, but the reader has to work hard to spell out the words and to sound out their meaning.

By contrast, when one turns the page, the Old English text is laid out very differently. The plain handwriting is still neat and attractive, but much more obviously practical and workaday. And although the script employs a few standard abbreviations to save space, and word division is just occasionally a little arbitrary, nevertheless each word usually forms a clear unit, each line of the text is written out in full, and there is much less attention to creating a visual effect on the page. With this text we have moved forward in time from the seventh century to the tenth, and the differences in attitudes to literacy and the practice of writing are palpable: writers now use the vernacular for practical workaday purposes, and the gospel book has become, as it were, a repository where a document can be deposited for safekeeping. This was not at the time felt to be a profane use of such a precious object; rather it evinces the respect that was lavished on the gospel book, for people placed trust in future generations to preserve the manuscript with great care.

As for the contents of this Old English document, it is an account of renders to be paid to St Augustine's Abbey every year from estates at Brabourne in Kent. The owner Ealhburg, whose family are known from other documents of the period, was a noble woman of some standing in the community of Canterbury or its environs in the 850s, who arranged for similar renders of food to go to Christ Church too.[12] There is a prosaic listing of the quantities of food required: '40 ambers of malt, 1 mature bullock, 4 wethers, 240 loaves, 1 wey of bacon and of cheese, 4 fothers of wood, and 20 hens'. All this comes as a surprise given the gospel context in which the list appears. But the render is evidently taken very seriously, as is shown by the imprecation against any neglectful successor, who will be excluded from God and all his saints and St Augustine for his or her failure to comply. Indeed the whole transaction is regarded as an act of piety that Ealhburg has undertaken on behalf of herself and her relatives.

In return for the donation, the monks of St Augustine's will pray for Ealhburg and her family and sing the *Exaudiat te Dominus* (Psalm 19), an appropriately triumphant psalm that fits the charitable bequest, since it is a bid for help in times of trouble and a petition to reward the giver, the one who offers sacrifices. In the Latin of the Vespasian Psalter, another time-honoured altar book that was certainly kept at Canterbury at the time, Psalm 19 begins as follows:

Exaudiat te dominus in die tribulationibus protegat te nomen Dei Jacob...

[May the Lord hear thee in the day of tribulation: may the name of the God of Jacob protect thee.]

The psalm is a prayer, in which the speakers ask for help and defence, rejoicing in God's salvation, declaring that while some 'trust in chariots, and some in horses' they instead will 'call upon the name of the Lord, our God'. It is possible, though certainly difficult to prove, that Ealhburg knew this psalm in Old English, her mother tongue. As well as all the psalms in Latin, the Vespasian Psalter contains an interlinear vernacular version of the text, added in the mid-ninth century, in the Mercian dialect of Old English.[13] By the time Ealhburg was making her donations to Canterbury, the Vespasian Psalter had become a bilingual copy of the Psalms. Clearly written Old English was being used more widely, for a variety of purposes; it was gaining in status, assuming functions that had previously been reserved only for Latin. And it may also be the case that literacy in English was replacing literacy in Latin rather than simply supplementing it.

Psalm 19, verse 3, if addressed to the Lady Ealhburg, would have been a suitable and appropriate message in terms of her gift to St Augustine's and the reward she hoped to receive, no doubt in all due humility, for her act of piety. In the interlinear Old English translation in the Vespasian Psalter, the verse reads as follows:

> Sende the fultum of halgum and of Sion gescilde the.
>
> [May [the Lord] send thee help from his saints and from Zion, may he shield thee!]

Ealhburg would surely have appreciated the benefit of such prayers, and there is some poignancy here, for she had good personal reasons to fear the Viking attacks. As the Anglo-Saxon Chronicle reports, her brother was killed in the year 851 fighting a battle on the Isle of Thanet against yet another army of Viking raiders.[14]

'I, AELFRED THE EALDORMAN ... PURCHASED THIS BOOK FROM THE HEATHEN ARMY ...'

A generation later, with King Alfred now established as the young ruler of Wessex, including Kent, the general level of Latin literacy had changed very little.[15] If anything, it had worsened. In the case of Kentish charters (official documents recording grants of land), we finds mistakes in the grammar, and faulty spellings based on pronunciation rather than rules of orthography; in one case, a scribe who was quite capable of writing in English nevertheless made a whole host of mistakes when writing in Latin.[16] It looks like there is some truth to the claim in King Alfred's preface to his *Pastoral Care* that people could no longer appreciate their books because they could not read or write the Latin language in which they were written.

The situation at the time is further illustrated by another splendid Latin gospel book in which a ninth-century scribe has added some English in the margins. The gospel book in question, now known as the Stockholm Codex Aureus, is a dazzling example of the manuscript illumination of the early eighth century.[17] It is most likely a Canterbury product, for its iconography seems to have been influenced by the Augustine Gospels, which of course was still present at Canterbury and available for the scribes and illuminators to use as a model. In the evangelist portraits for example, the gospel writer sits on a similar throne to that of the Augustine Gospels, and there is the same arched frame in which the symbol of the evangelist is depicted.[18] There are differences, however, for the pictorial narrative scenes which we saw in the Augustine Gospels are not present here. Moreover, the clothing is more stylised, less obviously Roman, the body flatter, the face, though naturalistic, has large eyes that gaze out at the reader, more like a Greek icon as seen in present-day Orthodox churches. The presentation is notably sumptuous, with some burnished golden display capitals, as found also in the Vespasian Psalter. The decoration on the page is complex and artistic: there are some patterns of linear interlace and 'Celtic' spiral patterns on the architectural features, showing influence from the great Northumbrian gospel books such as the Lindisfarne Gospels. The Codex Aureus is clearly another *de luxe* showpiece, but unlike the Augustine Gospels, it is of native manufacture.

In the late ninth century the Codex Aureus was stolen by some Vikings, who took it as plunder from one of the Kentish churches or monasteries. Perhaps the original book cover of wood and leather, decorated with precious metalwork, was removed for its bullion value, for it no longer survives. But the manuscript itself was saved. As we know from the Old English inscription written in the upper and lower margins of the opening page of the Gospel of Matthew, the book was then ransomed:

+ In nomine Domini nostri Iesu Christi. Ic Aelfred aldormon 7 Werburg min gefera begetan ðas bec æt hæðnum herge mid uncre claene feo ðæt ðonne wæs mid clæne golde 7 ðæt wit deodan for Godes lufan 7 for uncre saule ðearf[e] ond for ðon ðe wit noldan ðæt ðas halgan beoc lencg in ðære haeðenesse wunaden.

[In the name of our Lord Jesus Crist. I, Ealdorman Aelfred, and Werburg my wife, obtained this book from the heathen army with our clean money which was clean gold, and we did this for the love of God and for the need of our souls and because we did not want this book to remain any longer in heathen possession.]

Figure 3b St Matthew, Stockhom Codex Aureus, folios 9v and 10r

A nobleman of the region, who coincidentally shared his name, Alfred, with the young king who had just ascended the throne, reports how he redeemed the book, paid good money for it and then gave it to the cathedral of Christ Church, Canterbury, for the benefit of his soul and that of his wife and daughter.[19] From cases such as this may conclude that Latin gospel books were prized possessions, high in spiritual value. But notably, when Ealdorman Alfred chose to intervene in the margins of the text, the language he used was his English vernacular.

ASSER'S *LIFE OF KING ALFRED*

This, then, was the situation as King Alfred instigated his plan for the recovery of Wessex, a programme of educational reform and, to use a modern term, national defence. Precious books had become objects of barter, and it looks like competent literacy, at least in Kent, was confined to the vernacular. But it seems that a precedent had been lain down here: this was a culture in which the use of the mother tongue in literary production had become acceptable. This deliberate cultivation of the English language for use in administration, government and the Church was taken further by the king in pursuing his educational reforms. But first, in order to realise his aims, Alfred had to look abroad, outside Greater Wessex, in other words beyond the South Country, to find the assistance he needed.

One of the scholarly advisers whom Alfred summoned to his kingdom was Asser, bishop of St David's in the south-western region of Wales (or Cymru as it should really be called, since the name *Wales* derives from an

Old English word *wealas* meaning 'strangers'). Even more so than England in this period, Wales was a patchwork of independent regions, from Gwynedd and Powys in the north to Ceredigion and Asser's native Dyfed in the west and Yestrad Tywi, Brycheiniog, Glwysing and Gwent in the south. These principalities were far from united among themselves, despite some feelings of cultural and linguistic affinity, and they vied for the attention and support of the large powerful kingdoms of Mercia and Wessex in the 'Saxon' regions – as they called them – to their east. A likely motivation for Asser's work was to inform his compatriots in Wales about the policies and achievements of his illustrious patron.

The moment when Alfred and Asser first met was a pivotal one in the narrative, and it is treated with some attention in Asser's biography of the king (Chapters 79–80). Using the simile of the *apis prudentissima*,'the most prudent bee', gathering nectar from flowers,[20] it is made clear that Asser was one of the flowers, one of the scholars summoned by the king bee to the royal court (Chapter 76). Asser's journey and meeting is told in Chapter 79. As befits the perambulatory role of a king at that time, Alfred was not at home in Winchester, or indeed anywhere else in Wessex proper, when Asser answered his summons. Instead he was residing temporarily at the royal estate of Dean in Sussex. Led by his English guides, Asser was brought before the king and, we are told, given a warm welcome. Like the scene in Bede's *Ecclesiastical History of the English Nation* where King Æthelberht meets the missionary Augustine for the first time (for which see Chapter 5 below), the circumstantial details of the meeting are not given. The passage is therefore strikingly different in style to the arrival scene in *Beowulf*, the set-piece drama where Beowulf son of Ecgtheow arrives at the court of Hrothgar king of Denmark, an episode which is lent colour by the details of shining hall and boar-helmet, and made dramatic by formal speeches of challenge, welcome and response by the main characters.[21]

For a modern biographer this first meeting would surely have been the opportunity to describe the king's appearance and personality, along with some details of the occasion: the location, presumably the royal hall at Dean where they met and ate a meal, and its surroundings. Instead the narrative consists of indirect speech, a summarising report of what was said in the negotiation:

> When I had been warmly welcomed by him, and we were engaged in
> discussion, he asked me earnestly to commit myself to his service and to
> become a member of his household, and to relinquish for his sake all that I

had on the left hand and western side of the Severn. He promised to pay me greater compensation for it (which indeed he was to do).[22]

The style is somewhat detached: we do not hear the actual words spoken but only the gist, with verbs and expressions of reported speech such as *welcomed, asked, promised* and *replied.* Only once in fact are any words of the conversation quoted directly, at the moment when Alfred makes his final offer: 'If it is not agreeable to you to come on these terms, at least grant me one half of your services, whereby you would be with me for six months each year and the same length of time in Wales'.

Asser's *Life* is not a biography in the modern sense. It lacks the ongoing attention to detail, to that rich, vivid, even superfluous detail which most modern biographers bring to their work. There are indeed details present, sometimes even lively touches, but these appear in selected scenes only, and these scenes feature as anecdotes rather than as part of a consistent narrative style. We do not learn much from Asser about the personalities of Alfred's parents, the sights, sounds, and smells of his first home, his early schooling and the name of his first tutor, for instance, nor do we learn many of his inner thoughts or many of his personal opinions; we can guess, we can extrapolate, but we are not given any concrete discussion, for example, of how he felt about his warrior grandfather Ecgberht or his pious father Æthelwulf, who went to Rome when Alfred was a child. His literate mother has one cameo appearance, but is otherwise not mentioned. And Asser provides only a little analysis of personality or motivation. Where the modern biographer is influenced by the techniques of the novelist, the historian or the psychoanalyst, Asser's work is coloured by the narrative conventions of the hagiographer. And the writing of lives of the saints, in other words hagiography, is found everywhere in early medieval literature.

As a biography, however, Asser's basic model was Carolingian. The court of Charles the Great, otherwise known as Charlemagne (768–814), who ruled the empire of the Franks, i.e. the joint territory of present-day France and Germany, from his capital at Aachen, had produced two biographies of its renowned emperor, one of these being the well-known *Life of Charlemagne* by the writer Einhard (*c.*775–840).[23] There was a model to follow here. Other Carolingian biographies combined a chronicle style (a chronology or list of events) with biographical anecdotes based on personal connections or hearsay. Such is also Asser's approach in his *Life of Alfred*, a work divided into 106 chapters (like many biographies of the time, these chapters are quite short, often covering only half a page or so). Asser derives his chronology and structure from the Anglo-Saxon Chronicle and arranges his chapters to cover his ground year by year (chs 1–21, 26–72). The first of his digressions comes in Chapters 22–25. One of the best examples here is the king's own first-person account, as retold by Asser, of how his mother encouraged him to learn by heart a book of English poems. On his successful completion of the task she rewarded him with the book as a prize for his efforts. It is fair to say that for the present-day general reader such stories provide the main interest of the whole work, an interest that is partly biographical, in the details of Alfred's life, and partly literary, as narratives in their own right. And even if it were proved, as some have tried to do, that the text attributed to Asser was the work of a literary forger working in the eleventh century, these anecdotes would retain a good deal of force as insights into the ways of life and thought of the period.[24]

The second main digression occurs around the year 885. The Viking army was abroad in France, and the East Anglian Vikings were on the verge of treacherously breaking their peace agreement, as Asser announces in Chapter 72. But for a while, as it were, both the king and also Asser – in the process of writing his narrative – are granted a respite. They have the time and space to move away from military affairs and devote themselves to the many other activities of the royal career. Chiefly in Asser's case these consist of more anecdotes and personal information that he has gleaned from conversations with the king himself. Here we learn also some general assessments of the king's character, a few facts about his marriage and his personal piety, and his struggles with ill-health (ch. 74); we learn the names of his children and read about their education in the new literacy, with brief data about their later careers (ch. 75). At this point (ch. 76) Asser extols the cultural life of the kingdom and all the noble or courtly activities that take place there: the hunting and hawking, the craftsmanship, the reading aloud of books and the learning of English poems, the church-going, and not least the patronage and the generosity extended widely to all manner of nationalities.

The anecdotes from the two main digressions in Asser's *Life of Alfred* have been scrutinised over the years by historians and tested for their veracity. Some have wondered whether the stories of the king's poor health were inspired by saints' lives and so do not correspond realistically to the active life of a warrior as he fought his various wars against the Vikings. Others have questioned whether Alfred's mother was still alive at the time of the story of the poems. Moreover, an anecdote about a book of ancient poems in the vernacular is told by

Charlemagne's biographer (though this coincidence in itself does not disprove the existence of such books of poems in Wessex). But as the historian Richard Abels sensibly remarks, these narratives come from Alfred's memory, mediated through Asser the writer, and they are likely to be important personal memories for Alfred.[25] In that sense at least they can be taken seriously.

To return to the story of Alfred and the poems, one remarkable aspect is the feat of memory involved, so remarkable that it prompts the question of whether a young boy really could learn by heart such a large number of texts. How did he accomplish it? Here the work of historians of medieval culture supplies a clue, for the arts of memory were highly developed in the Middle Ages. Mnemonics, including mental image-making and meditational practices, helped to fix the key features of a text in the mind.[26] Even without such techniques, memories were trained also by sheer repetition, by the constant need to recall texts and passages to mind in a culture where books and writing materials were costly and scarce. As Asser tells the story, the young Alfred ran to his tutor for help with his task. School lessons in the period commonly involved reading aloud, listening and repeating, and Asser's text emphasises a number of times how Alfred had a habit of listening to books being read out loud. In the religious life the Psalms were learned by heart for use in church in the liturgy and for personal devotion and meditation. The Latin Psalter, or Book of the Psalms, became a textbook: people learned to read and write on the basis of a text they already knew.[27] Such was the memory culture in which the young Alfred so excelled.

As well as the king's personal memoirs, Asser also provides us with his own impressions of Alfred's energies and preoccupations, and again there is a ring of truth to his observations. So Asser tells in Chapter 88 of how the king met with Asser to discuss many and various matters and to listen to books being read out loud. This must have taken place on one of Asser's prolonged stays in Wessex, from March to December of the year 887.[28] On one occasion when Asser was reading to him he reports that the king suddenly showed him a little book in which all manner of religious texts had been collected, including psalms and prayers that he had learned by heart as a youth. Admiring what he had just heard, the king asked him to copy the passage into his book. What sounds convincing here is the king's reticence, the fact that he had held back from telling Asser about his book, perhaps until he had come to know his adviser more closely or perhaps until he had gained more confidence in his own intellectual abilities. The result was that the king and Asser together began to compile a new *florilegium* or 'handbook', as it was called, with the king listening to Asser reading and then making decisions as to which passages he would like to copy and preserve and then teach to others by translating them into English.

'JOHN THE WISE MAN'

As we have seen, Alfred's intellectual advisers and writers for the *Pastoral Care* and other literary projects came from abroad, men like John the Old Saxon from northern Germany or Grimbald of Saint-Bertin (the abbey in Saint-Omer, near Calais in northern France), not to mention Bishop Asser from St David's in Wales. Germans, French, Irishmen, Bretons, and many other nationalities also attended the court, and inevitably new ideas and policies were debated.

One of the 'new' policies briefly attempted was monastic reform, but it looks like the English Church of Alfred's day was not yet ready for such a radical step, which was not to be taken until the time of Bishop Æthelwold in the 950s and 960s (see Chapters 12 and 15). In one of the more colourful of narratives in his *Life of King Alfred*, Asser recounts – selectively though in some detail – the story of the attempted murder of an abbot. Like his narrative of his first meeting with the king, Asser lingers over the details here rather longer than usual. In his desire to revive the monastic life, so he tells us, Alfred had founded a monastery at Athelney, the very place in the Somerset fenland where some years before he had established his fortification against the Vikings, before his great victory at Edington. As abbot of the new institution he appointed one of his chief advisers, John the Old Saxon, or as Asser calls him in his biography: *Iohannem presbyterum et monachum, scilicet Eald-Saxonum genere* ('the priest and monk John of the race of the Old Saxons').

Presumably because there were no suitably trained Englishmen, Alfred gathered together a community of monks made up of foreigners from different nations, including even a young man of Viking extraction. As Asser tells the story (chs 93–6), however, he implies that these national differences eventually lead to rancour and dissension and then to the murder plot. It is the men of France (Gaul or Francia as it was then called) rather than Denmark or Germany who prove to be the problem, and perhaps we can speculate that John as an Old Saxon had linguistic difficulties communicating with them. These Gallic villains are not named, nor does Asser dwell on their motivation other than to say that they are a priest and a deacon, and thus important figures in the hierarchy of the monastic house, who are incited by the devil of envy to betray their lord and master, the abbot. Being of Gallic origin, presumably speakers of a kind of early French, they employ 'two slaves of the same Gallic race' to perpetrate the actual crime.

Asser is not aiming to be sensational. He is careful to make his position clear: he has no great wish to retell this story, because it is shameful to hear. But like most historians of his day – and a similar example is to be found in Bede's *Ecclesiastical History* in the dedicatory preface to King Ceolwulf (the Old English version is printed in Interlude II below) – he feels that the purpose of telling what has happened is didactic. Good deeds are to be emulated and the men and women who do them are to be praised, while evil actions are to be shunned and the perpetrators punished. So while he does not wish to tell the tale of this crime, and, so it is implied, while he has no intention to entertain, nevertheless his narrative is sufficiently vivid to capture the reader's attention. He begins by describing the plot that the conspirators were hatching (ch. 96). The anticipation is part of the fascination for the reader as he or she is drawn to picture the scene: the two murderers lying in wait in the unlocked church, the rest of the community 'sleeping soundly in blissful bodily peace', the abbot making his usual nocturnal visit to the church to pray on bended knees before the altar, the conspirators' plan to kill him savagely and dump his body outside the door of a prostitute in order to deflect attention from them and, in Asser's words, to 'heap crime upon crime'. In the next short chapter (ch. 97), having set up expectations, Asser satisfies our natural curiosity to know what happened next.

This is not a modern novel like Umberto Eco's *The Name of the Rose*, which also tells of murder in a monastery, nor is it the heroic poem *Beowulf*, with its careful building of tension in, say, the story of Grendel's attack on Heorot. The narrative that follows proceeds in the form of a detailed summary rather than a fully narrated story, but Asser fulfils expectations and creates suspense by the device of repetition, deliberately repeating the expected stages of the plot as they unfold:

> When all the evil plan had been clearly expounded and outlined by the evil conspirators to their evil accomplices, when the night had arrived and was thought propitious, and a promise of impunity had been given, the two armed villains shut themselves in the church to await the abbot's arrival. At midnight John entered the church secretly as usual (so that no one would know) in order to pray, and bowed down on bended knees before the altar; then the two villains attacked him suddenly with drawn swords and wounded him severely (ch. 97).

Asser now gives us a few details – he reminds us (though he had not mentioned it before) that John had had some experience in fighting from his earlier life before he entered upon his clerical vocation. This is not implausible: in the eleventh century for instance we hear in the Anglo-Saxon Chronicle of several important priests and monks fighting in the army on significant occasions. So John is able to fight back and resist, shouting loudly at his assailants.

The noise awakens the rest of the monks in the monastery. Unlike in *Beowulf*, the narrator does not present the details of the physical fight: this is summary rather than full narrative. Mostly we have reported speech rather than dialogue: we only hear the one word 'devils!' that Abbot John shouts, but we do not hear what words the would-be murderers uttered as they attacked him. However, the noise of the fight – heard by those outside – is reminiscent of *Beowulf*, as is the emotion of fear. Like *Beowulf* the would-be helpers who have gathered outside the building are so fearful that they hesitate to venture in. And so, like the monstrous Grendel who attacks the royal hall in *Beowulf*, the two criminals are unhindered: they quickly make for the door and escape into the fastness of the nearby fenland.

Here, rather abruptly, Asser ends his anecdote, although he notes briefly that in the end the criminals were captured and received their due punishment. And this, to put it quite simply, is all the historical record can tell us of the character and personality of John the Old Saxon. What we know from Asser can be summed up quickly: John the Old Saxon was a learned and gifted scholar, assistant to King Alfred, appointed as abbot to Athelney (Asser, chs 77 and 94). What we can infer from Asser's suspenseful anecdote is that John was a strong personality who inspired both envy and affection, that he was a man of physical strength and endurance, loud-voiced, and quick to express his anger in a desperate situation. Although he was so severely wounded in the attack that the monks had to carry him home in great sorrow, he seems to have survived.

The investigations of Michael Lapidge have cast a little extra light on the matter.[29] A grant of land recorded in a charter from the reign of Edward the Elder is witnessed by a certain Iohannes in the year 904. Since the name was not common in England at the time, this man is likely to have been the former abbot of Athelney. Much later, in the twelfth century, the historian William of Malmesbury recorded the epitaph of a certain *Iohannes sophista* or John the scholar, and he mentions a martyrdom, which may – arguably – refer to the attempted murder of John the Old Saxon, although William mistakenly interpreted the name as referring to the Irish philosopher John Scotus Eriugena, who was active at the Carolingian court in the same period. A further clue is provided by an eleventh-century text in Old English known as *The Resting Places of the Saints*, which mentions 'Iohannes se wisa', 'John the wise man', who was buried at Malmesbury.[30] Is this holy man in fact John the Old Saxon, who perhaps spent a quiet retirement at the peaceful haven of Malmesbury?

ASSESSING ALFRED'S REFORMS

The age of Alfred is rich in documentation, the *Life of Alfred* by Bishop Asser, despite the doubts expressed by some historians, being the great window on Alfred the man, with a number of cameo scenes and anecdotes on Alfred's life and preoccupations, such as his memorising a book of English poems as a young boy. There is no comparable discourse on the everyday life of a king until the eleventh-century *Life of Edward*, which we cited above in Chapter 2 for its anecdote of robbery and loyalty on the Via Cassia outside Rome. And both royal biographies show us more than just the figure of the king: they provide sporadic views of ordinary people responding to moments of need and crisis: Gospatrick the thegn claiming to be Tostig and thus allowing his lord to ride off to safety; Abbot John fending off murderers in a darkened church as his terrified monks gather outside, reluctant to go in.

But above all Asser's *Life* helps to corroborate the evidence of educational reform that is given to us, apparently in Alfred's own words, in the prose preface to the *Pastoral Care*. In the course of this chapter we have noted the growing use of English in the surviving Kentish documents of the ninth century; in the face of Viking raiding, there was a culture developing in which the use of the written vernacular was becoming acceptable. It is in this context that Alfred's reforms are best seen. He may have failed to regenerate the monasteries that might have been an active force for spreading his ideas and policies. But it is hard to deny his success with the existing institutions. The positive result was the series of translations and paraphrases – of what might be called the 'Christian Latin classics' – which appear in the manuscript record from the 990s onwards. Evidently they are inspired by Alfred and his court, if not actually composed or written there. The oldest such translation, and the one most strongly associated with the king himself, is the *Pastoral Care*, which is full of insights into the psychology of the ruler and his spiritual needs. It is to this Alfredian work that we now turn.

CHAPTER 4

The rule of government: 'The craft of all crafts'

Did King Alfred really write anything? This is the startling question raised recently by a distinguished scholar of Anglo-Saxon literature. Malcolm Godden's argument focusses on the philosophical texts traditionally attributed to the king, the *Consolation of Philosophy* and the *Soliloquies*, arguing that these scholarly paraphrases of works by Boethius and Augustine look like the products of a learned milieu rather than of a royal court.[1] Far from debunking the myth of King Alfred, however, Godden's discussion really highlights the 'Alfredian' influence that pervades the long tenth century. As later chapters of this book will indicate, Alfred set a cultural trend for literature in the vernacular: from his time on, literary, historical and philosophical works could be translated into English with the blessing of the king, or penned in the name of the king, the father of the dynasty. But despite the doubts about authorship, one literary work in particular seems very closely to reflect the intellectual interests and social concerns of King Alfred himself, as known from Asser's biography. This is the text and preface of the *Pastoral Care*, an English version of Gregory the Great's *Pastoral Rule*, probably the second of the various books to be translated in this period and (apart from Alfred's Lawcode) the one most certainly associated with the guiding hand of Alfred himself.[2] In this text the practice of ruling is described as 'the art of all arts', or to follow the Old English wording *cræft ealra cræfta*, literally 'the craft of all crafts'.

GREGORY THE GREAT

Why did Alfred choose Gregory the Great as an author to be translated into English? The two men are worlds apart, one a warrior king with an interest in books, the other a former Roman senator turned contemplative monk, who found himself drawn back into the life of the institutional Church. The reasons for Alfred's interest will require some further explanation.

Pope Gregory the Great, who held the papal see from 590–604, was known as the 'apostle of the English', the sponsor of the English mission that sent Augustine and his followers to Kent in the year 597. He was born in 540, the son of a Roman senator, and for the first half of his life pursued a secular career, eventually becoming Prefect of Rome in the year 571. But his religious vocation was strong and after his father's death he became a contemplative monk on the Caelian Hill in Rome. The experience was formative, and in the *Pastoral Rule* (II, 7) he later wrote:

> While a leader is preoccupied with exterior matters he must not lessen his solicitude for the inner life. Nor when he is preoccupied with his inner life should he relax his watch on exterior concerns. Otherwise, by being engrossed in the pressing duties that assail him, he will experience an interior collapse; or by keeping himself busy solely with things that concern his inner life, he will end up neglecting his external duties to his neighbours.

The push and pull of the inner life and the outer life is typical of Gregory's concerns, and it is this that seems to have struck a chord with King Alfred. Gregory stressed the importance of reading the Bible and the Church Fathers for their insights into human nature and the mind of God. Reading, thinking, meditating, putting thoughts into action: all this was an essential part of Gregory's philosophy.

From 579 Gregory had become papal representative in Constantinople; here he wrote his celebrated classic *Moralia in Job*, a biblical commentary that also served as a springboard for theological and philosophical reflections. On his return to Rome Gregory became abbot of the monastery of St Andrew, which he had earlier founded on the Caelian Hill.

Four years later he was elected Pope, and he left the contemplative life. He became a great statesman, dealing skilfully with the various Germanic nations that had risen to prominence since the collapse of the larger Roman Empire, securing peace with the Lombards in northern

Figure 4a   The Caelian Hill, Rome

Italy and friendly relations with the Franks and Visigoths.[3] He also continued to write, producing in his early years as Pope the *Pastoral Rule* and the *Dialogues*, both destined to become literary classics in Anglo-Saxon England, where they were read and studied in the minsters and cathedral schools and, in the Alfredian period, translated into English.[4]

The title itself of Gregory's *Liber regulae pastoralis* or the *Book of Pastoral Rule* reveals how it was indebted to monastic guidebooks such as the *Regula* or Rule of St Benedict (Benedict of Nursia: born 480, died 543 or 547) founder of the Benedictine Order, at the time a loose association of monasteries all following the same set of rules and customs for their daily practice. Gregory in his *Regula pastoralis*, to give it its short title, was aiming at a similar rule or manual to be used by the secular clergy, especially bishops and priests. In the *Regula pastoralis* there is a balance between withdrawal and active service, between contemplation of divine love and the active pastoral work of the clergy. There is also much practical psychology in the treatise, which considers the many different types of human character and behaviour and shows how the pastor should temper his teaching and guidance to fit the psychology of the particular type of person or persons involved.

'THE SHEPHERD'S BOOK'

The Old English *Pastoral Care* (hereafter referred to as the *Pastoral Care*) was probably completed by the king himself at his court, with the expert help of his clerical advisers. It seems that special plans were implemented for the 'publication' of the book, which was copied and distributed to all the bishops in Alfred's kingdom. The bishops could then use it for the training of priests and clerics, who were in their turn the main educators of the wider populace. Probably at least a dozen copies of the book must have been made and each was, according to the preface, furnished with a precious *æstel* worthy fifty mancusses (a mancus was a gold monetary measure equivalent to 30 silver pennies; in his will, for example, Alfred's sword is worth 100 mancusses). The æstel was perhaps a special mount or jewelled handle used to hold a pointer. The reader would place the book open on a lectern and read it aloud, using the pointer as a guide. The evidence for this is found in four precious metal objects furnished with apertures into which the pointer could be inserted, the most famous being the Alfred Jewel, now in the Ashmolean Museum in Oxford, which sports an inscription 'ALFRED ORDERED ME TO BE MADE'.[5]

In the Old English version, the *Pastoral Care* was called *hierdeboc*, 'Shepherd's Book', developing the image of the *pastor of a flock* which is implied in the Latin title. The preface is frequently cited and anthologised in many introductory textbooks of Old English, with good reason, but students of the period have disregarded the main text of the Old English *Pastoral Care*. This neglect is to be regretted, for it is not a literal translation but a paraphrase of the original Latin, which adds cumulatively a set of extra thoughts and imagery to the text; in fact the book is more than advice aimed only at bishops, and becomes an extended meditation on the themes of rule and authority, whether secular or religious.

Another feature of the *Pastoral Care* in its Anglo-Saxon textual guise is the additional metrical preface with which the text is supplied. Again this is little read or studied today, despite its availability in a well-used modern anthology of Old English verse,[6] and literary critics rarely discuss it. Without wishing to compare it to the highly crafted verse of such poems as *Beowulf* or *The Wanderer*, I think this text has some attraction as a historical document, and also some literary value as a poem. There is a striking use of the theme of the sea-crossing *ofer sealtne sæ* ('over the salt sea', a motif still current in modern-day folk songs) and there is a clear allusion to the story of Augustine's mission and the

conversion of the 'island-dwellers', which appealed to the general sense
of origins that Anglo-Saxon readers must have felt in the 890s:

> Þis ærendgwrit Agustinus
> ofer sealtne sæ suðan brohte
> iegbuendum

> [This message Augustine
> brought from the south over the salt sea
> to the island dwellers.]

Like the Gospels of Augustine, the *Regula pastoralis* is here referred to as a
book that Gregory's chief missionary and first archbishop of Canterbury
brought with him from Italy. The book, so the poet tells us, Gregory
himself *adihtode*, 'composed' – the word could almost be translated
'dictated' – it is, so the verse preface implies, the product of Gregory's
famed eloquence, a treasure hoard of thought and wisdom.

The earlier part of the *Pastoral Care* concerns the role of the teacher
or ruler, and stipulates how he should remain constant, avoid
complacency, and balance his duties carefully; the latter half of the
work treats the different types of people and personalities that the ruler
must deal with. As church historians have shown, Gregory had a
uniquely expansive and associative writing style based on sets of
loosely connected images that exemplified his point.[7] This aspect of his
style is reflected in the Old English version. In Chapter 4 of the *Pastoral
Care*, for example, the opening sentence states the theme as the worries
of teaching which divide the attention of the mind among many
different objects and so make it less effective.[8] The authority of the
biblical Solomon is cited in support of this thesis, and there is a little
exemplum of a man on a journey who is preoccupied with other affairs
until he forgets the actual aim and purpose of his journey. And a further
Old Testament parallel, Hezekiah, king of the Israelites is mentioned
(IV Kings 20: 1–21). At this point in the chain of examples the message
shifts rather abruptly and disjointedly to a warning against pride in a
ruler, and the well-known story of Nebuchadnezzar, the king of
Babylon, is cited, whose pride in his great city led to his temporary
downfall and madness (Daniel 4: 27). The logic of the connection
between lack of attention and pride is not explained, but the moral
point is clearly expressed. As a proviso, the text then makes the
following disclaimer, adding a further thought to the argument which
is not paralleled in the Latin:

Nevertheless, although I recount this example, I do not blame great works nor legitimate power: I blame the fact that, because of them a man will become arrogant in spirit.[9]

In such reflections there is an obvious application to Alfred the re-builder of Winchester, as we know him from archaeology, and to Alfred the ruler of ninth-century Greater Wessex, as we know him from our reading of Asser and the Chronicle.

A further feature of interest in the *Pastoral Care* lies in the process of transformation that the text underwent when it was put into Old English.[10] Gregory's colourful imagery seems generally to have enticed or invited further expansion by Alfred and his team of commentators and translators. For modern readers it is what they adapt, what they add and remove from the Latin in the process of translation that adds value and interest to the Old English text. A case in point is the developed architectural image that Alfred and his advisers add to the passage describing the structure of the work. The *Regula pastoralis* offers the division of *iste liber*, 'this book', into four parts, 'so that it may reach the mind of its reader by well-ordered means, *quasi quibusdam passibus*, 'as though by steps'. Here the architectural feature, the steps, is an abstraction, a mere analogy qualified by *as though*, and has become practically a 'dead metaphor'.[11] No one is thinking of real steps or even visualising the stages in the structure of the book as steps when they read this sentence.

In the *Pastoral Care* by contrast, there is a major difference. The process of study is explained by the more concrete, everyday image of a ladder. The discourse will rise into the learner's mind *on sume hlædre*, 'on a ladder', reaching up *stæpmælum*, 'step by step', until it stands firmly on the *solor*, presumably the boarded loft, or perhaps the upper room in a stone tower.[12] *Solor* is originally a loanword, related to *solarium*, an import from Latin that had been naturalised in the Old English language. The translators are here picturing the progress of the learner by means of a metaphor drawn from the *realia* of their own world and its characteristic architecture.[13]

Another architectural image in Gregory's *Regula pastoralis* chimes well with Anglo-Saxon everyday realities. This is Alfred's policy of *burh*-building for defence against the Vikings, which was so crucial for the final decade of his rule and for the reign of his son Edward the Elder. The passage in question occurs during a discussion of loquacity.[14] Drawing on the proverbs of Solomon, the writer compares the talkative person to a *burh* or city with its gates left open, leaving it vulnerable to attack. The expressions employed are *burh ðæs modes*, 'citadel of the mind', and *openre byrig*, 'open (i.e. undefended) city'. These metaphors surely had very particular associations for any person reading the passage in the context of the renewed Viking attacks of the 890s and the early 900s. This is not quite the wartime motto of 'careless talk costs lives', but the military image of the *burh* is clearly relevant to the political situation.

A favourite set of images in the *Regula pastoralis* concerns water and its properties, and it is demonstrable that this particular imagery resonated with the interests of Alfred and his team of writers, for the *Pastoral Care* expands on the image, adapts it and even uses it as a basis for the metrical epilogue, the interesting poem attached to the end of the treatise. Part of the problem with the metrical epilogue lies in the fact that it makes better sense if it is read not in isolation (which is how it is usually presented in modern anthologies) but in the context of the developing argument and imagery of the main *Pastoral Care* itself.[15] Before reading the poem, therefore, we need to explore the symbolic use and range of significances attached to the various images of water as a well or spring, as a watercourse or aquaduct and as a pool or weir.

As a source of fresh water, the drinking well was ubiquitous in the medieval centuries. A fundamental feature of human life in many cultures, it is also biblical, featuring as a focal point of social gatherings in Old Testament narratives. And as the water of life it also has rich symbolic associations from its use in the Psalms and Gospels. Early in the argument of the *Pastoral Care* (ch. I, p. 31), the text makes its first of many references to the well as a source of water for flocks and a source of wisdom for men and women: the bishop as pastor must draw clean water so that his flock will benefit from his teaching. Here the symbolism is very clear: water equates with wisdom, with spiritual sustenance. The text returns to the idea a number of times, in a passage near the end of the *Pastoral Care* reworking the theme of water as a drink for human beings, and as irrigation for the crops. This motif is pondered along with that of ownership, for water can be channelled in aquaducts and guided along routeways (*Pastoral Care*, p. 373, 1. 2).

Watermills powered by channels of water were a common sight in Anglo-Saxon towns and villages, employed to grind wheat and barley for bread. Excavated watermills and contemporary records provide evidence for the standard design.[16] Anglo-Saxon watermills were devices in which the water rushed along the channel from a dam or weir to drive the oakwood vanes of the horizontal wheel; cogs of elm redirected the power; the wooden shaft, also of solid oak, was

Figure 4b 'A very deep pool is dammed up in the mind of a wise man'; the City Mill, present-day Winchester

reinforced with iron. The obvious and necessary prerequisite for the mill was the water supply: the millrace had to be created by damming the channel or stream. The land in the south-eastern quarter of Winchester owned by King Alfred's wife Ealhswith contained two mill-ponds. As the description of the bounds of the estate imply, the ponds were filled with water diverted down channels from the fast-flowing River Itchen to the east of the town wall.[17]

The pool of water so created is deep and still, because it is *ge-wer-ed*, literally 'weired' i.e. 'dammed up'; this is one of its fascinations as a symbol of profundity:

se wisa Salomon sæde ðætte suiðe deop pol wære gewered on ðæm wisan monnes mode, ond suiðe lytel unnyttes utfleowe
(*Pastoral Care*, 279. 14–16)

[Solomon the wise said that a very deep pool is dammed up in the mind of a wise man, and very little will flow out uselessly.]

The pool, however, can have also connotations of danger: it is the power of the restrained water that creates the fascination in the water-as-speech metaphor; in the same passage about the undefended city we read of the weir or dam, the flow doubling back on itself, the water striving to find a way out. In the Old English paraphrase, the assonance (repeated vowels) and rhymes of the three verbs *miclath, uppath, fundath* (i.e. 'increases and rises and struggles') underline Alfred's message:

> Ðæt wæter, ðonne hit bið gepynd, hit miclað ond uppað ond fundað wið ðæs ðe hit ær from com, ðonne hit flowan ne mot ðider hit wolde.

> [The water, when it is blocked, increases and rises and struggles back towards where it came from, when it cannot flow where it would wish to.]

So the pressure builds up until the sluice is opened or the dam is breached, and the water flows out in a surge and is wasted in the fen.

In the metrical epilogue to the *Pastoral Care*, we are offered a poem celebrating the ideas of the book that the reader has just finished reading.[18] In theme it dwells on the need for constancy and commitment and there is an urgent call for readers to use their time and resources to the best advantage; this is a theme that is echoed at the end of Asser's *Life of King Alfred*. In style the metrical epilogue is not overly complex, for the syntax is straightforward and easy to follow. The interest lies in the chain of associated motifs, the one leading smoothly to the next:

> Ðis is nu se wæterscipe ðe us wereda God
> to frofre gehet foldbuendum.

> [This is now the wellspring which the Lord of hosts
> promised as a consolation to us dwellers on the earth.]

In this composite metaphor, the whole of the preceding book of the *Pastoral Care* becomes a *wæterscipe* or well-spring, a rich image that covers a range of ideas and connotations: a well or font, the drink of life, irrigation of the crops, watering of flocks, a deep pool, and the danger of flooding. All these images represent the concrete realities of the Anglo-Saxon world for which Alfred and his team were writing.

If we now cite once again the passage from the metrical preface discussed above we will see some interesting connections between preface and epilogue:

> Þis ærendgwrit Agustinus
> ofer sealtne sæ suðan brohte
> iegbuendum

> [This message Augustine
> brought from the south over the salt sea
> to the island dwellers.]

Figure 4c 'The water, when it is blocked, increases and rises and struggles back towards where it came from'; the City Mill, Winchester

The *message*, which according to the metrical preface, was brought by Augustine from Gregory 'to the island-dwellers' (*ieg-buendum*), has become, in the metrical epilogue, the *wellspring* brought by the Lord as a consolation 'to the earth dwellers' (*fold-buendum*). Gregory's message was wisdom, and according to Old English *Pastoral Care* and its epilogue, the ruler gains wisdom, then pours it forth for the benefit of others. The parallel is clear in the structure of the sentence, and in the structure of the two compound ideas both ending in the agent noun *buend*, meaning 'dweller'. The dwellers on the island have become the dwellers on the earth, who draw on their accumulated wisdom in order to practise just rule and government, the 'craft of all crafts'. The king clearly thought long and hard about this theme before composing the final passage of verse that serves as an epilogue to his work.[19]

CHAPTER 5

The importance of Bede

The wooden hall with a high gable roof stands tall and prominent in the landscape. At one end is a large wooden door, strengthened with metal braces in the shape of dragons, the doorframe richly painted and decorated with serpentine carvings. Inside the hall, when the door is flung open, is a mosaic floor and a neat central hearth made of stone; the fire throws out heat and further light is provided by torches or tallow candles. Such is the picture supplemented by the reconstructions of archaeology that we have of Heorot, Hrothgar's hall in *Beowulf*, its light 'shining across the lands' (*Beowulf*, line 311). The composite image of hall and hearth is an enduring feature of medieval life. In the central Middle Ages and later the hall formed an integral part of the castle, although the hearth was then moved to the side and built into the wall. But in early medieval times the hall was a feature in its own right, and it endured throughout the period from the seventh century to the eleventh. Seen from the outside, the hall was a landmark on the horizon, but on the inside it was an emblem of home, for round the communal hearth sat the 'hearth-companions', the lord and his retinue; the phrase is found in *Beowulf*, which is set in the distant past, but the same word recurs in *The Battle of Maldon*, a poem contemporary with the events it describes in the year 991.

And the image of the hall as the communal centre was not confined to epic poetry. By comparison there is is the so-called 'Parable of the Sparrow', the counsellor's speech to King Edwin, from the Venerable Bede's *Ecclessiastical History of the English Nation*:

I see, O king, this present life of men on earth seems to me, in comparison with the time that is unknown to us, as if you were to sit feasting with your ealdormen and thegns in winter-time, the fire kindled and your hall warmed, while it rains and snows and storms outside; and there comes a sparrow and quickly flies through the house, it comes in through one door, and departs through the other.[1]

The speech occurs at a great council summoned by the king at Yeavering in the year 626. Remarkably, the archaeology of this particular site in Northumbria seems to support Bede's narrative; near a large rectangular area with post holes that marks the site of the hall is a semi-circular structure resembling a kind of wooden stage with raised seating; here the counsellors sat at special assemblies to debate their decisions.[2]

BEDE'S *ECCLESIASTICAL HISTORY OF THE ENGLISH NATION* AND ITS INFLUENCE

The most famous work of history to emerge from early medieval England is the *Ecclesiastical History of the English Nation* by the Northumbrian monk and scholar Bede which he completed in the year 731.[3] In his learned Latin, Bede related the story of the settlement of southern Britain by various groups of people from Jutland and northern Germany, their eventual conversion to Christianity, and their gradual development of a common cultural identity in the history of the Church. In a preface, Bede dedicated his work to a contemporary, no less a person than Ceolwulf (pronounced 'Cheolwulf'), king of Northumbria, and he showed him a draft copy for his approval before sending him the final version. The king was a learned man, literate in Latin and sympathetic to Bede's project; six years later, in the year 737, he even abdicated and became a monk at Lindisfarne. In dedicating his work to Ceolwulf, Bede explained that the purpose of his history was to provide models of good and bad behaviour and to make available the deeds and sayings of the men *nostrae gentis*, 'of our nation'.

Bede was an excellent historian, a careful sifter of his sources who used oral accounts and traditions only when they could be verified by eyewitnesses, and he wrote to various leading figures in the Church of his day for further information, especially on the subject of the church in their region. So for example he tells us that his source in Canterbury was the very learned Albinus, a scholar of Greek (unusual for the time) who is reported to have read and spoken Latin as fluently as his mother tongue English (Bede, Book V, ch. 20). Albinus had historical resources available to him – he had become abbot of St Peter's and St Paul's monastery (later known as St Augustine's) at Canterbury in 709 – and obviously knew the local traditions. An intermediary between Bede and Albinus was Nothhelm, a priest in London and later archbishop, who even went on a fact-finding journey to Rome, where he discovered relevant letters in the papal archive. Bede cites such letters and other documents wherever appropriate. His treatment of the figure of Pope Gregory is a case in point. Gregory the Great, who had been the instigator of the Christian mission to southern England at the end of the sixth century, naturally received much attention in Bede's work. In Book I, Bede describes the start of the mission, quoting papal letters in full wherever appropriate and in Book II he reviews Gregory's career and character and quotes letters to King Edwin and his queen from Pope Boniface.

Despite his careful historical method, Bede wrote with a clear agenda, the literary construction of the *gens Anglorum* the 'English nation' (literally 'the nation of the Angles'), interpreting and shaping his theme of the early history of the English Church in the light of his own reading: on the one hand the history of the early church, on the other hand the Old Testament, particularly its stories of warrior kings. Thus Augustine, first archbishop of Canterbury, and Laurentius, his successor, are compared to St Peter, first bishop of Rome, and his successor St Clement. And in Book I, Chapter 34, Æthelfrith, an early pagan king of Bernicia (the northern half of Northumbria), is seen as an English counterpart to Saul, 'but with this exception, that Æthelfrith was ignorant of the divine religion'.[4] In describing him, Bede appropriates the words of the patriarch Jacob blessing his son Benjamin from Genesis 49, 27: 'Benjamin shall ravin as a wolf; in the morning he shall devour the prey, and at night he shall divide the spoil.'

In some respects this way of looking at the heroes of the pre-conversion period recalls the Old English epic poem *Beowulf*, and the two texts present similar figures and themes, dealing with societies of the northern world on the brink of change. In both texts there is a sense that the safety and wellbeing of society depends on the guiding hand of a strong and righteous king, as in the Old Testament tradition. However, where the *Beowulf* poet is apocalyptic, depicting the end of an era, Bede is teleological and optimistic. For Bede, history has a purpose, expressed notably in his vision of a series of seven kings who successively rule as overlord of southern Britain, gaining – with setbacks and recoveries – in strength, wisdom and quality of faith from generation to generation (the idea is important and will be discussed further below). The clarity and breadth of Bede's historical vision coupled with this theological and political agenda are obvious reasons for the popularity of his work. Here, within the pages of the *History*, are mirrors for princes and models for kings to follow.

The dedication to a lay person was important: Bede evidently had a didactic purpose, and envisaged King Ceolwulf and other lay people reading his *History* or hearing it read (which was a common practice). His expectations were fulfilled, for the Latin text of the *Ecclesiastical History* was indeed widely read, to judge by the number of manuscript copies that survive. In the late ninth century, the *Ecclesiastical History* was turned into English prose; the translation was done by a Mercian scholar and he was perhaps actually resident in Mercia, although his project chimed well with the West Saxon policy of educational reform. In short, there were two versions of Bede available in the tenth century: on the one hand there was the original Latin text, circulating in Europe among the Latin-trained elite, and on the other hand the Old English *Bede*, available only in England (since very few people in Europe knew Old English). In fact the Latin version arguably took second place in tenth-century England, while the Old English paraphrase was widely copied.[5] In either language it became a resource on which writers such as Ælfric or the various writers of the Anglo-Saxon Chronicle could draw.

In the process of translation the text was edited, abbreviated and adapted, the omissions tending to be details of Roman history, chronology, doctrinal disputes and papal letters, while the occasional additions are didactic and explanatory. As George Molyneaux points out, the dedicatory preface to King Ceolwulf was included, but the resulting text is more obviously a text designed for 'Christian instruction'.[6] And as Greg Waite has shown, this Old English preface was authored by yet another adapter, most likely a West Saxon: the Mercian scholar's translation of Bede was complemented by a West Saxon preface based on Bede but with clear applications to the new situation of Greater Wessex.[7] What was originally a Mercian work had been appropriated by the West Saxons.

Now in an Old English guise, the preface explains the uses of history to an audience facing a different world on the cusp of the tenth century (for the text, see Interlude II). New passages added by the Old English adapter, though still in the voice of 'Bede', include the following:

> For this reason it is good to praise the good and blame the evil, so that he may prosper who hears it. But if the other will not hear it, how else will he be taught? I wrote this for your need and for that of your people; and because God chose you as king: it is right and proper for you to teach your people.

As will be clear from comparison with the *Pastoral Care*, this injunction to the king himself to teach his people is 'Alfredian' in tone and subject matter, and it takes further the emphasis in the original Latin on learning from the models of history.[8] Here was an opportunity for later Anglo-Saxon readers to derive timely lessons, learning about kingship and sanctity and the benefits of monasticism, just as a new unified English nation was becoming a political reality under the tenth-century West Saxon dynasty.

THE CONVERSION OF ÆTHELBERHT

Book I of the *Ecclesiastical History* narrates the momentous events of the year 597, when Pope Gregory the Great sent a group of missionaries from Italy to the former Roman colony of *Britannia*. These were led by an Italian monk called Augustine (who seems to have been named after the great fourth-century theologian Augustine of Hippo). Arriving in Kent, the Italians were given a warm reception by Æthelberht (OE: Æðelberht) the pagan Anglo-Saxon king of *Cantia*, who reportedly gave them a place to live *in ciuitate Doruuernensi* or, as it is called in the Old English version, *in Cantwara byrig* (i.e. Canterbury).The Old English *Bede* reports this decisive moment as follows (Book I, ch. 14; cf. Bede, Bk I, ch. 25):

> Þa sealde se cyning him wunenesse ond stowe in Cantwara byrig, seo wæs ealles his rices ealdorburg, ond swa swa he geheht, him ondlifen forgeaf ond weoruldþearfe

> [Then the king gave them a place to live in *Cantwara byrig*, which was the capital city of all his realm, and just as he had promised he gave them sustenance and their worldly needs.]

This magnanimous gesture led to the establishment of the archbishopric of Canterbury, an institution which is taken for granted today, although it had not been part of Pope Gregory's original plan, since he had had the large port of *Londinium* in mind as the intended home for the chief bishop of the mission. But Canterbury had many ancient associations, and in the political climate of the time it was an expedient choice. *Cant*, from *Cantia*, is the old British name for the region inhabited by the tribe of the *Cantii*, originally adapted from the Celtic by the Romans to denote this area in the south-eastern corner of Britain. It is a reminder of the ancient associations which the *ciuitas Doruuernesi* had with imperial Rome.

Once a large Roman city during the days of the empire, Canterbury still had its ancient city walls, various grand public buildings and the old theatre, and shrines and churches; all these, though dilapidated, were still standing some two hundred years after the Romans had left.[9] The theatre had become a public meeting place, and the eastern part of the city within the walls was well populated, while the western part, prone to flooding from the river, was reserved for agricultural use.[10] The fact that the city walls still stood was important: this was a strong city able to defend itself, and eventually it came to be called *Cantwara burh*, literally 'the city of the dwellers in Kent'. They called it a *burh* with good reason. Also spelt *burg*, and *byrig*, the OE noun *burh* is connected with a verb *beorgan*, 'to protect, fortify', and it denotes a fortified place, a citadel, or city. It is one of the many walled towns, some Roman urban centres, others new Anglo-Saxon foundations, that were to play such a crucial role in the formation of England in the tenth century. This process of town-planning will be considered in more detail in chapters below, but it is worth remembering that not only the Old English institution of the *burh* but also the name itself is still with us; it gave rise to the modern word *borough* and the modern place-name Bury, both forms seen in numerous place-names occurring not only across the country from Canterbury to Banbury, Malmesbury and Glastonbury but also up the country, as far as Anglian influence extended, from Peterborough to Gainsborough, Bamburgh and even Edinburgh in the far north.

At crucial moments in his plot and for dramatic confrontations, Bede departed from his careful historical method and also used his imagination creatively to picture the scene. For example, the short cameo that he paints of Æthelberht's reception of the Augustan mission is vivid and interesting. Bede gives us authentic detail: the island of Thanet just off the east coast of Kent (in those days it was separated from the mainland by a channel), a description of its size and proportions, the arrival there, rather than on the mainland, of the cautious Augustine with his forty Italian clerics and acolytes, their message sent to the king, and the king's positive response. From Bede's description, we can picture their stately procession across Thanet to the meeting place, with the silver cross and portrait of Christ borne before them, all of which must have been intended to impress.

Of additional interest perhaps to the modern reader is the mention of Æthelberht's paganism, one of several rare nuggets that Bede gives us of the now forgotten old beliefs:

Some days afterwards the king came to the island and, sitting in the open
air, commanded Augustine and his comrades to come thither to talk with
him. He took care that they should not meet in any building, for he held
the traditional superstition that, if they practised any magic art, they might
deceive him and get the better of him as soon as he entered.[11]

With his belief in magic, Æthelberht sought to avoid threats to his person
indoors, where magic was more efficacious. It is fruitful to compare the
above passage with its paraphrase as rendered into Old English in the
ninth century, for where Bede had spoken of the practice of an old
superstition (*uetere usus augurio*) and magical art (*maleficae artis*), the
anonymous translator, as though sympathetic or aware of some basis for
the king's anxiety, uses the phrase *breac ealdre healsunge*, 'he employed an
old counter charm', and the compound notion of *drycræft*, 'the art of a
druid' or 'the craft of a wizard', to express the same ideas. Are we to
imagine that the king intoned a counter charm as he waited outside in the
open air for the foreigners to arrive? This is the implication of the Old
English wording.[12] It chimes with what we know of the use of protective
magic more generally in early medieval society. A number of protective
charms, mostly Christian in content or wording, survive in the margins of
Anglo-Saxon manuscripts including, coincidentally, a manuscript of the
Old English *Bede*.[13] The changes brought to the text by the Old English
translator are thus full of interest, for they suggest ways in which the text
was interpreted or re-interpreted in period from 850 to 930 (during which
period the translation was made).[14]

According to Bede, it was less than a year after his dramatic encounter
with Augustine that Æthelberht submitted to baptism, and thereafter he
became a great promoter of Christianity in Canterbury and the
surrounding region. He founded church buildings, including one on
Thanet; in particular he built a church within the eastern part of the city,
on the site of a temple or chapel associated with the ancient Church of
the Roman period. This was later to be called Christ Church, the
cathedral and seat of the archbishops of Canterbury that was to play a
key role in the religion and politics of Anglo-Saxon England, and far
beyond that time too. To the east, just outside the walls of the city,
Æthelberht and Augustine also founded the monastery of St Peter and St
Paul. The fact that Archbishop Augustine was a monk – as opposed to a
secular cleric – was another crucial factor in the coming of Christianity
to England, for it meant that the vocation of the monk was particularly
favoured, and it set a precedent for future monastic archbishops in the
tenth century such as Oda, Sigeric and Dunstan.

Right from the start St Peter's and St Paul's also served as a mausoleum for the kings of Kent and the archbishops of Canterbury, and it later became known as St Augustine's, the partner institution to Christ Church, and another dynamic force in the development of the Anglo-Saxon world. It was here in 716 on his death that Æthelberht was laid to rest after his long and eventful reign. As Bede presents him, his achievements were both cultural, the conversion to the new religion, and political, the assumption of national overlordship. Even though England did not exist either as a name or as a unified country in this period, and appears rather more like a set of clans or tribes, nevertheless there was some sense of common culture and language, even when one of these regions held a dominant position over the others. This was not yet England, but the seeds were being sown, as the dominant power shifted from Kent to Northumbria.

The word Bede uses in his Latin is *imperium*, 'empire, imperial power', though he qualifies this as 'imperium huiusmodi', the 'overlordship of this kind' to which all the kings and sub-kings south of the Humber were subject. Bede goes on to list the names of seven kings who had achieved this distinction, Æthelberht being the third in chronological succession. The list in many ways presents an agenda for the political history that Bede is aiming to cover, as if he is appealing to the reader to pay attention, for these names will prove important in the course of his book:

> The first king to hold such overlordship was Ælle, King of the South Saxons; the second was Cælin, King of the West Saxons, known in the speech of his people as Ceaulin; third, as I have mentioned, was Æthelberht, King of the Kentish folk; the fourth was Redwald, King of the East Angles, who even in the lifetime of Æthelberht was winning pre-eminence for his own people. The fifth was Edwin, King of the Northumbrians, that is, the people living north of the Humber, who was a powerful king, and ruled all the peoples of Britain, both Angles and Britons, with the exception of the Kentish folk. He also brought under English rule the British Mevanian Isles [Man and Anglesey], which lie between Ireland and Britain. The sixth was Oswald, also King of the Northumbrians but a most Christian one, who maintained the same frontiers; the seventh was his brother Oswy, who for a while ruled the same territory, and to a large extent conquered and made tributary the Picts and Scots in the northern parts of Britain. But I shall speak of these kings later.

It will be recalled that Redwald is a name often attached to the Sutton Hoo ship burial, for the grandeur of the burial mound with its fine East Anglian

Figure 5a   St Augustine's Canterbury

metalwork, Frankish Merovingian coins and Greek bowls befit the status
of a high king such as Bede is describing here. In the discussion below it
will be seen that Redwald plays a key role in the narrative of the
conversion of the Northumbrians under King Edwin, for it is Redwald who
offers refuge to Edwin as exile and fugitive, and enables him to defeat his
enemies and gain power as ruler in Northumbria.

BEDE'S ACCOUNT OF KING EDWIN

In Book II of his *History* Bede's principal focus is on Edwin, king of
Northumbria after the usurping reign of the pagan Æthelfrith, and on St
Paulinus, the Roman missionary who converts Edwin. Rather than give a
straightforward account in chronological sequence, Bede weaves the story
into the rest of his narrative, and he uses the technique of flashback to
vary the narration and underline the crucial moments in the story.
We will follow the account in Bede's original Latin first, before
considering what the later Old English paraphrase brings to the narrative.
    The story in Book II, Chapter 9 tells how Edwin marries a Kentish
princess, a Christian, and so comes under the sway of the new religion

and its representative: the recently consecrated bishop Paulinus, who has come up from the south in the company of the king's Kentish bride. A year passes, and the assassin Eomær appears in the province. Claiming he is on a diplomatic mission from the king of the West Saxons, he gains an audience with Edwin in the royal hall on the river Derwent near York. The murder is thwarted, however, by Lilla, *minister regi amicissimus*, 'the most loyal of the king's thegns', who dies in the act of shielding the king from the thrust of Eomær's poisoned dagger. Then, 'on the same night of holy Easter', the queen safely bears the king a daughter. Impressed by these events, and by his subsequent victory in a retributive expedition against the West Saxons, Edwin vows to renounce idols. But though he promises Paulinus that he will honour his wife's religion, Edwin delays his own baptism, since he likes to discuss with his counsellors or sit alone pondering his life and the ways before him.

Bede's *History* now records two letters from Pope Boniface to the king and queen (chs 10 and 11), before resuming the story in Chapter 12. Bishop Paulinus, by virtue of his sanctity, knows of another time many years before when Edwin had sat alone pondering his life and its purpose. At this point in the narrative, Bede reverts to that previous occasion. The flashback returns to the period before Edwin succeeded to the throne, when he had spent many years in exile, including a time at the court of Redwald, king of the East Angles. One night Edwin is called out of bed by a man outside. This 'most faithful friend' warns him that Æthelfrith (the aforementioned pagan king of Northumbria) is pursuing him and has sent messages persuading Redwald to betray and destroy him. As Edwin sits on a stone outside the hall pondering this fate, he sees a mysterious vision. A figure in strange garments promises him three things: deliverance from his enemies, a 'great gift in the future' of a powerful throne, and counsel to salvation and a better life, on condition that he will follow the salutary advice when it comes to him. The man lays his hand on Edwin's head and declares that this will be the sign for him. Then the figure disappears, and Edwin is left pondering the vision as he sits on the stone.

Suddenly his trusty friend reappears with good news: Redwald has relented, following the prompting of his queen that honour is 'worth more than all treasures', and has decided to help Edwin gain his rightful throne. Events turn out well: a sudden sally from East Anglia catches Æthelfrith unawares at Hatfield Chase, where he is defeated and killed. The flashback ends here, at the end of the chapter, and Bede returns us to

Northumbria to the figure of King Edwin sitting alone and pondering the way ahead. Paulinus now approaches him, places his hand on the king's head and calls on him to fulfil the promise he made in his vision.

This narrative, skilfully crafted by Bede, is clearly one of loyalty, of keeping to one's word, repaying services rendered. Edwin promises to convert because of his experiences and because of the benefits he will gain. At the same time, he is served well by the loyalty of his friends and followers. The final chapters of Book II recount the latter stages of Edwin's conversion narrative. In a famous scene, Edwin calls a council of his chief men, who decide to accept the new faith and destroy the pagan temples (ch. 13). But this is only an early stage in a greater story that Bede is unfolding. The narration of events accelerates: there are no more dramatic scenes and few set-piece descriptions. Edwin is baptised at St Peter's in York and begins the building of a stone church, an unfinished project that only his eventual successor St Oswald will complete. For the next six years until Edwin's fall in battle, Paulinus spreads the faith preaching and baptising with Edwin's support (Bk II, chs 14 and 15). By Chapter 16, a short account of the bishop's preaching in Lindsey, there is a sense that Bede is summing up, compiling a tally of the achievements of the reign. Bede praises the general peace and security that Edwin established, so that though a woman were to walk alone with her new-born child she could travel unharmed across the whole island, from one sea to the other. Also, on heavily travelled roads bronze cups were placed on poles near streams so that travellers could refresh themselves, and because of the authority of the king no one purloined them except for their own necessary use.

THE SET-PIECE SCENES AND THEIR OLD ENGLISH STYLE

One of the attractions of the *Ecclesiastical History* – in whatever language it is read – is its set-piece scenes, which accumulate to form a powerful evocation of the lost world of seventh-century Britain. The prose – whether Latin or English – recreates dramatic moments, makes arresting images and presents lively characters. But particularly in their Old English versions, these passages recall themes or imagery in Old English poems such as *Beowulf* or *The Wanderer*, and in this respect they are worth examining for their style and choice of word or phrase, for this in turn contributes to their overall meaning. A particularly vivid moment, for instance, is the scene on Thanet where Æthelberht receives his guests with cautious hospitality, delivers a fair speech in response to their mission, and grants them the use of the city of Canterbury. The scene could be compared fruitfully with the scenes of hospitality in *Beowulf*.

Particularly in his account of the reign of Edwin, to give another example, Bede presents situations in which characters live out the values of their society and face problems and dilemmas much as they do in *Beowulf*. One such value is a common issue in *Beowulf*, from the dispute with Unferth through to the cowardly flight of the retainers during the final battle with the dragon. This is the question of loyalty to one's king, or generally of keeping faith and holding to one's word. A clear parallel in the Old English *Bede* is the account of the assassin Eomaer's attack against Edwin, a scene reminiscent of the dramatic confrontations between king and guest that occur also in *Beowulf*:

> Then he entered, as if to deliver his lord's errand. And as with crafty lips he reported his feigned errand and falsely whispered, suddenly he got up, and drawing his weapon under his garment, rushed on the king. Now when Lilla saw this, who was the most devoted of the king's attendants, having no shield at hand to defend the king, he interposed his body to meet the thrust. And Eomaer thrust through the king's attendant and wounded the king. Then he was at once assailed with weapons on all sides. But still he slew with his wicked dagger yet another of the king's attendants in the tumult, who was called Forthere.[15]

No wonder Beowulf and his men are required to make a pile of their weapons at the door, and leave men to guard it, as they visit Hrothgar in his hall at Heorot. Heroic life is precarious and treacherous, and potentially brief and violent, if loyal retainers are not on hand as they are here. An added touch in the Old English version of this passage (as opposed to Bede's original Latin) is the mention of the assailant's *geswippre muþe* (literally 'cunning mouth'). The description of his concealed weapon as 'wicked' (*manfull*) translating Bede's Latin *nefanda* is an interesting personification of the treacherous weapon (OE *Bede*, Bk II, ch. 8).

The ideal of absolute loyalty also features in the episode of Edwin's exile at the court of Redwald, king of the East Angles. When Edwin appeals for protection he asks Redwald to be his *feorhhyrde*, 'life-preserver' (OE *Bede*, Bk II, ch. 9). This Old English poetic compound, which is made up of the two elements *feorh*, a word for 'life' occurring mostly in poetry, and *hyrde*, meaning 'keeper', implies in this context that Edwin has made a formal appeal to Redwald on the basis of a shared set of ethical conventions. Later he refers to the appeal as a *wære*, a formal compact. It is this solemn agreement that

Edwin feels he cannot break, despite the warning by Edwin's 'friend the most trustworthy' *his freond se getreowesta* (p. 126, l. 30). When the friend alerts him to the danger and offers to conceal him elsewhere, Edwin's gracious refusal sounds like a prose version of a speech from *Beowulf*:

> Eadwine replied: 'I am grateful to you for your offer and your love, but yet I cannot do what you advise, and wilfully forsake the compact (OE: *wære*) made with so great a king, seeing that he has done me no harm nor showed any hostility. And if I must suffer death, I would rather he put me to death than a meaner man.

His friend leaves him sitting despondently on a stone before the hall 'troubled with many a feverish thought' (p. 129, l. 11). The image is reminiscent of exile figures in Anglo-Saxon verse, from the speaker of *The Wife's Lament* sitting out the 'summer-long day' to the solitary of *The Wanderer*, musing alone on the truth 'that in a man it is a noble virtue / to hide his thoughts, lock up his private feelings, / however he may feel. A weary heart / cannot oppose inexorable fate, / and anxious thought can bring no remedy.[16] These poems eventually were copied in the Exeter Book anthology of *c.*975, but we imagine that similar writings in prose and verse were also being read earlier in the ninth or tenth century. It was a stock theme in the literature, with which late Anglo-Saxon readers would have been familiar.

Probably the best known and most often quoted passage in Bede's *History* is the arresting image of the sparrow flying through a hall in the dead of winter, the passage alluded to at the beginning of this chapter. This extended metaphor for human life occurs in a speech during the council that Edwin holds to debate the acceptance of Christianity. Bede's Latin is vivid enough, but the Old English gains in spontaneity and added detail:

> I see, O king, this present life of men on earth in comparison with the time that is unknown to us, as if you are sat feasting with your earls and thanes in winter-time, the fire kindled and your hall warmed, while it rains and snows and storms outside. A sparrow comes and flies swiftly through the hall – it comes in at one door and out at the other. So then, for the time that he is inside he is not touched by the winter storm, but that is a twinkling of an eye and a brief moment, and he proceeds from one winter to the other winter. So also this life of men appears for a short space of time: what may have gone before and what may follow after, we do not know. Therefore, if this teaching can bring us anything more knowledgeable or suitable, then it is worth our while to follow it.

In contrast to Bede's stately Latin, the Old English version of the passage prefers the dynamic quality of the verb rather than the static Latin noun. In the description of the storm, the clause 'while it rains and snows and storms outside' is rendered more dramatic by effects of rhythm, alliteration and half-rhyme in the Old English; in the following extract the symbols / and x mark stressed and unstressed syllables, the pattern of stresses (or lifts as they are called in Old English poetics) sounding out a particular rhythm:

x   x / x   x   / x   x   / x / x

ond hit rine ond sniwe ond styrme ute.   [*hit* = 'it'; *ute* = 'outside']

The Old English writer then adds the further detail of 'the twinkling of an eye' to capture the brevity of the incident and perhaps also to provide biblical depth and allusion.[17] The accumulation of small-scale stylistic effects serves to enrich the text further. Already a powerful image, it acts like a parable taking the reader or listener beyond the surface details of the event into a 'hidden realm ... overflowing with significance'.[18]

The style underlines the ultimate message. For the reader it is no surprise that Edwin decides to convert in the end, given the force of the arguments presented to him, and after the decision has been taken, the king consults Cefi, his former high priest, about the proposed demolition of the pagan temple, potentially a highly volatile situation, given that the decision of the king and council must now be accepted by the people. Cefi undertakes the first step himself, and the story moves to the crucial moment where he puts his words into action.

Again it is worth comparing and contrasting the differing emphases of the Latin and Old English versions if only imperfectly through the medium of modern English. The following is a rendering of the Latin version by Bede:

> And at once, casting aside his vain superstitions, he asked the king to provide him with arms and a stallion; and mounting it he set out to destroy the idols. Now a high priest of their religion was not allowed to carry arms or to ride except on a mare. So, girded with a sword, he took a spear in his hand and mounting the king's stallion he set off to where the idols were. The common people who saw him thought he was mad. But as soon as he approached the shrine, without any hesitation he profaned it by casting the spear which he held into it; and greatly rejoicing in the knowledge of the worship of the true God, he ordered his companions to destroy and set fire to the shrine and all the enclosures.[19]

By contrast, the Latin passage was adapted into Old English prose on the following lines (note the different way in which verbs are handled in the later version):

> And he at once cast from him the idle foolishness he had previously entertained, and asked of the king that he give him weapons and a stallion to ride on so that he could throw down the idols. For the bishop of their holiness was not allowed to carry weapons or ride except on a mare. So the king gave him a sword with which he girded himself; and he took his spear in hand and leapt onto the king's steed and proceeded to the idols. When the people saw him so equipped, they supposed that he did not know rightly any more and had gone raving mad. As soon as he approached the sanctuary, he shot his spear into it so that it stuck fast in the sanctuary, and he was overjoyed at his new understanding of worship of the true God. And he ordered his companions to throw down the whole sanctuary and burn the timbers.[20]

Again a brisker effect is created by a series of dynamic verbs of motion (here translated as 'gave', 'took', 'leapt', 'proceeded') and a vivid impression remains of the spear left quivering in the inner wall of the temple.

The sense that the Edwin story is an episode in a grander narrative is even more strongly conveyed in the final pages of the Old English version than it is in the Latin. Bede's reproduction of Pope Boniface's letters is omitted, thus placing greater symbolic weight on the events of Edwin's conversion story, as Sharon Rowley has argued, and also making the English rather than Roman or Continental aspect of the *History* far more prominent.[21] The writer is keen to tell the essential story and exclude all extraneous matter. To keep the focus on Edwin and what is to be his eventual fall in battle, the translator makes the radical decision to remove Chapters 17, 18, 19 in which Bede had reproduced three letters of Pope Honorius. Following the death of Edwin, both Latin and Old English texts now relate the aftermath: the cruelty of the victorious Welsh and Mercians after the battle, and the flight of Paulinus to Rochester.

Stylistically, the end of the story in the Old English is interesting, for it picks out rhetorical effects in Bede's Latin and heightens them further. Both the Latin and Old English texts are of course narrating the same events, and in both versions Book II ends on a similarly eulogistic note, even though the mission has suffered a setback with the fall of the king and the flight of the bishop. All is not in vain, for Paulinus 'left behind also in his church at York, an ecclesiastic of great holiness'.

This deacon, James, becomes a kind of rearguard who 'by his teaching and by baptism ... took much spoil from the old enemy'. But I would argue that the translator of the Old English *Bede* had the advantage of composing in the vernacular, in the immediately comprehensible mother tongue of his audience. Even more so than the Latin Bede, he reproduces the feel of an Old Testament narrative, like Moses before the Promised Land, and in the rhythmical and alliterative style of his Old English, adds an extra phrase *thæt is godra dæda* and more rhythm to the final cadence (Bk II, ch. 16):

> Ond he tha eald ond dagana full, thæt is godra dæda, æfter thon the haligu gewritu sprecað, thæt he fædera weg wæs fylgende.

The last four words are interconnected by alliteration on the sounds 'd', 'f' and 'w', by syllable count and rhythm, and by the final word *fylgende*, 'following', which highlights the message. James the Deacon leads a full life, teaching church music after times of peace have returned, and then 'old and full of days, that is of good deeds, as the scriptures say, he followed the way of his fathers.'

BEDE'S THEORY OF KINGSHIP

This chapter began with Bede's preface to Ceolwulf, in which he justified the relevance of history to the present day. It is clear that by turning the *Ecclesiastical History* into Old English the translator sought to present a similar message to his late ninth or early tenth century audience. A theological significance is attached to the king as a representative and role model for his followers, and he is praised for the great peace that he brings to the nation. In these ways, Edwin was a moral example of wisdom and governance, a model of kingship for later readers to ponder. As will be seen in Chapters 14–16, Edgar the Peaceable is presented in similar terms, in writings associated with Æthelwold and Winchester, echoing Bede's admiration for Edwin. The story of Edwin as told in the Old English *Bede* is an exemplum of an early king of Northumbria to whom the later rulers of a greater England could see themselves as worthy successors.

In the year 829, to give another particularly significant example, Alfred's grandfather Ecgberht defeated the Mercians in battle and overran their country. The Winchester version of the Anglo-Saxon Chronicle (probably written from the standpoint of the 880s) reports this event and dwells on its significance. Here is the first sentence; it opens atmospherically with the darkening lunar eclipse on the night before the mass of Midwinter, in other words, at Christmas:

> Here the moon darkened on the mass-night of Midwinter, and in the same year King Ecgberht conquered the kingdom of Mercia and all that was south of the Humber, and he was the eighth king who was *bretwalda* (overlord) . . .

For the Winchester Chronicler, the darkening moon was a portent of change. Ecgberht had conquered Mercia and become the eighth overlord of Britain (the term *bretwalda* will be considered shortly). Such a claim was not totally unjustified, since the Northern Welsh and the Northumbrians had also submitted to Ecgberht's overlordship, and he was effectual ruler of a Greater Wessex which included Sussex and Kent within its borders.

Ecgberht went on to further military gains thereafter. Carried away by the success of this new West Saxon overlord, the patriotic Chronicler breaks into a kind of loose poetic style as he lauds his king's victory at the Battle of Hingston Down. Though his text does not follow the strict rules of metre and poetic vocabulary that we find in *Beowulf*, there are rhymes on the verbs and alliterative effects on the sounds 'w' and 'f', all of which serve to highlight this report as a special event:[22]

> Her cuom micel scip-here on West-walas ond hie to anum gecierdon, ond wiþ Ecgbryht Westseaxna cyning winnende wæron. Þa he þæt hierde ond mid fierde ferde ond him wiþ feaht æt Hengest-dune ond þær gefliemde ge þa Walas ge þa Deniscan.

> [Here a large Viking ship-army arrived in Cornwall and they joined forces to wage war against Ecgbert, king of Wessex. When he heard this he moved up with his army and fought with them at Hingston Down and put to flight both the Cornish and the Danish.]

In this battle, the *Westwalas*, the 'Western Welsh' – in other words the Cornish, in alliance with a fleet of Danish Vikings, were defeated on the field of Hengestdun. There are two possible locations for this site, both called Hingston Down and both located in the west of England. The name 'Hengest-dun' literally means Stallion Hill, but contemporary readers of the Chronicle might have heard resonances of the name Hengest, legendary ancestor of Æthelberht, the first Christian king of Kent, who as we have seen was celebrated by Bede in his *Ecclesiastical History*. Moreover, Hengest is also the hero of the (unfortunately fragmentary) poem *The Fight at Finnsburh*, a tragic tale of feud and revenge which is also retold as an episode in *Beowulf*.[23]

Figure 5b   Eclipse of the moon

THE CONCEPT OF THE 'WIDE-RULER'

Since his historical writing was so widely read, Bede was inevitably an influence on the compiler of the Anglo-Saxon Chronicle, who adapted the earlier agenda of the *Ecclesiastical History of the English People* for his own purposes. Both Bede and the Chronicler were interested in the notion of Anglian/English identity, in the cultural connections between the various regions, and in the development of Christendom in Britain. But where Bede wrote from a Northumbrian viewpoint, the Chronicle is firmly West Saxon, and its author is likely to have been attached to the West Saxon court and perhaps based at the principal town of Winchester in the heartland of Wessex. Sometimes the Chronicler takes over a few ideas from Bede directly. This is very evident for instance in his treatment of Ecgberht, King Alfred's grandfather, especially in the account of the conquest of Mercia in the year 829. As we have seen, the Chronicler immediately links this conquest with the idea of the *imperium* or overlordship over Britain, which is one of the themes of Bede's *History*. Bede himself listed seven overlords and traced a pattern whereby the overlordship shifted from Kent to Northumbria. By the time Bede was writing his *History* in the eighth century that supremacy had gone to the Mercians, ruling as overlords and exacting tribute from the kings of the other regions.

In fact historians tend to speak of the Mercian Supremacy, meaning King Offa and the eighth century.

But now in the ninth century the West Saxons were in the ascendancy. And the West Saxon author of the Chronicle found one literary justification for *imperium* or overlordship in his reading of Bede. He takes over Bede's list and applies it to Ecgberht. There is no mention of the supremacy of Offa or the Mercians; it is Ecgbert who holds the *imperium*, and the Chronicler takes – or perhaps invents – a compound noun *bretwalda* and uses it as a title for this office. This is a West Saxon notion, at least as far as the records go, for Bede does not use it, nor does the Mercian translator of the Old English *Bede* seem to be aware of it. The word is clearly made up of two elements, but the first, *bret-* (or in one manuscript *bryten-*), is ambiguous; it seems to imply either 'wide-ruler', or even more ambitiously 'Ruler of Britain'. Historians have often applied this word retrospectively to the seven kings of Bede's history, but in fact the word *bretwalda* first appears in the ninth-century Anglo-Saxon Chronicle.[24] It is an indicator of the far-reaching ambitions of the Wessex dynasty at the end of the ninth century.

INTERLUDE II

The dedication to the king in the preface to the Old English *Bede*

It has been shown that this preface was composed by a West Saxon writer and found its way into three of the surviving manuscripts of the Old English *Bede*, originally the work of a Mercian writer who was active at some time in the late ninth or early tenth century. We do not know if it was found in the other two manuscripts extant, because they have lost leaves from the beginning.

Ic Beda Cristes þeow and mæssepreost sende gretan ðone leofastan cyning Ceolwulf; and ic þe sende þæt spell þæt ic niwan awrat be Angelþeode and Seaxum, ðe sylfum to rædanne and on emtan to smeageanne, and eac on ma stowa to writanne and to læranne; and ic getreowige on ðine geornfulnysse, forþon ðu eart swyðe gymende and smeagende ealdra manna cwidas and dæda, and ealra swyðost þara mærena wera ure þeode. Forðon þis gewrit oððe hit god sagað be godum mannum, and se ðe hit gehyreð, he onhyreð þam, oððe hit yfel sagað be yfelum mannum, and se ðe hit gehyreð, he flyhð þæt and onscunað. Forþon hit is god godne to herianne and yfelne to leanne, þæt se geðeo se þe hit gehyre. Gif se oðer nolde, hu wurð he elles gelæred? For þinre ðearfe and for þinre ðeode ic þis awrat; forþon ðe God to cyninge geceas, þe gedafenað þine þeode to læranne.

[I Bede, Christ's servant and mass-priest, hereby greet the dearest King Ceolwulf. And I send you this treatise that I recently wrote concerning the nation of the Angles and Saxons, for you to read and meditate at your leisure, and also to have copied and studied in more places; and I trust in your zeal, for you care a great deal for the words and deeds of men of the past and you meditate upon them, especially those of the great men of our nation. For this book either speaks good of good men, and those who hear this will imitate it, or it speaks evil of evil men, and those who hear it will avoid it and shun it. For it is good to praise the good man and to censure the bad man, so that they who hear it will prosper. And if they will not, how else will they gain an education? I have written this for your profit and for the profit of your people, and as God chose you as king it is your duty to instruct your people.]

PART III

The expansion of Wessex

In the year 899 when Edward the Elder came to the throne, he succeeded to the whole of the kingdom south of the Thames. His father had seen no point in sharing out the various regions of his dominion, leaving Wessex itself to one son or nephew and Sussex and Kent to another. This was to lead to internal strife, as we shall see, in the case of Edward's cousin Æthelwold, a member of the rival branch of the royal family. There were external conflicts too. Outside Wessex, the main threat came from the Danish Vikings, who after the Treaty of Wedmore were now established in the Danelaw beyond Watling Street. Eastern Mercia had become the region of the Five Boroughs, named after its five fortified towns of Leicester, Nottingham, Derby, Stamford and Lincoln. In addition there were the Danish-controlled regions of East Anglia and York.

As for Mercia, or rather, western Mercia (since the Five Boroughs now belonged to the Danes), this also formed part of Edward's kingdom, but at first it retained some autonomy, for it had been a separate country up to the time of Alfred's marriage to the Lady Ealhswith, a member of the royal house of Mercia. Being the son of a West Saxon father and a Mercian mother, Edward was well qualified to rule the two kingdoms. But by family arrangement, Mercia was administered by Edward's dynamic sister Æthelflæd, in conjunction with her husband, the Mercian ealdorman Æthelred. Eventually, however, Edward extended his power and influence here too.

A remarkably precise document that may date from this period is the Burghal Hidage. This catalogue of fortified towns in Wessex and Mercia allots a number of 'hides' to each town in the list. A hide was a unit of measurement, the amount of land sufficient for the needs of one farming family or household, and it was decided that each hide should provide one warrior to help man the defences of the wall of the town. On the basis that one 'pole' (i.e. 5½ yards) of wall required four men to defend it, the 'hidage' was calculated for each town depending on the length of its wall.[1] Archaeology mostly corroborates the document, demonstrating that the value of the 'hidage' corresponds in each case to the actual length of the town's fortifications.[2] There are grounds for assuming that the Burghal Hidage was compiled in the reign of Edward the Elder, perhaps before his successful campaign against the Danes in the year 917, a campaign which depended for its success on the network of fortress-towns that Alfred and Edward had created.

Overall, in a politically effective reign of twenty-five years, Edward the Elder followed wholeheartedly in his father's tracks: the revival of education and the consolidation of the fortified boroughs in Wessex and their extension into Mercia, the ultimate aim being to recover territory from the Danelaw.

CHRONOLOGY FOR PART III

899	Edward the Elder becomes king of the Angles and Saxons
early 900s	The Old English Fonthill Letter; records the misdemeanours of Helmstan
	The Old English literary production at Winchester: the Junius Psalter, Hand II of the Chronicle, the first copy of the OE *Orosius*
early 900s?	Old English *Boethius*
900	Edward's cousin Æthelwold seizes Wimborne, then flees to the north
901	Edward founds the New Minster, Winchester
902	Battle of the Holme: Edward's army defeats his cousin Æthelwold
909	Death of Bishop Denewulf; appointment of Frithestan as bishop of Winchester
909/10	Death of Asser, bishop of Sherborne and Alfred's biographer
911	Death of Æthelred, lord of the Mercians
	Edward and his sister Æthelflæd, Lady of the Mercians, begin offensive against the Danelaw, building fortified towns (*byrig*) at suitable locations
917	Edward's successful campaign against the Danes of the Danelaw
918	Death of the Lady Æthelflæd; Edward assumes power in Mercia

CHAPTER 6

The reign of Edward the Elder

Edward the Elder's first significant act when he became king was to fight a civil war to put down a rebellion by his cousin Æthelwold (who shares the same name with a famous bishop of the later tenth century). What began as a bitter dispute over Æthelwold's inheritance, soon became a rival claim to the throne. Despite the general consensus that overall Edward's reign was a political success, this was a crisis, and it is clear that matters might have turned out very differently.

Although Alfred had originally made careful provision for his son Edward in his will, the plan almost backfired. The problem, put simply, was that Alfred was the fourth of four brothers to rule the West Saxon kingdom, and the previous king, Alfred's brother Æthelred, had also had children of his own. There were two sons, male heirs with some claim to power, and in accordance with the terms of the agreement that Alfred had made with their father (and these terms are even recorded verbatim in Alfred's will) they had expected to receive more of their father's royal property on Alfred's demise. But the facts of the matter speak for themselves. Here in the words of the bequest, is the record of land granted by Alfred to his son Edward, and it is easy to see that Edward's inherited properties are very numerous:

> First, I grant to Edward my elder son the land at Stratton in Triggshire, and Hartland, and all the booklands which Leofheah holds, and the land at Carhampton, at Kilton, at Burnham, at Wedmore – and I entreat the community at Cheddar to choose him on the terms which we have previously agreed – with the land at Chewton and what belongs to it; and I grant him the land at Cannington, at Bedwyn, at Pewsey, at Hurstbourne,

at Sutton, at Leatherhead, at Alton, and all the book lands which I have in Kent.

As Keynes and Lapidge show in a very revealing map in their translation and edition of the *Life of Alfred* and other Alfredian writings, nearly all these lands and estates are located in central Wessex, in present-day Somerset, at the very heart of the old kingdom.[1] By contrast, here is the original bequest of three estates in Surrey to Alfred's nephew Æthelwold:

> And to my brother's son Æthelwold the estate the estate at Godalming, at Guildford, and at Steyning.

Contrary to the spirit of the agreement that he had made with Æthelred his brother, and (it might be added) contrary to the philosophical writings associated with his court, Alfred was not beyond showing partiality. Quite blatantly Alfred's will delivered lands in central Wessex to his son but gave precious little to his two nephews, and this precious little only on the peripheries.

Alfred's will thus provides a clear motivation for the older nephew's grievance, and Æthelwold, according to the Anglo-Saxon Chronicle entry for the year 900, lost no time in niceties: 'in this year,' it reports, Alfred died, Edward succeeded, and Æthelwold rode to Wimborne and seized it 'without leave of the king or his *witan* [council]'. Such is the so-called *parataxis*, the characteristic disjointed style of the Anglo-Saxon Chronicle: three sentences, three events, without logical connectors. The reader is left to draw out the implications. Clearly Æthelwold felt that more land was owing to him than the terms of the will allowed, and he decided to take the law into his own hands. He rode to Wimborne, because, as we know from earlier in the Chronicle, it was here in the minster church that his late father King Æthelred I, King Alfred's brother, had been buried.

At this point in the story, despite his laconic mode of writing, the Chronicler lingers over the action. In a few sentences he presents the beginning of the revolt as a dramatic stand-off. There are some similarities to another famous story of a revolt that took place in the year 786 in a long text that was interpolated into the usually short annals of the Chronicle for the 700s. This confrontation, between King Cynewulf's men, as besieging forces, and the rebel Cyneheard, holed up in a manor at a place called Merton, was presented as a short two-way dialogue: a demand and a refusal that led tragically and inevitably to a fight to the death for Cyneheard and his men.[2] In the case of Æthelwold, the Chronicler must surely have known the Cynewulf and Cyneheard story, since it was available for consultation in his Winchester copy of the Chronicle.[3] Nevertheless he chose not to imitate its length or its two-part structure. But there are certainly echoes of its dramatic style in his summary account, for the Chronicler preserves some of the actual words spoken by Æthelwold as he confronts his royal cousin from behind (or above) the locked gates of Wimborne. Here is the passage (the Old English requires a little padding in a modern paraphrase to capture its implications):

> And Æthelwold remained in the estate with the men who had given their allegiance to him, and he had blocked all the gates guarding the way in to him, and he said that he would do one of two things: live there or lie there. But then in the meantime he stole out by night and got away, and joined the Viking army in Northumbria, and the king ordered his men to ride after him, but they were unable to catch up with him.

As in heroic poems such as *Beowulf* or the later *Battle of Maldon*, Æthelwold, in the lull before the fighting begins, defies his assailants, but then rather shamefully, or so it is implied, he steals away by night. Here are his actual words of defiance, as reported by the Chronicle (note the parallelism and sound patterning):

> sæde þæt he wolde oðer oððe þær *l*ibban oððe þær *l*icgan.
>
> [he said that he would do one of two things: live there or lie there.]

Interestingly, Æthelwold's parallel expression 'live there or lie there' alliterates, perhaps for emphasis or rhetorical flourish, alliteration being a standard embellishment in English poetry, traditional verse, proverbs and sayings. It is still found, for instance, in the saying *live and let live*.

Æthelwold's stealthy retreat from Wimborne under the cover of darkness is not quite the end of the episode, for the Chronicler has one more point to make, which in fact underlines his partiality. His final sentence is a rather mean-spirited parting sally to Æthelwold, who managed to escape his pursuers, although his wife did not:

> Þa berad mon þæt wif þæt he hæfde ær genumen butan cynges leafe and ofer þara biscopa gebod, forðon ðe heo wæs ær to nunnan gehalgod.
>
> [But they did catch up with the wife whom he had taken without the king's leave and against the bishop's command, because she had been consecrated as a nun.]

The Chronicler has no more to say about the wife, but eloping with a nun was a serious crime in the time of King Alfred and his successors, and it will be seen that the Chronicler's words even echo the relevant paragraph of Alfred's Lawcode:

> Gif hwa nunnan of mynstere ut alæde butan kyninges lefnesse oððe biscepes, geselle hundtwelftig scillinga, healf cyninge, healf biscepe ond þære cirican hlaforde ðe ðone munuc age.

> [If anyone should abduct a nun from a monastery without leave of the king or the bishop, let him pay one hundred and twenty shillings: half to the king and half [divided equally] to the bishop and the patron of the monastery which owns the nun.[4]]

As the lawcode goes on to declare, an eloping nun was denied legal status, which meant that Æthelwold's wife (or indeed his widow, to anticipate the final outcome of the story) would have had few prospects for a comfortable life thereafter.

But who was this mysterious nun, and why did Æthelwold take such trouble to wed her? Nuns were often important members of the nobility. There are many cases in Anglo-Saxon history of ladies from the ruling elite taking monastic vows, often for reasons of personal faith. But there were also young women who attended nunneries to complete their education, while others took refuge there in times of war. This latter option was particularly common at the time of the Norman Conquest, when even the daughter of the king of Scotland found refuge in an English nunnery, and there was a controversy when the opportunity arose for her to marry as to whether or not she had taken full vows. The Scottish king even turned up at the monastery in support of his daughter's ambitions.

In point of fact, at the time of Æthelwold's rebellion at Wimborne, there was at least one quite famous nun living nearby, though she was not in the nunnery attached to the minster complex at Wimborne itself. We should recall *The Life of King Alfred*. When reporting the careers of Alfred's children, Asser gave the following accounts of the two daughters:

> Æthelflæd, when the time came for her to marry was joined in marriage to Æthelred, ealdorman of the Mercians; Æthelgifu, devoted to God through her holy virginity, subject and consecrated to the rules of monastic life, entered the service of God ...[5]

Later, Asser speaks of Alfred's foundation of monasteries, including one at Athelney, headed by his spiritual adviser John the Old Saxon, and one at Shaftesbury, to provide for the spiritual vocations of women:

King Alfred ordered the other monastery to be built near the east gate of Shaftesbury as a residence suitable for nuns. He appointed as its abbess his daughter Æthelgifu, a virgin consecrated to God, and many other noble nuns live with her in the same monastery, serving God in the monastic life. Alfred abundantly endowed these monasteries with estates of land and every kind of wealth (ch. 98).

Shaftesbury lies about twenty miles north of Wimborne Minster. As Alex Woolf has tentatively suggested, this might be the nunnery where Æthelwold acquired his wife.[6] And even more speculatively: was it actually Æthelgifu, the daughter of King Alfred, whom he chose as his would-be spouse?

The canon law of the Church at the time prohibited such marriages of closely related kin, but that was no deterrent for Æthelwold (after all, his uncle Æthelbald had married Judith, his grandfather's wife and consecrated queen). By marrying his cousin, Æthelwold would have secured an alliance between the two rival factions of the royal family and increased his own credibility as a claimant to the throne. Two generations later, this was certainly the issue of the day: the ruling monarch at this time was Edwy (OE spelling: Eadwig), a descendant of Alfred, who elected to marry the lady Ælfgifu, a descendant of Alfred's brother Æthelred. In the end, Oda, the archbishop of Canterbury, annulled the marriage on grounds of consanguinity, although as cousins several times removed they were hardly closely related. The question divided the ruling elite as both clergy and laity took sides in the dispute (see Chapter 13).

As far as Æthelwold was concerned, his setback at Wimborne was only temporary, for he was not content merely to escape after his failed attempt to recover his landed property. According to the Chronicle, he proceeded at full speed to Northumbria, where he joined forces with the infamous *here*. A common term in the Chronicle, the noun *here* was pronounced as two syllables 'he-re' and derived from the verb *herigan* 'to harry, raid, plunder'; it signified – at least from the perspective of the main Anglo-Saxon Chronicle with its West Saxon bias – that Æthelwold had taken up with the old enemy, 'the raiding army', i.e. the Vikings. Æthelwold may have seen it differently: Anglo-Scandinavian York had recognised him as king, and for a brief period he even issued coinage in his own name.[7]

Æthelwold now persuaded a Viking fleet to sail down the coast to East Anglia. He seems to have gathered more English support as well, which makes some historians suspect that he was nearly successful in pursuing his claim to the throne, for it looks like he had been recognised as king in several of the English regions. The bitter end, however, came a couple of years after the escape from Wimborne. A rather chaotic battle was fought, probably in 902, at a place called the Holme, in which the Kentish men fighting on King Edward's side deliberately and repeatedly ignored his order to withdraw. Their stubbornness probably came from their ranking in the army: since the Kentishmen traditionally made up the vanguard they felt honour-bound to cover the rear while the rest of the West Saxon army behind them withdrew. The character Beowulf expresses a similar sentiment in one of his retrospective speeches shortly before he goes out to face the *gryregiest* the 'terrible guest' or 'dreadful visitant' of the dragon. He recalls how in his earlier career he always preferred 'to be with the footsoldiers in the forefront' of his lord Hygelac's army:

Symle ic him on feðan beforan wolde (*Beowulf*, lines 2497–9)

In the case of the Kentishmen, the Chronicler is typically as laconic as usual, but he rises to the occasion to provide at least a few details of the fateful encounter: many of Edward's Kentish contingent fell in the battle, including, as we know from another source, Ealdorman Sigehelm (see Chapter 14 below). The Danes perhaps held the day, but if so it was a pyrrhic victory, since they lost most of their leaders, and the 'rebellion' was over. As events turned out, the pretender (to view Æthelwold from the West Saxon perspective) also fell in the fighting. But to reverse our sympathies for a moment and take Æthelwold's point of view is to see the whole episode in a different light. As a man who was able to gather support from both English and Danes, Æthelwold was an exceptional figure in the politics of the time and he might have acted as a force for Anglo-Danish unity. His loss changed the course of history.[8]

KING EDWARD AND BISHOP DENEWULF

At this time Anglo-Saxon England was still mostly a rural society, but the construction of the defensive *burh*, with its walls, gates, new streets, market and official mint, signalled the beginnings of urbanisation. Winchester, for example, proto-capital of West-Saxon England, went from strength to strength. As archaeology has shown, Alfred restored the originally Roman city, leaving intact both the city walls and the original high street that crossed the city from the west gate to the east gate. This street, now the High Street, was known at the time as the 'cheaping' or 'cheapstreet' (OE: *Ceapstræt*), from an Old English word for 'buying' or 'place for purchases'). Otherwise Alfred completely redesigned the grid of streets, which no longer corresponded to the Roman streets that now lay buried beneath the developing town.[9] The process was repeated elsewhere. Today the Anglo-Saxon street patterns are the ones that still pertain in many towns and cities in England.

The development of Winchester continued after Edward succeeded to the throne. Edward's mother, Ealhswith, the Mercian who married Alfred in 868 and who eventually died in 902, was involved in the founding at Winchester of the Nunnaminster, a monastery for nuns, later known in the Middle Ages as St Mary's Abbey. Ealhswith was evidently very devout, like her husband King Alfred, and she is associated with the Book of Nunnaminster, a prayer-book of Mercian origin.[10] And as was noted in Chapter 4, Lady Ealhswith was a property owner in Winchester, owning a tenement near the east gate and south of the main street. The evidence for Ealhswith's ownership is contained in an Old English description of the property entered into a blank space after one of the Latin prayers in the Book of Nunnaminster (the document is S 1560 in Sawyer's Catalogue). It is this estate in the south-eastern corner of the city that eventually came to form the precinct of the Nunnaminster itself. In short, Ealhswith granted her land to the nuns for their use as a nunnery.

For his part, Edward founded another monastery in Winchester. The New Minster was a large church with an aisled nave covering 790 square metres; by contrast the small, ancient cathedral (thereafter called the Old Minster) was already 250 years old, and measured a mere 354 square metres. Built right next to it, the New Minster dwarfed its old neighbour.[11] Edward's purposes in building this church are not set down in writing, but they can be extrapolated. His new royal foundation was 'a political action, underlining the king's power in the refortified borough as against that of the bishop who had previously been the most prominent figure in the area'.[12] The New Minster became the burial site of kings, an important ecclesiastical centre for the *burh* (S 1443).[13] The building is no longer extant though its outline can be seen, laid out in its original position near the present cathedral at Winchester. An impression of the grandeur of Anglo-Saxon churches can be gained from visiting early medieval buildings abroad, for example in Germany or Italy; perhaps the grandest Anglo-Saxon church still standing is St Helen's at Brixworth in Northamptonshire (Figure 6a).

Edward gained his new site by a mixture of negotiation and power politics. As Alexander Rumble has shown, the royal policy was to take control of a place and then offer other settlements or estates in

Figure 6a   Brixworth church

exchange.[14] A good example is Portchester, which was a former Roman
coastal fort that is remarkably well preserved, probably because of its
later usefulness. Offering Bishop's Waltham in Hampshire in exchange,
the king acquired Portchester for his defensive policy and converted it
into a *burh* or walled fortification. Rumble cites other instances of royal
requisition, and in some cases it is not clear that the original holders of
the estate were entirely happy with the exchange forced upon them by
the king's command.

A fascinating document and highly relevant in this context is the
declaration sent by Denewulf, bishop of Winchester, to King Edward,
informing him that he had finally persuaded the two communities at
Winchester, i.e. the Old and the New Minsters, to lease an estate for the
king's use.[15] In the style of its opening phrase 'I hereby declare to you
what happened with the estate at Beddington' it recalls the better known
Fonthill Letter (discussed in Chapter 7 below), and Denewulf uses the
same verb 'to declare' and *min leof*, 'my dear', a similar mode of address,
to his lord the king. The document is mostly objective and informative,
listing the various crops, animals and people that belong to the estate.[16]
The crucial clause comes at the end: a request, slightly defiant, from the
bishop, that the king should not in future make any more demands on

land or estates belonging to the minsters in Winchester. It looks like the bishop had lost patience, and was not willing to tolerate any more royal requisitioning.

EDWARD AND ÆTHELFLÆD

The Anglo-Saxon Chronicle continued to be written in Edward's reign at Winchester, in the full expansive style that is found also in the entries for the reign of King Alfred. Scribe II of the manuscript, who wrote the entries for the years 891–920,[17] closely follows the king's military career, his successes and occasional setbacks, and his policy of constructing fortresses in the territory recovered from the Danes. Especially in the middle years of his reign, following his defeat of the Northumbrian Danes, Edward turned his attention to the Five Boroughs and East Anglia, where he built or refortified *burh* after *burh*, and the word becomes a recurrent motif in the text of the Chronicle, particularly for the years 914–21.[18] With their frequent naming of places gained or conquered by the steady advance of West Saxon forces, the annals resemble the boundary clauses of charters, describing the territory and providing proof of occupation or ownership.[19] As each *burh* was built, the steady advance was consolidated. In the Chronicle entry for the year 917 Edward is seen as the saviour of East Anglia, the conqueror and rebuilder of the fortified towns of Passenham, Towchester, Huntingdon, Colchester; in each case those who remain seek his peace and protection.

For the Chronicler, it was *anno Domini* 918 that proved crucial; the year saw the death of Edward's sister and ally Æthelflæd, Lady of the Mercians, effectively governor, or even queen, of Mercia since her marriage to Æthelred, the Mercian lord and ruler of the region. In Alfred's time this royal couple had turned Mercia into a stalwart ally of Wessex in the struggle against the Vikings. But Edward revealed his opportunism, riding to Tamworth and seizing the *burh*, along with the allegiance of all the people of the region who had previously owed their loyalty to Æthelflæd. According to the Chronicler, all the people (OE: *þeodscype*) who had once been subject to his sister Æthelflæd *him cierde to*, 'turned to him'. And according to the same Winchester Chronicler, when Edward then proceeded to Nottingham, capturing the city, refortifying it and filling it with supporters, these were of both ethnic groups, *ægþer ge Denisc ge Englisc*, 'both Danish and English'. Meanwhile, the various leaders of the Welsh recognised Edward as their *hlaford*, their lord or overlord. The record of these events in Chronicle A, the

Figure 6b   City wall, Winchester

Winchester copy of the Anglo-Saxon Chronicle, thus emphasises the overlordship of Edward. This is the language of nation-building.

An alternative perspective on Edward's extension of his kingdom is provided by a rival chronicle written in Mercia, perhaps in response to version A, but outside the influence of the royalist circles in Wessex. Found as an interpolation in manuscript B, where it is copied as a new section after the main text or 'common stock' (the part shared with manuscript A), this so-called Mercian Register is a set of mostly brief annals that record different events and focus on different participants. Like Chronicle A, its language speaks of lordship and authority, but unlike Chronicle A the Mercian Register favours Æthelflæd, 'the Lady of the Mercians', as the active agent rather than her brother Edward.[20] Accordingly it is Æthelflæd who is able to bring Chester into her authority (*geweald*); it is to Æthelflæd that the men of York make their promises, some giving pledges and others swearing oaths. The record of Æthelflæd's death here does not mention her brother Edward's immediate seizure of power; instead the entry in the Mercian register for 918 becomes a kind of royal epitaph: it affirms that she 'justly and rightly' (*rihte*) held 'power and lordship' (*onweald* and *hlaforddom*). It is worth noting here the gendered language describing her *hlaford-dom*, literally her 'lord-ship'.

The Mercian Register now speaks of her final resting place at Gloucester in the church of St Peter, just as earlier annals in the Chronicle had recorded the burial and final resting place of a great king such as Offa of Mercia, ruler of the Mercian Hegemony in the eighth century.[21]

There is much that is left unsaid here, but the silences and implications point to brother and sister as allies on equal standing, rather than one having authority over the other. All this was to change once Æthelflæd was gone. The Mercian Register – brief but nevertheless informative – shows, to Edward's discredit (although it avoids mention of his name) how Æthelflæd's daughter was deliberately removed from power (onweald) and taken to Wessex. Once again, at the departure of a ruler, there was no question of power-sharing, or of dividing the territory with a successor. The keynote is expansion, but the two Chronicle texts – both the West-Saxon and the Mercian – are loath to condemn their rulers for sounding this note. By the end of his reign Edward was ruler of all the West Saxons and the Mercians; and the Northumbrians and the Welsh, at least in theory, were also his subjects.

CHAPTER 7

The lessons of history: 'Edwardian' literature

CONTINUING THE REVIVAL OF LITERACY

It is arguable that literacy and literature were – at least at first – low on King Edward's priorities. The point was taken up by historians in the twelfth century such as William of Malmesbury, who compared Edward unfavourably with his father Alfred as a patron of letters.[1] Certainly Edward was peculiarly reticent about issuing royal charters, and for the second half of his reign none survive, the obvious reason being that the constant military campaigning focussed his attention.[2] But Edward evidently continued his father's literacy campaign in the Anglo-Saxon kingdom. And as a number of manuscripts indicate, the written vernacular continued to be fostered by the ruling elite, who had certainly benefited from the great drive to teach their sons – and perhaps also their daughters – to read in Old English.

There was no immediate change of personnel. The main leaders of the educational revival of the previous reign continued under Edward. Grimbald of St Bertin in Flanders, an appointee of Alfred, remained as bishop of Winchester until 908. Asser, biographer of Alfred and bishop of Sherborne, did not die until 909 or 910. Plegmund, the Mercian churchman and scholar whom Alfred appointed as archbishop of Canterbury in the year 890 continued actively in that office through the whole reign of Edward, until his death in 923.[3] As archbishop, Plegmund must have officiated at King Edward's coronation. It is during Plegmund's time that we have evidence of a minor revival of Latin literacy in the writing of a few formal Latin land charters, which as we have seen had been in decline in ninth-century Kent. Two concrete examples still survive, issued by the archbishop and extant in their original single-sheet form as witness to their authenticity.[4]

Another literary project attributable to Edward's reign was the Junius Psalter, which contains an interlinear word-for-word translation of the Psalms from Latin into English, the result being similar to the ninth-century Vespasian Psalter cited in Chapter 4 above.[5] These so-called 'glossed psalters' were essential works, since the Psalms were the basis of services in church, a textbook for learning to read, and an object of biblical study and commentary.[6] Furthermore, a version of the first fifty psalms in Old English prose is attributed to King Alfred, who may have intended a full-scale translation project, of which only these fifty psalms survive. It is therefore no surprise to see that an English gloss of the psalter was made during the reign of his son. It is even possible to make an educated guess about the author of this English psalter. At the centre of Wessex in Winchester was the new bishop Frithestan (who was to hold office from 909 to 931). It is possible that Frithestan glossed the Junius Psalter, perhaps following the lead taken by his predecessor, Alfred's friend and adviser Bishop Grimbald.[7] Apart from this 'official' literary project, there are nevertheless signs that more informal vernacular literacy continued to develop.

Figure 7a   Fonthill, Wiltshire

'AND, DEAR KING, WHEN IS ANY CLAIM ENDED?'

Narrated in the first person, the 'Fonthill Letter' is a declaration sent to King Edward the Elder at the beginning of his reign concerning a lawsuit that had been started in the time of his father King Alfred. The ownership of an estate of five hides (100 acres) at Fontial in Wessex (present-day Fonthill, south of Warminster in Wiltshire) was in dispute, following a theft by a certain Helmstan, who was living on the property and who just so happened to be the godson of the author of the letter. This author of the letter is not in fact named in the despatch, although many have assumed him to be Ealdorman Ordlaf, who is indeed mentioned in the course of the dispute.[8] The inevitable brevity of the document (all such declarations normally covered one page) means that some details of the events are obscure or debatable. Nevertheless the language of the piece is relatively informal and vivid, sometimes even unnecessarily wordy for a relatively short account: we are given insights into the working of early English law; but more than that, we see and hear the ordinary colloquial language of the period; there is even a brief vignette of King Alfred washing his hands in the royal chamber, before he listens to the details of the dispute. It is another window on the life of the period.

The letter opens with a standard address to the king: *Leof ic ðe cyðe*, which can be modernised as *Leof, ic the cythe*, 'Dear, I hereby declare'. The writer then declares 'what happened with the estate at Fonthill, the five hides to which Æthelm Higa lays claim.' The one word *leof* meaning 'dear' or 'beloved' – rather than the later mode of address to the king as 'Sire' – indicates the workaday terms of affection in which business was conventionally done in the early English kingdoms. The population was small, and the maintenance of personal relations was the way in which both the smaller and larger affairs of the country were enacted. The verb *cythe* (from *cythan*, 'to make known') is connected with modern English *couth*, the opposite of *uncouth* (*couth* is now of course an obsolete word). It means literally 'to make *couth*, i.e. to make known', or in other words 'to declare, to notify', and it identifies the genre of the piece of writing to the recipient; on reading this or hearing it read, King Edward would have known broadly what kind of writing he was dealing with, namely a legal *declaration* or notification.[9]

The opponent in the dispute is a man called Æthelm, short for Æthelhelm, and the name is furnished with the additional byname Higa. Short familiar forms of names were probably more common than is often realised, and by-names were often necessary in early medieval times, since surnames were unknown, and many people bore the same name. This Æthelm Higa, for some unstated reason, has laid claim to the estate that is now held by the narrator.

In this case, however, all would have nevertheless gone well for Helmstan had he not so foolishly committed the *undæde* – literally the 'undeed' as the narrator, his godfather, puts it – of stealing a belt. At first sight this crime seems rather petty and insignificant, but the stolen object, if it resembled any of the elaborate pieces of ornate Anglo-Saxon metalwork that have been uncovered by archaeologists, was certainly an expensive item. The Sutton Hoo belt buckle for instance is made of 14 ounces of gold, with elaborate animal interlace, and later artefacts of the ninth century such as the fine finger ring associated with King Æthelwulf, or the famous Alfred Jewel associated with his son, though less sophisticated than the earlier artefacts of Sutton Hoo, are nevertheless still precious works of art.[10] In view of the penchant among the Anglo-Saxon nobility for high-status personal accoutrements, then the seriousness of the theft is more readily understandable.

As the narrator goes on with his story it seems that as soon as Helmstan made himself vulnerable by stealing the belt, then Higa and others took their chance to 'make a claim against him' (the Old English word here is *specan*, literally 'to speak against him'), in order to obtain the estate that this malefactor had in his possession. Helmstan therefore appeals for help to the narrator, the one 'who had received him from the hands of the bishop', in other words, his godfather. The recurring theme in this wholly typical process of Anglo-Saxon litigation is 'speech'. So here Helmstan asks his godfather to be his *forespeca*, 'the one who speaks before him', in other words, his advocate. As the narrator then puts it, picking up on the wording of the previous sentence, *tha spac ic him fore*, 'then I spoke before him', in other words, 'then I spoke as his advocate'. He goes on to say that 'I interceded' (OE *thingade*) on his behalf before King Alfred, the word *thing* having connotations of a legal parley or encounter of some kind (one might compare the cognate Old Norse *Thing*, the name of the traditional Icelandic assembly or parliament, and place-names in English such as Thingwall or Dingwall, where assemblies may have been held). Then in his own words, the narrator reports King Alfred's response to his 'intercession', the word in Old English is *forspæce* (the pronunciation of this word sounds similar to 'for-speech'):

Ða, God forgelde his saule, ða lyfde he ðæt he moste beon ryhtes wyrðe for minre forspæce & ryhtrace wið Æðelm ymb ðæt lond

[Then, God reward his soul, the king granted that Helmstan would be worthy of justice because of my advocacy against Æthelm for the land.]

Here 'justice against Æthelm' involves gathering a legal assembly with witnesses. And justice is indeed seen to be done. Helmstan, who still possesses the charter for the estate in question – or the 'land-book' as it is known – takes it to the assembly at Wardour. The document is read out formally, and all present are able to see and confirm the presence of the *hondseten*, literally 'the hand-setting' or ratifications. These names of witnesses on the charter are the equivalent of modern signatures; each witness, whether literate or not, 'sets his hand to it', placing his finger on the mark of the cross next to his own name as he declares his physical presence at the agreement. It seems now that Helmstan will inevitably win the suit, for nothing can stand in his way. Æthelm now plays for time, declaring to the king that he is unwilling to agree (this is the celebrated scene at the royal chamber where the king first washes his hands before attending to the matter in hand). Nevertheless it is agreed that Helmstan is ready on the appointed day to take an oath to clear his name.

The appointed day duly arrives, and Helmstan asks his godfather to help him with an additional oath, to which he agrees, but only in return for payment, the condition being that his godson will grant him the actual ownership of the estate. Next, almost like an eighteenth-century duel, each party with a second or witness rides out to the agreed meeting place. 'And we all heard,' says the writer, how Helmstan delivered the oath fully and appropriately. There the matter should rest, thinks the narrator, for this claim or 'speech' is now formally 'ended':

And, dear king, when is any claim ended, if it cannot be ended by payment or by oath?

In asides like this, exclamations of strong feeling, rhetorical questions, the writer of the Fonthill Letter demonstrates the command of his own 'voice', expressed here in the written medium of his own language.

As I hope to have shown, the Fonthill Letter is certainly worth further reading and would repay further study; there is more to the story for the interested reader to explore.[11] One other fact should be mentioned: the letter is untidily written with various corrections, indicating that the scribe was not a practised writer. But that only adds to its interest. This is a small but significant example of the development of literacy among the laity – rather than exclusively in the ranks of the clergy – in early tenth-century England.

THE OLD ENGLISH *OROSIUS*

An exemplary work of world history, in some ways complementary to the work of Bede, is the *History against the Pagans* by the Late Antique writer Orosius, whose overriding aim was to prove the benefits of Christianity by giving his own perspective on the history of Rome. Orosius was a contemporary of Augustine of Hippo, the famous Father of the Church, who effectively commissioned Orosius to write a polemic against the then prevalent view in pagan circles in Rome: that Christendom had brought more wars and troubles into the world; that Rome had fallen to the Goths in the year 410 precisely because it had earlier converted to Christianity under the Emperor Constantine. Orosius's aim was to refute all this. So he shows, for example, that the Christian Goths who seized Rome in 410 under King Alaric treated the inhabitants humanely. He makes much of the forebearance and mercy shown by Alaric, despite his 'barbarian' origins as a leader of the Visigoths (i.e. the Western branch of the Gothic nation). Above all, Orosius wanted to demonstrate how things had actually improved since the coming of Christ, and he is therefore at pains to picture the disasters and calamities of earlier history, before Christendom. His work was popular in the early Middle Ages and widely read.

In our period, Orosius's *History* was turned into English, and there are some reasons to link this version with the contemporary 'Alfredian programme', the fashion for translating or adapting selected Latin classics for English readers.[12] As Malcolm Godden has argued, the ensuing adaptation of Orosius is shorter than the original, but despite adverse comments by earlier twentieth-century critics it is certainly well written, presenting a series of lively stories from ancient history.[13] Interestingly, the earliest manuscript of the Old English *Orosius*, known as the Tollemache or Lauderdale *Orosius*, is dated not to Alfred's but to Edward's reign. As a quick glance at any facsimile reproduction will show, the manuscript is a finely presented book with wide margins.[14] And as palaeographers have argued, it was written at Winchester by the same scribe responsible for Hand II of the Anglo-Saxon Chronicle and the Latin text of the Junius Psalter, both attributed to Edward's reign.[15]

Figure 7b   Artist's impression of Alaric, king of the Goths (d. 410)

The *Orosius* opens with an interesting description of the regions of the world, which links this text to the *mappa mundi* discussed in Part I above. There is a characteristic emphasis in the Old English version on the spoken word: the whole book is presented as an oral account, the formula *cwæth Orosius*, 'as Orosius said', is repeated several times, along with the sayings of others. One such speaker is the heathen *scop* or poet who (in a characteristic departure from the original Latin) tells the story, ultimately biblical, of Joseph in Egypt. In particular, the Old English version also adds new travel accounts. These are told by Ohthere and Wulfstan, two contemporary Scandinavian traders who made voyages along the coasts of Denmark, Norway and Lapland in the reign of King Alfred. They then reported their experiences to the West-Saxon court (where they seem to be in the service of the king), telling of conditions for trade in fur and other commodities, and describing local customs, hunting and horse-racing, and even funeral practices.

Evinced here is a certain Anglo-Saxon curiosity about the great wide world, its ethnography, its geography and its history, which must lie behind the Old English *Orosius*. In Ohthere's narrative of his travels, for instance, he reports on his voyage back south to the great Danish trading port of Hedeby and the 'regions where the Angles used to live, before they came to this country'.[16] The Old English name for the port *æt Hæthum* means 'at the heaths', an apt name for this trading place at the end of the long narrow fjord of the Schlei.[17] The region is now part of Schleswig Holstein on the border between Germany and Denmark, and appropriately the Hedeby Viking Museum (or in German the Wikinger Museum Haithabu) now houses the famous Hedeby Viking ship, discovered by a scuba diver in 1953 beneath the old harbour.

Ohthere's Anglocentric remark is revealing, for it implies an interest in his courtly audience in the history of the Angles, before they settled 'in this country', in other words, in the island of Britain. The travel accounts by Ohthere and Wulfstan have often been anthologised,[18] and make for fascinating reading, but the fascination perhaps distracts from the ultimate purpose of the Old English adaptation of Orosius's *History*. Like the contemporary entries for Edward's reign in the Anglo-Saxon Chronicle, its main theme has been shown to be *onweald*: power and dominion.[19] Building on this approach, Francis Leneghan has made a good case for seeing the Old English *Orosius* as a history of empire-building. This makes sense in the context of the expansive ambitions fostered by the West-Saxon kings in the early decades of the tenth century. Probably the West Saxons saw themselves as taking over the Romanising mantle of empire from the Carolingian dynasty of Charlemagne, emperor of the Franks. This tradition had begun in the ninth century: there was, for instance, Æthelwulf's journey to Rome and his marriage to Judith, great-granddaughter of Charlemagne (as discussed in Chapter 2). Then, coincidentally – just as the Carolingian empire collapsed and divided into various smaller kingdoms in the late ninth century – Alfred and afterwards his son Edward began their bid for power and extension of their territory. It follows therefore that the West Saxon interest in empire is reflected in the text of the Old English *Orosius*, in the various omissions and changes made to the text.[20]

Accordingly, at the beginning of Book I (the work is divided into six books), the Anglo-Saxon author omits the prologue on the creation of the world which he finds in the original Latin, in order to focus more clearly on his main theme of empire-building. The Old English version now begins with Book I, Chapter 1, telling of the first man to rule in world history: Ninus, king of the Assyrians, who spent his fifty-year reign in war and plunder *mid ungemætlicre gewilnunge anwaldes*, 'with an immense desire for dominion (*anweald*)', until he had forced all of Asia to submit to his power (*geweald*). But finally he makes the mistake of waging war against the men of the northlands in Scandinavia (*on Sciððie þa norðland*) – men who had once lived their lives in harmless innocence but who have now acquired great skill in war – it perhaps seemed appropriate to an Anglo-Saxon writer that it is the Scythians (in other words the Scandinavians) who are the fiercest men in the world at that time. In one of these forays, Ninus is killed by an arrow whilst launching an attack on a town (*on ane burh*). However, this does not put an end to the wars, for Ninus's wife Semiramis succeeds to the kingdom and rules for another twenty-four years, during which, 'with a woman's hostility' (*mid wiflice niðe*), she attacks the innocent people of Ethiopia and wages long and ultimately unsuccessful war against India. In this narrative, Semiramis is a treacherous and lustful woman who acts with immense wickedness (*mid ungemætlicre wrænesse*); again the text highlights the *immense*, excessive nature of this monarch, the who murders her lovers and even sleeps with her own son. For Semiramis, the immense and excessive desire for *anwald* which the king her husband had bequeathed to her is insufficient for her needs.

This story of the wicked rule and aggressive wars of Ninus and Semiramis is like a counter-example to the just rule and legitimate expansion of Edward and Æthelflæd, as told in the two rival versions of the Chronicle. Where Edward gains lordship over his neighbours and Æthelflæd holds Mercia with just and lawful *onweald*, Ninus and Semiramis behave in excessive manner, without restraint or measure (*gemet*). As the Old English *Orosius* comments:

Greed and war were grimmer *then* than they are *now* because men were not acquainted with any models for behaviour such as they know now, and they lived their lives in naïve simplicity.

In ancient times, so the writer asserts, men lived simple lives, either for good or bad, because they did not have any more complex models to emulate. The key factor is the concept of the model (OE: *bysene*). This is crucial to the purpose of the Old English writer's text, and more generally to his philosophy of history, for he believes it is by examples from the past that men and women acquire models for their own behaviour. This approach recalls the purpose of the Old English *Bede*, as stated in the preface to that work (for which see the discussion above in Chapter 5 and the text in Interlude II):

> For this book either speaks good of good men, and those who hear this will imitate it, or it speaks evil of evil men, and those who hear it will avoid it and shun it.

In the very last chapter of the Old English *Orosius*, the behaviour of the Goths is seen as likewise exemplary, in a positive sense, for when Alaric, the Christian king of the Goths, seizes Rome, his men carry out their actions with very little hostility (OE: *mid swa lytle niþe*), in contrast to the hostility of Semiramis in the opening chapter of the narrative, and Alaric issues orders that no one is to be killed, nor are the churches to be damaged or harmed. This is the positive note on which the author ends his work. It might be compared with the account in the Mercian Register for the year 918 of how Æthelflæd was able to take the city of Leicester *gesibsumlice*, 'peacefully', without bloodshed. In the Old English *Orosius*, the new ruler of Rome is *Alrica se cristena cyning ond se mildesta*, 'Alaric the Christian king, the most generous', with an echo of the final epitaph in the closing lines of *Beowulf* in which the poet praises his hero as *wyruldcyninga manna mildust ond monðwærust, leodum liðost ond lofgeornost* (*Beowulf*, lines 3180–2), employing superlatives with mostly positive associations 'of kings of the world the most generous and the kindest of men, the most loyal to men and the most eager for fame'.[21] There is a suspicion among commentators that the Anglo-Saxon who has translated Orosius's *History* secretly admires the Scythians and the Goths, for they are related to his own nation, part of Germania.[22] In the final reckoning the author of the Old English *Orosius* is an optimist, for he feels that now, since the establishment of Christendom, men do indeed have good examples to follow.

THE OLD ENGLISH *BOETHIUS*

But what of the negative examples to avoid, of which there are many, for not all rulers are just? A few generations later than Orosius, the Latin theologian Boethius (born *c.*480, sometimes also known as St Severin), a Roman consul under the Gothic kings, became painfully aware of this issue when he fell out of favour with Theoderic, the Ostrogoth king of northern Italy. King Theoderic, who ruled from his capital at Ravenna from 493 to 526, came to power after making peace with his predecessor, King Odoaker, and then treacherously murdering him and his dependents. In 523, after he had briefly taken political office, Boethius was accused of treason, arrested and eventually done away with, but while under arrest he wrote his *Consolatio Philosophiae*. This is the famous *Consolation of Philosophy* that was later admired and translated by Geoffrey Chaucer in the fourteenth century and by Queen Elizabeth I of England in the Tudor period. In the *Consolation*, Boethius presents his ideas in the form of a dialogue between the narrator and Lady Philosophy, who appears to him in a vision in his prison. In coming to terms with his lot, Boethius ponders the tyrannical figures of the past, such as the emperor Nero, and of the present, such as King Theoderic himself. Then, on the basis of these *exempla*, Boethius wrestles with ideas of fortune and providence and – as his title proclaims – seeks a solution to his plight through the discipline of meditation and hard thinking.

The Old English version of this treatise is attributed to King Alfred in its prefaces. That authorship cannot be demonstrated as certain; one problem is the date: the two earliest manuscript copies date from the mid-tenth and early twelfth centuries.[23] An added complication is that Boethius originally wrote a prosimetric work (i.e. in prose, with interposed passages of verse), but the original Old English *Boethius* seems to be in prose – only at a later date were poetic versions of the Metres then added to the text.[24] Whoever the author is, he or she adapts the original text, adding new material, some of which is rooted in the longstanding commentary tradition: Boethius's Latin text had been studied and annotated by generations of European scholars, whose ideas circulated through the schools. In his new version, the Old English writer recasts the story as a personification allegory, a dialogue between the characters *Mod* (Mind) and *Wisdom*, a male figure (grammatically, *wisdom* is a masculine noun) who also appears in female form as *seo Gesceadwisnes* (a feminine noun), meaning Reason or

Discernment. The change probably allows for more flexibility, while also increasing the relevance of the text to its new long-tenth-century audience. The poetic version of the text, completed later, added another layer of interest to the text.[25]

Inevitably the rise of the House of Wessex lies behind this text, and with this consideration in mind we can see the relevance of the Old English *Boethius*. For its time, it is the most complex and sophisticated contemporary thinking on the theme of power and the desire for power. Certainly the *Pastoral Care* had lessons to impart on this subject – it takes for example the Old Testament figure of Nebuchadnezar as an image of kingly pride to avoid. The main force of its message, however, is concerned with human psychology and the need for the ruler to temper his rule according to the different types of behaviour in the men and women under his authority. The Old English *Boethius*, by contrast, penetrates further into the nature of power and into the motivations of the good and bad ruler, and because – at each stage in the argument – the text is presented in the form of a Socratic dialogue, it even debates, questions or deconstructs earlier statements which at first sight had seemed well founded.

In Chapter 16, for example, Wisdom compares Nero and Theoderic to a raging fire, declaring that power (*anweald*) is never good unless he who has it is good. The point is illustrated with further examples and exposition of Nero's crimes.[26] In Chapter 17 it is now the turn of Mind to take up the challenge and give his considered response.[27] The passage is a famous one, often cited, for it is well expressed in powerful prose, and it is an elaborate Old English expansion of a single sentence of Boethius's Latin. It deals with the notion of three communities, of 'praying men and fighting men and working men', that form the 'tools' of government and hold a society together; indeed, this is the first expression of the idea of the Three Estates in the history of European thought.[28] As Scott T. Smith has observed, in this passage also, Mind emphasises that the king's 'material' for his task of government is 'land manned fully', highlighting the vital importance of landholding in the West Saxon administration of the country.[29]

Slightly later in the passage Mind repeats his idea of 'land on which to live, and gifts and weapons and food and ale and clothes and whatever else is required by the three communities'; above all the speaker pleads for 'wisdom' in order to use these tools and materials with success. He begins this speech on a modest note, as though he never really wished for power, but he ends it with a rather striking formulation:

To be brief, I may say that I desired to live worthily while I lived, and that after my life, to leave to men who came after me the memory of me in good works.

These stirring cadences sound like a personal declaration: is this the voice of King Alfred himself? Is this the voice of the royal court, as it were intervening in the debate? Many would be tempted to reply in the affirmative, but as Godden and Irvine rightly point out in their edition, we may be treating the passage out of context.[30] As critical readers we need to keep listening to the dialogue, for after a moment's silence, once Mind has finished his speech, Discernment (Wisdom) begins speaking, and she launches into a hefty critique of what she has just heard (Chapter 18, lines 1–2):

Eala mod eala, an yfel is swithe to anscunianne.

'O Mind, listen,' she declares, 'One evil is very much to be shunned.' Here the intensifier *very* is a sure indicator of the tone of her rebuke as she leaves the listener waiting, until she rather damningly castigates the final statement of his speech in a triple variation on the same idea:

… that is to say, the desire for vain boasting and unjust power and the immoderate fame of good works over all the people.

Nothing could be clearer as the argument proceeds: men in the world desire power – and here one is tempted to think of the desire for

Figure 7c   Wayland's Smithy, Berkshire

anweald expressed in writings associated with Alfred and his successors – because they would want to have good fame, even though they are not worthy to have it, and moreover the most wicked of all men desire the same thing. But, as the rest of the chapter affirms, fame is nothing at all, it is like the tiny size of the world in the vast cosmos, like a pin-prick in a board, so insignificant that it is like many peoples living their separate lives 'in this little park' *on thissum lytlan pearroce*.[31] Moreover, in the next chapter, Wisdom launches into an elegiac *ubi sunt* passage of elegy in which she asks, famously:

> Hwær synt nu þæs Welondes ban, oððe hwa wat nu hwær hi wæron?
>
> [Where now are the bones of Welond, or who knows now where they were?]

Welond, or Wayland Smith, is a figure of folkore deriving from ancient Germanic legend, mentioned in *Beowulf* and the poem *Deor*. Where Boethius had written Fabricius, the Old English author perhaps makes a play on the name and its etymological link with *faber*, 'goldsmith'.[32] In brief, fame is fleeting, and the desire for power is a kind of vanity.

INTERLUDE III

'When the sun most brightly shines', from the Old English *Metres of Boethius*

The Old English poem is Metre 6 in the mid-tenth-century manuscript of the Old English *Boethius*.

Ða se Wisdom eft   wordhord onleac,
sang soðcwidas   and þus selfa cwæð:

Ðonne sio sunne   sweotolost scineð,
hadrost of hefone,   hræðe bioð aðistrod

ealle ofir eorðan   oðre steorran,
forðæm hiora birhtu   ne bið auht
to gesettane   wið þære sunnan leoht.
Ðonne smolte blæwð   suðan and westan
wind under wolcnum.   þonne weaxeð hraðe

feldes blostman,   fægen þæt hi moton.
Ac se stearca storm,   þonne he strong cymð
norðan and eastan,   he genimeð hraðe
þære rosan wlite,   and eac þa ruman sæ
norðerne yst   nede gebædeð,

þæt hio strange geondstyred   on staðu beateð.
Eala, þæt on eorðan   auht fæstlices
weorces on worulde   ne wunað æfre!

[Then Wisdom again unlocked his word-hoard.
His tales of truth he sang as follows:

When the sun most brightly shines,
gleaming in heaven, it quickly obscures
over the world all other stars;
for their brightness is nothing at all,
when set against the sun's light.
When softly blows from south and west
the wind beneath the heavens, then quickly grow
the flowers of the field, glad that they can.
But the severe storm, when it strongly blows
from out of the north-east, how quickly it takes
the beauty of the rose! The spacious ocean too
by the northern wind is helplessly afflicted
until, strongly heaving, it beats on the shore.
Alas, that in the world no firm foundation
lasts for long on this earth!]

Figure 7d   'The spacious ocean ... beats on the shore'

PART IV

War, poetry, and book-collecting

THE POEM 'ADALSTAN'

Probably the earliest writing in honour of Edward the Elder's son and heir Æthelstan is a Latin *acrostic*, a short poem which uses the initial letter of each line of verse to spell out a name or message. In this poem the name ADALSTAN is spelled vertically down the page, and here also there is a telestich, in which the final letter of each line spells vertically a meaningful word, in this case the name IOHANNES:

A rchalis clamare triumuir nomine sax I
D iue tuo fors prognossim feliciter aeu O
A ugusta .Samu. cernentis rupis eris .el. H
L aruales forti beliales robure contr A
S aepe seges messem fecunda prenotat altam iN
T utis solandum petrinum solibus agme N
A mplius amplificare sacra sophismatis arc E
N omina orto petas donet precor inclita doxu S

To reproduce the original effect of this enigmatic acrostic/telestich it is necessary, I think, to delay glancing at the modern English translation in the endnote.[1] An Anglo-Saxon reader at the time would have had to show good knowledge of Latin, plus some ingenuity, to solve the riddle of the additional wordplay in this text, for example the name *Samu-elh* being divided so that the '-elh' falls at the end of line 3. Did Æthelstan himself peruse this poem, reading his own name and working out the linguistic puzzles? The idea which the poet explores is that 'Æthelstan' means 'noble stone'; in other words that it is a significant name, like the name of the famous bishop Æthelwold, which is interpreted as the 'noble benevolent one' by his biographer and contemporary chronicler.[2] Because Æthelstan is a 'stone' or 'rock', he will be able to stand against his enemies, but in times of peace (and with a mixing of metaphor) the poem foretells 'a great harvest', since this noble rock is 'endowed with the holy eminence of learning'.

The poem has been added by a scribe at the end of an anthology of Latin poetry, including major poems by the early Anglo-Saxon poet Aldhelm and the late Roman poet Prudentius. Both poets were masters of classical Latin. Aldhelm, a contemporary of Bede and son of the West Saxon king Centwine (676–85), served as abbot of Malmesbury and bishop of Sherborne. As a Latin poet, Aldhelm was famed for his complex style; he wrote a then-popular and still fascinating set of Latin riddles. Prudentius, by contrast, was a late Roman Christian author writing around the year 400, whose most famous poem is the highly influential *Psychomachia*, an allegorical epic in verse, composed in the style of Virgil's *Aeneid* or Statius's *Thebaid*, on the struggle between virtues and vices, all of which are personified as female warriors engaged in battle.

The two authors were popular in the tenth-century schools, and students and scholars pored over their poems and annotated them with glosses and translations and explanatory notes in simpler Latin. This was the kind of poetry to which students aspired. And this particular anthology of poems (the manuscript is now in the Bodleian Library, Oxford, at shelf mark Rawlinson C. 697) is here given a royal stamp of approval by the acrostic dedicated to the king. The implication is that King Æthelstan encouraged such studies, and other evidence supports this view. There were Latin poets at Æthelstan's court (see Chapter 8), and the Anglo-Saxon Chronicle contains two Old English poems celebrating the victories of Æthelstan and his brother Edmund (Chapter 9 below). Two famous scholars and teachers of Latin poetry even took up the study of Aldhelm and Prudentius enthusiastically in their schools. It looks like the very same manuscript, Rawlinson C. 697, was used as a textbook at the school of Glastonbury by Abbot Dunstan in the 940s and 950s (see Chapters 10 and 11).[3] Dunstan's former protégé Æthelwold, who studied with Dunstan at Glastonbury, also became a teacher of Latin poetry, first as abbot of Abingdon and later as bishop of Winchester (see Chapter 13).

There are two possible dates for the composition of 'Adalstan'. In his edition, Michael Lapidge has plausibly argued that the poem was written by John the Old Saxon (the adviser to King Alfred whose narrow escape from murderous monks was related above). This would explain the name 'Iohannes' in the right-hand column. If this is indeed the work of John, who died perhaps in 904, then he must have composed the text when Æthelstan was a youth. In an alternative approach, Gernot Wieland sees the poem as celebrating Æthelstan's coronation as king in September 925, when the 'cornfields were promising a good harvest', as the poet declares. On this view, 'Iohannes' was perhaps a special name conferred on the king at his consecration.[4] Whatever its precise date, the poem is a prediction: the poet sees himself as a biblical prophet like Samuel, foretelling a glorious career for Æthelstan as both a great political leader and a patron of the arts.

Part IV contains four chapters: two concerned primarily with the activities of Æthelstan, and latterly also of his brother, Edmund, who became king in 939, and two concerned with the life of Dunstan and the development of the school at Glastonbury. Chapter 8, 'King Æthelstan the Pious', focuses particularly on the king as a collector of books and saints' relics, and it explores in particular the growing veneration in the south of England of Cuthbert, that epitome of Northumbrian sanctity, as West Saxon power and influence moved northwards. Chapter 9 is concerned with literature relating to Æthelstan's victory at Brunanburh, and the Old English poem celebrating that event; this includes some discussion of the poem on Edmund's victory, *The Capture of the Five Boroughs*, and some thoughts on the context of *The Metres of Boethius*. The growing importance of Dunstan is charted in Chapter 10, while Chapter 11 looks at his school at Glastonbury with its rather surprising curriculum that included, as a set text, *The Art of Love* by Ovid.

CHRONOLOGY FOR PART IV

687	Death of St Cuthbert, bishop of Lindisfarne
720	Bede's prose *Life of St Cuthbert*
793	Lindisfarne attacked and pillaged by Viking raiders
800s	St Cuthbert's community leave Lindisfarne
883	The community settle at Chester-le-Street, Northumbria
early 900s?	The poem 'Adalstan' added to an older anthology of Latin poetry
910?	Birth of Dunstan
924	Death of Edward the Elder, after dealing with a revolt in Chester
925	Æthelstan becomes king of England after a disputed succession
926	Æthelstan's treaty with Sihtric, king of York
927	Æthelstan asserts power in Northumbria, the meeting at Eamont (Cumbria)
930s	Dunstan present at the court of King Æthelstan
934	Æthelstan visits the tomb of St Cuthbert at Chester-le-Street; presents a copy of the *Lives of St Cuthbert* to the community
937	The great battle, commemorated in the poem *The Battle of Brunanburh*
939?	The poem *King Æthelstan the Pious*
939	Olaf becomes king of York
942	Old English poem *The Capture of the Five Boroughs*
940s	The story of King Edmund and the hunting of the hart
940s and 950s	Dunstan head of the school at Glastonbury
940s and 950s?	Origin of the OE poems *Solomon and Saturn* and *The Metres of Boethius*
960s	The cleric B., Dunstan's biographer, moves to Liège
990s	B. Completes his *Life of St Dunstan*, probably in Canterbury

CHAPTER 8

'King Æthelstan the Pious, famed throughout the wide world'

As far as King Alfred's immediate successors are concerned, at least one shared his enthusiasms for literacy: certainly his son Edward continued his educational policy, but it was Alfred's grandson Æthelstan who was an avid collector and donor of books. Which is why we know so much about his interests, for the surviving medieval libraries of England contain about a dozen titles donated by Æthelstan, with suitable inscriptions and dedications recording the king's generosity. Like Alfred, Æthelstan had an interest in reading the lives of saints, and apparently he also appreciated poetry, but otherwise his tastes differed from those of his grandfather. The younger king has been described as the 'Pierpont Morgan of his age' for he seems to have preferred *de luxe*, lavishly illustrated books, such as copies of the Gospels and the Psalms. He has also been called the 'Isaac Wolfson of the tenth century' because of his generosity, and as the books were written in Latin they could be imported from abroad and distributed to all and sundry.[1] But perhaps these epithets are misleading, and we should attach a rather different significance to the book donations of Æthelstan. A poem added to one of his book donations, to be considered in the next chapter, sums up the king fittingly, in its opening line:

King Æthelstan the Pious, famed throughout the wide world.

Rather than simply love of books, it is poetry, piety and politics that here seem to walk hand in hand, and cannot too easily be separated.[2]

THE FREEING OF A SLAVE

King Edward the Elder unexpectedly died in the summer of the year 924 while at Farndon on the river Dee, in what was then Mercia; according to William of Malmesbury, the king had just dealt with a rebellion in nearby Chester (the town had allied itself with the Welsh). Unlike his father Alfred, Edward passed away without leaving any written instructions with regard to the royal succession. The two athelings (as Anglo-Saxon princes were called), the half-brothers Æthelstan and Ælfweard, were both of age, and both considered themselves 'throne-worthy'. The incomplete jigsaw of evidence indicates that Æthelstan had Mercian support: it is likely that as a young boy, after his father had remarried, Æthelstan was fostered and educated in Mercia at the court of his aunt Æthelflæd. Thereafter he may well have served in the Mercian contingent of the English army.[3] Moreover, Æthelstan must have been in Mercia at the time of his father's death, for the Mercians immediately elected him as their king. In the south, however, the West Saxons chose Æthelstan's half-brother Ælfweard as king. It must have looked as if Edward's 'kingdom of the Anglo-Saxons' was falling apart along the old West-Saxon/Mercian divide.

But fate intervened. The half-brother died, within a matter of a few weeks, and he was buried beside his father at the New Minster in Winchester, Edward's own foundation. There were other eligible half-brothers, including a certain Edwin, who later proved difficult, and there were Edmund and Edred, the two sons of Edward's third marriage with the Lady Eadgifu (Ediva). But all were too young at the time. Æthelstan accordingly succeeded as king of the Anglo-Saxons. Thereafter his relations with the New Minster at Winchester remained cool – and perhaps never warmed, for Æthelstan himself favoured Malmesbury as his final resting place at the end of his life. At the beginning of his reign, therefore, it was evidently not practicable for Æthelstan to hold his inauguration at Winchester. A year passed before the tensions relaxed, and the twelfth-century historian William of Malmesbury mentions rumours of revolts and dissatisfaction. In the end Æthelstan chose to have his royal consecration at Kingston-on-Thames, the river effectively forming the boundary between the two regions of Wessex and Mercia. Rival parties could proceed to this location as a suitable half-way house.

The inauguration ritual duly emphasised Æthelstan's election as king of two separate peoples, the West Saxons and the Mercians. The aim was to heal the rift. According to some recent research, the ceremony was a new one, for it was the first English *coronation* in the strict sense of the word *corona*: Æthelstan was consecrated king with a crown, not with a helmet as in earlier times, and the archbishop of Canterbury anointed him with oil, investing him with a ring, a sword and a rod and sceptre as the regalia of royal office.[4] From the 930s onwards, coins issued in the name of the new king picture him wearing a kind of crown. As was noted in Chapter 1, the first piece of writing in the Vercelli Book is a sermon on Christ's Passion, and it contains a passage explaining to the reader or congregation the nature of a *corona* or crown.[5] In tenth-century England, this was not general knowledge that a preacher of a sermon could take for granted in his congregation.

To celebrate his royal consecration, the king followed the usual practices of the period and made gifts of land to deserving beneficiaries. A thirteenth-century copy of an older document records his restoration of some land on Thanet to the monastery of St Augustine's at Canterbury. This took place on 4 September 925, the actual day of his consecration as king. The text, which appears to be genuine, describes Æthelstan as *rex Saxonum et Anglorum*, 'king of the Saxons and Angles'. This was the goal that Edward the Elder had aspired to, and after a year of political uncertainty the son had now inherited the same title. But as he consolidated his position such relatively modest territorial ambitions were about to change.

Already at this stage the young king was an avid collector of books. In his collection was an old Northumbrian gospel book, originally made in the eighth century (the book is now preserved at London in the British Library, shelfmark Royal 1. B. VII).[6] This is a workaday manuscript, with minimum decoration and colouring, not as elaborate as the *de luxe* items described above in Chapter 3, and therefore, to put it in material terms, not too expensive. It is an appropriate item to be found in the household of a young prince who had not expected to be propelled so suddenly to royal power. The Old English inscription in the book charts his response:

> King Æthelstan freed Eadhelm immediately when he was first [declared] king. This was in the presence of Ælfheah the mass-priest and the household [*se hired*] and Ælfric the reeve and Wulfnoð the White and Eanstan the provost and Byrnstan the mass-priest. Whoever would change this, may he have the disfavour of God and of all the *halidom* I have acquired in England by the favour of God. And I grant to the children the same as I grant to the father.[7]

The text records an act of manumission, a formal freeing of the slave
Eadhelm, in the presence of the king's household, including his two
priests and a provost. Slavery was a fact of life in the tenth century, but it
was also possible to free slaves and their families, and such
manumissions were recorded for posterity in precious books such as
the Gospels. Often the acts of manumission were reinforced by
maledictions, calling down severe threats on anyone who tried to
contravene the agreement.

Interestingly this particular malediction throws light on the role of
the king and the attitudes that he held, for Æthelstan felt he had the
support of a whole host of saints through the power granted by their
halidom or relics, since these were relics that he now owned. The word
halidom in the above passage means literally 'holiness, sanctity', but used
concretely the word here denotes holy objects, i.e. the relics of the saints.
And like his grandfather before him, Æthelstan was a great collector of
such objects and artefacts, for they were believed to have special potency
and virtue. A text in Old English added to another sacred book, the
Leofric Gospels, lists the many such relics that Athelstan generously
donated to the cathedral at Exeter.[8] According to the later writer William
of Malmesbury, Æthelstan's store of relics also included gifts from Hugh
Duke of the Franks, who sent his messengers to Æthelstan in the year
926. The king received the spear of Longinus, the Roman soldier present
at the crucifixion, the standard of Maurice, the early Christian martyr
and legendary leader of the Theban legion, a fragment of the true cross
and a sprig of the crown of thorns. In return, the duke received the hand
in marriage of Æthelstan's sister Eadhild.[9] Here Æthelstan's *halidom*
played its part in the cementing of a political alliance.

'A FAITHFUL THEGN'

Æthelstan was clearly well educated, with poetic sensibilities. The
recent biography by Sarah Foot argues that poetry was actively
promoted at Æthelstan's court; certainly there are various surviving
examples of contemporary poetry in Latin, and these are apparently
intended for the court. It seems likely that poems in Old English were
performed there too. Perhaps literature in other languages was also
heard, for many foreigners, sons of royalty and nobility from France,
Brittany, Germany, and Denmark became guests of Æthelstan's
household. There were even Viking adventurers serving the king, and
according to *Egil's Saga* one of them composed poems specifically for

Æthelstan. To what extent the king would have understood a poem in Old Norse is not known, though the two languages were close enough for simple everyday communications. He may have known more than one language. Like his grandfather Alfred and his father Edward before him, Æthelstan issued laws in the mother tongue, but he also seems to have understood Latin.

After being relatively neglected by father and grandfather, Latin charters and land-grants flourished in Æthelstan's reign. A royal diploma of the year 926 is of particular interest.[10] It records the king's grant of land at Chalgrave and Tebworth in Bedfordshire to his 'faithful thegn' Ealdred; this was former Danelaw territory, and it is clear that the estates had once been in Danish hands. But Æthelstan now confirmed his thegn as the new holder of the land, and Ealdred was granted the freedom to bequeath the two estates to whosoever he wished. This was typical of estates granted by the king as a *boc* or 'book', in other words as a royal charter. *Bocland* or Bookland, as it was called (the term even became the place-name Buckland in many parts of the country) was highly coveted among the ruling elite, because it was not on loan, in other words, it was not a temporary lease like *lænland*, to be returned to the lender after two or three generations. As is the case with most royal diplomas, the main language of the text is Latin, but it switches to English for the important boundary clause, and it is interesting to see yet again (as was noted in Chapter 2) how a Roman road, in this case Watling Street – *Wæclinga stræt* in the Old English – serves as one notable landmark bordering the estate.

The author of this charter may have been a Breton at the English court, in exile because of Viking depredations in his native Britanny; he was widely read, and his Latin style demonstrates his literary inclinations and sensibilities. After the invocation *In nomine Domini nostri Iesu Christi*, 'in the name of our Lord Jesus Christ', the writer begins the proem, the initial theological reflection, with his thoughts on the transitory nature of the visible affairs of men when compared with the invisible and hidden things that are governed by the eternal Judge. A monetary image is employed, for 'the divine documents of the scriptures' (*diuina scripturarum documenta*) offer promise to those who are worthy that they can acquire (*adipisci*) and purchase (*mercari*) these things by the full grace of God.

The act of buying – this time on an earthly rather than a spiritual level – is mentioned a further three times. First the text emphasises that the thegn Ealdred – at the instigation of Athelstan's predecessors King

Edward in Wessex and Ealdorman Æthelred in Mercia – had originally been required to purchase (*emerat*) the estates 'from the pagans', i.e. from Danes living in the Danelaw, 'with the appropriate money of his own' amounting to ten pounds of gold and silver. Secondly the document declares that the aforesaid land is free from any secular burden except for bridge and fortress building, and except for the *expeditio*, in other words 'military service', which in Old English is *fyrd*, the act of going on expedition (related to *faran*, 'to go'). There is however a condition attached. In return, the king received from Ealdred 'an adequate sum of money ... 150 mancusses of gold'. The transaction has become a gift exchange. This is mentioned yet again, for a third time, but now the text switches once more to English in the closing sentence before the list of witnesses:

> Þis sind þa land þe Æþelstan cyng gebocade Ealdred wið his clæne feo on ðas gewitnesse þe her on sind...
>
> [There are the estates which King Æthelstan booked to Ealdred in exchange for his clean money in the presence of the following witnesses ...]

There is no record of what Ealdred thought about the justice or otherwise of first having to buy the estates from the Danes and then, on the succession of the new king, having to pay good money yet again for the right to hold the land.

The actual speech act which confirms that the king 'booked' (i.e. granted) the land, is put into a first-person declaration by the king. It is legitimate to wonder whether this was spoken out loud, perhaps by the king himself, perhaps by one of the Latinate scholars attached to his court:

> Quapropter ego Æthelstanus Angulsaxonum rex ... dabo
>
> [Therefore I, Æthelstan, King of the Anglo-Saxons ... will give]

The text incidentally reveals the title used to describe the king at the onset of his reign, and although he is, at this stage in the year 926, merely the ruler of the Anglo-Saxons, he is nevertheless honoured (*infulatus*) and raised up (*sublimatus*) in great dignity (*non modica dignitate*). This theme of exaltation is reflected generally in the solemn register of the Latin employed in the charter.

Such a style of Latin was to attain even greater heights of eloquence in subsequent charters, which are usually ascribed to the same writer at a later stage in his development and are given the convenient label of 'Æthelstan A'. Scott T. Smith has shown, in a study of the 'literary showmanship' of this now rightly celebrated if anonymous writer, how he employs amplification, alliteration and assonance and other sound effects, and draws on the writings of the seventh-century writer Aldhelm for the wording of his high-flung phrases, as well as employing grecisms, i.e. words and expressions derived from Greek vocabulary lists.[11] These two features, the Greek-derived vocabulary and the use of neologisms were characteristic of the complex tenth-century Latin taught in the schools. The 'Hermeneutic' style (so called because it draws its vocabulary from word lists and glossaries) makes the Latin of the period mysterious and obscure to the non-initiated. It has led later writers (not only historians such as William of Malmesbury in the twelfth century but also modern literary scholars) to dismiss it as uncouth and barbaric. The heavy influence of Aldhelm is significant and will be discussed further below. But the literary graces of Æthelstan A can serve as evidence of the poetic interests of the royal court in the period. Even on the occasions of ceremonial gift exchanges and land transactions, the court was hearing the echoes and allusions, words and phrases of one of the most admired and most frequently studied of the Anglo-Latin poets.

A MEETING AT EAMONT

As a patron of literary work, Æthelstan did not only donate books, so leaving traces of his movements and career. He seems to have had a number of poets present in his company, who recorded his significant deeds. In the next chapter we shall have occasion to hear the Norse praise-poem composed by Egil, as recorded in *Egils's Saga*. Then there is the work of the 'Adalstan' poet, possibly named Iohannes, as discussed above. Another such poet names himself Petrus, which like Iohannes is another biblical name, and unusual for the onomastics of the time. Petrus composed his poem, perhaps *ex tempore*, on a very specific occasion: Æthelstan's first expedition to the north in the year 927, when various kings and rulers of the north swore their allegiance to their West Saxon overlord at a place called Eamont, near Penrith in Cumbria. The year before, the king's sister had been married to Sihtric, ruler of York, but when Sihtric suddenly died, Æthelstan quickly proceeded north, and Constantine (the king of the Scots who later opposed him at Brunanburh) promised him his allegiance. The likely location for the meeting can still be seen today, at the confluence of two rivers north of Ullswater, with the steep mountainous fells of Lakeland to the west forming a dramatic backdrop to the encounter between the two kings.

Figure 8a   Eamont Bridge, Cumbria

Æthelstan's diplomatic triumph was immediately celebrated in this occasional poem, which was apparently communicated by a messenger travelling on horseback and on board ship, who delivered it to the royal court in the south. The evidence suggests that Petrus composed his verses directly, perhaps on the ubiquitous wax tablet that every scholar wore at his belt, the equivalent of today's notebook. The messenger then perhaps memorised the poem by heart before his departure. We can imagine that the news was eventually celebrated in suitable manner once the news-bearer had reached his destination and explained in his own words what had happened. Perhaps he even declaimed the Latin poem to the assembled household at Æthelstan's royal palace, which is mentioned in the poem.

But was this messenger literate? And how competent was his Latin? A faulty oral delivery of the poem might explain the garbled transmission of the actual text, which is to be found in two very divergent versions in two extant manuscripts. Perhaps the poem was passed on by word of mouth from one speaker to the next, and in this process, like the party game 'Chinese whispers', the author's verses were mangled, words changed and the spellings altered. Here is the opening of the poem as recorded by one scribe, writing many years later, in the lower margin of yet another gospel book, the Durham Gospels; the text is more or less as it appears there:[12]

> Quarta dirie gressus p maria nauigans stellarū que spaciū ad regē spalacium:-
> Regē primū salute non aclitunē clerū conditū armites milierum:-
> Illic sitric defuncto armature plio sex annū exces sitū uiuit rex adelstanum:-
> Costantine

Probably the first phrase or line should be restored correctly as *Carta, dirige gressus, per maria nauigans* and translated: 'Letter, direct your steps, sailing across the seas'. However, for the strict scholar or teacher of Latin, at any time or place in the last thousand years of the teaching of the subject, this scribe's Latin is simply 'wretched'. It is full of lexical errors, phonetic spellings and grammatical mistakes. What, for example, is the first word *quarta*? It must be the noun *carta* meaning 'parchment, letter, message', given in an idiosyncratic spelling. As for *dirie* – this might be explained as the imperative verb *dirige* 'direct'. The faulty spelling may be phonetic, since an Old English speaker who knew how to write in his own language would pronounce the letter combination 'ge' as 'ye' (as in modern English 'yes') and so write it 'ie'. Such errors continue through the whole text, and modern editors have had to work hard to restore the original message of the poem.[13]

A NEW PATRON SAINT

In the light of the king's *halidom*, his veneration for saints mentioned above, another famous royal book donation falls into place. This is a copy of Latin writings concerning Cuthbert (*c*.635–87), the famous Northumbrian hermit and bishop from the golden age of Northumbria, whose life was recounted in a number of writings by Bede and others. Cuthbert's story follows a pattern familiar from other lives of holy men, torn between the life of contemplation and the active life of politics and pastoral care. Indeed Cuthbert is the quintessential hermit, associated with the old coastal monastery of Lindisfarne, or Holy Island as it is called, and with the remote seal-haunted Farne Islands further out to sea, where he spent a period as a solitary contemplative.

Stories of Cuthbert's piety often concern his long pastoral journeys through the countryside and encounters with animals and wild beasts, with which the saint appears to have a special relationship. So a horse pulls hay from the thatch of a roof to reveal a loaf hidden away for the provision of the travellers; or an eagle provides fresh fish as food on the journey. Most famously, there is the story of Cuthbert's spending hours standing in the cold North Sea at prayer, observed by a monk who has secretly followed him from the nearby monastery. The monk sees Cuthbert emerge from the sea to be met by two otters on the beach, who use their fur to dry the water from his limbs and keep the holy man warm. The monk later repents for his inappropriate curiosity. Such was the holy and ascetic life in which Cuthbert persisted until he was called to become bishop of Durham, an office he accepted with reluctance but pursued with great zeal; he finally retired to spend his last days back on Farne.[14] A saint of this calibre was a great spiritual warrior, and any king would wish to associate himself with such piety and sanctity.

In this respect Æthelstan was no exception. In the summer of the year 934, Æthelstan was again on the road north with his army, with the firm intention of asserting his authority over the Scots: so much is known from the brief entry in the Anglo-Saxon Chronicle. On the occasion of that expedition, the king inevitably passed through Northumbria, where he stopped at Chester-le-Street (now in County Durham), for it was here that the coffin of the revered saint had been moved from Lindisfarne because of the danger of damage and theft by Viking raiders. (In the late eighth century, Lindisfarne had been one of the first monasteries to be attacked and plundered.) At Chester-le-Street, Æthelstan visited Cuthbert's shrine in order to pay his respects, perhaps also to promise delivery of his precious gifts; listed in the fine gospel book that formed the main present, these gifts included some finely embroidered ecclesiastical robes and a number of sacred books decorated with gold and silver, including a 'Life of St Cuthbert in verse and prose'.

The latter item refers to the two *Lives* of Cuthbert that the writer Bede composed in different media and for different types of reader. For the literate monk there was Bede's *Metrical Life of St Cuthbert*, a complex Latin poem which required attention and careful meditation. For the more general reader there was the *Life of St Cuthbert* in prose, a more informative but also more easily readable, didactic work.

This particular 'twinned life' of Cuthbert still survives, now in the Parker Library at Corpus Christi College, Cambridge (CCCC 183). On the evidence of the script and of an illustration in the manuscript, it looks like King Æthelstan specially commissioned the book, and he probably sent it to Chester-le-Street after his return from Scotland. The frontispiece shows the crowned king standing on the left, with head slightly bowed (the paint on his face now degraded), presenting or perhaps

Figure 8b   King Æthelstan and St Cuthbert

reading the open book to the saint, who stands haloed, in a gesture of greeting or blessing, at the entrance to a stone church. There are a number of historical moments embodied in this illustration. For one, it is the first painted portrait of a king in English history; royal images on coins exist in abundance, but this is the first time that an artist has attempted to portray a king in action as an illustration to a book made in England.[15] The illustration marks also a significant political moment, in that it demonstrates how the West Saxon kings were cultivating support for their policies of expansion by appealing to local sensibilities. Cuthbert was a Northumbrian holy man, but now the West Saxons too wished to find inspiration and support from veneration of this saint. A narrative called the *Historia de Sancto Cuthberto* (*The History of St Cuthbert*) written perhaps later in the tenth century, will take this development further, for it relates how King Alfred too had seen visions of the saint; at moments of crisis he too found help and support through the merits of the holy man of Farne.[16]

Another index of this widening of Cuthbert's influence is seen in the great Lindisfarne Gospels, a seventh-century copy of Matthew, Mark, Luke and John, perhaps the most famous illustrated gospel book from Anglo-Saxon England, and arguably the finest. In their formally perfect calligraphy and elaborate decorated initials, with the carpet pages and evangelist portraits which introduce each of the four gospels, and the mixed cosmopolitan influence of Italian liturgy, Germanic sculpture and Irish metalwork in the designs, this book was and still is an impressive work of art and craftsmanship. Describing a similar gospel codex in the twelfth century, probably the equally well-known Book of Kells, the Norman writer Gerald of Wales spoke of the 'work of angels', and no one feels inclined to disagree.[17] This was a precious book for which the library and scriptorium of the seventh-century community in Lindisfarne had devoted much of its resources and time, all in honour of God and St Cuthbert. Later, to escape from the clutches of the marauding Viking raiders, the unique copy of the Lindisfarne Gospels travelled with the refugee community of clerics to Chester-le-Street, where it was kept safely, no doubt with a certain modicum of pride, on the altar of the church.[18]

When this community later moved to Durham, the book went with them; it is clear that it was on display and known widely, for its iconography can be detected in another gospel book that was completed with illustrations in the eleventh century. The scene is a portrait of the gospel writer Matthew in the act of putting pen to parchment. As was shown in the discussion of Canterbury books in Chapter 3, such evangelist portraits were an expected constituent of the early medieval gospel book. Here the image made at Lindisfarne is of a man peering round the edge of a curtain towards the evangelist; its meaning is debated, but the figure of the man perhaps represents Christ. Someone writing and illustrating the later gospel book used this rather unusual idea to create a new evangelist portrait.[19] The borrowing demonstrates the steady influence of the (by then) ancient and highly revered Lindisfarne Gospels on the culture of later Anglo-Saxon England.

There is also internal evidence, additions written in the book, for the continuing use of the Lindisfarne Gospels, and hence the increasing importance of St Cuthbert, in the culture of the new kingdom of the English. In 950s and 960s, the book was given a new lease of life by the provost of Chester-le-Street, a Northumbrian by the name of Aldred, who wrote his famous 'colophon', an epilogue in Old English at the end of the book, describing how the Lindisfarne gospel book was put together, copied and decorated. In addition Aldred spent a great deal of time and effort on a continuous running gloss in Old English, which he added painstakingly and consistently between the lines of the Latin gospel text.[20] Aldred's career extended through the reign of Edgar, but it seems appropriate to consider the work of this northern writer in this chapter, before our attention shifts back to the south.

English was now used widely alongside 'Book-Latin' throughout the Anglophone regions of Britain, for writing and glossing of books, and Aldred participated in this trend. Though it is tempting for modern viewers to see his work as an undesirable intervention in the beautiful late seventh-century text, his gloss is another act of devotion. In each sentence, the Old English words are written neatly and attractively in a smaller and very different style of script (Insular minuscule) over the significant words of the Latin.

In Figure 8d, the acclaimed Chi-rho page, where the two Greek letters *chi* and *rho* and a capital letter *I* serve as an abbreviation for *Christi*, 'of Christ', Aldred's additions can clearly be seen. At the top of the page, for instance, is the Latin rubric for the beginning of the Gospel of Matthew, with Aldred's Old English written above it:

Old English: Onginneð godspell æfter Matheus.

Latin: Incipit evangelium secundum Mattheum.

                [Begins Gospel according to Matthew.]

Just above the Chi-rho image itself, is the little explanatory word *Cristes* (meaning 'of Christ'), and next in the left-hand margin an explanatory translation:

Witedlice suæ wæs Cristes cneunesso.

[Indeed thus was Christ's genealogy]

The word *witedlice* ('indeed, truly') is neatly corrected to the more usual spelling *witodlice*: the scribe has written an *o* over the first letter *e* to mark the correction. Lower down, at the tail of the stem of the letter *rho* where an decorative beast's head can be seen, there is the inscribed gloss *suæ vel ðus*, 'so or thus'. Aldred's glossing served many purposes: above all it aided the Anglo-Saxon reader to understand the Latin scripture, and where necessary it gave alternative synonyms and occasional explanations.

The kind of English that Aldred writes is Northumbrian. In other words, the 'northern accent' of English was different, even in those far-off days: Aldred has an alternative vocabulary and grammar to that of his West Saxon contemporaries, although they probably understood him when he came into contact with them. He certainly travelled south on at least one occasion, probably in the entourage of his bishop, Ælfsige of

Figure 8c   Lindisfarne, monastic ruins

Chester-le-Street, who had duties at the court of King Edgar. And he even mentions the date (10 August 970) and location where he stayed, 'besuthan Wudigan Gæte æt Aclee on Westsæxum', in other words 'to the south of Woodyates at Oakley in Wessex' (Oakley Down, Somerset). This comment appears in the Durham Ritual, another liturgical text that Aldred glossed meticulously and carefully in his fine handwriting. On that occasion we find him sleeping in a tent as he continues his work of elucidating the text. A hint of a personality emerges from a study of the patient work of this genial, if shadowy, figure of the tenth-century world.[21]

***

The fact that Aldred the Northumbrian found himself so far south is a sign of the times, for Northumbrian sanctity and Northumbrian culture were attractive and in demand. The kings of England were now rulers in

Figure 8d   Chi-Rho page, Lindisfarne Gospels, with Aldred's Old English gloss

the north as well as the south, and high-ranking Northumbrians (such as Aldred's bishop) attended the West Saxon court at its various meeting places across the south. In short, the whole political constellation of southern Britain had shifted. And the reason for that shift can be traced back to the achievements of Æthelstan, and to the military might that the king was able to muster. At various occasions in his reign, Æthelstan formally asserted his power: his coronation in 925, the meeting at Eamont in 927, his gift of the Lives of Cuthbert. Finally came the battle at Brunanburh in 937. The next chapter will examine this 'power and glory' and how it was celebrated in at least three languages, in the poems composed around the end of Æthelstan's reign.

CHAPTER 9

The 'Great War' and medieval memory

THE DEVELOPING REPUTATION OF ÆTHELSTAN

The late tenth-century historian Æthelweard the Chronicler has surprisingly little to say about Æthelstan, first king of all England. For his account of the whole reign he offers only one short chapter, of about half a page, and seems to know very few facts. Indeed he has only one event to report, 'the huge battle fought [in the year 937] against the barbarians at *Brunandun*, for which reason it is still called the Great War by the common people'[1]. His selection of the 'Great War' as the major event of the reign is of course significant. For the common people, as his remark demonstrates, this Great War was memorable and epoch-changing. A struggle of several nations, Brunanburh (or 'Brunandun' as Æthelweard calls it) was a long and bloody battle which ended in triumph for the English army (mainly West Saxons and Mercians) over a combined force of Scots, Strathclyde Welsh and Dublin Vikings. The battle established the English king as ruler of, broadly, the territory that is now called England. Its significance was certainly felt at the time, and it lived on in the collective memory.

Frustratingly for the present-day historian, there are no eye-witness accounts, and the mentions in near-contemporary documents lack any detail; in one case, in the *Annals of Wales*, there are just the two words 'Bellum Brune' ('War at Brune').[2] The contemporary Latin poem cited in the previous chapter, *Rex pius Aethelstan* ('King Æthelstan the Pious') will be seen to allude to the battle but remain very brief, mainly giving a general eulogy of the king. And we will see shortly that even the relatively long Old English poem *The Battle of Brunanburh*, though impressive enough on its own terms, nevertheless gives us little factual information. The two leaders of the English, Æthelstan and his brother Prince Edmund, and the two leaders of the enemy forces, Constantine King of the Scots and Anlaf (Olaf) King of the Dublin Norse, remain shadowy figures.

Here, for the benefit of the present discussion, are the opening lines of the poem *The Battle of Brunanburh*, which give some idea of its tone and style:

Æþelstan cyning,   eorla dryhten,
beorna beahgifa,   and his broþor eac,
Eadmund æþeling,   ealdorlangne tir
geslogon æt sæcce   sweorda ecgum
ymbe Brunnanburh

[In this year King Æthelstan, lord of men, ring-giver of warriors, and also his brother, atheling Edmund, gained lifelong glory when they fought in battle with the edges of swords around Brunanburh.]

The king is not described here, or indeed elsewhere in the poem, in personal terms. We do not see him as a speaking character in dialogue with his men, and his actions are very briefly summarised: he gained glory, he returned triumphant. In this respect the Æthelstan of the literary work *The Battle of Brunanburh* differs not only from the character Beowulf in the poem of that title but also from Byrhtnoth, the leader of the English in *The Battle of Maldon*, a poem that is also based on a historical event. In these two poems, Beowulf and Byrhtnoth are men who speak and act: they give orders, make promises, declarations, challenges; they express their emotions and their inner feelings. By contrast, the poet of *Brunanburh* presents Æthelstan only in terms of his role. He is a 'lord of men' and a 'ring-giver', two Old English poetic terms that express the authority and generous patronage that he was supposed to embody. As a historian and biographer of Æthelstan has recently remarked on the task of writing a biography of a king for whom the sources are relatively thin, it is legitimate to wonder whether 'Æthelstan the man still remains largely invisible'.[3]

But if contemporary poems fail to show us the man himself at the moment of his great triumph in 937, later writers from the twelfth century onwards are guilty of the opposite fault: invention, in other words embroidering too much new material onto the scanty contemporary records. Perhaps the most informative of these authors is William of Malmesbury, in his *Gesta regum* (*History of the Kings*), whose account of Æthelstan's reign seems to be based on a lost tenth-century source. But William also admits to taking his information from *cantilena*, 'popular songs', which retold and reworked the legends of King Æthelstan.[4] William's remark bears witness to the stories and ballads of Æthelstan that must have circulated among the populace for generations, but they do not inspire total confidence in the accuracy of the portrait of Æthelstan which he then paints. As Sarah Foot has shown, the twelfth-century legends fed into the pool from which the later medieval English accounts drew. One well-known fourteenth-century Middle English poem capitalises on 'Athelston' as the name of a famous Anglo-Saxon king from an earlier era and uses the historical king as a fictional character in a story set in the Old English past.[5] It looks like the real Æthelstan has been lost from sight. But there remains one other account of Æthelstan's Great War, and on an initial impression this looks far more convincing.

EGIL'S SAGA

Perhaps the most popular and enduring of the medieval literary reworkings of the story of Æthelstan and the Battle of Brunanburh comes not from England but from medieval Iceland. *Egil's Saga* is a work of historical fiction composed in the thirteenth century, one of the well-known prose sagas which are Iceland's major contribution to world literature. Iceland was settled in the ninth and tenth centuries by Norse farmers, who established a kind of republic or commonwealth that lasted until a political crisis in the thirteenth century, when the Norwegian kings asserted their rule over the island. That crisis marked a loss in autonomy for Iceland's independent-minded farmers but a definite gain for literature. Thirteenth-century Iceland was a traditional but also highly literate society that cultivated the spoken and written vernacular (the language they spoke was Old Norse, the same language spoken by the tenth-century Viking invaders and settlers of Britain). Embedded in the thirteenth-century Icelandic prose sagas are older poems, or passages from older poems, which the saga writers claim were composed by the skalds, the Old Norse poets of the tenth century.

    An example in *Egil's Saga* is the poem *Aðalsteinsdrápa*, which offers the following passage (the translation is here adapted from a version by John Hines):[6]

Nú hefr foldgnárr fellda
– fellr jǫrð und nið Ellu –
hjaldrsnerrandi, harra
hǫfuðbaðmr, þría jǫfra;

[Now, towering over the land, – the land falls under the kinsman of Ælla – the enhancer of battle, the king's [or kings'] foremost scion, has felled three kings.]

The text goes on to declare that 'Aðalsteinn of vann annat', in other words, the kinsman of Ælla, i.e. Æthelstan, 'achieved more', for now 'the high reindeer hills' are under his rule.[7] Most linguistic and stylistic studies indicate that this text is a genuine tenth-century poem. The diction and choice of word, the use of elaborate similes and riddling metaphors known as kennings, the obscure allusions in highly wrought language – all this is characteristic of the Old Norse skaldic poet. It is also evidence that the genre of the Norse panegyric, or praise-poem, was flourishing in tenth-century England. The poem, preserved in the later saga text, demonstrates the international prestige that Æthelstan achieved in the course of his reign. But since the poem is quoted only in part, what of the saga itself – what should we make of its portrayal of the king as a patron of poets?

Since it lay outside the European mainstream, and continued to cultivate traditions of poetry going back to the Viking age, thirteenth-century Iceland developed its own unique literature, a staple of which was this new genre, the long narrative prose *saga*, a kind of historical novel. Where literate people in the rest of Europe were reading or hearing verse romances about chivalry and courtly love, often set at the idealised court of the legendary King Arthur, at the same time the literate population of Iceland was reading 'the Sagas of the Icelanders' and the 'Sagas of Fargone Days': tough, realistic prose narratives set in the turbulent times of Viking-age Scandinavia and northern Europe. *Egil's Saga* is one of the highlights of this genre.

The saga tells of a family of farmers and warriors who escape the oppressive rule of King Harald Fairhair of Norway by seeking refuge in the new world of Iceland. A good many of the characters in the saga are historically attested elsewhere, which adds to the verisimilitude. The story moreover is well told by the standards of modern prose fiction, with convincing detail: we see the family's feud with the king, hear the recriminations and confrontations, follow the family's flight, and witness the dangers and rituals of voyage and landfall in Iceland. As in a modern novel, details are piled up in the narrative, not for their symbolic import but for their own sake, and the accumulation of facts and minor details thus contributes to the overall naturalistic effect. As modern readers, we find it believable. There is a convincing determinism of character, for two personality types recur in the family over the generations: a tall, pleasant extrovert and a dark, ugly-looking melancholic with touches of poetic genius. Egil, protagonist of this saga, clearly belongs to the second type. He is a fascinating anti-hero in a plausible plot which involves members of his family in a long-standing feud with King Harald of Norway and his aptly named son Erik Bloodaxe (who later rules as king of York). Members of this Icelandic family, in particular the resourceful Egil, return to northern Europe at intervals and involve themselves in the deeds of kings, including – to come to my main point – those of Æthelstan, king of England.

Since the nineteenth century when it was first published and translated, there has been a temptation to give too much credit to the narrative of Æthelstan's great victory as described in *Egil's Saga*. The saga is in fact highly imaginative, a work of creative reconstruction of the past. This is its attraction and its danger. Based no doubt on oral traditions and some historical knowledge, its author recreates a history of events that took place 300 years before, in his own way and for his own purposes, but at the same time he bends or distorts the historical facts considerably. Here are two examples. First, *Egil's Saga* presents as exact contemporaries Æthelstan in southern England and Erik Bloodaxe in the kingdom of York, while their reigns were in fact more than twenty years apart. Second, the saga presents Æthelstan's opponent Olaf as king of Scotland, whereas – according to the contemporary sources – Olaf was the Norse king of Dublin, and his ally Constantine was king of Scotland. Furthermore, it is stated that the battle itself was arranged in advance by negotiation, and the field marked out with hazel rods, almost like a tournament (*Egil's Saga*, ch. 52); here the saga sounds closer to the fictional reworkings of Middle English poems mentioned above. It is clear therefore that *Egil's Saga* should not be read as *bona fide* history.

With this proviso in mind, *Egil's Saga* can be read and appreciated for what it actually is: an imaginative and creative reconstruction in which not so much the historical facts as the circumstantial details ring true. Unlike any modern historical novelist who writes about this period, the thirteenth-century Icelandic saga writers were much closer in their mindset and attitude, in their traditions and lifestyle, to the men and women of tenth-century northern Europe. It is in the mood and mentality, in the descriptions of everyday life, ways of thought and expression, attitudes to feud and recompense that the historical interest lies. Here we can learn from the saga, for its author lived in a society, different, but not too different, from the world of an Anglo-Saxon thegn.

Let us now return to the stock expression 'ring-giver' which the tenth-century poet of *Brunanburh* used to describe Æthelstan. For an audience steeped in the traditional words and phrases of Old English verse a *beag-gifa*, meaning a 'ring-giver', was a king, in other words a royal patron who rewarded his followers for services rendered. In Old English, a *beag* was a ring, but probably a large arm-ring is intended rather than a *hring* or mere finger-ring. Such arm rings are found in treasure hoards of the tenth century, for example the Cuerdale Hoard, found near Preston in Lancashire; made of silver, the *beagas* are items of portable wealth which a Viking could remove as plunder or a king use as a gift for a supporter. Coincidentally, an episode in *Egil's Saga* (ch. 55) illustrates this splendidly. Egil, the dark and melancholy protagonist, dangerously erratic when depression afflicts him, sits on one side of the ceremonial hearth in the hall of King Æthelstan after aiding him to his great victory in battle. Egil is mourning his brother Thorolf, and a foul mood has descended upon him. He has received no compensation from the king.

In this context, the physical setting of the scene becomes all-important. A feature of early medieval society that the passage illustrates is the reliance on compensation as a redress for wrong. This was a common practice in Iceland, and a similar system pertained in Anglo-Saxon England: many of the laws of Anglo-Saxon kings, for instance, stipulate the amount of money to be paid to those who have been subjected to theft or bodily harm. As Peter Baker suggested in a recent discussion, it was not only a case of the guilty party paying money to the victim's friends and relations. For example in *Beowulf*, Hrothgar the king pays Beowulf for the loss of Hondscioh, who has been killed by the monster Grendel, though no one blames Hrothgar for the killing (*Beowulf*, lines 1053–5). A compensation payment therefore had many social functions: it was a public recognition of loss, it was a way of restoring the honour that a man loses when his kinsman or supporter is killed.[8]

In such a society, a large arm-ring was a valuable item of portable wealth, and accordingly in this particular episode in *Egil's Saga* it is considered to be the appropriate token of recognition to pay to an important man when his brother (in this instance Egil's brother Thorolf) has fallen in battle:

[Egil] refused to touch a drink even though people were serving him, and did nothing but pull his eyebrows up and down, now this one, now the other.

King Æthelstan was sitting in the high-seat. He, too, had laid his sword across his knees and so the two men sat for some time. Then the king drew his sword from its scabbard, took a fine big bracelet from his arm, and hung it on the sword-point; he stood up, stepped down to the floor and stretched over the fire with it towards Egil. Egil got to his feet, drew his sword and stepped down himself to the floor. He put his own sword-point inside the arc of the bracelet, lifted it towards him and went back to his place. Then the king sat down on the high-seat.

As soon as Egil was seated he put the bracelet on his arm and his eyebrows went back to normal. He laid down the sword beside him along with the helmet, picked up the horn that had been offered him and drank it down.[9]

Here the saga author evokes the layout of the early medieval hall with its rectangular hearth located in the middle of the living space, around which the men sit at the mead-benches, while any smoke from the glowing fire is able to escape through the louver, or smoke-hole, far above them in the roof. The scene can be vividly pictured. And although the narrator does not state explicitly what the two men are thinking or feeling, he shows it in his stage directions, in the descriptions of the men's gestures and behaviour: the king sitting in the high seat, deliberately calm, the warrior betraying his desperate grief by his facial expressions. The hearth now becomes the setting for the dramatic confrontation between king and courtier, for Æthelstan is taking no chances with his dangerously aggrieved Viking warrior.

The king carefully keeps the security of the central hearth between himself and Egil, and he offers the compensation literally on the point of his sword across the fire: if events should turn nasty he is ready to defend himself.

There are various early medieval parallels for this kind of cautious parley with weapon in hand. A possible analogue is a scene in the eleventh-century Bayeux Tapestry where the keys of the fallen city of Dinan in Britanny are surrendered to the besiegers: the knight, identified by the Latin caption as Conan, reaches down from the parapet with his spear to a mounted knight, who takes the keys on the point of his lance.[10] A more obviously dramatic confrontation is found in the ninth-century German poem *Hildebrandslied* (*The Song of Hildebrand*). Here the protagonist finds himself facing a young warrior in single combat who turns out to be his own son. Hildebrand offers a parley, with gifts, but the young hothead refuses to accept his father as the real thing, declaring that the only way to accept a gift is on the point of his spear.[11] Closer to home in Anglo-Saxon England is the poem *The Battle of Maldon* mentioned above. Again there is an opening parley, and here the Viking spokesman offers to depart with his fleet of ships if only the English army will pay them to leave. To this outrageous demand the English leader Byrhtnoth has only one ironic response (Lines 45–8). 'Do you hear, seaman,' he asks the Viking, 'what this English army has to say?' He continues:

> What they will pay   is spears they will send
> with poisoned points   and their family swords,
> those heriot weapons   not for your profit.[12]

A 'heriot' (Old English *here-geatu*) meant literally 'military equipment', but it came to be used as a legal term for the payment of an inheritance tax, rendered to the king on the death of a thegn or retainer. The various surviving Old English wills of the tenth-century Anglo-Saxon aristocracy often stipulate in their opening clauses that a heriot of horses, weapons and equipment should be paid to the lord their king. So there is obvious ironic force here in the promise of heriot weapons to the Vikings. But the English leader Byrhtnoth makes his ironic remark all the more pointed; the Vikings will be paid literally with English spears and swords, *ord ond*

Figure 9a   Viking sword, modern reconstruction

ecg, 'the point [of the spear] and the edge [of the sword]', being a
recurrent motif. In contrast to the scene in *Egil's Saga*, violence will
inevitably ensue: there will be no payment, and no reconciliation.

It is telling that in *Egil's Saga* the figure of Æthelstan as a great lord
and ring-giver does not become a fully rounded character, even though
there would have been ample opportunity to paint his portrait in the
fictionalised narrative. We imagine that the saga writer had few written
sources to work with, but this does not prevent him from composing a
lively portrait of other historical characters, such as King Erik. The
writer clearly intends Æthelstan to be a good king, a foil to Erik
Bloodaxe, but Erik is given far more weight and attention in the telling
of the tale. The fact is that Æthelstan speaks very little in the five
chapters set in England (chs 51–55) and what he does say is often
reported in summary; he remains a rather distant figure. In terms of
actual direct discourse, he at one point delivers a rebuttal to the
Scottish king just before the battle, then in the scene just discussed he
offers Egil compensation for his brother; at the end of this section there
is the friendly farewell where he extends his invitation to Egil should he
ever return again to his kingdom. These speeches tally with what was
generally known about the reign: to judge by the records, Æthelstan
was decisive in military action, generous to his allies, and hospitable at
his court. Perhaps the saga writer made educated guesses from what he
knew of the king's reputation, but he shied away from presenting a full
and detailed character.

OCCASIONAL POEMS AND CHRONICLE POEMS

In terms of subject matter, the celebratory theme of Egil's *Aðalsteinsdrápa*
recalls *Rex pius Aethelstan*, cited in Chapter 8 above. Again, like other
occasional pieces, this is found in a gospel book (London, British Library,
Tiberius A. ii), in this case one made on the Continent, and with clear
political connections: it was once owned by Otto I, the German emperor,
and the queen mother Matilda, who presumably sent it as a gift to King
Æthelstan. According to the description in the poem, Æthelstan had the
headings or titles in the book adorned with gold plate, and its wooden
boards seem to have been decorated with precious stones. Again we see
how books were valued objects that could serve to cement political
friendships. As the poem goes on to declare, Æthelstan for his part
donated the volume to Christ Church, Canterbury, where it rested for
posterity.

Rex pius Aethelstan is a eulogy to the king, praising him for his piety and strength. Like Christ who treads down the serpent, or like the personified Virtue who treads down Vice in Prudentius's poem *Psychomachia*, so Æthelstan treads down his enemies. Here are the opening lines of the poem, with a translation; the name of the king is capitalised as in the manuscript copy:[13]

Rex pius AEÐELSTAN patulo famosus in orbe,
Cuius ubique viget gloria lausque manet,
Quem Deus Angligenis solii fundamine nixum
Constituit regem terrigenisque ducem
Scilicet ut valeat reges rex ipse feroces
Vincere bellipotens colla superba terens.

[King Æthelstan the Pious, famed throughout the wide world, whose glory flourishes everywhere and whose praise endures; whom God established as king of the English people, supported on the foundation of his throne, and leader of his earthly people, so that this king powerful in war would conquer fierce kings, treading their proud necks.]

The obvious allusion is to Brunanburh, the king's great triumph over fierce kings, a reminder of the Old English poem on that battle.

Perhaps on the model of the Latin poems intended for the court, the making of Old English political poetry seems to gather momentum at the end of Æthelstan's reign. The evidence is found primarily in copies of the Anglo-Saxon Chronicle. Version A of the Chronicle, neglected at its home in Winchester, was partly revived around the middle of the tenth century, but it did not return to the full prose narratives found in the entries for the reigns of Alfred and Edward the Elder. Some historians see this as a decline, arguing that the flow of the Chronicle 'dries up in the tenth century'.[14] At first the scribes reverted to the older style of a list of years with short notices attached to each year. But then a new policy was introduced. Evidence for this can be seen on the pages of the manuscript itself, which are adapted, and the list of dates erased to make room for lengthier text. The scribe had to rethink his working practice. So for the year 937, instead of the date and brief text, the scribe adds a whole poem, *The Battle of Brunanburh*; there follows one short notice recording the death of Æthelstan (actually 939) and the succession of his brother Edmund; then for the year 942 there is the poem *The Capture of the Five Boroughs*. A mere handful of short entries now cover the brief reigns of Edmund, Edred and Edwy, but for the longer and more significant reign of Edgar two further poems are included. So although there is low coverage of mid-century events in the Chronicles, the poems add a new literary dimension to the text.

As to their style, all four of these poems are written in the traditional Anglo-Saxon poetic metre. In this respect, as I have said, the style of *The Battle of Brunanburh* is similar to that of *Beowulf*, and it has been shown that the poet aimed for gravity and a high poetic effect using archaic words and metre.[15] But the purpose of the poem *Brunanburh* is very different. Like *Rex pius Aethelstan* this is a commemoration rather than a proper narrative; it is a panegyric in praise of the West-Saxon royal dynasty. The poet emphasises that the English army acted in tandem, with both the West Saxons and the Mercians sharing equally in the action. It was 'natural' for them to defend their land, so the poet declares, because their ancestors had lived there so long. In brief, the poem is political, and it charts the growing sense of a nation with a shared heritage becoming a cohesive whole.

When compared and contrasted with *Beowulf*, the tone is far less personal, less involved with the details of action and character. We are told that the warriors broke the enemy's defensive formation, known as the shield wall, and the image is elaborated, with elegant variation on the weaponry. But we do not see how it happens, the narrator does not show us the action, and we do not know the details. There is no monologue or dialogue; and no dramatic confrontation is shown to us – everything is reported at a distance. Even when the two poets use a similar image there are differences. In *Beowulf*, for example, the passage of the sun is charted as it crosses the sky, but the focus then shifts to Beowulf himself on the beach, the rumour of his coming, and the preparations for his arrival (lines 1963–76):

> Then the redoubtable warrior set off with his retinue across the sand, stepping across the sea-meadow and the wide shores. The candle of the world was shining, the sun eager on its journey from the south. They finished their journey, marched on resolutely, to where, as they had heard, the young and worthy warrior king, protector of good men, slayer of Ongentheow, was dealing out rings in his fortress. Hygelac was immediately told of Beowulf's journey, that the protector of warriors, the shield-companion had come back safe and sound from the play of battle and was at the outer precincts and making for the court. Quickly, at the command of the king, the hall was cleared for the guests.

Although this is summary – and the passage of the sun across the sky seems to prompt this kind of hurried narration – there are nevertheless snatches of human speech. The men have heard that Hygelac is at home, the messengers hurry to tell him who has arrived; the king orders the hall to be prepared.

In *The Battle of Brunanburh*, there is a similar passage where the sun moves across the sky and events are quickly summarised, but the effect is rather different. There is no coming down to earth, no homing in, no descent to the level of human dialogue. Here is the prose translation by Hallam Tennyson, son of the Victorian poet Lord Tennyson:

> The spoilers cringed, the Scottishmen crouched; and the ship-crews fell: they were doomed to the death; the field flowed with the blood of warriors, from when the sun on high, the mighty star in the morning-tide, the bright lamp of God the everlasting Lord, glided over earth, even until this noble creature sank to his setting.[16]

Hallam Tennyson adds a footnote by the Cambridge professor of Anglo-Saxon, W.W. Skeat, explaining that *cringed* was once a strong verb, *crungon* (meaning 'they fell'). Hallam's prose translation here captures the meaning, and wherever possible the connections with modern English, but it cannot render fully what Skeat calls the 'swing' of the original metre and rhythm. The elder Tennyson later consulted his son's text when writing his version of the poem and rearranged accordingly, though he also added stanzas for a more ballad-like effect. Here is his equivalent passage, which forms stanza III of his poem:

> Bow'd the spoiler,
> Bent the Scotsman,
> Fell the ship-crews
> Doom'd to the death.
> All the field with blood of the fighters
> Flow'd, from when first the great
> Sun-star of morning-tide
> Lamp of the Lord God
> Lord everlasting,
> Glode over earth till the glorious creature
> Sank to his setting.

Although this is certainly spirited and dynamic, it does not do full justice to the poetic craftsmanship, the elaborate compounds and kennings, and the rhetorical patterns of the action.[17] Nevertheless, even in translation, the poem's lively form can be seen to have literary value, even though thematically it is a rather blatant glorification of war and conquest. In this well-crafted passage, in fact, the poet gives a sun's eye-view of events, and the passing of time during this eventful day is conveyed by a description of the sun as a noble creature moving across the sky. We realise now that the battle is over, and night is falling, and that the sun has departed and left the enemy dead lying all over the battlefield.

The theme of departure now comes to the fore. Essentially all the leaders leave the field of the battle, although with different motivations and responses. The enemy of course is forced to flee: Anlaf the Viking leader by ship and Constantine the Scottish king by land. In a kind of grim irony, there is no cause for them to rejoice – the Vikings go home *æwiscmode*, 'ashamed'. Here the theme of celebration is rehearsed in its absence, until the poet turns finally to the English homecoming: Æthelstan and his brother Edmund, the two leaders of the English army, return *wiges hremige*, 'triumphant in battle'. As Matthew Townend has argued, this practice of naming and shaming and naming and celebrating is characteristic of Norse praise poetry, and is perhaps imitated here by the Anglo-Saxon poet.[18]

The Capture of the Five Boroughs is a much shorter poem than *Brunanburh*, but there is the same attention to the role of the king. Like Æthelstan, King Edmund is lauded for his role rather than his person, with several compound epithets that describe his role as 'king of the English', 'protector of men, 'doer of deeds', 'protector of warriors', 'son of Edward':

> Her Eadmund cyning,   Engla þeoden,
> mæcgea mundbora,   Myrce geeode,
> dyre dædfruma,   swa Dor scadeþ,
> Hwitanwyllesgeat   and Humbra ea,
> brada brimstream.   Burga fife,
> Ligoraceaster   and Lincylene
> and Snotingaham,   swylce Stanford eac
> and Deoraby.   Dæne wæran æror
> under Norðmannum   nyde gebegde
> on hæþenra   hæfteclommum
> lange þrage,   oþ hie alysde eft
> for his weorþscipe   wiggendra hleo,
> afera Eadweardes,   Eadmund cyning.

[Here King Edmund, lord of the English, protector of men, the well-loved doer of deeds, occupied Mercia, as far as it is bordered by the Dore, the Whitwell Gap and the wide sea-stream of the Humber river. Five boroughs,

Leicester and Lincoln and Nottingham, and Stanford and Derby. The Danes had been subjugated under the yoke of the Northmen, the captive chains of heathen men, for a long time, until *he* released them through his worthiness: the protector of warriors, Edward's son, King Edmund.]

There is a theme of release, or even salvation. Like poems such as the *Advent Lyrics* from the Exeter Book in which Christ the Saviour releases mankind from the chains of darkness, so Edmund is a saviour figure.[19] In its briefer style, it picks up on the theme of territorial expansion that was found in the annals of Edward's reign (see Chapter 6 above), and this fits well with a set of entries that emphasise Edmund's successes rather than his setbacks, for there is no mention in these annals of the fact that Edmund had failed to retain this territory when he first came to power.[20] The poem now goes further, for it takes the technique of listing the names of towns and fortresses found in the annals of Edward the Elder's reign and reworks it into a poetic catalogue of *burga fife*, 'five boroughs', recovered from the Northmen. It is important to emphasise that the enemy is no longer the Danes but the heathen Northmen, who must be invaders from the Norse-controlled kingdom of York.[21] The Danes are now members of the English kingdom, royal subjects, who are released from captivity by the king of the English.

Why are such poems added to the Chronicle? It looks like the royal court at some stage in the middle of the tenth century began actively intervening in the record-keeping, keen to promote its unifying policies.[22] National poetry became the new fashion, deriving from the tradition of Viking panegyric, as well as other sources. Opinions differ as to whether the poems were composed specifically for the Chronicle. I am inclined to the view that the poems on Æthelstan and Edmund circulated elsewhere, and were added to the Chronicle later, while the poems on Edgar may have been written by the Chronicler himself.[23] In these texts, there is a growing sense of national identity in the titles invested on the king. Æthelstan, as we have seen, is *eorla drihten* 'lord of men' but Edmund is *Engla theoden* 'king of the English' and as we shall see, Edgar in the poem on his coronation is *Engla waldend* 'ruler of the English'. We will return to Edgar's reign in Chapter 13. First we need to direct our attention to some other fruitful sources for the mid-tenth century period.

THE METRES OF BOETHIUS

Around the middle of the tenth century a scribe made a copy of a rather different set of Old English poems. In the Cotton collection of the

British Library is to be found a manuscript of the Old English *Boethius*, which has preserved the so-called 'prosimetric' version of the text, in which passages of prose are also interspersed with occasional poems.

As we discussed earlier, from the evidence that survives it seems that the original English translation of Boethius's *Consolation of Philosophy* – whether or not literally by King Alfred – was done in the medium of Old English *prose*. But when somewhat later – and not necessarily by the same writer – the translation was reworked, passages of poetry were inserted into the prose in order to reflect the alternating prose and poetry of the original.[24] Boethius himself had had in mind the earlier Roman poet Ovid (43 BC – 17 AD), who, like Boethius, had also lived out his days in exile, banished from Rome to Tomis on the Black Sea by the emperor Augustus in 8 AD. Following his model, Boethius in his *Consolation of Philosophy* imitated the style of Ovid's poetic elegies and wrote his accompanying poems in many and varied genres and metres. To a certain extent, the Old English *Metres of Boethius*, even though they are done in the Old English alliterative metre used by the poet of *Beowulf* or the poet of *Brunanburh*, capture the variety of the original Latin. It has been suggested that the Old English *Metres* belong to a new 'Southern mode' of Old English poetry that developed in the late Anglo-Saxon period.[25] And one scholar argues that the poet of the *Metres*, with his slightly looser style and approach, has created not necessarily masterpieces but, in some cases, new poems 'that stand among the most unusual products of OE literature'.[26]

Metre 9, for example, is presented as a song sung by Wisdom to further the progress of the argument of the treatise. It begins with the traditional call for attention '*Hwæt!*' ('listen, attend') that occurs at the start of many Old English poems. It then retells the wicked deeds of the emperor Nero, King of the Romans, which the poem asserts 'we all know' (line 1).[27] This first person plural 'we' of the opening gambit is inclusive, assuming an audience, as in *Beowulf*, who share with the poet the same knowledge of the past:

> We have heard in days long gone of the glory of the kings of the Danes, how those princes performed great deeds (cf. *Beowulf*, 1–3).

But where the Danish kings are said to have practised *ellen* (courageous action), the emperor Nero does its very opposite, namely *ærleaste*, literally 'deeds without honour', and, as the poem goes on to declare, he has committed 'a multitude of evil deeds', and he has thought 'the evil thoughts of the unjust man'; yet despite the enormity of his crimes he remained 'slaughter-cruel' (cf. C Metre 9, lines 1–8, 37–8). Thus the emperor Nero in the *Boethius* is like Heremod in *Beowulf*, the king of the Danes who preceded the saviour-figure Scyld in the genealogies, the man with the 'blood-cruel' heart who killed his table-companions in his swollen anger (*Beowulf*, 1709–19). In the famous so-called 'sermon' or admonitory speech in *Beowulf*, Hrothgar the aged king urges the young warrior Beowulf to benefit from this admonitory exemplum and see the virtue that he must emulate: 'learn from this and perceive the virtue!' (1722–3):

> þu þe lær be þon / Gumcyste ongit!

Virtue, it seems, can be learned even from wholly negative models of behaviour. And Hrothgar continues, in his long speech, to warn Beowulf of the onset of pride that will destroy the moral integrity of a ruler at the height of his power and joy. Similarly Metre 9 ends with an admonitory proverb, again employing the first person 'we' that includes its audience in the evaluation; its message resonates with the famous dictum of Lord Acton, a thousand years later, that power corrupts and absolute power corrupts absolutely (Old English *Boethius*, version C, Metre 9, lines 61–3):

> It was very clear there what we have often declared:
> that power (*anwald*) does not do any good at all
> if he who has the power (*geweald*) does not wish for good.

Literature is not always harnessed to the wagon of the powers that be. Thoughtful Old English poets in the middle of the tenth century may have had reason at least to question the ruler's desire for *anweald*. Were there dissidents in the ranks? Or perhaps moralising churchmen? There are, I think, many ways in which this proverb might have been applied to the expansionist ambitions of the dynasty. As to who its author might be, that must remain a moot point, but if the Metres are not Alfredian, they must have been composed by someone in a school or place of learning, someone with intellectual and moral confidence, someone who was not afraid to question the authority of the king. Malcolm Godden has suggested that the author of the Old English *Boethius* was 'someone like Dunstan', in other words someone who could behave like an uncompromising prophet, a biblical Elijah or Ezekiel, in his relationship with the king and the royal court.[28]

CHAPTER 10

'Prophet in his own country': The early life of St Dunstan

Statesman, visionary and intellectual, archbishop of Canterbury from 959 to 988, Dunstan, as we have already seen, looms large in the political, religious and literary developments of the tenth century. Though his date of birth is not known for sure, he lived through nearly all the reigns of the tenth-century kings: Edward the Elder's three sons Æthelstan (924–39), Edmund (939–46) and Edred (946–55), then Edmund's two sons Edwy (955–9) and Edgar (959–75), and finally Edgar's two sons Edward the Martyr (975–8) and Æthelred the Unready, who was consecrated as king by Dunstan in 978. Exploring the life of Dunstan is an essay in tenth-century English history, for Dunstan witnessed, and indeed took part in, the various succession crises; he was well acquainted with all the important men and women of his age, from dowager queens such as Eadgifu (pronounced, broadly, as Ediva) who was the mother of King Edmund and King Edred, to churchmen like Æthelwold, the reforming bishop of Winchester in Edgar's reign.

In short, through his long life, Dunstan was party to all the new developments; he witnessed the growth of towns and the reconquest of the Danelaw; he participated in the monastic revival, both at Glastonbury where he was abbot, and at Canterbury where he eventually became archbishop; he supported the reform of education at Winchester, Worcester, Canterbury and elsewhere.[1] And when Dunstan spoke to kings, such as Edmund or Æthelred, they felt compelled to listen to him, even if they did not immediately appreciate what he said.

THE AUTHOR OF THE *LIFE OF ST DUNSTAN*

> To the most wise lord archbishop – that is to say Ælfric – B, remotest of all priests and worthless native of the Saxon race, [wishes] the joys of high heaven.

So begins the *Life of St Dunstan* by the anonymous B., completed most likely at Canterbury by an author who had recently returned from abroad. Known only by his pen-name, B. was a man who lived in Liège from the 960s but who had known Dunstan personally in his earlier life and had been taught by him at the school of Glastonbury.[2] B. completed his biography in the 990s, in the period after his return to England, when he seems to have been an author looking for a patron, and sending letters of introduction to bishops and archbishops in pursuit of this aim. He eventually found a patron in Ælfric, not the already mentioned writer and abbot of Eynsham, but a man of the same name, the archbishop of Canterbury and successor to Sigeric, who served in that post from 995 to 1005. Following a precedent set by other hagiographers before him, B. set about the task of writing his Latin *Life of St Dunstan*. He writes mostly in the ornate and difficult 'Hermeneutic' Latin prose that was fashionable in the tenth century, embellished with exotic Greek vocabulary; sporadically also, he included purple passages of fully fledged Latin verse, although his sources seem mostly to be the Christian Latin poets like Juvencus and Prudentius rather than classical poets such as Virgil.

It is important to emphasise one credential in B.'s curriculum vitae. Although B. was educated at the monastic school at Glastonbury, he was a cleric and not a monk. The distinction is highly relevant, because it is crucial to understanding tenth-century English debates on the organisation of church and state. In Anglo-Saxon terms, a cleric is a member of the so-called secular clergy, for he is probably a canon, and has taken orders and eventually may become a priest. Once he has achieved priestly status he may well become a resident in a minster community from which he goes out regularly to serve the smaller dependent churches in the countryside as the need arises. Alternatively he may be a member of a cathedral community, which he helps to run, in which case he perhaps follows more intellectual or educational pursuits as part of his weekly labours. But the fact that he is not a professed monk means he is permitted to have his own property; he may entertain and dine with the local citizens or nobility; he may even be married, as were the clergy at Winchester before the reforms of Edgar's reign.

A monk, by contrast, is a member of a different kind of community or household, namely a monastic order that follows a rule. He is celibate and shares all his property with his brethren or fellow monks in the monastery. His daily life is extremely closely ordered and regulated by the monastic Hours, i.e. the daily round of services, which all the monks attend in order to sing the Psalms and the liturgy. In between these set times in church there is space for work, either manual or intellectual labour, according to the individual vocation of the particular monk. Daily life for the monk, therefore, is more disciplined and ascetic, and the hours of work apparently more productive and efficient, than it is for his cathedral or minster counterparts. In the tenth century, English monastic communities followed the Rule of the Benedictine Order, which had been undergoing a process of radical change on the European Continent, particularly under the lasting influence of Carolingian monastic reformers such as Benedict of Aniane and Smaragdus of Saint-Mihiel. From the reign of Edmund, the reforming ideas started to filter into England. By the time of King Edgar, the monastic party was in the ascendancy, and their success is tangible: much (though not all) of the surviving art, metalwork, architecture and manuscripts, both literary and religious, can be attributed to the spread of the monasteries across Greater Wessex and the south of England from the middle of the century onwards. Dunstan was to play a significant role in all these developments.

Being a cleric rather than a monk, the author B. found himself an outsider on his return to England in the 990s. The world had changed, for the monastic life had taken over in the major centres such as Winchester and Canterbury. Naturally B. has little to say about Dunstan's role in the monastic reforms, for the simple reason that he had lived abroad and was not present to witness Dunstan's activities as archbishop. Nor, as a cleric, did he have any wish to place great weight on this monastic aspect of Dunstan's career. Moreover, perhaps B. is right not to emphasise Dunstan as a purist monastic reformer. It is certainly true to say that Dunstan was less consistent than colleagues of his such as Æthelwold, who ordered all the clerics to be ejected from the Old Minster at Winchester, whereas Dunstan was quite happy to preside over mixed communities of clerics and monks, both at Glastonbury and Canterbury.

B.'s Latin prose is – linguistically – difficult to read. But in more ways than one, it is fair to say, he has had a bad press. As far as historians are concerned, he is surprisingly ignorant about even well-established facts, such as the names of the kings who preceded Æthelstan. To judge by remarks in his preface, it may be that B. was also completing his work under time constraints, and without ready access to new information. For Latin classicists, his style is felt to be clumsy or overly elaborate. Clearly, he lacked the full rigour of the classical education that contemporary monastic writers such as Æthelwold, Lantfred and Wulfstan of Winchester had enjoyed, although he had studied enough to write some of his chapters in verse. By the usual standards he falls short, and the two authors of the recent masterly edition of B.'s *Life of St Dunstan* are not complimentary about his literary style, his prolixity, and (especially) his rather 'clumsy' or 'mediocre' Latin verse making. As they point out, B.'s ambition to write a prosimetric work soon falters, and he returns to prose for most of the work.[3]

Where B. arguably captures our attention is his choice of anecdotes to include in his story. These interesting narratives aptly illustrate Dunstan's qualities not only as an abbot with a prophetic turn but also as a man with an artistic and creative side to his character. And although B. is writing within the constraints of the genre of hagiography, not all the anecdotes are miraculous, while some provide insights into the mentality of the man and the times in which he lived. From a literary point of view, it might be argued that they add authenticity to the main structure of the story. And in their narrative content rather than their poetic form, perhaps these anecdotes go some way to redeeming B.'s reputation as an author. This chapter, then, offers a revisionist thesis. It will be argued that B. is a writer whose saving grace is his ability to tell a significant or colourful anecdote.

DUNSTAN'S SAINTLY CHARACTER: THE DREAMS

B. depicts Dunstan as a holy man in his propensity to dream dreams and see visions. Typically, following the usual earlier models for such lives, B. as a hagiographer finds evidence for Dunstan's later character in his experiences as a youth: in other words, the child is father of the man. He illustrates this idea with rich anecdotal detail. In his Chapter 3, for example, as we saw at the beginning of this book, he shows us Dunstan as a very young boy accompanying his father Heorstan on a visit to Glastonbury 'with its curving shores spread wide', in order to worship there.

According to B. the site 'dedicated to the holy service of God' covered only a small area. First there was the celebrated Old Church, which stood on the site now occupied by the medieval Lady Chapel (one of the few buildings still intact in the present day, among the ruins of the abbey). Dedicated to St Mary, the Old Church was a wooden building so ancient that the first West Saxon Christians at Glastonbury did not know who had built it and when. Next to it was the stone church dedicated to Christ and St Peter, built in the conversion period, as B. tells us, although typically he does not appear to know that it was constructed during the reign of Ine (Ina), king of the West Saxons (688–726).[4] Such facts are not, on his own admission, available to him.

But continuing his story, B. tells us that here at this church Dunstan and his father stayed overnight to pray. Falling into a deep and peaceful sleep, Dunstan dreams of a man in snowy-white clothes, who takes him on a walk round the monastic site and even shows him the positions of the future buildings that will be built during his abbacy. In terms of medieval dream theory this must surely be taken as a prophetic dream sent by God: the abbey site will expand considerably under Dunstan's future leadership.

The boy Dunstan undergoes a prophetic dream experience of a rather different kind some years later once his parents have sent him to live at Glastonbury. At this stage the community is not a monastery proper but a community of unreformed clerics, and here the young Dunstan begins his studies at the school (B., *Life of St Dunstan*, Chapter 4). During a severe bout of illness and fever, he takes to walking in his sleep. One night he leaps up suddenly from his bed, grabs a stick and brandishes it as though he is fighting off a pack of dogs; he then makes his way to the stone church and climbs the workmen's ladder onto the roof, where he walks about unharmed. In the morning he is found sleeping next to the two watchmen on the inside of the church, but he has no idea how he got there, for the church doors had been barred from the inside. Clearly intrigued by this incident, B. highlights its perils and dangers by shifting to verse.

In the resulting 42-line poem 'Sed quod contulerat', the author in time-honoured fashion addresses directly the 'good reader' of his work (lines 35–7):

Optime nunc lector, celeri sermone fatere
Quid tibi veredico videatur in hoc pusione,
Si talem dubites superum conscendere templum...

[Good reader, now, tell me the truth quickly:
What do you make of this lad?
Have you any doubt that such a man climbed to the top of the temple...?][5]

B. ends this poem with an appeal to his reader to draw the right moral from the narrative, namely that Dunstan's climbing the temple is a sign that he will afterwards show 'by teaching and example how the humble sufferer rises and the proud man falls headlong'. Here is the original language (lines 41–2):

> Dogmata distribuens necnon exempla relinquens,
> Ut surgat patiens humilis ruat atque superbus.

The Latin is quoted here to show that despite his problems with the diction of classical verse, and despite his uncertainty about long and short syllables (evidence that he was not indeed so well versed in the writing of hexameters), B. nevertheless has some skill with the weighing of words. In these two lines he employs alliteration (dogamata ... distribuens; surgat ... superbus) and rhyme and assonance (distribuens ... reliquens ... patiens; surgat patiens ... ruat atque) to underline his message. In addition, the final line is so constructed as to emphasise the parallel and the contrast: that the sufferer (*patiens*) will rise (*surgat*), while the proud man (*superbus*) will fall (*ruat*). Is B. thinking here in English rather than Latin? Embellishments such as parallelism were also used effectively by the authors of Old English religious poems, sermons and homilies, for example in the Vercelli Book, and it is not beyond possibility that B. was also influenced by that tradition in the writing of his poem.

As told by B., Dunstan's youthful dreams prepare for those of his mature years, when after his time at Æthelstan's court Dunstan returns to Glastonbury, first as a student and then, in the reign of Edmund, as abbot of the community. There is, for example, the appearance of the late departed Wulfred in a prophetic dream in Chapter 9 of the *Life*. On another occasion, Dunstan, standing in prayer at the door of the church, sees a beautiful vision of a white dove, its wings scintillating with light as it crosses the evening sky on the occasion of the death of the Lady Æthelflæd (Chapter 11). Again, in Chapter 20, shortly after he has rejected his friend King Edred's offer of the bishopric of Crediton, Dunstan dreams that Andrew, one of Jesus's apostles, appears to him in his sleep, rebukes him first for refusing to join their company, and then strikes him with his staff. On waking, Dunstan clearly still feels the effect of the blow, for he asks a fellow monk, presumably his servant, who it was that had the temerity to strike him. The servant is unsure:

> At ille 'Nullus' inquit 'te quiescentem liquo percussionis tactu me sciente contigerat.'

[The reply was: 'No one, so far as I know, gave you a blow while you were still asleep.']

As with many other medieval biographical writings – and so far we have principally considered those of Bede and Asser – there is of course no reason to suppose that the young monk's reply, as recorded here in B.'s literary Latin, is any reflection of the way that the monk actually spoke. But the same cannot be asserted for Dunstan's rather colloquial response, at first hesitant, then slowly more confident:

> Is ergo premeditatus ait: 'Modo, fili mi, scio, modo a quo sim percussus agnosco.'
>
> [He thought it over, and then said: 'Now, my son, I know: now I realise who hit me.']

After a moment of confusion on first waking, Dunstan's thoughts become clear and he remembers his dream; the repetition of 'now' reflects his dawning realisation, and adds the authenticating detail. The king has been urging Dunstan to accept the position as bishop, and has even asked the queen mother Ediva (Eadgifu) to visit Dunstan to press his case further. But Dunstan has persuaded them to accept an acquaintance instead. Now however, touched by their entreaties, Dunstan has had second thoughts, and these regrets are reflected in the dream that he experiences in the following night. Not all episodes in medieval hagiography can be rationalised in this way, but it surely makes sense to interpret Dunstan's dream here in terms of his motives and aspirations.

THE ROLE OF ANIMAL IMAGERY IN THE STORY

As was already seen in Chapter 1, there are a surprising number of dog-like figures and wild animals in B.'s *Life of St Dunstan*. Some of these are to be taken as authorial similes and metaphors while others are more concrete and tangible. Sometimes Dunstan sees these creatures in his dreams, but often he perceives these animals with his physical senses, and sometimes they even attack him, although in the end it turns out that they are apparitions or sendings created by 'the Old Enemy', in other words the devil. In this respect such animals belong in a long tradition of saints' lives, going back to the ferocious 'spectres in the form of lions, bulls, wolves, vipers, serpents, scorpions and even leopards and bears' in the Latin *Life of St Antony* by Evagrius of Antioch in the fourth century.[6]

Two examples of the recurring dog imagery have already been mentioned. The first comes in the sleepwalking episode. Here is B.'s narrative describing the onset of the young Dunstan's adventure:

> After being long weighed down like this by the mass of the invisible ill, lo and behold! he suddenly moved, leapt up, rose briskly, and snatched a thin stick that he chanced to find at that moment. Away he went with it, slashing at the air on either hand as though defending himself against mad dogs.[7]

B. perhaps deliberately makes mysterious this anecdote about warding off invisible dogs. It certainly is an arresting moment, all the more effective for being left unexplained, a disconcerting view of a small boy slashing about wildly with a stick while he walks in his sleep. Another of Dunstan's encounters with dogs comes in B.'s Chapter 6, the incident when his kinsmen and rivals at Æthelstan's court throw him into the swamp (discussed in Chapter 1 above). Here the reference to dogs begins as a complex biblical metaphor: Dunstan, it is implied, is like the lamb led to the slaughter which never opens its mouth to complain (Isaiah 53: 7) while his enemies are like barking dogs, an image perhaps borrowed from the writings of the fourth-century scholar St Jerome, the famous translator of the Vulgate Bible.[8] But if the dogs in the first instance are an illusion, and if these dogs here are a literary echo, in the very next scene of Dunstan's story the dogs are by contrast all too real, rushing out of his friend's farmhouse to bark at the strange monstrous figure coated in mud who has come blundering onto the premises hoping to find refuge and a bath.

Again, as with the stories of dreams, the youthful episodes about dogs prepare for the reappearance of the motif later in the *Life*. In his Chapter 15, as we saw earlier, the author B. takes stock of Dunstan's achievements: the winning of souls for the company of heaven, the success of the school at Glastonbury under his abbacy in training 'many priors, deans, bishops and even archbishops' (among whom Sigeric should be included). Chapter 16 now relates, as is common in hagiography, how the devil attempts to disrupt the saint's good work. Known traditionally as 'the Enemy', the devil sends a series of apparitions which are meant to distract Dunstan from his spiritual practice of prayer and meditation in the cloisters of the monastery. First he sends a frightening bear, next a savage dog intended to distract him from his prayers, then an ugly fox. But to no avail, for Dunstan sees the 'devilish monsters' (as B. calls them) with the eyes of the spirit.

He smiles, makes the sign of the cross, and as in many hagiographies the Enemy vanishes.

In Chapter 17, however, the Enemy is back, now described as the *seductor antiquus* (Old Seducer) and the *illusor* (the Deceiver), appearing in the form of 'a shaggy bear, huge and frightening'. The exhausted Dunstan, it seems, has fallen asleep in the middle of reciting a psalm, and in this momentary lapse he has left himself open to attack. This time the bear appears so convincing that Dunstan, briefly, is taken in: it advances on him, puts its front paws onto his shoulders and prepares to tear him apart. But at the last moment Dunstan manages to get hold of his staff and strike back. At once he is woken by the noise that his staff has made as it strikes the inner wall of the church, and, losing no time, he immediately resumes his recital of the psalm at the point where he left off: 'Let God arise ... so let the wicked perish at the presence of God' (cf. Psalm 67 (68): 1–3). As in many such stories, the text of the psalm being read is more than coincidentally appropriate.

But B. prefers not to end this episode on the supposition that it was after all only a dream. Here are his closing words to the chapter:

> They say that at the very moment he resumed singing, the deceiver could be vaguely seen beating a baffled retreat, like a pitch-black shadow of the shape I have described.

The vision was a dream but, disturbingly, it also had a palpable if shadowy reality. From the perspective of the writer B., and no doubt that of Dunstan too, the spiritual world is just as real as the physical, and the two spheres impinge on each other inextricably.

DUNSTAN'S DEALINGS WITH MEMBERS OF THE NOBILITY

Even as a youth Dunstan had stood out from his compatriots for his literacy and learning, but there was also something obdurate about his character, something that won him friends and enemies in equal numbers. This may also be connected with the role of adviser to the king or prophet in the Old Testament sense that Dunstan assumed at various times in his career.[9] Nowhere is this better seen than in his dealings with members of the West Saxon nobility and royal family, with whom Dunstan also enjoyed ties of kinship.

Among his close friends are a number of retired but influential religious women, including elderly widows of important members of the ruling elite; one of them is even the Lady Ediva, widow of King Edward the Elder, who is given a passing mention in B.'s narrative (see Chapter 13 below). Another is the Lady Æthelflæd, whose mystical death-bed scene and Dunstan's vision of the flight of the white dove has just been alluded to. An earlier instance of this friendship is found in the story of the copious mead at Lady Æthelflæd's hall. This occurs in the part of the *Life* dealing with the reign of King Æthelstan, and it paints yet another cameo portrait of that king as a man fond of ceremony and feasting yet perceptive and generous towards others. The anecdote is miraculous, told for its spiritual message, and since it bears a resemblance both to the biblical Marriage at Canaan and also to an episode in Wulfstan of Winchester's contemporary *Life of St Æthelwold*, it may not have much basis in actual historical events. Nevertheless the story has some literary qualities, and the incidental details once again create a window on the everyday life of the times that other texts and genres fail to provide.

As has already been remarked, it was a custom of the time for the English king to travel around from place to place to visit his subjects, deal with issues of law and order, and generally smooth and lubricate the governance of the country. The king needed to be seen and heard if he was to maintain his rule effectively. The anecdote in the *Life of St Dunstan* shows a household preparing for just such a royal visit, which inevitably was a drain on a household's resources, since the king travelled with his whole court: reeves and other royal officials, thegns, soldiers, scribes and servants; and all these had to be accommodated and provided with suitable food and drink, for as long as they needed to stay. In B.'s narrative, the king sends his chamberlains ahead to alert his niece, the Lady Æthelflæd, to his imminent arrival (Chapter 10).[10] All is well, they report, apart from the supply of mead. Typically B. presents the crucial moment as direct speech, a dialogue between the lady and the king's thegns:

> After inspecting everything, they said to her, 'You have all you need for the entertainment, as long as you don't run out of mead.'
> She replied, 'My lady Mary, the holy mother of my Lord Jesus Christ, does not wish me a shortage of that or anything else needed to honour the king.'[11]

Immediately B. has her hurrying into the Old Church to pray to its patron St Mary.

Figure 10a   The Lady Chapel, Glastonbury, *c.*1900; site of the Old Church

Lady Æthelflæd's petition is heard. When the king eventually arrives 'with a great retinue' (*multo ... comitatu*) they first attend mass in the church, then adjourn to the lady's hall for the *prandium*, or 'meal'. Inevitably, however, there is no mention of food: as in the scenes at the mead-benches in the royal hall of *Beowulf* the occasion calls for mead.[12] And since this is a royal visit, the mead supply is practically exhausted by the end of the first round of drinks; but amazingly (for those present) and also expectedly (since this is the life of a saint) it continues to flow. The servants continue pouring out the mead all afternoon 'from horns, goblets, and other vessels, large and small, as is the custom at royal banquets' (*ut adsolet in regalibus conuiuiis, cornibus, scifis aliisque uasibus magnis et modicis*). The description is reminiscent of feast scenes in Anglo-Saxon manuscript art, for instance the feast in the Tiberius work calendar discussed in Part I, where the feasters drink from various horns and goblets, and the servants replenish their drinks from large pitchers held with a towel in their hands. Such is the scene also at the Lady Æthelflæd's hall, and the implication is that since this drinking has gone on all day it surely threatens to continue all night. But the king finally relents:

'We have greatly sinned by burdening this servant of God with our great company.' So he got up, saluted his niece, and went his way.

It is left to King Æthelstan to have the last word and leave the lady before they drink her out of house and home.

It is not clear if Dunstan was present on this occasion, whether as friend of the lady of the household, or as member of the royal retinue. From what B. subsequently relates in Chapter 12, it is clear that Dunstan was still heavily embroiled in his studies, which were remarkably wide-ranging. B. takes the trouble to mention that Dunstan's interests cover biblical, literary, artistic, and musical studies. He is even involved in designs for textiles, assisting in the making of a cope with Æthelwynn, another noble lady. During their work together, his harp, which he had hung on the wall, spontaneously sounds out a tune, all on its own, to the great consternation of those present. There are resonances here of the much later literary work 'The Eolian Harp', by the poet Samuel Taylor Coleridge:

> And what if all of animated nature
> Be but organic Harps diversely framed,
> That tremble into thought, as o'er them sweeps
> Plastic and vast, one intellectual breeze,
> At once the Soul of each, and God of all?

Or even Shelley's 'Ode to the West Wind', another meditation of the ethereal resonances of a wind harp:

> The trumpet of a prophecy! O Wind,
> If Winter comes, can Spring be far behind?[13]

Modern scholars cite the incident with the harp for its art historical interest, the fact that a scholar like Dunstan was involved in the design of a stole or bishop's garment which was to be decorated with gold and gems.[14] B., on the other hand, sees this wind harp as a sign of imminent change: the new king, Æthelstan's half-brother Edmund, is about to summon Dunstan to service at the royal court.

KING EDMUND AND THE HUNTING PARTY

A crucial scene in the *Life of St Dunstan* takes place at Cheddar in Somerset, not far from the royal hall or hunting lodge that archaeologists discovered there in the 1970s.[15] At this point in the plot, Dunstan is now firmly attached to King Edmund's court and participating in one of the king's long perambulatory tours of Greater Wessex. The royal party has reached Cheddar and is preparing for the hunt. But for Dunstan, recent history seems to be repeating itself. Once again, as at Æthelstan's court, he has fallen foul to the machinations of various unnamed courtiers, who appear to have a grudge against him, for reasons of envy. Again the king is persuaded by their reports, summons Dunstan into his presence and in a furious rage orders him to be stripped of his possessions and banished from the kingdom. He is, however, given a time of respite to arrange his affairs, during which he appeals for help to sympathetic visitors from an 'eastern kingdom'; possibly these are Greeks or Franks, though no further information is given. The point is that Dunstan is about to leave the country.

The repeal comes unexpectedly, on a day set aside for a royal hunt (*Life of St Dunstan*, Chapter 12):

> One day soon afterwards, the king went out with his men to enjoy the hunt as usual. When the huntsmen arrived in the woods, they competed to race on different sylvan tracks.

Such a hunting tableau is a common one in medieval sources, both literary and historical. Illustrations of hunting often form a background to other events, or serve as a decorative theme on an embroidery or tapestry. In Anglo-Saxon art there are hunting scenes in sculpture, in illustrated calendars, in the margins of the Bayeux Tapestry. But a hunt also has symbolic potential. In religious contexts the hunted hart or stag recalls the first verse of Psalm 41 (Psalm 42 in modern versions of the Bible), a text with an obvious allegorical interpretation as the yearning for God, which reads as follows in the bilingual Junius Psalter of the early tenth century:

> Swa swa heorot gewilnað to wiellum wætra swa gewilnað sawl min to ðe god
> *Sicut cervus desiderat ad fontes aquarum ita desiderat anima mea ad te deus.*
>
> [As the hart panteth after the waterbrooks, so panteth my soul after thee, O God.][16]

A classic pictorial rendering of this verse occurs in the Utrecht Psalter, an illustrated Book of the Psalms that was kept in the late tenth century at Christ Church Canterbury, at the very scriptorium or library where B. is likely to have been completing his work. Highly influential on the development of Anglo-Saxon art in the tenth century, this Carolingian psalter in a classicising style acted as a model for numerous artists, and the whole psalter was copied and reworked as the Harley Psalter in the late tenth and early eleventh centuries.[17] It pictured each psalm with a lively illustration in which every verse provides an image for the composition: a warrior, a horse, a deer, a fountain. In the Utrecht Psalter, the picture accompanying the psalm shows a deer realistically drawn in outline in pen and ink. The detail is very clear: this is a stag with full antlers, leaping up onto the crags towards a stream in the centre of the picture. Behind the stag are two large wolfhounds straining forward in hot pursuit, jaws panting.[18] Such a scene would fit very well as an illustration to the scene at the royal hunting lodge in Cheddar in the *Life of St Dunstan*.

Generally speaking, if a hunt features in any detail in medieval writings it usually signals that something untoward is on its way. In historical works, it is hunting accidents that attract attention, the best known in the context of the Anglo-Saxon Chronicle being the annal for the year 1100 which reports the death of King William Rufus, son of William the Conqueror, in the thirteenth year of his reign, 'on the morning after Lammas, while out hunting, [he was] shot with an arrow by one of his own men'. An earlier example is the death of Carloman, killed in the forest while hunting a boar, as reported by the Anglo-Saxon Chronicle for the year 855. Literary examples include two of the stories in the Welsh *Mabinogion*, possibly composed in the tenth century. In Old English, there is a brief hunting scene in *Beowulf* and a more elaborate hunting episode in a legend popular in England from the middle of the tenth century onwards, the *Life of St Eustace*.

Figure 10b   Illustration to Psalm 41 in the Harley Psalter

In *Beowulf* the hunt is mentioned by King Hrothgar during a long speech he makes in his hall of Heorot, a name which itself means – perhaps significantly – 'hart' or 'stag'. At lines 1366b–1372 Hrothgar is in the process of explaining to Beowulf the location of Grendel's Mere, a gloomy lake set in woodland which Beowulf must seek out if he is to deal with the second monster of the poem, Grendel's vengeful and murderous mother. The passage is eerily atmospheric, a rhetorical set-piece with echoes of descriptions of hell found in contemporary sermons, both in Latin and Old English.[19] Here the figure of the stag or hart (named *hæthstapa*, 'the heath-stepper', or *heorot*, 'hart', in the Old English text) becomes a kind of *exemplum*, or illustrative story (lines 1366b–72):

> No þæs frod leofað
> gumena bearna,   þæt þone grund wite;
> ðeah þe hæðstapa   hundum geswenced,
> heorot hornum trum,   holtwudu sece,
> feorran geflymed,   ær he feorh seleð,
> aldor on ofre,   ær he in wille
> hafelan beorgan;   nis þæt heoro stow![20]

[There is no child of man so wise that he knows the depth of it. Even if the heath-stepper, harried by hounds, the strong-horned hart, were to seek that wood, pursued from afar, nevertheless he would give up his life and breath on the shore, rather than plunge in to save his head. It is an unpleasant place!]

Even though the stag is pursued to the point of death by the hunting hounds, nevertheless it would rather halt at the water's edge than dive into the uncanny waters and make its escape.

In the *Life of St Eustace*, set in the pagan Roman empire during the time of the Christian martyrs, the stag assumes some of the divine associations and symbolic significance that it has in Psalm 41. And like the stag in *Beowulf*, it is again a solitary creature, separated from the rest of the herd and harried relentlessly by the hounds. The Old English text of the *Life of St Eustace* lingers over the preparations for the hunt, before it homes in on the protagonist, in this Old English version named 'ealdorman Placidas', at the moment when he starts up the enormous stag:

> Þa hi ealle ymb þone huntað abysgode wæron, þa æteowde him sylfum an ormæte heort, se wæs ormætre mycelnysse ofer ealle ða oþre, and wlitig, and þa gewende he fram þam flocce, and ræsde into þam wudu þær he þiccost wæs. Þa þæt Placidas geseah, þa gewilnode he þæt he hine gefenge, and him

geornlice æfter ferde, mid fæwum geferum. Þa æt nixtan wurdon hi ealle
geteorode, and he ana unwerig him æfterfyligde.[21]

[When they were all occupied in the hunt an enormous stag appeared to
him, much greater in size than all the others, and beautiful, and then it
turned aside from the herd, and rushed into the wood where it was thickest.
When Placidas saw this he desired to catch it, and went after it eagerly with
a few companions. But in the end they all tired and he alone continued to
follow unwearying.]

It is the separation from the others that marks out these narratives of
the chase; first the stag separates itself from the herd, then the hero
finds himself alone following the stag as the other men become weary
and drop out of the running. In this Old English passage the alliterative
technique (a repetition of 'm' and 'f' sounds) is used to embellish the
style. The Eustace legend culminates in the scene on the mountain crag
where the stag stops and turns to face him, and a figure of Christ
appears between the antlers asking Eustace why he is persecuting him.
It is of course a Damascus moment. Eustace has a change of heart; he
converts from paganism to Christianity, with all his family.

Stories such as these constitute the echoes and resonances behind
the incident of King Edmund and the stag as told in B.'s *Life of
St Dunstan*. The narrative takes the reader from the noisy preparations,
with the dogs barking and horns blowing, to the king's choice of a
single stag to follow by himself; the chase is long, up many winding
paths 'with his lively horse and pursuing dogs', until suddenly and
unexpectedly the precipice of Cheddar Gorge appears, and the stag and
leading dogs leap into the abyss and are lost. The problem for the king
is that he is close behind in full career and his spirited horse will not
stop. Here is the translation in the recent scholarly edition:

Behind them came the king, his horse flying on at a great pace. Suddenly he
saw the precipice, and did all he could to stay the horse's onrush. But it was
a stubborn and stiff-necked beast, and would not respond.

The original Latin text bristles with alliteration here, in particular the /k/
sound represented in the Latin by spellings with 'c' and 'qu' and in one
case 'x' (not to mention other effects with 's' sounds), and the
consonantal 'v' of *voluntatis, venit, viso* and *viribus*):

Similiter autem et rex sequens ceruum et canes cum magno voluntatis equi
impetus venit, et statim viso precipitio cursum accelerantis equi quantum
quibat viribus retinere conatus est; sed quoniam colli contumacis et rigidae
cervicis erat non potuit.

Through the texture of the /k/ sounds, I would argue, B. is aiming to convey the urgency and inevitability of the impending disaster. The only solution for the king is to resort to prayer; and as he prays he recalls that he has harmed no one save Dunstan alone, and he vows to make amends if his life is spared. 'At these words' *ad quod dictum*, we are told that the horse stopped, by the merits of the saint, with its hoofs on the very brink as it is just about to plunge down into the depths.

At this point we might recall the episode of the young Dunstan on the roof of the church at Glastonbury, along with the moral message that B. attached to it, namely that the patient sufferer will rise and the proud upstart will fall. At Cheddar Gorge, King Edmund in his pride very nearly fell, and he is swift to make amends. Dunstan is summoned; the king rides with him to the church at Glastonbury and amid tears of contrition personally leads him to the priest's chair and installs him as abbot of the community.

What is the modern reader to make of this? B. clearly has some literary ability to tell a tale and tell it well, but to what extent can we believe him as a writer of history, *wie es eigentlich gewesen* ('as it really happened')? A historian such as Nicholas Brooks is cautious.[22] He points out that Dunstan in fact rarely signs any of the surviving charters of King Edmund (who reigned from 939 to 946), in direct contrast to the many charters that Dunstan witnesses during the reign of King

Figure 10c   Cheddar Gorge

Edred (946–55) when he is much more firmly established in his position in royal government. The conclusion Brooks draws is that Edmund and Dunstan certainly were reconciled, but that Edmund's solution to this recalcitrant monk – this able and gifted administrator but outspoken critic, this holy man but difficult friend – was to promote him to the abbacy of Glastonbury. In so doing, Edmund freed Dunstan from attendance at court, where many personal tensions and political rivalries had arisen. Liberated for the rest of Edmund's reign from political duties, Dunstan was able to rebuild the abbey and to develop the monastic life there, including the school.

CHAPTER 11

'By skill must love be guided': The school of Glastonbury

'THE LIBERAL ART OF GRAMMAR'

By the middle of the tenth century, Glastonbury had become a prosperous monastery and great school, the equivalent of a medieval university.[1] For many years in the first half of the tenth century – due to the Danish takeover in York, East Anglia and the Danelaw – it had been the major institution of its kind in southern Britain, perhaps for a time the only significant school still in working order. And it was highly successful, for Dunstan's students went on to prominent positions in the English kingdom:

> later very many shepherds of churches, trained by his teaching and example, were in demand for diverse cities and places where saints rest, chosen to give instruction there in the holy rule and the standards of justice, as priors, deans, abbots, bishops, and even archbishops.[2]

According to B., the school taught standards of justice and good works – what might be called law and ethics in modern parlance – as well as 'instruction in the holy rule', which seems to refer to the Benedictine Rule for monasteries. Overall B. emphasises the political impact of Glastonbury on what was becoming a unified England.

The facilities at Glastonbury were by the standard of the day considerable: under Dunstan the abbey was extended into a large precinct bounded by an embankment and ditch. To the east of the Old Church, Dunstan's workers enlarged the main church (dedicated to saints Peter and Paul), and to the south they built a cloister, where traditionally, at least in summer, classes and study sessions could take place. Described by archaeologists Philip Rahtz and Lorna Watts as 'one of the earliest to be found in England', the cloister also housed industrial workshops; excavations have uncovered pigments for frescoes, pottery, and glass for vessels and windows.[3] Evidently various arts and crafts were practised there, as well as literary activity, and all this is corroborated by statements in B.'s biography.

The 'very many shepherds of churches', the company of 'priors, deans, abbots, bishops, and even archbishops', are not named in B.'s biography, but they were important men, for the late tenth century was the time when the monastic party came into its ascendancy, when monks held positions of power in the united England of Edgar and his successors. Wulfstan of Winchester, in his *Life of St Æthelwold* (ch. 11), names as former alumni the Glastonbury cleric Osgar, who eventually became abbot of Abingdon after Æthelwold, and Foldbriht, who became abbot of Pershore, and Ordbriht, who became abbot of Chertsey and bishop of Selsey. These were minor posts, but the archbishops of Canterbury who were possibly taught by Dunstan must include Æthelgar, Dunstan's immediate successor from 988 to 990, and Sigeric (in office from 990 to 994), whose journey to Rome was traced in Part I. And thereafter the Glastonbury school continued to send its important alumni out into careers that led them to high positions in the life of the church and the nation.[4] But the most famous alumnus of the School of Glastonbury was clearly Æthelwold, later abbot of Abingdon and subsequently bishop of Winchester, who was to become, alongside Dunstan, one of the two foremost men of Edgar's kingdom (see Chapter 13).

According to his biographer Wulfstan Cantor, Æthelwold came to Glastonbury shortly after Dunstan's appointment as abbot, during the reign of King Edmund (939–46). At this point in his tale, Wulfstan adds a few remarks on Dunstan's teaching at the school and Æthelwold's subsequent studies:

> [Æthelwold] profited greatly by Dunstan's teaching, and eventually received the habit of the monastic order from him, devoting himself humbly to his rule. At Glastonbury he learned skill in the liberal art of grammar and the honey-sweet system of metrics; like a provident bee that habitually flits around looking for scented trees and settling on greenery of pleasant taste, he laid toll on the flowers of religious books.[5]

The curriculum evidently included the teaching of the Rule of St Benedict, the essential guide to Benedictine monastic life. But the emphasis seems to be markedly literary, for alongside studies of the Rule

Figure 11a   Glastonbury Tor

came Latin grammar, and the rhythm and metre of Latin poetry, and classical poets were read as well as the usual Christian authors. They were often studied in extracts, anthologies and florilegia, hence the reference to the 'provident bee' choosing its nectar from the best flowers in the field, an image also used by Bishop Asser, the biographer of Alfred (see Chapter 3 above).

But whole books were also studied, and in some cases the manuscripts still exist, furnished with the additions, marginal notes or interlinear glosses that both Dunstan and Æthelwold added to them. One book, for example, is a copy of Augustine's *Enchiridion*; a scribe has added a poetic epilogue, an acrostic/telestich poem rather like the poem 'Adalstan' discussed earlier; but where the main theme is the Trinity, the telestich (the vertical column on the right-hand side) spells out the name of 'Dunstan, unworthy abbot'. Another book by Augustine, or at least attributed to Augustine (though now identified as the work of Caesarius of Arles), is a commentary on the biblical Apocalypse (Revelation); the manuscript has an inscription at the end, on the very last page:

> Dunstan abbas hunc libellum scribere iussit.

The colophon unequivocally declares that 'Abbot Dunstan ordered this book to be copied'.[6]

A third book fits very well into Wulfstan's description of the curriculum. This is the manuscript containing 'Adalstan', an anthology of poems copied in north-eastern France in the ninth century. For convenience in the following discussion, it will be referred to by its

Bodleian Library shelfmark as Rawlinson C. 697. The English monastic reader of this volume would have had much to ponder. First of all he could have read the riddles of Aldhelm, poems in a high literary register on topics ranging from everyday objects such as a candle or a pillow to the phenomena of nature and the night sky. Secondly there is a set of unusual poems on the letters of the alphabet, starting with 'K'. Thirdly he could have meditated on the lives of saints in Aldhelm's hagiographical *Carmen de uirginitate*. The fourth text is *Psychomachia*, 'The Struggle of the Soul', in which the late Roman poet Prudentius offered the reader a strange violent allegory of a war between the Virtues, personified as women warriors, and a similarly attired host of Vices.

All in all, this is a varied set of poems for a student of Christian Latin poetry to tackle, treating the world and the cosmos in the first two items, and hagiography, moral theology and church history in the third and fourth. Now as we know from B., Dunstan was present at King Æthelstan's court in the 930s, and perhaps saw the Rawlinson manuscript there. Once Æthelstan had died, his personal library may have been given away to suitable recipients.[7] Perhaps Dunstan acquired the book then, for it contains some intriguing notes made by a scribe who has come to be known as 'Hand D'.

Hand D is an example of the new Caroline handwriting that spread to England from the Continent in the middle of the tenth century.[8] This scribe's annotations are visible in a variety of books: a commentary on the Benedictine Rule, Bede's work on time and the seasons, Primasius's commentary on the Apocalypse, the poetry of Aldhelm and Prudentius, and the philosophy of Boethius. Fairly confidently, the Hand D glosses can be ascribed to the great abbot himself, and they provide a 'preliminary indication of the books studied at Glastonbury by Dunstan and his students'.[9]

'ST DUNSTAN'S CLASSBOOK'

The best known of the manuscripts annotated by Hand D is the famous compilation known as 'St Dunstan's Classbook'.[10] Originally this was made up of three booklets, one from Britanny and two from Wales, all copied in the ninth century, which Dunstan re-assembled into one volume in three parts:

(1) *The Art of the Verb*, Book I, by Eutyches, a Latin grammatical treatise,[11]

(2) *The Book of Commoneus*, a unique anthology or florilegium of biblical extracts and other texts,[12]

(3) *The Art of Love*, Book I, by Ovid.

Evidently Dunstan used this book for teaching, and, as with other textbooks from the period, it looks as though grammar, biblical readings and chronology, and poetry and metrics were studied together. And like Asser and Alfred before him, Dunstan – as the likely maker of this book – combines texts not normally associated, in order to create his own personal anthology or florilegium.

On folio 1r, the opening page, there is a large frontispiece. It seems that Dunstan added – or commissioned – a full-page pen-and-ink drawing of a haloed Christ with long dark hair and billowing robes, holding in his right hand a staff, or rod of justice, and in his left hand a book on which is written in Latin 'Come, ye children, hearken unto me: I will teach you the fear of the Lord' – this is a quotation from the Psalms which also appears in both the Rule of St Benedict and in Smaragdus's commentary on that Rule, two other books that Dunstan knew and studied.[13] Dunstan himself features in the picture, a small figure at Christ's feet: he appears as a tonsured monk in profile, wearing his monastic habit and shoes, kneeling with his head pressed into the ground, his left hand pointing to Christ's feet, his right hand to his eyes, as though to indicate emotion or contrition. And above the figure of the monk in the picture is a short verse distich or couplet, evidently by Dunstan, and written in the recognisable handwriting of D. Washes of red lead pigment are used to colour not only Christ's halo but also the end of the rod, and the hem of Dunstan's hood and robe. The same colour is used to highlight the initial letters of the verses: clearly both picture and writing belong together, and it is possible that Abbot Dunstan added both script and pigment to complete the image (see Figure 11b).

In its original Latin word order, the distich is a kind of prayer from Dunstan, whose name occurs at the beginning of the line, directed towards Christ in the second half of the line; it reads as follows:

Dunstanum memet clemens rogo, Christe, tuere
Tenarias me non sinas sorbsisse procellas

[I ask you, merciful Christ, that you watch over me, Dunstan; do not allow the Taenarian storms to swallow me.]

Despite its brevity, this poem contains an allusion to a celebrated abbot of the previous century, Hrabanus Maurus (c.780–856), the great Carolingian scholar and poet, abbot of Fulda and archbishop of Mainz.[14] Hrabanus was the author of the popular work *De laudibus sanctae crucis* (*In Praise of the Holy Cross*), a poetic meditation using acrostic images in which text and picture are linked to form messages, a genre known as figurative poetry, similar in technique to twentieth-century concrete poetry. It is possible that a particularly splendid copy of Hrabanus's work, now in Trinity College, Cambridge, was also owned by Dunstan at Glastonbury.[15] Arguably, then, the poem and picture in Dunstan's Classbook combine a number of sources to present something new: one of the first authorial self-portraits in the history of English art and literature.

There is even a classical echo. The phrase 'Taenarian storms' in the second line of the poem transports the reader to Taenarum, a promontory and bay on the southern coast of the Peloponnese in Greece. The likely source is a passage from the Roman poet Statius's epic *Thebaid*, Book II:

> There is a place – named Taenarum by the Inachian folk – where foaming Malea's dreaded headland rises into the air, nor suffers any vision to reach its summit. Sublime stands the peak and looks down serene on winds and rain, and only to weary stars affords a resting-place. There tired winds find repose, and there the lightnings have their path; hollow clouds hold the mountain's midmost flanks, and never beat of soaring wing comes nigh the topmost ranges nor the hoarse clap of thunder. But when the day inclines towards its setting, a vast shadow casts its fringes wide over the level waters, and floats upon mid-sea. Around an inner bay Taenaros curves his broken shore-line, not bold to breast the outer waves.[16]

According to legend, a mysterious cave in this storm-tossed region provided a portal granting access to the Underworld, the Land of the Dead. Dunstan's poem, then, is a rare expression of his fears and hopes, in which – as elsewhere in the manuscript – we find a mixture of Christian learning and classical scholarship.

On the next page of the Classbook, just as the grammatical work by Eutyches begins, there is another poetic couplet written in the middle of a blank space below the preface to the grammar; it is also in the conspicuous handwriting of 'D'. This is an extract from *De bono pacis* (*On the Goodness of Peace*), an epigram by Eugenius, archbishop of Toledo in Spain during the time of the Visigothic King Chindaswith (who ruled Spain from 642 to 649):

Figure 11b   Portrait of Dunstan at the feet of Christ in 'St Dunstan's Classbook'

Qui cupis infestum semper vitare chelidrum
Cordis ab affectu pace repelle dolum.

[You who desire always to avoid the hostile serpent,
repel treachery from the disposition of the heart of peace.] [17]

Like the previous distich, there is a definite 'protective function' to this short piece, which takes on new meanings through the associated texts and contexts.[18] Both the Taenarian storms and the hostile serpent are dangers to be avoided, by means of prayer and meditation.

In the second booklet of the Classbook, at folios 19–36, we again find fascinating juxtapositions of texts. Hand D is particularly busy: he adds further comments to assist in the reading of a Paschal Table (a diagram providing the dates of Easter over a 19-year cycle). Later (folios 35r-35v) he completes a biblical text, so that the whole passage conveniently appears on one page at the end of the booklet. The text is bilingual, in parallel columns of Latin and Greek arranged as readings in church during the liturgy of Easter and Whitsun Vigils (which is unusual, since few people in England or western Europe knew Greek at this time).[19] The reading is an Old Latin text of Genesis 22, the story of Abraham and his attempted sacrifice of his son Isaac, prevented at the last moment by God, who rewards Abraham for his obedience under pressure. The text relays God's ensuing promise to Abraham (verses 16–17):

> Per memetipsum iuravi, dicit Dominus: quia fecisti uerbum hoc, et non pepercisti filio tuo dilecto propter me: benedicam tibi, et multiplicans multiplicabo semen tuum sicut stellas cæli, et velut harena quæ est ad litus maris [in littore maris]. Et hereditabit semen tuum ciuitates aduersariorum.

> [By my own self have I sworn, saith the Lord: because thou hast performed this word, and hast not spared thy beloved son for my sake: I will bless thee, and I will multiply thy seed as the stars of heaven, and as the sand that is at the sea shore: thy seed shall possess the cities of their enemies.][20]

There are messages here about God's favour to a chosen nation, which may have struck a chord with the West Saxons at this particular point in their history.[21] In St Dunstan's Classbook, the text originally finished at verse 17, so in order to complete the liturgical passage for the reading, Hand D added the final two verses:

> Et benedicentur in semine tuo omnes gentes terræ, quia obedisti vocem meam. Reversus est Habraham ad pueros suos, et surrexerunt et abierunt simul ad puteum orationis, et habitavit Habraham ad puteum orationis.

> [And in thy seed shall all the nations of the earth be blessed, because thou hast obeyed my voice. Abraham returned to his young men, and they rose and went to the Well of the Oath together, and he dwelt at the Well of the Oath.]

According to Mildred Budny, the part copied by Dunstan, with its emphasis on obeying the Lord's voice, recalls the psalm verse on the rod of justice in the illustration of Christ on the first page of the volume, where the Lord calls upon his children to hearken to his voice. In Budny's words, this combination of texts 'proclaims the Lord's omnipotence, just judgement and salvation for those prepared to carry out his precepts'.[22] It is likely then that these texts had particular personal spiritual meanings for Dunstan when he reworked them for his own florilegium.

The third booklet of St Dunstan's Classbook is a copy of Book I of Ovid's *Art of Love*. It opens with the title *Ouidii nasonis ars amatoriae liber*

primus incipit, 'Here begins Book I of Ovid's *Art of Love*'; the usual opening
lines then follow:

> Siquis in hoc artem populo non novit amandi,
> Hoc legat et lecto carmine doctus amet.
> Arte citae veloque rates remoque moventur,
> Arte leves currus: arte regendus amor.

> [If anyone among this people does not know the art of loving,
> let him read this, and having read the poem be skilled in love.
> By skill swift ships are sailed and rowed,
> By skill fast chariots are driven: by skill must love be guided.][23]

This is poem from a very different context and of very different concerns
to those of an abbot and his students in a tenth-century school. But the
classics still have their lessons to teach. 'By skill must love be guided' –
arte regendus amor – this is the message which underpins the text.

The original ninth-century Welsh scribe copied most of the Ovid, but
for some reason the last section is missing (lines 746–72). Hand D now
steps in and copies the end of Book I of the *Ars Amatoria*. The passage
copied concerns different ways to entice the hearts of many different
types of women, using images from horticulture such as vines, olives and
wheat, and from the changing aspects of nature: waves on water, a lion, a
tree, a wild boar (lines 757–62). This is not obvious reading matter for a
monastic school; but it is beautifully written, a model for the writing of
verse, and it has a certain moral and psychological relevance (for the
whole passage, see Interlude IV below). Perhaps the rest of the poem was
available to Hand D, but he chose not to copy it or include it in the
Classbook.

OLD ENGLISH POETRY AT THE SCHOOL OF GLASTONBURY?

It is distinctly possible that Old English poetry was studied at
Glastonbury. We should recall the Rawlinson anthology, which offers
evidence of the acquisition of books and pursuit of poetry at
Æthelstan's court. The manuscript contains a copy of Aldhelm's Latin
Riddles or *Enigmata*, a wide-ranging set of one hundred riddles or
enigmatic poems in a classical style. These were available then as a
source for Old English poets. It has long been realised, for example, that
Exeter Book Riddle 35 translates Aldhelm's riddle 'Lorica', and this is
evidence of a long-standing tradition of translating riddles in Anglo-
Saxon England.[24] It has also been shown that Rawlinson C. 697

contains the actual (rearranged) text of Aldhelm's Enigma 100 that was used as the source by the Old English author of Exeter Book Riddle 40.[25] On this argument, Riddle 40 must be a tenth-century poem, perhaps composed at Glastonbury. This raises a whole host of questions, not all of which are amenable to quick and convenient answers. But literary historians are starting to wonder whether the famous Exeter Book, which had found its way to Exeter Cathedral Library by the mid-eleventh century, could have been assembled at a large and active monastic school such as tenth-century Glastonbury.[26]

A recent case has been made for associating the colorful and idiosyncratic Old English *Solomon and Saturn Dialogues* with Dunstan and the school of Glastonbury. Certainly such an assertion is not susceptible to absolute proof, but the chain of connections presented by the editor Daniel Anlezark is plausible.[27] First, there is the subject matter, which fits very suitably with poems available for study at Glastonbury as outlined above. For a flavour, the following is my interpretation of the mystical passage on the verbal power of the Paternoster (i.e. the Lord's Prayer) in the poem *Solomon and Saturn I*.

The two speakers in debate are Saturn, representative of worldly knowledge, and Solomon, the spokesman of Christian wisdom. In the passage I have in mind, Solomon takes up one of Saturn's challenges, claiming that the 'palm-twigged Paternoster' has the power to open up heaven, bless the holy, and make the Lord merciful, to strike down murder, extinguish the devil's fire and kindle the Lord's fire. Saturn's agnostic reply questions the notion that the Paternoster 'strikes down murder' (*morðor gefylleð*); he speaks of his anxiety and curiosity, his heart is *bysig æfter bocum* 'busy in pursuit of books' where he hopes to find the answers, and he employs a metallurgical image that Daniel Anlezark sees as characteristic of the poem (lines 53–6):

> Ac hulic is se organ   ingemyndum
> to begonganne ðam   ðe his gast wile
> meltan wið morðre,   mergan of sorge,
> asceadan of scyldum?

Here is Anlezark's translation, which deliberately leaves the word *organ* in the text as a rather unusual use of a loan word, a tenth-century scholar-poet's borrowing of the word *organum* from Latin into Old English:

> But how is the organ to be applied in memory by him who should wish to smelt against murder, to purify from sorrow, separate from sin?

In another recent translation, Robert E. Bjork interprets *organ* as 'the song, the Pater Noster':

> But how is the song, the Pater Noster, to be revered
> in memory by the one who wishes to refine
> his spirit from the dross of crime, to purify it from sorrow,
> to separate it from faults?

Saturn is in doubt, and seems to be saying that however wonderful the Lord's Prayer may appear, he is anxious about how to use it, how to pray it. Solomon's consolatory reply *Gylden is se Godes cwide*, literally 'Golden is the utterance of God', is extraordinary for the exuberance of its metaphors (lines 63–7):

> Gylden is se godes cwide,   gimmum astæned,
> hafað sylfren leaf;   sundor mæg æghwylc
> ðurh gastes gife   godspel secgan.
> He bið seofan snytro   and saule hunig
> and modes meolc,   mærþa gesælgost.

> [Golden is God's utterance, studded with gems, has silver leaves. Each one separately can proclaim the Gospel through the Spirit's grace. He is the spirit's wisdom and soul's honey and the mind's milk, the most blessed of glories.][28]

The passage describes the Lord's prayer (God's utterance) in terms of fine metalwork, glory and wisdom, and sustenance (milk and honey). It has been shown that much of this imagery and rhetoric derives from Hiberno-Latin, i.e. Irish sources.[29]

The colourful rhetoric and arcane subject matter are unusual, but appropriate if the context is a school that also studied Aldhelm as its principal poet, along with other arcane texts such as *Versus cuiusdam Scoti de alphabeto*. The Hiberno-Latin influence is also significant given the story in B.'s biography of how Dunstan was reading literature brought to Glastonbury by Irish scholars and pilgrims, as we saw earlier. Anlezark's argument for placing the *Solomon and Saturn* in the school of Dunstan weaves many threads together. In sum, Anlezark highlights such factors as the use of Greek vocabulary, the fascination with letters and names, the influence of the violent imagery of the Latin poem *Psychomachia*, the love of riddles and enigmatic imagery. In all this, the likely presence at Glastonbury of the Rawlinson anthology of verse is a key factor, possibly a catalyst for the new directions taken by Old English poets at this time.

INTERLUDE IV

A Passage from 'St Dunstan's Classbook'

FROM OVID'S *ART OF LOVE*

The passage below covers a whole page, folio 47r, in Oxford's Bodleian Library, manuscript Auct. F. 4. 32. It was copied by Hand D as the last page of the third booklet, in order to complete his text of Book I of Ovid, *Ars Amatoria*, Book I, lines 747–72. The context of Ovid's argument at this point is that when it comes to love, your friends are not to be trusted, and anyone who hopes for trustworthy friends may as well wish for the return of the Golden Age. The usual process of copying texts in Antiquity and the Middle Ages inevitably led to many variants, editorial changes, new readings and misreadings of the original texts, which cannot therefore be reconstructed in a 'pure' form. In particular, Classical poems were often transmitted in defective versions, and it is clear that Dunstan must have copied his model faithfully, faults and all. The passage as given here is not a critical edition; it reproduces the text as copied by Hand D, with variants placed in italics wherever D's text differs from the standard modern editions.[1]

> Siquis *item superat iacturas* poma myricas
> *Supet* et e medio flumine mella petat
> *Nihil tibi* turpe iuvat: curae sua cuique voluptas
> Haec quoque ab alterius grata dolore venit   750
> Heu facinus non est hostis metuendus *amandi*
> Quos credis fidos effuge tutus eris
> Cognatum fratremque cave carumque sodalem
> Prebebit veros haec tibi turba metus.

[If anyone still *hopes*, let him *hope* for tamarisks dropping apples, and let him seek honey in the middle of a river (lines 747–8).

Nothing repugnant pleases you, [but] no one cares for anything except his own delight, and that is agreeable when it comes from another's pain (749–50).

How wicked this is! A lover has no need to fear an enemy.

Avoid those who you think are loyal, and then you will be safe (751–2).

Beware your kinsman, brother and close friend;
they will cause you real fears (753–4).]

> Finiturus eram, sed sunt diversa puellis   755
> Pectora: mille animos excipe mille modis
> Nec tellus eadem parit omnia: vitibus *illis*
> Convenit *hic* oleis *hic* bene farra virent
> Pectoribus mores tot sunt, quot in *orbe* figurae
> Qui sapit innumeris moribus aptus *erat*,   760
> Utque leves Prot*heus* modo se tenua*bat* in undas
> Nunc leo nunc arbor nunc erit hirtus aper
> *Hic* iaculo pisces *illic* capiuntur ab hamis
> *Haec* cava contento retia fune trahunt
> Nec tibi conveni*at* cunctos modus unus ad annos   765
> Longius insidias cerva videbit anus.
> Si doctus videare rudi petulansve pudenti
> Diffidet miserae protinus illa sibi
> Inde fit ut quae se timuit committere honesto
> Vilis *in* amplexus inferioris eat.   770
>
> Pars superat coepti, pars est exhausta laboris
> Hic teneat nostras ancora iacta rates. *FINIT*

[I was about to finish, but diverse are women's
hearts: for a thousand minds you need a thousand methods (lines 755–6).

The same earth does not bear all crops: it suits these vines;
here it suits olives, *here* wheat grows well (757–8).

There are as many fashions of the heart as there figures in the *world*: he who is wise *was* adaptable to the many fashions, and like Proteus *would* now become light waves, now become a tree, now a lion, now he will be a bristling boar (759–62).

Here fish are caught with a spear, *there* with hooks;
these others are dragged in full nets with firm ropes (763–4).

One method *may* not suit you for every age-group:
a grown hind will consider the snare from further away (765–6).

If the simple one finds you educated, and the modest one finds you crude, she will immediately distrust herself (767–8).

So it happens that she who is afraid to commit herself to an honest man, will fall into the embrace of a worthless inferior (769–70).

Part of my task remains: part of my labour is done.
Here may the dropped anchor hold our boat secure. *END*]

PART V

Building the nation

According to medieval theories of onomastics, as we saw in the case of the poem 'Adalstan', a good deal of promise was latent in a name. From the time of Edmund, who succeeded Aethelstan in 939, through the middle years of the tenth century, there is a series of kings, all members of the ruling house of Wessex, whose alliterating names echo each other: Edmund (son of Edward), his brother Edred, and Edmund's two sons Edwy and Edgar. And the common element in their compound names is the first element *ed-* or *ead-* meaning 'blessedness' or 'prosperity'. The word is connected to an adjective *eadig*, later appearing in medieval English as *edi*, meaning 'blessed':

> Edi beo thu, Hevene Quene
> folkes frovre and engles blis,
>
> [Blessed art thou, Queen of Heaven,
> the people's comfort and angels' bliss]

The adjective is still to be heard in this thirteenth-century choral piece, a hymn addressed to the Virgin Mary.[1]

Eadmund, the first in this series of mid-tenth-century royal figures, means 'prosperity-guardian'. As we have seen, Edmund's two most significant actions were arguably the appointment of Dunstan as abbot of Glastonbury in or around the year 940 and the seizure of the Five Boroughs from the Norse Vikings in 942. His victory was then celebrated in the short English poem *The Capture of the Five Boroughs* entered in the Anglo-Saxon Chronicle for the year 942. On his early death, Edmund's two sons were still minors and the crown therefore passed to his brother Edred (Old English *Eadred* 'prosperity-counsel'), who reigned from 946 to

955. Edred was of similar calibre, arguably even more successful in war against the Norse, though there are no extant poems celebrating his martial deeds.

Like Æthelstan, Edred died without a son and heir, and for a while joint rule passed to his two nephews, Edwy (i.e. *Eadwig*, 'blessed war') and his younger brother Edgar (*Eadgar*, 'blessed spear'). Power-sharing had been a ninth-century theme, as we saw in Part I. Like the House of Lancaster during the reigns of the Yorkist kings in the fifteenth-century (in the period of the Wars of the Roses), the descendants of King Alfred's brother King Æthelred remained as a separate minor branch of the West Saxon royal family. But unlike the fifteenth century there was no protracted civil war, though there certainly were bitterly felt divisions. A notable member of the lesser branch, as will be seen shortly, was the Lady Ælfgifu, who married King Edwy in the year 956. Edwy may well have had strong feelings of affection for Ælfgifu, and this may have been his main motivation for the marriage. But he also wished to secure his claim to the throne, in this case against his younger brother Edgar, who was clearly a serious rival. Edwy's other motive, then, for marrying Ælfgifu was dynastic; any heirs he produced from the union would have had a double claim to being throneworthy. In the event Edwy died early, and his wife Ælfgifu became the last of the line to enjoy royal power.

Later in the tenth century, a prominent member of the same minor branch of the family was Æthelweard, an ealdorman or provincial governor of the western provinces of England during the reigns of Edgar and Æthelred II (i.e. Æthelred the Unready). Known as Æthelweard the Chronicler, this ealdorman was both an enthusiast for monastic reform and a historian in his own right. With his son Æthelmær he founded monasteries at Cerne Abbas and at Eynsham, and in the 990s he energetically promoted the career of the prolific religious writer Ælfric, whose work *On the Times of the Year* is included in the Tiberius Miscellany (see Chapter 2).[2] By the standards of the laity of his day Æthelweard was particularly well educated, and rather impressively the chronicle that he wrote for the benefit of his German cousin Matilda was composed in Latin. That in itself is not surprising, since it was normal for literary works aimed at an international audience to be written in the Continental *lingua franca*. But it is distinctly unusual for a non-clerical author to have gained the necessary language skills, and above all the concomitant literary ability, for it is one thing to have a command of Latin for reading history, or for understanding sermons and prayers, it is quite another matter to be able to write letters or compose longer literary works in Latin prose or verse.

The cousin to whom Æthelweard dedicated his literary endeavour, Matilda (949–1011), was the granddaughter of the German Emperor Otto I and his English queen; probably because of her royal connections, she became Abbess of Essen at an early age, and she perhaps corresponded regularly with her English royal cousin. In response, Æthelweard addressed Matilda directly on a number of occasions in the course of his work. In the general preface, he dedicates his work to her, and emphasises his lineage, the fact that he was descended from King Æthelred I, his great-great grandfather, just as Matilda was descended from King Alfred. Both could bask in the glorious achievements that the West Saxon royal house had gained in the course of the ninth and the tenth centuries.

Family and kindred seem to come first. In his selection of important events to cover in his relatively short Chronicle, it is illuminating to note Æthelweard's partiality, for no event is allowed to sully the memory of either branch of the family. Naturally he praises his own illustrious ancestor Æthelred I in glowing terms; and he also has nothing but good to say for his cousin Matilda's ancestor, King Alfred. In his *Chronicon*, as he calls his Chronicle, he covers the reigns of both brothers in some detail, and he declares in the course of his fourth and final book:

> Accordingly sweet cousin Matilda, having gathered these things from remote antiquity, I have made communication to you, and above all I have given attention to the history of our race as far as these two kings, from whom we derive our descent. To you, therefore I dedicate this work, most beloved, spurred by family affection.[3]

Æthelweard seems to be reconciled to the fact that his immediate family no longer has claims to the English throne, but although he deals in his text with the Battle of the Holme, he omits all mention of his kinsman Æthelwold's rebellious involvement. And when it comes to his reporting of Edwy's reign, the tone is appreciative although the coverage is very brief: in fact he has little to tell except that this king was a man graced with good looks and worthy of praise. He certainly does not mention the uncomfortable fact that his kinswoman Ælfgifu's marriage to Edwy was annulled for reasons of both canon law and politics, even though he probably knew more about it than he

was willing to admit. His source was a text similar to version A of the
Anglo-Saxon Chronicle, culminating for Æthelweard in the reign of the
great Edgar the Peaceable, at which point, so he declares, he ends
'happily' the fourth and final book of his *Chronicon*.

871	Alfred the Great succeeds to throne after his brother Æthelred I
902	Rebellion of Æthelwold (Æthelred's son) ended at the Battle of the Holme

***

946	Murder of King Edmund at Pucklechurch
	Scots swear oaths to King Edred
947	Edred meets the Northumbrians at Tanshelf
	The Northumbrians elect Erik Bloodaxe as king of York
948	Edred's punitive foray into Northumbria, burning of Ripon Minster
949	Reculver Charter, prominence of Ediva the queen mother
950s	Dunstan prominent in governing of the country
952	Edred imprisons Wulfstan, archbishop of York
954	Erik finally expelled from York
	Æthelwold appointed as abbot of Abingdon
955	King Edred's will
	Dunstan confronts King Edwy at his coronation feast
	Edwy marries Ælfgifu, descendant of Æthelred I
956	Edwy's charters rewards land to 'new men'
955–7	Dunstan in exile in Ghent
957	Kingdom divided between brothers Edwy in the south and Edgar in the north
959	On Edwy's death, Edgar inherits the whole kingdom
	Dunstan become archbishop of Canterbury
960s	New laws
963	Edgar appoints Æthelwold as bishop of Winchester
964	Clerics expelled from Winchester and replaced by monks
965?	'Clearance' of the south-east of Winchester
966	Charter of the New Minster, Winchester (with portrait of King Edgar)
970s	Æthelwold writes *Regularis Concordia* (in Latin) and *King Edgar's Establishment of the Monasteries* (Old

English) as preface to his Old English version of the Benedictine Rule

The Fleury monk and writer Lantfred resident in Winchester

Copying and compilation of the Vercelli Book in Kent

Copying and compilation of the Exeter Book

970?	Council of Winchester
971	Translation of the relics of St Swithun into the Old Minster, Winchester
973	Second coronation of King Edgar, at Bath
	Edgar's overlordship acknowledged at Chester, on the River Dee
	Reform of English coinage
974 onwards	Old Minster enlarged, with a new westwork
971 x 984	Benedictional of St Æthelwold written for the bishop
975 x 983	Æthelweard, ealdorman of the Western provinces, and descendant of Æthelred I, writes his Chronicle.

CHAPTER 12

The reign of King Edred: Dealing with the Northumbrians, the queen mother, and the archbishop

'IT WAS WIDELY KNOWN HOW HE ENDED HIS DAYS'

King Edmund's untimely death is something of a mystery. He appears to have become involved in a dispute between his steward and a thief, perhaps a thief caught in the act, at the royal palace. The Anglo-Saxon Chronicle has little or no circumstantial detail to offer, the contemporary version of the Chronicle merely reporting that the king died after a reign of seven and a half years. A later version of the Chronicle, compiled in the north of England in the eleventh century, offers a little more information (version D, for the year 946):

> Her Eadmund cyning forðferde on Sancte Agustinus mæssedæge, þæt wæs wide cuð hu he his dagas geendode, þæt Liofa hine ofstang æt Puclancyrcan.

> [Here King Edmund ended his days on the Feast of St Augustine; it was widely known how he ended his days, that Liofa stabbed him at Pucklechurch.]

Since it is *wide cuð*, 'widely known', even 'notorious', how Edmund met his end, so the chronicler declares, there is no need for him to tell the story again here. Entries like this betray the limitations of the Anglo-Saxon Chronicle as a memory aid, for the risk is run that, as the generations pass, the details of the matter are lost to posterity. The last man who claims to know more about the incident than this was John of Worcester, a chronicler writing in the twelfth century, already many generations later; it is on his authority that we know that Edmund was attempting to assist his steward when the mishap or murder took place.

The new king was Edmund's younger brother Edred (Eadred), another man of action. Edred continued where his brother Edmund had left off; his aim it seems was to restore the English kingdom to its full size under West Saxon rule. This meant dealing with the Northumbrians, in particular the Anglo-Scandinavian kingdom of York that was asserting itself with considerable weight against the upstart southerners.

EDRED AND THE NORSE KINGDOM OF YORK

We have already noted the separateness of Northumbria from the rest of the English kingdom and the way that Æthelstan took care to establish his authority over it, even paying tribute to its great saint in his gifts to the clerical community of St Cuthbert at Chester-le-Street. Anglo-Scandinavian York had existed as an entity since the Great Army had conquered the city in the year 866 and then settled it in 877. Its name, which in Roman times had been Eboracum, had been Anglicised as Eoforwic, a popular 'rationalisation' of the older name into a compound of *eofor* 'boar' and *wic* 'trading settlement'.[1] Under the Norse, the city's name was transformed into Jorvik, and typical street names such as Coppergate, Mickelgate, Stonegate and Petergate point to the new and dominant language of the city (*gata* means 'street' in Old Norse). As shown by the famous Coppergate excavations (now housed in the Jorvik Viking Centre), the city became a thriving centre of trade and industry, with craftsmen working in wood, antler, amber and jet, glass and textiles. It developed its own artistic traditions, visible in stonework and metalwork. As befitted the second archbishopric, this city had the only mint for the issuing of coins in the north of England. In fact, it was the only major city in the north. As for its ruling monarchs, these seemed to change with alarming rapidity in the middle of the tenth century, for York was contended and fought over by the West Saxons, the Viking kings of Dublin, and by the Norwegian Erik Bloodaxe. Politically, although the ultimate ruler was the king, the kingdom of York was run by the Northumbrian *witan*, a Council or Assembly, often in conjunction with the archbishop, who had considerable power.[2]

In his policy towards the North, Edred seems to have acted just as resolutely as his late brother Edmund, and also with setbacks, but ultimately with more political success. In the entries of the northern recension of the Anglo-Saxon Chronicle (manuscript D) Edred appears as a successful warrior king. First, he reasserts control over the Land of the Northumbrians, i.e. the kingdom of York:

> þa æfter him feng Eadred æþeling his broþor to rice, and gerad þa eall Norðhymbra land him to gewealde. And þa Scottas him sealdon aþas þæt hi eall woldon þæt he wolde.

> [Then after him his brother the atheling Edred succeeded to the kingdom, and conquered and subdued the land of the Northumbrians; and the Scots swore oaths to him that they all would do what he would do.]

The idiomatic expression *gerad þa eall Norðhymbra land him to gewealde* throws light on the chronicler's attitude; it means literally 'then he rode over all the land of the Northumbrians into his authority'. The verb *ge-rad* with its perfective prefix *ge-* implies that he 'rode (*rad*) and acquired', and *to gewealde* sounds the note of *anweald* (power, dominion) that we have heard in much of the political records of the West Saxon dynasty. This is mingled with a recurring motif of loyalty and pledges of loyalty that will be heard again in the account of Edred's reign. This annal for 946 nevertheless reads very like that of 944 only two years before, where Edmund had also attempted to reassert control over the land of the rebellious Northumbrians, who apparently wanted no truck with the southerners. The West Saxon ambitions to rule a greater England were running into difficulties.

As Chronicle D surveys the events of the reign, however, it shows Edred as particularly active in the military sphere, especially in the early half of his reign. The annal for the next year (D 947) reports that Edred went to Taddenesscylfe, the town of Tanshelf situated south of York between Doncaster and Leeds, where he met with the Northumbrians and with one of their leaders: Wulfstan, the powerful archbishop of York (now known as Wulfstan I to distinguish him from Wulfstan II, the later writer and archbishop of the same name). The meeting is treated with some significance by the D Chronicler:

> Her com Eadred cyning to Taddenesscylfe, and þær Wulstan se arcebiscop and ealle Norðhymbra witan wið þone cyning hi getreowsoden, and binnan litlan fæce hit eall alugon, ge wed and eac aþas.

> [Here King Edred came to Tanshelf, and there Archbishop Wulfstan and all the *witan* of the Northumbrians pledged their loyalty to the king, and within a short while they broke both their pledge and their oaths.]

In the opinion of the D Chronicler, the Northumbrians literally 'lied about it all' (*hit eall alugon*): they were not to be trusted, for they soon broke their word. In the following year he reports that Edred invaded Northumbria once again and plundered the region, 'because the Northumbrians had taken Erik as their king', i.e. the Norwegian Erik Bloodaxe (one of the main characters in that vivid piece of historical fiction, *Egil's Saga*, as we saw in Chapter 9).[3] During the plundering, 'the great minster at Ripon which St Wilfrid had built was burned down', the passive *wæs forbærnd* perhaps disguising a deliberate action on behalf of Edred's men. The situation escalated when Edred's men were ambushed. Determined on vengeance, he became hard to appease – the adjective *gram*, 'angry, hostile', is the Chronicler's telling choice of word. He forced the Northumbrian *witan* to abandon Erik and come to an agreement on his terms. All was not over yet, for Erik apparently managed to regain power later. The annal in D for 952 has further punitive actions to relate: Edred ordered Wulfstan to be thrown into prison at a place called Iudanbyrig, evidently a stronghold; he then attacked Thetford in revenge for the killing of the local bishop Eadhelm. But 954 is the triumphal year: Erik was finally expelled,[4] and Edred recovered Northumbria. As for Wulfstan, the D Chronicler makes the following short statement: 'Here Archbishop Wulfstan again received a bishopric at Dorchester.' This is open to interpretation. Perhaps in a gesture of conciliation, perhaps as a means of detaining him in the south, Wulfstan was given episcopal power at Dorchester, close to the West Saxon heartland.

Finally, the Chronicler reports the death of King Edred, which took place in 955. Such are the bare facts of Edred's reign as they are told in the annals of text D of the Chronicle. For further information the historian has to look to the royal documents of the period, which show that Edred was styling himself 'Ruler of the Northumbrians' in 946, 949–50, and 955. These charters evidently reflect Edred's changing fortunes in these years. Similarly for the archbishop of York, the presence or absence of his name in the witness lists of the charters and land transactions demonstrate his fluctuating role at the court of the Anglo-Saxon king. A prolonged absence from the witness list over several successive charters indicates a period when the archbishop and king were more enemies than friends.[5]

A contemporary poem on St Wilfrid provides another indicator of changing circumstances. Composed at Canterbury in the elaborate Hermeneutic style of the Anglo-Latin poets, its author was a Frankish scholar named Frithegod, whose patron was Oda, the reformist archbishop of Canterbury. Here is part of the prose preface; the voice is that of Oda, though the style is that of Frithegod:

> Certain men carried away the venerable relics of Wilfrid, the blessed confessor of Christ, [which were] decayed with the unbecoming mould of a bramble-covered abyss, even – what is fearful to say – neglected by the hair-raising wilfulness of prelates, I reverently received them and established them within the apse of the metropolitan church, over which by God's grace I preside.[6]

The text thus documents the recent theft of the relics of St Wilfrid, the grand seventh-century prelate and northern saint, which were removed from Ripon and taken to Canterbury. Again the text is so worded as to remove any explicit agency for these actions. Oda and Frithegod avoid mention of the burning of the minster, and they avoid blaming Edred or his men for the removal of Wilfrid's remains (theft of relics was common in the period, often for political reasons). Instead, their preface emphasises the Northumbrians' neglect of the original shrine and argues that Wilfrid's relics are now housed more respectfully at the metropolitan see, and now honoured fittingly with a new poem on his saintly life.

'WITH HER WOMAN'S ELOQUENCE'

The pages of B.'s *Life of Dunstan* also provide more incidental detail on the reign of Edred, though they paint a rather different portrait of the king than does the Chronicle. Partly this is due to the hagiographical element in the *Life*: here Edred appears as a warm, pious and affectionate character, who, in contrast to his older brother and predecessor King Edmund, promotes Dunstan within the hierarchy of his government. In this version of the reign of Edred, the abbot of Glastonbury now finds himself involved once again in court politics, for, as we saw in Chapter 10, the king even offers him the bishopric of Crediton. The offer apparently takes Dunstan by surprise: he counters with excuses and then a firm refusal.

At this point we are introduced to the queen mother, Ediva (Old English *Eadgifu*). In the account by B., King Edred asks his mother to persuade the reluctant abbot to accept the vacant bishopric. B. imagines that the king spoke as follows, the choice of word and phrase (*O mi dilectissima mater*, 'my dearest mother') expressing the affection that the king felt for his mother (*Life of Dunstan*, 19.4):

> The king accordingly made his own mother speak for him. 'Dearest mother', he said to her, 'I want you to ask our particular friend Dunstan to

dine with you. During the agreeable conversation of a cheerful occasion, use your woman's gift of words to urge him to accede to my proposal and become bishop of the church that has lately been vacated.'

The slightly later account by Adelred of Ghent rewords this, making the Queen more actively involved:

> She sent for Dunstan and entertained him at a royal banquet (*regio convivio*). During the feast she began to try to persuade him to become a bishop, revealing the king's intentions (Aldred, *Lectiones*, ch. IV).

However, despite speaking with *feminali facundia*, 'with her woman's eloquence', as B. describes it, Ediva was unable to persuade Dunstan. His final refusal has already been mentioned (see Chapter 10); it led to punitive dreams.

In the end, the bishopric was given to another candidate, for Dunstan was not yet ready for this kind of ecclesiastical promotion. According to the later biographer, Dunstan would not leave the court because of his affection for the king. B. too describes a warm personal friendship between the king and the abbot; perhaps Dunstan was reluctant to give up this position of influence. As for the queen mother, Ediva, she was able to exercise her influence on another promising reformer. We are told in the biography of Æthelwold by Wulfstan Cantor that Ediva succeeded in preventing him from travelling abroad, appointing him instead to a newly created post as abbot of Abingdon.

'WRITTEN WITH THE JOINTS OF MY OWN FINGERS'

Contemporary charters corroborate the biographers' accounts. From being a shadowy figure in the reign of her stepson Æthelstan, Queen Ediva emerged as a powerful figure during the reigns of her two sons Edmund and Eadred, 'the first important queen of the tenth century, thanks to her landed power, especially in Kent'.[7] After her husband King Edward the Elder's death she had probably remained living at the royal household in Winchester, but during Æthelstan's reign she kept a low profile and did not take part in the royal perambulations round the kingdom that were so important to royal governance in the period. Now in the reign of Edred, she becomes particularly prominent in the records: clearly she was active at the royal court.

Similarly with Dunstan; he is merely a young courtier in the time of Æthelstan, and he is hardly ever named as a witness in the charters of Edmund, suggesting that he did not take part in day-to-day business at the royal court. The exception proves the rule. A document from the Glastonbury archive dated 946 records a lease of land at *Wodtone*, i.e. North Wootton, Somerset, by King Edmund to a thegn called Æthelnoth, on condition that he sent annual renders to the Old Church at Glastonbury Abbey.[8] Both the text and the witness list of this charter are unusually short. The four named witnesses are the king, the two archbishops and the abbot, each ratifying the agreement with his *hondseten*, i.e. with his finger on the sign of the cross and his name, and declaring a brief first-person testimonial:

> + Ego Edmund rex impressione signi sancte crucis hoc donum ministro meo et censum illi sancte ecclesie depingere iussi. + Ego Wolstan archiepiscopus consensi et subscripsi. + Ego Oda episcopus consensi et subscripsi. + Ego Dunstan abbas nolens sed regalibus obediens verbis haunc cartulam scribere iussi.

According to the above passage, the king places his finger on the charter and declares, 'I King Edmund by touching the sign of the cross ordered a record to be made of this gift to my thegn and this render to that holy church'. Archbishop Wulfstan and Bishop Oda both say 'I agreed and subscribed'. Dunstan's subscription is rather different. One interpretation is that the modest, 'unwilling' abbot, 'obedient to the king's words, ordered this charter to be written'.[9] However, the phrase *abbas nolens sed regalibus obediens verbis*, literally 'abbot unwilling but obeying the words of the king', has been taken to mean that Dunstan 'was obeying the king's commands with reluctance'.[10] If such an interpretation is permissible (and this is questionable), then Dunstan appears rather like Bishop Denewulf only reluctantly agreeing to the wishes of King Edward (see Chapter 6). However we understand his words, this is a rare instance of Dunstan present and actively taking part in a land transaction.

But now, during the reign of Edred, Dunstan is far more engaged in administrative work. Famously, there is his involvement in the well-known Reculver charter, in which, in the year 949, King Edred granted the minster of Reculver in Kent (now a royal estate but with a long history as a minster) with all its lands and properties to Archbishop Oda and Christ Church Cathedral, Canterbury. The fame of this document rests on its witness clauses. Ediva the Queen Mother is again prominent and audible 'with a heart rejoicing' (*animo letabundo*), and Dunstan witnesses immediately afterwards, declaring that he himself wrote the charter with his own hand, or, as he prefers to put it, 'with the joints of my own fingers':

+ Ego Eadgifu regis genetrix prefati animo hanc prefatam letabundo in Christo largitionem ob optabilem remunerationem concessam. signi corroboratione salutiferi humillime consignaui. + Ego Dunstan indignus abbas rege Eadredo imperante hanc Domino meo hereditariam kartulam dictitando composui. et propriis digitorum articulis perscripsi.

[+ I, Ediva, mother of the aforementioned king, with a heart rejoicing at the aforementioned generous gift to Christ have most humbly marked with the corroboration of the mark bringing salvation [i.e., the cross] + I, Dunstan, unworthy abbot [of Glastonbury], at the behest of King Eadred my lord have composed by dictation this charter of ownership and have written it with the joints of my own fingers.][11]

The phrase *propriis digitorum articulis*, 'with the joints of my own fingers', is sufficiently unusual to call for comment. If Dunstan himself actually spoke – and indeed wrote – the words, then it is likely that he was echoing a great predecessor. The writer and deacon Alcuin of York (735–804) was appointed as court scholar of the Frankish empire by Charlemagne; he became a teacher at court, who taught the leading lights of the Carolingian world in the 780s and 790s and ended his career as Bishop of Tours (796–804). Dunstan is alluding to one of Alcuin's letters (and letters in the middle ages were collected and studied as models). In an 'intensely personal' letter of greetings and close friendship to Bishop Arno of Salzburg, Alcuin addresses him by his Latin nickname *Aquila*, playing on the meaning of his correspondent's name, for *Arno* means 'eagle' in Old High German, Arno's mother tongue. This is a meaning that Arno would recognise if Alcuin called him *earn*, eagle, in his own, Old English, mother tongue. In his exuberant expression of friendship, Alcuin promises that like the Old Testament prophet Habbakuk who seemed to fly through the air in his prophetic vision, Alcuin will embrace and kiss *manuum et pedum singulos digitorum articulos*, 'every single joint of your fingers and toes'.[12] It is no coincidence, moreover, that the Hebrew name Habbakuk has the meaning 'embrace'. Such are the literary echoes that Dunstan is calling forth in the charter ostensibly penned by his hand.

Dunstan's authorship is significant. First, it is a reminder that scribal work was considered to be hard, laborious work and that scribes could be important people in Anglo-Saxon society. Secondly, the script is Anglo-Saxon square minuscule. It shows that in the year 949 Dunstan was still using the older style of handwriting, and had not yet switched to the Caroline script that we saw in use by Hand D on the pages of Dunstan's

Classbook. The authenticity of this Reculver charter has been doubted, some experts arguing that it was written in the late tenth century, by a forger at Canterbury.[13] Such deceitful practices were common in the Middle Ages; it was felt to be justifiable to concoct a charter if none was available, especially if a minster or cathedral was convinced of its land-holding rights. In this case, however, there are good reasons to see both the script and contents of this charter as genuine, given that the phraseology matches that of other charters in which Dunstan was involved. Throughout the reign of Edred, as research has shown, Dunstan participated actively in the administration of the country, witnessing most if not all of Edred's charters.[14]

Dunstan's active involvement is confirmed by B.'s biography. According to B., King Edred even entrusted part of his treasury to Dunstan for safekeeping at Glastonbury. The relevant passage is worth quoting in full for the light it casts on contemporary financial practices (ch. 19.2):

> In this spirit of trusting affection, the king handed over to Dunstan his most valuable possessions: many land charters (*plures ... rurales cartulas*), the old treasure of earlier kings (*veteres precedentium regum thesauros*), and various riches of his own acquiring, all to be guarded faithfully behind the walls of his monastery.

The passage illustrates the value of documents, even in a world where many of the users of these documents were only partially literate; the *rurales cartulas* of this Latin text correspond to the *landbec* in Old English writings, the 'land-books', not literally books, but charters proving that a land transaction had taken place, demonstrating that land had been 'booked' to a recipient in perpetuity. Such documents were valuable, to be stored alongside money and precious objects. The issue was where to keep such wealth. Royal treasuries had to be held in secure places, but there were no banks in Anglo-Saxon England. For the king, a monastery enclosure such as Glastonbury was clearly a suitably strong place for depositing his wealth. As Brooks wryly comments, however, this decision was 'likely to have created jealousies'.[15]

'THIS IS THE WILL OF KING EDRED'

To judge by the Chronicle, Edred had been a man of action, who spent his reign on active campaigns in the north. Other sources give a different spin. It is left to B., for instance, to provide the information that, like

King Alfred, Edred suffered from ill-health 'all through his reign' (ch. 20.3), a fact not otherwise apparent in the records. Edred's last will is another useful document, for it casts light on the political divisions of the kingdom at the time of his death. The main beneficiaries of the will are the church institutions at Winchester, his mother Ediva, and the thegns and members of his court. But like Alfred's will, which was partisan and potentially divisive (see Chapter 6), Edred also excludes the one person who needed support, his nephew Edwy, King Edmund's son and heir.

In its style, King Edred's will is carefully constructed to present a hierarchy of gifts and recipients. It opens with a Latin invocation, then addresses itself to the first and arguably the most important of the various beneficiaries, the Old Minster at Winchester. The third-person pronouns 'he' and 'his' impart an objective tone to the pronouncement:

> *In nomine Domini.* Þis is Eadredes cinges cwide. Þæt is þænne ærest, þæt he an into þære stowe þær he wile þæt his lic reste twegra gyldenra roda and twegra gyldenhiltra sweorda and feower hund punda.[16]

> [*In the name of the Lord.* This is King Edred's will. Which is, first of all, that he grants – to the place where wishes that his body will lie – two golden crosses and two golden-hilted swords, and four hundred pounds.]

The precious objects were certainly a special gift, and it is fair to say that this reflects contemporary values and attitudes. As the art historian C.R. Dodwell has shown, golden crosses were particularly precious in the period.[17] The word for 'cross' or 'crucifix' is *rod*, pronounced with a long vowel *rōd*; this same word has become modern English *rood*, as in *rood screen*, and is used in the Vercelli Book poem *The Dream of the Rood*. Here the dreamer narrating the story in the opening lines of the poem has a vision of a mysterious object, a wonderful tree in the air, the brightest of beams, a beacon *begoten mid golde* (line 7a), in other words covered or 'infused' with gold.[18] This object in the dreamer's vision is of course a cross, conceived enigmatically as both a tree and a precious object. Swords were likewise felt to be special: they were prized heirlooms, symbolic as well as practical, passed on from generation to generation. The hero of the poem *The Battle of Maldon* bears a *fealohilte swurd*, 'a golden-hilted sword' (line 166), which, it is implied, is an ancient heirloom, literally an 'old sword' (*ealde swurd*, line 47). A later illustration from the next century captures the grandeur and munificence of such royal gifts. A golden cross and a gold-hilted sword are depicted in a portrait of King Cnut from the eleventh century. With his right hand the

king presents a golden cross to the altar of the New Minster at
Winchester; in his left hand he holds his personal sword with its tri-
lobed pommel, displaying it prominently to the viewer of the book.[19]

As well as the precious objects in his will, Eadred leaves three estates
to the Old Minster, three estates to the New Minster, and three to the
Nunnaminster, thus covering all three major monastic institutions in
the south-eastern quarter of tenth-century Winchester, essentially the
royal centre or capital city. Some money will go to churches, but the next
provision is striking, since it explicitly involves Dunstan, among others,
for its implementation, and concerns the needs of the whole nation:

> Þænne an he his sawla to anliesnesse and his ðeodscipe to þearfe sixtyne
> hund punda to þan ðæt hi mege magan hungor and hæþenne here him
> fram aceapian gif hie beþurfen.

> [Then he grants, for the redemption of his soul and the needs of his people,
> sixteen hundred pounds, so that they can combat hunger and buy off a
> heathen army, should they have need to.]

For Edred, the two direst imaginable threats to the nation are famine and
pagan invasion: for both eventualities, the money is to be kept in hand
as insurance. According to this clause in the will, various bishops and
church leaders, including Dunstan, are to hold the money in safe
keeping, and should anything happen to them, the local shire assembly
is to take responsibility for the use of the money. In times of famine it
could be used to buy grain and food. And, as is implied in some of King
Alfred's earlier dealings with the Vikings, it could be used to buy off a
'pagan invasion'. In other words it was sometimes expedient to pay
money to Viking raiders or invaders to persuade them to leave without
fighting. Such was the purpose of Edred's provision in his will.

For the more personal bequests that follow, Edred now changes his
style and switches to the first person form of address:

> Þænne an ic minre meder þæs landes æt Ambresbirig and æt Waneting and
> æt Basingum, and ealra minra boclanda þe ic on Suðeseaxum hæbbe and
> on Suðrigum and on Cent, and ealra þæra þe hio ær hæfde.

> [Then I grant to my mother the estate at Amesbury, and at Wantage and
> Basing, and all my book-lands that I hold in Sussex, Surrey and Kent, and all
> of those that she once held.]

Edred leaves nearly all his landed wealth to Ediva. Next he proceeds
down the ranks of society bequeathing money to archbishop, bishops,
ealdormen, thegns, and then to the minor officials of his court:

his chamberlains, stewards, mass-priests and other priests, and to anyone else who may have held office at his court after he succeeded to the throne – expressed in the familiar Old English idiom 'took to power' (*to anwalde feng*).

Conspicuously Edred's nephew, Edwy (Eadwig), receives nothing at all, not even a mention in the will. Accordingly, it looks like Edwy came to the throne seething with resentment directed at both his grandmother, Ediva, and at the abbot of Glastonbury, Dunstan. Both were about to lose their positions and all their landed possessions in the turbulent months that followed.

CHAPTER 13

Politics, monasteries, and the rise of Bishop Æthelwold

THE CORONATION OF EDWY

The four-year reign of Edwy, or Eadwig in the Old English spelling, began, according to the story in the *Life of St Dunstan*, with a sexual scandal. In a sensational anecdote B. claims that the young king, after his consecration, left his seat at the feast in the hall and stole away to his chamber with two ladies of the court. The crown – symbol of his coronation – rolled from his head and was left abandoned as he indulged in lascivious play with the two women. Sitting at the feast in the royal hall at Kingston was Archbishop Oda (Dunstan's predecessor as archbishop of Canterbury), who clearly disapproved of this untoward absence but did not wish to intervene directly. Instead, B. states that he sent Abbot Dunstan, with his kinsman Cynesige, bishop of Lichfield, as support, to haul the reluctant king back to the feast.

If that exercise of power by an abbot over a king seems unlikely, it should be remembered that Edwy was fifteen years old at the time and perhaps had not reached full adulthood; probably he was no match physically for the energetic Dunstan. But there is reason to wonder about the truth of 'what actually happened'. The two women were Æthelgifu, a member of the royal family (a distant cousin), and her daughter Ælfgifu, whom King Edwy soon married. And the later will of Ælfgifu, which survives in full, suggests that she was a perfectly respectable member of the Anglo-Saxon nobility. As was noted above, Ælfgifu's brother was the ealdorman Æthelweard (that is, Æthelweard the Chronicler) who in his chronicle has only a little to report about the reign of his brother-in-law, though all of that is positive. According to Æthelweard, who naturally favoured a member of his branch of the family, the king was known as 'Edwy the All-fair'.

B.'s sympathies, on the other hand, lay with the Dunstan–Oda–Cynesige–Ediva faction. The 'child Edwy' (as he is called rather dismissively in a later document associated with Ediva) was marrying into a rival branch of the West Saxon family, who were equally throne-worthy. If they had children and male heirs, Edwy and Ælfgifu were removing the younger brother Edgar's chances of succession. It looks like this incident was part of an ongoing dispute between rival branches of the royal family and their supporters. Dunstan, who was distantly related to the royal family, had already fallen foul of kinsmen when he was a young man, as the incident in the Somerset marshes makes all too clear.[1] Now the tables were turned.

But not for long: as in the two earlier disputes, first between Dunstan and King Æthelstan and then again between Dunstan and King Edmund, the king naturally had the power to dismiss or banish a difficult courtier. In 956 Edwy issued a huge number of charters, about sixty grants of land in total, to a whole range of supporters, all new men on the political scene, and he appointed new ealdormen from his family to prominent positions. Temporarily, Bishop Cynesige's name disappears from the documentation concerned with the *witena gemot*, the assembly of counsellors, for a period of more than a year.[2] He was evidently out of favour at court. Ediva, as intimated earlier, was deprived of her estates, despite being the new king's grandmother. And the unruly Dunstan was summarily dismissed from his position and ordered to leave the country.

'EXILE IN THE CAUSE OF JUSTICE'

This time there was no last-minute royal reprieve. Dunstan's biographer adds that none of his friends were able to support him. Even his students, whom he had steeped in 'the nectar of his teaching', are said to have 'connived at the wicked conspiracy', much to Dunstan's astonishment. Perhaps the words of the old Roman poet whose work he copied in the Classbook passed through his mind:

> Quos credis fidos, effuge, tutus eris.
> Cognatum fratremque cave carumque sodalem:
> Praebebit veros haec tibi turba metus.

> [Avoid those who you think are loyal, and then you will be safe. Beware your kinsman, brother and close friend; they will cause you real fears.][3]

We can only speculate on what Dunstan thought as he copied these lines. But betrayal by friends was an experience that Dunstan had felt keenly on a number of occasions in his career. Dunstan's erstwhile student Æthelwold was perhaps numbered among these dubious friends. Æthelwold was now established as the new abbot at Abingdon, and clearly thought differently about the whole business. The new king gave his support to Abingdon, and in return Abbot Æthelwold supported King Edwy's marriage to Ælfgifu.[4]

To judge by a similar case in the eleventh century, Dunstan was perhaps given a limited number of days to cross the border or reach the coast and embark on a ship. Otherwise his safety would have been forfeit. B. adds the colourful and rather suspect story that Ælfgifu – now the king's wife, and presented as a vindictive and villainous Jezebel figure – ordered her men to pursue Dunstan and blind him. But to no avail, for Dunstan was already sailing the high seas, making the 'dangerous voyage across the mad billows of the tossing ocean', as B. describes it.

As for Dunstan, rushing from one danger to the next, he perhaps recalled his own prayer that the 'Taenarian storms' would not swallow him. That prayer (as shown in Chapter 11 above) alludes to the stormy seas around Taenarum, entrance to the classical Underworld described in Vergil and Statius.[5] Certainly B. feels impelled to make allusions to the Roman poets as he describes Dunstan's getaway voyage; as he puts it in his neo-Classical style, the sea-crossing proceeded *rapido cursu* 'rapidly' *equoreas uias* 'along the seaways', the two phrases echoing Vergil and Ovid respectively.[6]

Dunstan duly crossed the English Channel to Flanders, where the ruling magnate Count Arnulf offered him asylum.[7] His hosts were the monks of St Peter's in Ghent, a monastery also known as Blandinium, which rather like Æthelwold's Abingdon was in the process of being reformed and rebuilt. The biographer B. makes no specific mention of Dunstan's location in exile, but more information on his 'exile in the cause of justice' is provided by Adelard of Ghent, who was indeed a monk of that monastery:

> Dunstan, an exile in the cause of justice [*exilio pro iusticia asscriptus*], crossed the sea, and approached Arnulf, a great man of royal stock. This man was at the time engaged in restoring to new splendour a noble monastery called Blandinium, founded of old by St Amand. Thither he translated, in conformity with God's will, the [relics of the] great priest of God Wandregisil, and two archbishops with him.

The blessed Dunstan spent some time there, and left brilliant examples for others to follow.[8]

It might be objected that Adelard's narrative sounds more like a sermon than a history. But there is good reason for its homiletic style: the text was intended to be delivered as part of a series of readings in church, and this explains the more overtly hagiographical perspective of the above passage. But the information given rings true. Dunstan certainly stayed at the abbey, situated, like the late medieval abbey that succeeded it, on a hill overlooking the old city, with steep slopes descending through monastic vineyards and orchards to the river below. According to B., Dunstan was homesick in exile (*in exilio*), particularly when he recalled the grand religious life (*religionis celsitudinem*) which he had left behind in his monastery. Perhaps he found some solace in the Old English exile poems, if he knew them, such as *The Wanderer* or *The Seafarer* (which were later anthologised in the Exeter Book, copied in about the year 975). Perhaps he consoled himself with reflections on power (*anweald*) and its abuses such as are found in the Old English *Metres of Boethius*.

The prolonged sojourn at St Peter's nevertheless had its benefits, for it led to Dunstan making friends with the reforming monks of Ghent. Later, as archbishop of Canterbury, Dunstan came to be regarded as their patron. Wido, who was abbot of St Peter's from 980 to 986 and who had perhaps known Dunstan personally, sent delegations to him on at least two occasions asking for financial aid. Their pastureland, probably reclaimed salt marshes, had been damaged and the crops had failed. The previous incumbent, Womar, abbot of St Peter's from 953 to 980, who certainly knew Dunstan during his stay in 956–7, was remembered with affection by the monks of the New Minster in Winchester, for his name was entered in the *Liber Vitae*, their splendidly illustrated *Book of Life* that was compiled in the eleventh century.[9]

At the great Council of Winchester in around 970 in Edgar's reign – and this was long after Dunstan had been restored to royal grace and appointed archbishop of Canterbury – Dunstan reciprocated the hospitality of the monks of St Peter's Ghent by inviting some of them to be present at the discussions. Along with participants from Fleury, the monks of Ghent had an advisory role, and Womar himself seems to have spent time at the Old Minster in Winchester, advising Bishop Æthelwold on the writing of the *Regularis Concordia*, or 'Monastic Agreement', the great document regulating monastic life that was compiled after the Council.[10]

'HE RAN NO RISK OF BECOMING PROUD'

One of Edred's last significant acts as king had been to appoint a new man, Æthelwold, the dean of Dunstan's Glastonbury, as abbot of the newly refounded monastery at Abingdon. Once again in this decision we see the prominent role played by the queen mother in the policy-making of the kingdom. But fully to understand the rise of Æthelwold we need to review his early biography, as told in the *Life of St Æthelwold*. Its author, Wulfstan Cantor, was writing in the 990s, about the same time as B. was completing his *Life of St Dunstan*.

Wulfstan tells us, then, that Æthelwold joined the community at Glastonbury during the reign of Edmund, where he studied under Dunstan, eventually being made a monk:

> Though he was universally loved for his holiness and was made dean of the monastery by the abbot, he ran no risk of becoming proud; indeed he set those below him such a standard of humility that he performed manual labour every day, cultivating the garden and getting fruit and different kinds of vegetables ready for the monks' meal.[11]

Wulfstan writes purposefully here, alluding to the text of the Benedictine Rule in order to demonstrate how assiduously Æthelwold lives up to its ideals in terms of its guidance on the practice of humility, on the measures and allowances of food, and on the need for manual labour (*Benedictine Rule*, chs 7, 39, 48).

Reading between the lines, we see that Æthelwold was not entirely content at Glastonbury. Dunstan seems to have been a tolerant rather than strict father to the members of his household, for he allowed monks and clerics to live and work alongside each other, without insisting on absolute unity of practice, which would be the norm in a Benedictine community sticking closely to Benedict's Rule for Monasteries. Æthelwold, on the other hand, had different views. He wanted, as Wulfstan says, *monastica religione perfectius informari*, 'to receive a more perfect grounding in a monk's religious life' (ch. 10), the comparative *perfectius*, 'more perfect', suggesting that, like reformers in other hagiographical writings, he needed more than Dunstan and Glaston-bury had to offer. Æthelwold even talked of studying monasticism abroad, but Queen Ediva 'forestalled his plans', preventing his departure. Instead, the king – at his mother's suggestion, and with her financial support – gave Æthelwold a site at Abingdon in the Thames valley. Abingdon had once been a monastery, but after the golden days of Abbot Hean in the early eighth century, and after destructive attacks by Vikings in the ninth century, the site had become a royal manor with a church of canons attached to it.[12]

To judge by the biographies, Æthelwold at Abingdon certainly was stricter than Dunstan at Glastonbury. Admittedly both abbots cultivated music, poetry and the arts, but Dunstan's interests were wider. Where Dunstan dreamed his prophetic visions and dined with noble ladies, Æthelwold taught his monks the virtues of humility and obedience. Nevertheless Æthelwold earned the respect of like-minded seekers, and men abandoned their careers and came willingly to Abingdon to join him in his new project. For example, three Glastonbury clerics – and it is significant that they were still clerics – also left Dunstan's Glastonbury to become monks at Abingdon, and one, Osgar, was soon sent overseas to study monastic customs at Fleury, near Orléans in the Loire Valley. Now known as Saint-Benoît-sur-Loire, Fleury is once again a revived monastery, with an imposing Romanesque church and a shrine containing the relics of Benedict of Nursia, author of the Rule and founder of the Benedictine order (hence the modern name of the village). In the tenth century the acquisition of those relics was still a celebrated event, and after a visit from Odo of Cluny in the year 930, the monastery became an important centre of the Reform movement.

During his stay at Fleury, Osgar may have met another English monk, Oswald, a remarkable man, by all accounts. Oswald was a man of the tenth century, a descendant of an Anglo-Danish family whose uncle was Oda, archbishop of Canterbury (941–58) and whose grandfather, it seems, was a Viking and member of the Great Army that plundered across the country in the 870s. Oswald was later, in the reign of King Edgar, to become a reforming bishop of Worcester (961–92) and then also archbishop of York (971–92).[13] And Osgar himself was destined to become the next abbot of Abingdon, once Æthelwold had embarked on the more overtly political phase of his career, as Bishop of Winchester, from 963 onwards. Men who stayed at Fleury clearly returned to England filled with a zeal and ambition for reform. The stay at Fleury was also significant for the history of writing, for it is through contacts such as these that the new Caroline style of script reached England, and Anglo-Caroline, as it was called, was the script used by the new reformed monasteries.[14] But calligraphy was not the only practice that the English visitors learned. With hindsight we see that these reformers were planning ahead: the contacts with the Continent affected not only the arts but also the religious and political organisation of the English kingdom.

Figure 13a   Fleury monastery, now St Benoit-sur-Loire

'WHAT KIND OF MAN SHOULD THE ABBOT BE?'

Æthelwold is a rare figure in Anglo-Saxon literary history, a securely named author, with a datable career, who wrote not only in Latin but also in Old English. His substantial literary output includes a translation of the Benedictine Rule into Old English, which was widely circulated to the many new monasteries that were founded once Edgar came to power. The preparatory work for this translation must have been considerable. According to Wulfstan, Æthelwold's initial studies were carried out while still under the guidance of Abbot Dunstan at Glastonbury, and it is likely that he began the translation there.

One possible textbook, furnished with glosses, corrections and annotations by Hand D (who is likely to be Dunstan) is a copy of Smaragdus's *Commentary on the Rule of St Benedict*.[15] This is familiar ground on which we might expect a monk or abbot to linger. The Benedictine Rule had been one of several in use in monasteries in western Europe, but in the eighth and ninth centuries reformers had attempted to impose its use universally. Smaragdus of Saint Mihiel Abbey, near Verdun in France, a monk and abbot during the reign of the Carolingian emperor, Louis the Pious (778–840), was one such monastic reformer, a proponent of the reforms initiated by the Synods of Aachen in the years 816–19.[16] A synthesiser and prolific writer of scholarly works and florilegia, Smaragdus wrote a line-by-line commentary and exposition of Benedict's Rule. In the context of a growing interest in monastic reform in mid-tenth-century England, it is an obvious work for Hand D to be reading and annotating.

If Dunstan followed this guide as a basis for his teaching he probably taught the Rule intensively, with close attention to detail, following Smaragdus's concern with textual accuracy, with defining terms, with finding parallels in other literature. There is a reminder here of B.'s description of Dunstan at work by the light of the dawn correcting mistakes in books and getting rid of false readings (B., *Life of St Dunstan*, ch. 37.2). Overall, the main purpose of Smaragdus's work is to explain the Rule and demonstrate how it impinges on the daily life of the monks. Of undoubted relevance is Smaragdus's comments on Chapter 2 of the Rule, 'What Kind of Man the Abbot should be' (here the words in **bold** derive from Benedict's Rule):

> Wishing to show in the following what characterises a good shepherd, blessed Benedict first asked, **What kind of man should the abbot be?** The positive answer to this must be: A good person, certainly, and such as the apostle describes when he says: *Without reproach, as a servant of God, not proud, not given to anger or to wine or to physical violence, not desirous of base gain, but hospitable, kind, sober, just, holy, continent, so that he may be able to exhort by sound doctrine and to refute those who contradict* [Smaragdus quotes Titus 1: 7–9]. Precisely this kind of man, no doubt, must **an abbot be who is worthy to rule over a monastery**, and **he must always remember what he is called.** For he is said to be, and is called, abbot, that is, father. If he is a father, let him love them in a fatherly way and, when necessary, chastise, reprove, beseech and reproachfully reprimand them in a fatherly way (Smaragdus, *Commentary*, ch. 2, pp. 123–4).

The explanation hinges on the etymology of *abbot* as 'father'. It seems that monasticism was returning to the idealism of the original Rule, in which an abbot should engage personally with the men under his care. According to the Reformers, an abbot should not act like a great lord and landowner, remaining aloof and distant from the other men in the monastery.

In terms of the question 'What Kind of Man the Abbot should be', Abbot Æthelwold clearly interpreted the guidance in the Rule of Benedict and in the commentary by Smaragdus rather differently to Abbot Dunstan. In this respect, the story of the monk Ælfstan's 'stealing obedience' in Chapter 14 of Wulfstan Cantor's biography is a much-discussed example of how Æthelwold viewed his role as abbot.

'YOU HAVE STOLEN THIS OBEDIENCE FROM ME'

Wulfstan begins the relevant section of his biography of Æthelwold by relating how at this time (the year must be 957) Dunstan was made bishop of Worcester after his recall from exile, a staging post on his way to becoming archbishop of Canterbury (for more details of Dunstan's rehabilitation, see my next chapter). There follows in Wulfstan's account a brief listing of Dunstan's qualities: persistent, learned, active, 'beautiful as an angel, strong in alms and prophecy' (*Life of St Æthelwold*, Chapter 14). It is this that reads like a contrast to Æthelwold, who in the next sentence of the passage, is described as sending Osgar to Fleury to learn there the way of life according to the Rule (*ut regularis obseruantiae mores illic disceret*) and to teach it to the monks on his return to Abingdon. In this way, Wulfstan declares, Æthelwold could follow the *normam monasticae religionis*, literally the 'norm of monastic religion', or as Winterbottom and Lapidge translate, the 'regulations of monastic observance', and in so doing they would avoid the *deuia* or 'by-ways' which prevent their proceeding on the straight path to the heavenly kingdom. This preamble presents two reformers of different types: the one, Dunstan, as a holy man and prophet, the other, Æthelwold, as a man of integrity and reformer of the rule.

The anecdote about 'stealing obedience' begins here, immediately, in the same chapter. Wulfstan introduces the monk Ælfstan as a 'straightforward and highly obedient man' – the emphasis on his obedience being important – whom the abbot has ordered to cook food for the workers and craftsmen that are rebuilding the monastery. This, it could be noted in passing, was exactly the kind of manual work that Æthelwold had done while he had been a monk under Dunstan at Glastonbury. According to Wulfstan, Ælfstan works assiduously (*devotissima*) at his tasks of cooking meat, serving the builders, lighting the fire, fetching water, cleaning the pans. So much so that the abbot suspects he has had the help of an extra servant. The said incident occurs at this point in the story. Presumably the abbot and the monk are in the meadows just outside the walls of Abingdon, where the monastic building work is proceeding, and Wulfstan reports that Æthelwold is on his customary tour of the site; here is the text, with a translation slightly adapted from that of the standard edition:[17]

> He happened to see this monk standing by a boiling cauldron in which he was preparing food for the craftsmen, and he went into the room. Finding all the pans sparkling and the floor swept, he said to him with a cheerful countenance: 'O brother Ælfstan, you have stolen this obedience from me [*hanc oboedientiam mihi furatus es*] in doing it without my knowing [*quam me ignorante exerces*]. But if you are the soldier of Christ you look to be, put your hand in the boiling water and fetch me a bit of food from the bottom. Quick about it!'

The question here is whether Æthelwold is right to blame a monk for acting on his own initiative, i.e. 'stealing the obedience' that a subordinate 'owes' to his superior by not waiting for specific instructions. For an abbot such as Æthelwold, Ælfstan has exceeded his remit and done more than he was asked to do.

This is obviously a kind of miracle story with a moral of monastic discipline, and there are hints of the practice known as the *ordeal* (the word and concept are originally Old English) that was used for making difficult decisions in Anglo-Saxon court cases. In the ordeal, the accused had to carry a hot iron bar for a stipulated distance, or remove a stone from a cauldron of boiling water, and the speed and quality of the healing process would determine his or her guilt (for the writer Lantfred's account of the ordeal, see Chapter 15 below).[18] Ælfstan of course obeys without hesitating, and removes the morsel of food from the pan, but without feeling any pain and without harming his hand. In this case, all ended well, as Wulfstan affirms. Ælfstan later achieved the rank of abbot (probably at the Old Minster in Winchester) and he later became bishop of Ramsbury. These, it is implied, are the rewards of absolute obedience.[19]

Is this the only message of the anecdote? The author of the biography, Wulfstan Cantor, always views Æthelwold in a favourable light, and he employs some of the standard hagiographical motifs as he recounts the life of his admired abbot. He is writing with hindsight, from the standpoint of the 990s. But he also knew his own teacher well, and to that extent he is a reliable witness to the many aspects of Æthelwold's character. So the question arises as to whether Æthelwold was unduly authoritarian in demanding this action of his efficient, if too self-sufficient, monk.

The key statements in this anecdote are highlighted above. Ælfstan is a man of obedience, Æthelwold is cheerful and confident: the feeling is, of course, that nothing can go wrong. But the abbot's assertion that Ælfstan 'stole his obedience' by working efficiently sounds positively despotic. And it contrasts in various ways with Dunstan's more kindly interactions with his monks in the stories told in B.'s *Life of St Dunstan*.[20] We are reminded of a later response to Æthelwold as a strict reformer (Wulfstan, *Life of St Æthelwold*, ch. 19), when, after his consecration as bishop and his forcible takeover of the minsters in Winchester, some disgruntled clerics tried to poison him (cf. the attempted murder of John the Old Saxon, abbot of Athelney, discussed in Chapter 3 above).

'THE BENEVOLENT BISHOP ÆTHELWOLD'

Strangely, perhaps, there are no reports that Æthelwold was unpopular among his more immediate charges. Wulfstan is clear about the 'severity of his discipline', but he also declares that Æthelwold tempered it with gentleness towards the humble and obedient. Generally speaking, later texts support the idea that Æthelwold was a genial teacher and friend. He even provided extra drinks for the members of his household, and as in the similar miracle story told in the *Life of St Dunstan*, Wulfstan Cantor in his biography reports that Æthelwold entertained King Edred and his Northumbrian thegns to a drinking session in which the drink never ran dry. (The mention of Northumbrian thegns adds an authentic note to the story, since Edred had spent much of his time on campaigns in the north.) In the thirteenth century the Abingdon monks still remembered with affection the *bolla Æthelwoldi*, 'Æthelwold's bowl', the large measure of mead that was dispensed for their enjoyment and sustenance.[21]

As we have seen, Wulfstan also describes Æthelwold as 'benevolent', punning on the meaning of his name (the adjective *æthel*, 'noble, good' and the verb *wolde*, 'wanted, was willing'), and the Anglo-Saxon Chronicle repeats this sobriquet when it reports the death of Bishop Æthelwold in 984, calling him *wel-willenda* (literally 'well-wanting', i.e. 'benevolent'): *se wellwillenda bisceop Aðelwold*, 'the benevolent Bishop Æthelwold'. Elsewhere in the *Life*, we are told that Æthelwold loved to teach young men through the medium of English rather than Latin.

This practice had important repercussions for the high status of the English language in late Anglo-Saxon England, since many of these students in turn went on to higher positions in the reign of Edgar (959– 75) or of Edgar's son Æthelred (978–1016). And it is clear that the use of written English spread widely.

Most significantly for the new developments, one of Abbot Æthelwold's students was Edgar himself, a young royal orphan who had been fostered away from the royal court, perhaps for his own protection. During the reign of Edgar's father Edmund, the nobleman Æthelstan Half-King had risen to prominence, becoming ealdorman of a huge territory – the whole of the eastern Danelaw including East Anglia – from 943 to 956. The by-name that he gained in his lifetime of 'Half-King' served to distinguish him from the other Æthelstan, the late departed king of the same name. In a period where people had only one name, this was practical. But the unusual by-name also indicated, and even reinforced, his high status as one of the most powerful men in the country. His family shared his good fortune: one brother was ealdorman of the south-east from 940 to 946 while another held a similar position in Wessex from 942 to 949.[22] It is significant that Æthelstan Half-King was the foster-father of the young orphan Edgar, who must have been

Figure 13b   Ruins of Abingdon Abbey

sent to Half-King's court after his father had been murdered. This fostering was to have far-reaching effects, for Æthelstan was a supporter of the monastic reformers, and it appears that he later arranged for Edgar to be educated at Abingdon, where Æthelwold himself was his tutor.

While at Abingdon, Edgar became good friends with Æthelwold, who fired him up with enthusiasm for the Benedictine ideal. Here is the twelfth-century historian William of Malmesbury, who had access to a full text (now otherwise lost) of Æthelwold's preface to the Old English translation of the Rule:

> For instance as I have read in the prologue of someone who translated the Rule of St Benedict into English, Edgar was on one occasion practising his skills at archery when he noticed some way off buildings of some size, but defaced by neglect and collapse. He asked his companions about them, eager to search out the truth. They told him that here had once been a splendid monastery there, but that it had been destroyed by enemy action or the arrogance of tyrannical kings, and now had only a few inhabitants. Edgar lifted his eyes, and bound himself by a vow: if he should ever be king, he would restore this place and others like it to their original state.[23]

In a quasi-Romantic tableau, Æthelwold pictures the young prince Edgar out in the fields near Abingdon, practising his archery and seeing the ruins of an ancient monastery, which impresses him so much that he vows to rebuild it when he comes to power. The decision was to have far-reaching effects.

CHAPTER 14

Lawsuits, law-books and sermons: Archbishop Dunstan and King Edgar

THE ROAD TO CANTERBURY

The chief events in Dunstan's rehabilitation and return from exile were not originally recorded in manuscript A of the Anglo-Saxon Chronicle. But around the year 1000/1001 it appears that this copy of the Chronicle was taken from Winchester to Canterbury. There, a new scribe, who was something of a local patriot, noticed that the annals, sparse as they were, conspicuously failed to make mention of his city's saintly archbishop. So he filled in the gaps with relevant entries of his own. By this time the great man's sanctity had been well established, so the scribe notes Dunstan's death against the year 988, calling him 'Sancte Dunstan' (in a mixture of Latin and Old English). Earlier, he found in the entry for 955 that 'Edwy succeeded to the kingdom, the son of King Edmund' and so felt compelled to add the further information that Edwy also *aflæmde Sancte Dunstan ut of lande*, 'exiled Saint Dunstan out of the country'. The next entry (alongside the year 958) marks the accession of Edgar as follows in the original text:

> Her forðferde Eadwig cyng on kalendas Octobris, and Eadgar
> his broðor feng to rice.
>
> [Here King Edwy passed away on the first of October, and his brother Edgar
> succeeded to the kingdom.]

For the next two years our Canterbury scribe found no entry at all in the Chronicle, just the running dates in the margin, so he added the following passages:

Her he sænte efter Sancte Dunstane and gæf him þæt bisceoprice on
Wigracæstre and ðæræfter þæt bisceoprice on Lundene.

[Here he sent after Saint Dunstan and gave him the bishopric in Worcester
and thereafter the bishopric in London.]

Her gewat Odo arcebisceop and Sancte Dunstan feng to arcebisceoprice.

[Here Archbishop Oda died, and Saint Dunstan succeeded to the
archbishopric.]

These entries are in fact attached to the wrong years (the correct years
being 958 and 959), but their content is confirmed by the writings of
Æthelwold, by B.'s biography and by other sources.[1]

As soon as Edgar came of age in 957 he was able to share power with
his brother Edwy, and the English kingdom was divided along the
border of the Thames. Because his jurisdiction was north of the
Thames, in Mercia, Edgar was free to recall Dunstan and install him in
two bishoprics (simultaneously and uncanonically) in the Mercian
province. Events took a drastic turn in 958, the year of Oda's death.
Edwy appointed as archbishop of Canterbury his loyal follower Ælfsige,
who was a traditional churchman, married with at least one son and
unsympathetic to the monastic reform movement. In the winter of
958–9 Ælfsige made a rash decision to set off on the prescribed journey
to Rome to collect his pallium (following the routes outlined in Part I of
this book). He never reached the 'Romulean city', as B. describes his
destination in his *Life of St Dunstan*.[2] The Alps were covered in heavy
snow, and Ælfsige succumbed to hypothermia. When the news reached
Edwy of this *infortunium in predictis montibus*, 'the disaster in the
mountains', he immediately appointed one Byrhthelm, formerly
Bishop of Wells, who, wisely perhaps, delayed his journey to Rome.
In the meantime Edwy himself died, and Edgar became sole king:

> Then, exercising divine authority and with the support of his *witan*, [Edgar]
> promoted Dunstan to the archbishopric, well knowing *him* to be steadfast
> of purpose (B., *Life of St Dunstan*, ch. 26.3).

The implication was that Byrhthelm lacked the necessary 'steadfastness'
and discipline. In B.'s opinion, Byrhthelm was *mitis et modestus, humilis
et benignus*, 'mild and modest, humble and kindly', but these were not
necessarily the qualities needed for the correction and care of his people
in the holy church of Canterbury. Byrhthelm perhaps acquiesced out of
humility towards his former abbot Dunstan;[3] he certainly did not

contest the new decision, and he was duly returned to his bishopric at Wells.

Dunstan, as we have seen, was certainly steadfast in his opinions, and he was evidently felt to be a more suitable candidate to fill the position at Canterbury. Fortitude, persistence, steadfastness of character: these are qualities that we can detect in B.'s biography of Dunstan, and they are confirmed by two case studies from Dunstan's early years at Canterbury (a period for which B. has relatively little to report). It is to these we now turn.

Both narratives concern disputes over land, the first the history of a property at Cooling in Kent belonging to Ediva, that is, the queen mother Eadgifu, who was last seen (in Chapter 12) witnessing a charter 'with her heart rejoicing'; the second a dispute over the possession of an estate at Sunbury in Middlesex. In both narratives, after various dramatic events, the estate passes to Dunstan's archbishopric at Christ Church Canterbury. Which probably explains how we know about them. By chance or design, the archives of Christ Church and Westminster have preserved the two single sheets of parchment that tell these tenth-century stories of clan rivalry and claim and counter-claim. As seems to be common with such documents, their chronology covers a long period of time, and it will be necessary to recall the events of the reigns of Edward the Elder and Æthelstan as we trace the somewhat tortuous plots of the two documents, written mostly in summary, with occasional lively dialogue and reported speech, in an interesting if rather allusive prose style. As modes of writing, these are 'short short stories' and I will draw on a range of historians and critics to interpret them. The second narrative in particular, the History of Sunbury, throws light on the character of Dunstan, supplementing what we know of him from B.'s biography.

THE HISTORY OF THE ESTATE AT COOLING (THE STORY OF EDIVA)

In the end the voice of Ediva the queen mother is heard. This is essentially the theme of the history of the estate at Cooling, a *declaration* or administrative document in which the queen mother, who had played such an important role in the reign of Edred, finally sees justice done.[4] Once her son Edred had died, the new king, Edwy, took umbrage at her close support of Dunstan and deprived her of her landed property. Suddenly Ediva found herself practically destitute, and with no obvious supporters to turn to. This in essence is the history of her estate at Cooling in Kent, which she had inherited from her father many years previously.

Again the political events of the tenth century form the backdrop to the narrative. It begins with an account of a battle, told not from the point of view of the people who fought (as, for instance, in the heroic poems of Æthelstan's reign) but rather of those who stayed behind. The year was 902, in the early years of the reign of King Edward the Elder, and Ediva's father, a certain Kentishman called Sigehelm, or Sigelm for short, was summoned to the Holme, site of the great battle at the time of the war against Edward's cousin Æthelwold, a battle in which many of the Kentish vanguard fell (see Chapter 6 above). But before he departed the estate at Cooling was still in the possession of a man called Goda, in exchange for a loan of thirty pounds, and Sigelm needed to pay back the sum in order to secure the estate for the young Ediva. In a single sentence, the writer sums up the father's need to leave his affairs in order and implicitly hints at the father's sense of duty towards his daughter:

> But Sigelm her father did not want to go to war with any man's money still unpaid.

He therefore paid off the loan and bequeathed 'both land and book' to Ediva his daughter (there is often an emphasis in these texts on correct legal procedures). The author now describes the inevitable:

> When [Sigelm] fell in the war then Goda denied any receipt of the money...

Goda now kept the estate until six years had passed, but litigation was in progress on behalf of Ediva, until the *witan* decided that she should, as the text puts it, 'cleanse her father's hand', in other words, as Harmer translates it, 'she should purge her father's possession by [an oath equivalent to] that amount of the money'.

As we saw in Chapter 6 in the case of Helmstan at Fonthill, the swearing of oaths was a serious business in tenth-century England, and Ediva duly swore her oath at Aylesford and cleared her father's name.[5] That normally should have been the end of the affair, for as the writer of the Fonthill text had feelingly declared:

> And, dear king, when is any claim ended, if it cannot be ended by payment or by oath?

But it appears that this was not enough after all, for Goda refused to move, and he continued to hold the estate until Ediva's friends finally appealed to King Edward to have Goda evicted. Edward now intervened more actively, and he clearly had other motives, for at some stage in these protracted proceedings Edward married Ediva, probably around the year 919.

Significantly the text does not mention the crucial fact that the king and Ediva were married, except to say that afterwards King Edward accused Goda 'so severely' that he deprived him of all his landbooks and property, in fact of 'all that he owned', and gave them to Ediva. Her response is nuanced, for she seems to cherish charitable feelings towards the now disgraced Goda. Again the text signals the crucial moment in the narrative by recourse to dialogue:

> Then she said that before God she did not dare to pay him back as he really deserved of her, and she returned to him all his estates apart from two sulungs at Osterland; and [she said] she did not want to return the landbooks before she knew how faithfully he would treat her with regard to the estates.[6]

Technically, from a grammatical point of view, this is indirect speech rather than verbatim report. But the impression given is that the writer reproduces at least in part some of the words that Ediva actually spoke. Rather cautious about whether she can trust Goda, she retains the landbooks, i.e. the charters or title-deeds (and it is interesting to see how much weight is given to the value of the written word, in a society where not everyone could read). Her speech is a mixture of justice and fairness with a modicum of caution. It turns out in the later course of events that her reticence was justified.

The transition here from one reigning king to the next is signalled by a suitable temporal phrase. Here are the three transitions as used in this text, with Harmer's translations:

Þa gewat Eadweard cyncg and fencg Æþelstan to rice

[Then, King Edward died and Æthelstan succeeded to the kingdom.]

Þa Eadred geendude and man Eadgife berypte ælcere are

[When Edred died and Ediva was deprived of all her property...]

Þæt þa swa wæs oþ Eadgar astiþude

[That then remained so until Eadgar came of age]

These three phrases mark the three distinct stages in the fluctuating career of Ediva as told in the story. The first, during the reign of Æthelstan, sees Ediva coming to an amicable agreement with Goda at a meeting of the royal *witan* in the presence of the king. However, Goda waited for a change of monarch before petitioning the new king for the return of his landbooks. But Ediva delivers them peacefully, and Goda thanks her humbly, and swears an oath that the case is now settled.

The second temporal phrase marks for Ediva the disastrous reign of Edwy (Eadwig), who according to the text immediately deprives her of all her property. As we know, Edwy felt considerable resentment towards the supporters of the previous king, his uncle Edred. Goda's sons now take their chance and seize the estates at Cooling and Osterland claiming 'to the child Edwy who had then been elected king that they were more rightfully theirs than hers'. Again the reported speech rounds off this stage in the story.

Finally we have the temporal marker 'Þæt þa swa wæs oþ Eadgar astiþude', which Harmer sees as the 'coming of age' of King Edgar. The wording is important and perhaps significant, and we will return to it below. For now, it is sufficient to note that as in the Sunbury dispute which we are about to consider, the efficient and rather radical Edgar reverses the decision made by his brother Edwy and restores the disputed property to Ediva. In her gratitude, and as a suitable final gesture for a woman now advanced in years, Ediva donates the property to Christ Church Canterbury:

> Then Ediva, with the permission and witness of the king and all his bishops, took the landbooks and entrusted the estates to Christ Church [and] with her own hands laid them upon the altar, as the property of the community for ever, and for the repose of her soul.

The scene before the altar echoes other moments in similar narratives where the king lays the charter on the altar to confirm the episcopal rights of a new bishop or to refound an institution.[7] But the symbolic moment is no less moving for all that. A story that began some sixty years previously has now reached its conclusion.

THE HISTORY OF SUNBURY

The History of Sunbury offers an equally interesting tableau. In the early part we hear a confrontational dialogue between two brothers, reported in full direct speech, as though the writer had all the time in the world to tell his story. As with the history of the estate at Cooling, the medium is a single sheet of parchment, and the writer really could not afford to waste any space. This suggests that the reported dialogue has some vital importance to the case.

Initially, the situation is a case of theft, of the woman Thurwif, who presumably is a servant or slave (her name is perhaps Scandinavian in origin). The accused is a certain *Æþelstan æt Sunanbyrg*, in other words Æthelstan of Sunbury, yet another man bearing this name, who is identified by his place of abode, and must be a property-owning thegn, presumably of some standing. Now Æthelstan has failed to turn up at the assembly to clear himself of the accusation. Because of his deliberate absence, the local ealdorman, i.e. the governor of the region, who had probably presided over the assembly, demands that Æthelstan pay a fine amounting to his full *wergild*. In other words he must pay the legal value set for a person of his rank and status. Given the brevity of the genre, the text does not describe the situation in which this conversation takes place.

But it seems likely that, having made his decision, the ealdorman has ridden over to Sunbury with his men and is confronting Æthelstan there, on the land itself, perhaps before his hall or manor. But Æthelstan is adamant in his refusal. Here is their exchange in full:

> Then Æthelstan said that he had nothing to give him.
> Then Edward, Æthelstan's brother, called out and said: 'I have the land-book for Sunbury, which our parents left to me. Hand the estate over to me, and I will give your wergild to the king.'
> Then Æthelstan said that he would rather it went to fire or flood than ever allow that to happen.
> To which Edward said, 'It is worse that neither of us should have it.'
> But that was what happened.[8]

It is curious to find one brother, Edward, holding the title deeds, while the other, Æthelstan, has possession of the property; one explanation may be that the two brothers once held the property jointly.[9] The style of the above exchange is vivid and dramatic, and it resembles that of an Icelandic saga, or the straightforward narrative of a modern writer such as Ernest Hemingway, a plain style that disguises its artfulness.

The art that conceals itself is heard, as Scott T. Smith points out, in the occasional alliteration and rhythmical language that the author uses to enliven the telling of his tale.[10] In the above confrontation, for example, when Eadweard asks for sole possession of the estate he says '*læt me þæt land to handa*' (*læt* and *þæt* and *land* and *handa* being linked also by rhyme for further rhetorical effect), while Æthelstan in rejecting his offer talks of '*fire and flood*', a common alliterative pairing even in the present day and one that adds further emphasis to his speech. We can almost believe these were the very words that he said.

In terms of content, it is clear that fraternal rivalry is a recurring theme of the text. Here lies the motivation for including such extended dialogue at a crucial moment in the story, and the conversation is so constructed as to reflect the personalities of the two brothers in various subtle ways. As Smith shows in his analysis, it is Eadweard, the more sensible of the two, who speaks in direct speech, while Æthelstan (the suspected thief) is given indirect speech in the subjunctive mood: this is use of language which detracts somewhat from the reliability of what he says. And he certainly is unreliable, for as soon as King Edred has died and the new government of King Edwy has taken power, Æthelstan returns to Sunbury illegally and resumes his possession of the land.

Smith's interpretation may be taken one step further. A land dispute such as this has affinities with Old Norse saga narrative (as seen for example in the extracts from *Egil's Saga* in Chapter 9 above). Despite the occasional alliterative adornment, the History of Sunbury and Send narrates its matter in a plain prose structured on the pattern 'then this happened, then that' (a structure known as *paratactic* syntax); the narration has minimal authorial comment; it employs dialogue not only for dramatic effect but also to point up differences in character. All these are typical features of the saga as a genre. And in terms of subject matter the saga often deals with land disputes, confrontations at the assembly, legal wranglings and demands for compensation.

Unlike saga, of course, there is the brevity of this particular text, in which the narration of events proceeds much more quickly than in a lengthy saga, given the lack of space available on the single sheet of parchment. Interestingly, recent research traces the origin of the Norse saga to similar short accounts of legal disputes, which were later expanded into longer, more novelistic narratives. In the story of Æthelstan and Eadweard, then, as in the Fonthill Letter, we appear to have a short saga narrative in embryo form.

Further interest in the story comes at the two transitions between the reigns of the kings. At each transition, the narrator employs a pointed turn of phrase as a temporal marker:

binnan ðam wendun gewyrda (lines 15–16)

[in the meantime events changed]

gemang þam getidde þæt Myrce gecuran Eadgar to cynge (lines 19–20)

[meanwhile it came about that the Mercians elected Edgar as king]

The transition from Edred's reign to Edwy's is attributed to happenstance, the word *gewyrda*, 'events' or 'fates', being the same as used at the beginning of the Exeter Book poem *The Ruin*, where 'disastrous events' brought down the city. By contrast, the accession of Edgar is attributed to human agency, to the fact that the Mercians chose him as king and gave him full 'control' (again this is the usual term *anweald*). In short, Edgar is given full control 'of all royal rights' (*ealra cynerihta*).

At this crucial point, the text becomes a key source for the early reign of Edgar, since it reports that the Mercians actively sought out and elected the young prince as their king. Why they would do this is not made clear. The author B., who is decidedly partial, has a similar story. He asserts that the Mercians were unhappy with Edwy's reign and his choice of counsellors and wanted a different ruler (*Life of St Dunstan*, ch. 24). Some historians are sceptical: they believe that the two royal brothers had planned in advance to share power once Edgar came of age. Whatever the reason, the kingdom of England was now divided between the two rulers, with the river Thames as the border, something that had happened before at the beginning of Æthelstan's reign. The situation was to last for two years until Edwy's death, which the author of the History of Sunbury finds no cause to mention, though it is clear by the end of the narrative that Edgar has succeeded to the whole of the English kingdom.

The pattern the writer has set up by telling a story of fraternal rivalry continues in the middle part of the document, where he implicitly compares Edwy and Edgar. As Scott T. Smith again demonstrates in his very insightful reading of the narrative, the writer of the document deliberately chooses different verbs to represent the similar actions of the two royal brothers. Accordingly, when Edwy heard that Æthelstan had illegally taken over the property, he 'gave' (*gesealde*) the land to one of his men, Byrnric, who promptly 'ejected' Æthelstan. This is the language of peremptory authority, and there is an implied criticism, for the king is not necessarily behaving correctly.

But the wily Æthelstan now appeals to Edwy's co-ruler, the other king. He must be hoping, we assume, to reverse the decision. So Edgar with his Mercian council duly hears the same case. But Edgar comes to a similar decision. Since once again the obviously stubborn Æthelstan refuses to pay his wergild and once again refuses to allow his brother Edward to pay it for him, King Edgar decides to grant the land to a more deserving recipient. So now, with Edwy's favoured recipient Byrnric out of the way (perhaps Byrnric had been forced to give up the estate on the accession of Edgar), the new king grants the land to another Æthelstan, an ealdorman, i.e. a member of the nobility. But the original tenant, Æthelstan of Sunbury, receives nothing for his pains.

   The king's attitude is not stated, it is implied by the choice of word and phrase, for unlike Edwy, who 'gave' (*gesealde*) the land away, it is said that Edgar 'booked' (*gebecte*) the estate to his ealdorman. As if to underline the legitimate nature of Edgar's transaction, the writer now adds an appropriate legal comment, that Edgar granted him the land in perpetuity, 'to be held and granted, during his lifetime or at his death, to anyone he pleased'.[11] This is the language of legitimate royal government, for that is how a king should behave, not simply 'giving' but 'granting' the land correctly in front of witnesses, with an appropriate royal charter or *land-book*.

THE MYSTERIOUS CASE OF ECGFERTH

The two land-hungry brothers are now 'out of the story', as a Norse saga would put it, but the estate is soon acquired by a new buyer, whose name is Ecgferth. Again it is stated that the sale is conducted lawfully and correctly: Ealdorman Æthelstan sells 'both land and book' to Ecgferth, in the presence of the king and his *witan*, and Ecgferth then 'held it and enjoyed it until his end' (another legal phrase). At this point we are told that Ecgferth entrusted 'land and book' to Archbishop Dunstan, again in the presence of the king. Dunstan's role, then, will be to protect the interests of Ecgferth's widow and child. As in the previous section, the narration now speeds forward to that moment of dialogue when the participants declare their differences:

> When he was ended [i.e. when Ecgferth's life was at an end], the archbishop rode to the king and reminded him of the guardianship and his witness to it.
>   Then the king said to him in reply: 'My *witan* have declared forfeit all Ecgferth's property, by the sword that hung at his hip when he drowned.'

Again there is a concrete image, not this time of fire and flood, but the very tactile one of the sword that '*h*ung at *h*is *h*ip' (*þæt swyrd þe him on hype hangode*), the alliteration serving once again to emphasise the message conveyed. The mysterious fate of Ecgferth is not explained. Did he drown by accident? Was it a trial by ordeal? Why was he still bearing his sword, symbol of his noble rank? There are no certain answers to these questions. Whatever happened, the king then 'gave away' (*forgef*) the estate to Ealdorman Ælfheah, one of his followers.

As in his dealings with earlier kings, however, Dunstan was certainly not afraid to oppose the king's wishes, for he clearly felt had a duty to support Ecgferth's widow. The dispute that now developed between bishop and king is again recorded in the form of a dialogue:

> Then the bishop offered the king his *wergild*.
> Then the king said: 'That might be offered in exchange for his Christian burial, but I have left the whole case to Ælfheah.'

The king drives a hard bargain and will not budge on his decision. Dunstan will presumably pay out Ecgferth's *wergild* to lay him decently to rest, but the estates will go to the king's man instead.

Nevertheless, there is a coda, or resolution, to the story. 'Six years later', the narrator tells us, Dunstan bought two estates from Ealdorman Ælfheah, paying two hundred mancusses of gold for Sunbury and ninety pounds for another pertinent estate at Send; the sale was conducted correctly, in front of witnesses, and was 'unopposed and uncontested' by any man. So now Dunstan may claim possession of the lands legally, since he has had them from Ælfheah, the man who had obtained them lawfully from the king, as his *witan* or counsellors had decreed. On this legal note the declaration ends (for the full text and translation see Appendix I).

Interestingly, the story is partly corroborated by another document (S 702 in Sawyer's catalogue), a Latin charter in the name of King Edgar, who hereby grants Sunbury to Ealdorman Ælfheah. It is possible that Dunstan had this particular copy of the charter made on the occasion when he bought the estates from Ælfheah in the year 968, in order to make the transaction legally secure.[12] Though the bulk of the charter is composed in Latin, the bounds of the estates are written in Old English, and a summarising sentence in Old English confirms that King Edgar *gebocode*, 'booked', this land to Ælfheah, who is identified as his 'kinsman', the family relationship helping to explain why the king was so insistent in his dispute with Dunstan. But if Edgar had acted illegally when he had originally given (*forgef*) the land, the matter had now been resolved to the satisfaction of both the king and his archbishop.

'WHEN EDGAR GOT TOUGH': THE LAW-BOOKS

Unlike earlier occasions when Dunstan had quarrelled with the ruling monarch, this difference of opinion did not lead to Dunstan's banishment and exile as it had done in the reign of Edwy, and very nearly had done also with Æthelstan and Edmund. It would be pleasing to know more details of the working relationship between Dunstan and Edgar, but the brevity of the original documents does not allow it. In such cases, therefore, close reading of the texts is the only way forward. Interpretation must rest heavily on the writer's choice of word or expression. In the History of the Estate at Cooling one verb in particular still requires our further scrutiny, since it potentially throws light on the character of King Edgar. Here again is the wording of the relevant sentence:

Þæt þa swa wæs oþ Eadgar **astiþude**

[That then remained so until Eadgar **came of age**]

Harmer's translation takes the rare verb *astiþian* to mean 'come of age'; in other words she argues, quite reasonably, that the verb indicates that the action was taking place in the year 957, when Edwy's younger brother Edgar, hitherto a minor, 'came of age' and was elected king of the Mercians. But *astithian* (to give it a more modern spelling) derives from an adjective *stith* meaning 'stern, severe, hard'; it is often used for stern or strict behaviour by rulers or kings, for example in the poem *Genesis A*, when God sternly tests Abraham by ordering him to sacrifice Isaac, or again in the Anglo-Saxon Chronicle for the year 1087, writing on the 'severe' rule of William the Conqueror. It seems therefore more logical to translate the phrase as 'when Edgar got tough'. As we shall see in the following pages, there is plenty of evidence that the young Edgar certainly did 'get tough' as he established and consolidated his power.

A genre of text that has been referred to in passing is *domboc*, literally the 'law-book' or law-code. As we saw in Part II, the tradition of West Saxon kings issuing their own laws in the English language had been revived by King Alfred and continued by his son Edward the Elder. Thereafter, each successive English king, with one or two exceptions, issued his successive lawcodes, each furnished with a short preface in which he explained the circumstances in which he was promulgating the new set of laws. Often in these texts the king would attempt to add to or improve on his earlier attempts at law-making or those of his predecessors. King Æthelstan's laws, for instance, are salutary in this respect, for each responds in different ways to the same problem, and we seem to see the king shifting his opinion and changing his mind. Apparently the main issue, at least in times of peace, was rampant theft. And it is clear that King Æthelstan changed his tune with regard to the severity of the punishment, abolishing the death penalty for young offenders out of sympathy for their tender age. His brother King Edmund seems to have had other ideas: in his third edict issued at a place called Colyton (known conventionally as III Edmund) all men are required to swear an oath of allegiance and loyalty to the king 'favouring what he favours and discountenancing what he discountenances'.[13] In other words, as in the laws of Charlemagne, a crime such as theft was treated as a breach of loyalty, a kind of treachery, a crime against the king, to be dealt with by royal punishments.[14] It is in this context that we can evaluate the severity and 'sternness' of Edgar's contributions to the making of law. For Edgar's reign there are four surviving texts, and the report of what perhaps is a fifth in the writings of the monk and biographer Lantfred on Edgar's 'law of great severity' (the severe law is important and I will return to Lantfred's treatment of this theme in Chapter 15).

The earliest lawcode attributed to Edgar goes by the title the Hundred Ordinance, and by all accounts it marks a development in the administration and law-keeping of the country. The shire was a West Saxon administrative unit, which then spread under the West Saxon kings to the rest of England. The hundred was a sub-division of a shire, and though its size varied, in Mercia where the new system was imposed relatively quickly, each hundred amounted to a hundred hides. The hide was an even smaller local unit of land, which was originally intended to represent the amount of land that would support a peasant farmer and his family. In a society without maps the hide was a useful term for measuring areas of land and assigning duties such as food rents and the manning and repairing of the walls of the fortified *burhs*.[15] Once the system of shire, hundred and hide was in place all over Edgar's England it must have led to a degree of uniformity and efficiency in the running of the English kingdom.[16]

The Hundred Ordinance seems to have been promulgated in the middle years of the tenth century, setting out the rules for the running of the hundred, which as well as being a unit of land was also the name of a law court. The hundred assembly was to meet every four weeks, and it has been pointed out that this relatively frequent gathering must have constituted the ordinary person's experience of royal government (since the shire assembly was a higher court that met only twice a year and the towns had their borough courts meeting three times a year). The main function of the hundred assembly, then, was to do justice: all the chief men of the hundred were to go out in pursuit of thieves, and if they caught the thief the value of the stolen goods was to be returned to the owner, while the rest of the thief's possessions were to be shared between the hundred and the local lord. Those who neglected these duties or opposed the workings of the hundred were to be fined, while persistent offenders were threatened with banishment. The final clause declares that *folcriht*, 'common law' (literally 'people-justice') should be enjoined in every suit.[17] Clearly all this served to prevent the frequent cattle-rustling and generally to preserve law and order.

At some stage early in his reign Edgar called an assembly of his *witan* at Andover. Laws issued here are now preserved as the documents II Edgar and III Edgar. As Simon Keynes shows, they present business as usual: ensuring protection of the church and the rule of law and regulating business practices.[18] By contrast the next law-book that Edgar issued, at a place called Wihtbordesstan, marks a distinct change: the text known as IV Edgar is a particular response to a year of famine. The explanation offered is in the form of a sermon; the preacher's theme is divine anger, because God's dues are not being paid to his Church. To illustrate the point, an elaborate exemplum is offered, like a parable, of a landlord making increasing demands on his tenant who persistently refuses to pay his *gafol*, the word for tribute, tax, or rent, even though the landlord sends his bailiffs, *bydelas*. At times, as the historian Patrick Wormald points out, we hear in IV Edgar a different style of writing, a different royal voice, with imperial overtones.[19] But the final exhortation, after all the dire threats, is friendly and almost personal:

> Ic beo eow swyðe hold hlaford þa hwile þe me lif gelæst, and eow eallum swyðe bliðe eom, for þy þe ge swa georne ymbe frið syndon.

> [I will be a very gracious lord to you as long as my life last. I am very well pleased with you all, because you are so zealous for the preservation of the public peace.]

THE COMPILATION OF THE VERCELLI BOOK

The homiletic voice of IV Edgar invites comparison with homilies and sermons composed or compiled during the reign of King Edgar. Here the most fruitful source is the Vercelli Book, datable by palaeography to around the year 970, near the end of Edgar's reign. Perhaps taken by a pilgrim to Rome, this book is Kentish. We have already seen in Chapter 1 that it is a florilegium copied and put together, as the researches of Donald Scragg have shown, from a number of separate texts and groups of texts taken from books available in the monasteries of Kent: Rochester and/or Canterbury being the principal cathedrals and centres of learning, and St Augustine's Abbey, Canterbury, being the most likely place of origin. The organising rationale for this anthology has been debated, since it contains a rich variety of poems and prose pieces. The criteria involved in the choice of texts could be mixed, and critics have suggested the following: devotion to the cross, sacred narrative, penance, the practice of Rogationtide and Lent, and the mixed life of contemplation and action.[20]

Canterbury was of course part of the Benedictine reform movement, but it was not the epicentre of Æthelwold's reform, which was Winchester. The presiding force here at Canterbury was Archbishop Dunstan, and it cannot too often be emphasised that Dunstan, though clearly a reformer, was flexible in terms of the kind of community he liked to build; unlike Æthelwold's exclusive communities of monks Dunstan allowed both clerics and monks to cooperate alongside each other. This diversity of clergy and monks at Canterbury may help to explain the diversity of texts in the Vercelli Book. Some of the poems – such as *The Dream of the Rood* – are demonstrably old by the time of the Reform in the tenth century. Other texts, such as Vercelli Homilies XIX– XXI, have plausibly been assigned to Archbishop's Dunstan's day.

The single authorship of the latter three sermons has been demonstrated on the grounds of style and use of sources.[21] It was rare in those times for a sermon writer to compose freely – much more common was for him to base his work on a selection of other texts and sources: other sermons, Latin biblical commentaries and religious treatises. There was no law of copyright, and writers simply selected their passages and sewed them together like patches in a quilt. A favourite Latin sermon collection that was put together in the Carolingian period is known as the St Père Sermonary after a manuscript copy of this text kept at St Père de Chartres. It circulated widely at this time. Old English sermon writers used this source as a treasure chest of examples, ideas, themes, motifs. The author of Vercelli Homilies XIX–XXI, who seems to have been active at Canterbury in the time of Archbishop Dunstan, is no exception, and it has been shown how carefully he translated extracts from the Latin sermonary and then adapted and fitted them together to make his own sermons.[22] Vercelli XIX is one such sermon or homily, which retells the story of Jonah and the whale, and provides opportunity for the homilist to demonstrate the message of the repentant king in Nineveh doing penance to avoid divine wrath. Thematically this resembles the exemplum in the lawcode IV Edgar.

Images of kingship appear in a number of the homilies: Vercelli I, V, VI, IX and X being good examples. In Vercelli I there is an exegesis of the word *crown* (see my discussion in the Introduction). In Vercelli IX the figure of the king appears as part of an exotic exemplum on the joys of heaven, which are compared to the joys of a rich royal court (see Chapter 1). Vercelli X is another example – available with text and parallel translation in Elaine Treharne's *Old and Middle English: An Anthology*. In Vercelli X it is the transience of kings and emperors that is emphasised in an *ubi sunt* passage on the passing of time:

> Where are the kings and Caesars that once were?

The message is not unlike similar passages in the poems *The Wanderer* and *The Seafarer* from the contemporary Exeter Book.

But in terms of images of imperial kingship, the Nativity homilies V and VI are arguably the most striking. Vercelli Homily V is a sermon on Christ's Nativity based on Chapter 2 of Luke's gospel, which records Christ's royal birth in Bethlehem, and the visit by the shepherds to the stable. Like many of these sermons, it begins with the biblical reading, and then proceeds with a verse-by-verse commentary interspersed with explanations and illustrations of the main themes. The translation of the biblical reading is of considerable interest for the way in which not only the words of the text but also the cultural concepts are translated from Latin into Old English. Here is an example of this text, which is more strictly paraphrase than translation (cultural additions to the biblical text are in italics):

> Swa sanctus Lucas se godspellere be þan wrat and cwæð: In þa tiid wæs *mycel gemot* gebannen fram Aguste þam casere þætte gewriten wære eall ymbhwyrft middangeardes. Þæt gewrit wæs ærest ongunnen fram þære mægðe *gerefan* þe Syria hatte, þæs mannes nama wæs Cyrinus. And þa eodon ealle, anra gehwylc on his ceastre, *þætte hie onfengon þam bebode þe þa gebannen wæs þætte æghwylc mann sceolde þam casere gaful gildan.* Þa ferde se eadga Ioseph fram Galilea, of þære ceastre *þe Nazaret hatte*, to Dauides ceastre *sio is nemned* Bethlem, forþamþe he wæs Dauides cynnes, *þætte hie þær sceoldon onfon þam bebode þæs gafoles þe þa gebannen wæs*, mid Marian þe him wæs to wife beweddod.[23]

> [Thus Saint Luke the gospel-writer wrote concerning this and said: At that time *a great assembly* was summoned by the Emperor Augustus that the whole extent of the world should be described. The description was first begun by the governor (*gerefa*) of the region called Syria, which man's name was Cyrinus. And then everyone travelled, each to their own town, *so that*

*they could receive the decree that had been issued that every man should pay
tribute to the emperor.* At that time the blessed Joseph travelled from Galilee,
from the town *that was called Nazareth,* to David's town *which is called*
Bethlehem, for he was of David's line, so that he should *receive the decree to
pay tribute which had been issued,* with Mary who was pledged to him as
wife.]

It is remarkable, even in this translation of the biblical passage, to see the
emperor Augustus summoning a great assembly (*mycel gemot*) just like an
Anglo-Saxon king, and then implementing this policy by means of his
reeve (*gerefa*), just like the town reeves and shire reeves of the new and
highly organised administration of Edgar's enlarged English kingdom.

As the author of Vercelli V continues his sermon, long passages are
devoted to apocryphal stories of miracles and wonders that took place
in the empire of Caesar Augustus at the time of Christ's birth (see
Appendix II for further extracts). There is a scene of royal triumph,
when a ring appears round the sun as Augustus enters the city of Rome
in pomp and splendour. Another passage treats the theme of the
Augustan *peace* at the time of Christ's birth as depicted in Luke. As for
the census itself, this is described as a *gafol* or tribute, and spiritual
analogies are found for its meaning rather like in IV Edgar. In these
homilies the emphasis is on the glory of kingship, the power and
onweald of the ruler. The parallels with the peaceful if severely governed
kingdom of Edgar are not difficult to see.

CHAPTER 15

Winchester, chief city of Edgar's England

THE STORY OF SWITHUN

On 15 July in the year 971, a grand ceremony was held at Winchester, presided over by Æthelwold, the former abbot of Abingdon, who had been, since 963, the reformist bishop of Winchester. There was a great procession, and the relics of Swithun, a ninth-century bishop, were moved from their prominent tomb near St Martin's tower and 'translated', as it is called, into the Old Minster. The ceremony marks the origin of St Swithun's Day, which is celebrated in the well-known lines of folklore verse:

> St Swithun's Day if thou dost rain:
> For forty days it will remain;
> If on St Swithun's Day it really pours:
> You're better off to stay indoors.

The occasion in 971 was well documented, commemorated in two literary works by Winchester writers, one writing in Latin prose, the other, a generation later, writing in verse. This was normal practice. Examples in earlier literature are Aldhelm's *De Virginitate*, in a verse and prose version, and likewise Sedulius's *Carmen Paschale*. Bede coined the term 'twinned life' and wrote his own *Lives of St Cuthbert*, in verse and in prose, which, to judge by King Æthelstan's gifts to Chester-le-Street, were still being read in the tenth century (see Chapter 8). A new trend was to employ an outsider: foreigners such as Asser or Frithegod were commissioned to write *Lives*, bringing with them new ideas and different approaches. In this chapter the focus will be on the *Translatio et*

Miracula S. Swithuni, 'The Translation and Miracles of St Swithun', by the Frenchman Lantfred, who was writing at Winchester in the 970s. And we will look briefly at the *Narratio Metrica de S. Swithuno* 'The Metrical Narrative of St Swithun', the later poetic reworking of the same story by the local monk Wulfstan Cantor, director of music at the Old Minster in Winchester and author, as we saw in Chapter 13, of the *Life of St Æthelwold*.[1]

In works of this kind, biography vies with hagiography. In his preface, for example, Lantfred admitted that he had been unable to discover much about the earthly life of Swithun when he was bishop of Winchester. But Lantfred's remit was to record how Swithun's sanctity had been rediscovered. To make up for his lack of biographical data on Swithun, Lantfred instead provides perspectives on the ordinary everyday lives of the Winchester citizens. In addition, he offers an interesting double-take in his style: he delivers the expected tenth-century 'Hermeneutic' high style in the narrative passages, but he switches to a more intimate and colloquial register in the conversations. His outsider's point of view is fascinating because he records what he sees and hears, retelling the stories he has heard from the smith (ch. 1), the local moneyer (ch. 2), the local landowner (ch. 3), anecdotes of everyday life but also tales of miracle and wonder, even stories of terror, strange supernatural events occurring out on the mule pastures by the river Itchen to the south of the city. And more interest is generated when Lantfred's version is compared to that of Wulfstan, who supplements the main plot with new chapters and extra passages on Winchester and its role in the course of events.

THE SETTING

What kind of writing is this? Clearly it is hagiography, but in particular, it belongs to a sub-genre of the saint's life known in Latin as a *translatio*, a 'translation account', for which there are many continental parallels. In a translation account, the saint usually appear to a certain person in a vision, miracles take place to convince and persuade, and the saint is then moved, i.e. *translated*, to a more appropriate resting place in a church, sometimes at a new location. But in more general terms, Lantfred's story is a wonder tale, and it tells of two worlds in contact: the world of the saint and the world of the citizen. There is a kind of tension in the plot. Will things turn out well? Will the saint be given his due?

The story takes place during the reign of King Edgar and is set in Winchester, which by this time was the second, if not the foremost, city of the kingdom. London was the principal port, but Winchester in the heart of Wessex was the seat of the West Saxon dynasty that was now ruling the country; it was the cultural centre. In general, cities were becoming increasingly important. As we saw in Parts II and III, the main development had been the building of 'boroughs', begun by King Alfred and then continued by his son Edward the Elder. The annals of the Anglo-Saxon Chronicle chart this policy, as Edward built one *burh* after another *burh*, in order to establish power over the Danelaw. In practice this meant that the walls of the old Roman cities were rebuilt and new walled towns were created.

Archaeologists used to regard the tenth-century *burh* as a refuge in times of war, but this view was overturned as urban archaeology developed in the 1970s. The archaeologist Francis Pryor puts it well in his *Britain in the Middle Ages: An Archaeological History*:

> In a well-known paper written jointly with David Hill, Martin Biddle suggested the existence of a whole series of planned Saxon towns, with non-Roman grid-like streets. In 1971 this was an astonishing revelation for everybody, except a few people ... who were working in urban archaeology. For most of us, even in the profession, it came as a revelation, because it seemed to go against everything we had been taught about the Saxons, who we believed were essentially rural people.

It is worth asking whether literary critics have also tended to think of Anglo-Saxon literature as essentially rural. There are no cities in *Beowulf* or the *Dream of the Rood*, and in the elegies such as *The Seafarer* or *The Wanderer* the city is generally a ruin, the *eald enta geweorc*, 'the old work of giants', the word 'giants' alluding to the Romans, the great men of the past, who knew how to build. But now, as the poet of the Exeter Book elegy *The Ruin* puts it, *brosnath enta geweorc*, 'the works of giants crumble'.[2]

Some Anglo-Saxon poets, however, seem to be aware of the changes. There is *Maxims II*, a piece of wisdom poetry added as a kind of preface to an eleventh-century copy of the Anglo-Saxon Chronicle (manuscript C). The poem celebrates rather than laments the cities in the landscape, and he praises them as *orthanc enta geweorc*, 'the cunning work of giants':

> The king's duty is to rule a kingdom. Cities are seen from afar,
> the cunning work of giants, those that are seen upon this earth,
> the splendid construction of wall-stones.

Perhaps this poem reflects the changing urban scene of the late tenth century. The celebrated *burh*-constructing of Edward the Elder's defensive policy has become urbanisation; the boroughs have developed into administrative centres. By Edgar's reign a typical town had a wall, a market, an assembly, a mint for producing coins, a cathedral and churches; there were town reeves to implement royal policy and regulate trade, and trading was only allowed to take place within the walls of the town. In *Maxims II* there is no longer any mention of ruins. Evidently, these towns 'seen from afar' were a feature in the landscape: new towns like Oxford, Wareham and Wallingford, but also a newly restructured town like London or Winchester. In reality the 'giants' who built or rebuilt these towns were the kings of a united England.

It is worth considering the situation in Winchester in the year 964, a key date for the narratives of Lantfred and Wulfstan. In the course of the tenth century Winchester had changed beyond recognition. Back in the time of Alfred and Edward the Elder the streets had been redesigned on a new grid that did not follow the pattern of the former Roman streets. The exception was the main street linking the west gate and the east gate – this still followed the Roman high street for obvious reasons, and in the tenth century it became the *cyping*, 'the cheaping', or the *ceapstræt*, i.e. the market street.[3] North of this street was the business and residential quarter, where the trades and professions flourished, which is reflected in the later medieval names of the streets: Tanner Street, Fleshmonger Street, Shieldmakers' Street. All this is relatively richly recorded in charters and administrative documents from Winchester and in the Winton Domesday of the twelfth century that was based closely on a survey of the city done in the time of Edward the Confessor.

Further changes came with the founding of the Nunnaminster by Alfred's wife Ealhswith and then the building of the New Minster by Edward the Elder in the centre of the city south of the market (see Chapter 6). The New Minster became a kind of rival to the Old Minster, designed to bolster the authority and presence of the king in the city: the two buildings stood side-by-side near the royal hall, although each had a large parcel of land attached to it. As was seen in Chapter 4, these minster estates made use of the new technology of the horizontal water-mill. According to Rahtz and Bullogh in their celebrated study of the parts of an Anglo-Saxon mill, such water-mills were used primarily by the royal court; only later did the technology go into widespread use. Streams and channels from the River Itchen were used to power the mills in the eastern quarter of the city and elsewhere; as befitted a royal centre, this was a modern city with up-to-date technology.

Later, during the reign of King Edgar, came the radical policies of the Benedictine Reform. In 964 a new royal policy was set in motion, practically the opposite of what was to happen with the dissolution of the monasteries in the sixteenth century in the reign of Henry VIII. Ironically, for Edgar in his day the *dissolution* of monasteries had been the result either of neglect of the monastic life or the assaults of Viking raiders. Now instead, the monasteries became the *solution*: all over southern England dozens of monasteries were founded or refounded on Benedictine principles. The main agent of this policy, and the most thoroughgoing, was Æthelwold. This is seen in the pages of the Anglo-Saxon Chronicle, where only a handful of annals exist for the reign of Edgar, but prominence is nevertheless given to Æthelwold's activities at Winchester once he had been appointed bishop. Æthelwold was consecrated on St Andrew's Day in 963. A year later, the Chronicle briefly reports that King Edgar *dræfde tha preostas*, 'drove out the priests', from the Old Minster and the New Minster and replaced them with monks.

It is Wulfstan Cantor in his *Life of St Æthelwold* who fills in some of the details of what happened that day, and his account of the monastic takeover naturally takes a more moral and spiritual line. Wulfstan asserts that the cathedral canons who were living there were guilty of

Figure 15a   Site of Old Minster, Winchester

'wicked and scandalous behaviour, victims of pride, insolence, and riotous behaviour' (end of ch. 16), so much so that Æthelwold could not tolerate it, and he replaced them with monks from Abingdon. In his Chapter 17, Wulfstan then explores the spiritual meanings of this event, the divinely appointed coincidence that when the monks arrived at the Old Minster, the canons and clerics were starting to sing the words of Psalm 2:11 for the mass-chant:

> Servite Domino in timore et exultate in tremore.
>
> [Serve ye the Lord with fear: and rejoice unto him with trembling.]

The monk Osgar, who had now returned from Fleury (see Chapter 13), was able to quote the rest of the psalm at the clerics as a kind of reproach for their lack of discipline, and generally Psalm 2 is concerned with the divinely appointed king and his power over the Gentiles. Osgar was speaking from a position of spiritual strength.

In his Chapter 18, moreover, Wulfstan reveals the physical power behind the event: the party of monks is accompanied by the king's thegn Wulfstan of Dalham, almost certainly backed by his soldiers, who forces the clerics to make the choice of either becoming a monk or leaving the cathedral. The narrative moves quickly at this point, there are no extended anecdotes or dialogues, and all is in summary – apart from the details of the reciting of the psalm – so we lack full details on how Wulfstan of Dalham behaved on this occasion. But it is clear that the clerics were terrified. Most of them, we are told, left Winchester for good, apart from Eadsige (a name to remember), and two others, a certain Wulfsige, and Wilstan the priest. We will return to the aggrieved Eadsige, for he features also in Lantfred's narrative.

THE CLEARANCE AT WINCHESTER

In the period thereafter, as the many documents edited by Alexander Rumble in his *Property and Piety in Early Medieval Winchester* demonstrate, the three minsters expanded, along with the bishop's palace, to cover the south east of the city. This expansion was referred to as a *rymet*, a 'clearance' of citizens' town houses, in order to make room for the monks and nuns and their new monastic buildings:

> Here in this writing is declared how King Edgar ordered that the monasteries in Winchester should be given privacy by means of a clearance, after he, through the grace of God, had turned them to the monastic life, and that he ordered it to be devised that none of the

monasteries within that place should have any dispute with another because of the clearance.[4]

The Old Minster, as we shall see later, was rebuilt on a grand scale and became far more important.

The New Minster in turn was given a special refoundation charter by the king. This lavish 'Golden Charter' emphasised that the New Minster was now run by monks living by the Rule of St Benedict, and that they needed to be given privacy and protection and be kept apart from the ordinary citizens. The document contains a frontispiece celebrating the almost priestly status of the king as Vicar of Christ: it shows Edgar in the act of presenting the book to Christ, while saints and angels look on.[5] As we know from other records, the abbots continued to pursue a policy of acquiring relics to enhance their institutions, and new saints' lives were composed accordingly, for example, a *Life* of the Breton saint Judoc, whose final resting place was a shrine at the New Minster.[6]

Archaeology confirms the historical record. Houses were cleared, and each monastery was surrounded by a high hedge; chalk streams were diverted to supply drinking water and run the water mills. This was not quite like the Norman Conquest, with its enforced evictions and clearances of whole streets for the purpose of building a castle. Citizens seem to have acquiesced in the clearance, but some documents record compensation arrangements and exchanges of land between prominent citizens and the monasteries. Inevitably, perhaps, there was also trouble between the various institutions, since for historical reasons the Old Minster and New Minster had ended up next door to each other, and there were problems with noise during the services. The site of the two churches is still visible a few yards to the north of the present-day cathedral.

But the greatest cause of dispute among the monasteries was water supplies. When the Old Minster building was enlarged, it encroached on New Minster land, and the bishop had to pay compensation, for as the same text continues:

> For that reason, therefore, Bishop Æthelwold, in the witness of the king and of all his cathedral community, has granted two plots of ground outside South Gate to the New Minster in exchange for the latter monastery's mill which stood in the cleared space that the king had had cleared for the Old Minster.

But improvements to the New Minster likewise caused disputes. The same document records how Æthelgar, the recently appointed abbot of the New Minster, diverted a stream to provide his institution with water.

The diversion 'ruined' a mill belonging to the third of the three institutions, the Nunnaminster:

> Abbot Æthelgar ... has assigned [two mills] to Abbess Eadgifu ... in exchange for the watercourse which he, with the king's permission, has diverted into the New Minster, and which formerly belonged to the community of nuns – and the diversion ruined a certain mill of theirs – and he has granted to the king in acknowledgement 120 mancusses of red gold ... in return for the land through which the water flows.

The dispute raged over access to running water. Compensation and exchange of gifts had to be arranged by the king, literally 'for the sake of peace and conciliation' (*to sibbe and to sóme*).

THE SCHOOL OF WINCHESTER

Æthelwold's work as a teacher and literary scholar at Winchester cannot be underestimated. He brought his school and literary projects with him from Abingdon, and he seems to have been the catalyst for a minor renaissance. The city became a powerhouse of spirituality and education; there was a Winchester School, which specialised in Latin literature, Old English writing and the arts, especially sculpture, architecture, manuscript drawing and painting. From the late 960s, then, as well as being a centre for royal government, Winchester became also a force for cultural renewal.

Much of this must come down to the personality of the chief player. This is Wulfstan's report on Æthelwold's style of teaching:

> Dulce namque erat ei adolescentes et iuuenes semper docere, et Latinos libros Anglice eis solvere, et regulas grammaticae artis ac metricae rationis tradere, et iocundis alloquiis ad meliora hortari. Unde factum est ut perplures ex discipulis eius fierent sacerdotes atque abbates et honorabiles episcopi, quidam etiam archiepiscopi, in gente Anglorum (ch. 31).

> [It was always agreeable to him to teach young men and the more mature students, translating Latin texts into English for them, passing on the rules of grammar and metric, and encouraging them to do better by cheerful words. Many of his pupils accordingly became priests, abbots, and notable bishops, some even archbishops, in England (trans. Lapidge and Winterbottom).]

The emphasis on the use of the mother tongue should be highlighted here; this was a centre for the teaching of Latin grammar and poetry, but it was also a place where the mother tongue was taught. Long before the

Figure 15b   King Edgar's New Minster Charter

founding of Winchester College, there was probably a 'Winchester accent', and arguably a kind of Standard English was promoted at the school. Certainly Old English, which had many dialects, went through a process of standardisation in this period. As it is spoken in the present day, Standard English originates in the variety of English used in the East Midland triangle formed by London, Oxford and Cambridge. In the Anglo-Saxon period, on the other hand, the standard was based on the West Saxon pronunciation and spelling. But what Æthelwold and his Winchester School further achieved was a standardised vocabulary, so that the written vernacular as used by many Old English writers in the late tenth century onwards contained certain preferred 'Winchester words' such as *modignes* (pride), *miht* (virtue), *gerihtlæcan* (to emend) where Old English writers elsewhere used other words such as *oferhygd, mægen, gerihtan.*[7]

As a writer, Æthelwold wrote in both Latin and in Old English, often with a practical purpose. He began probably at Glastonbury with the glossing of the psalter, a work of fine, meticulous scholarship. At this stage also, or perhaps at Abingdon, he completed his translation of the Benedictine Rule into English, which he then issued after his appointment at Winchester.[8] The Old English preface, nowadays entitled 'Edgar's Establishment of the Monasteries', gives an impression of Æthelwold's written English:

Æfter his forðsiþe Eadgar, se foresæda cynincg, þurh Godes gyfe ealne Angelcynnes anweald begeat and þæs rices twislunge eft to annesse brohte, and swa gesundlice ealles weold þæt þa þe on æran timan lifes węron and his hyldran gemundon and heora dæda gefyrn tocneowan, þearle swiþe wundredon and wafiende cwædon: Hit is la formicel Godes wunder þæt þysum cildgeongum cynincge þus gesundfullice eallu þing underþeodde synt on his cynelicum anwealde; his foregengan, þe geþungene wæron on ylde and on gleawscype swiþe bescawede and forewittige, and on ænegum gewinne earfoþwylde, næfre þisne andweald on swa micelre sibbe smyltnesse gehealdan ne mihton, naþor ne mid gefeohte, ne mid scette.[9]

[After his [brother's] death Edgar, the aforesaid king, obtained by God's grace the whole dominion of England, and brought back to unity the divisions of the kingdom, and ruled everything so prosperously that those who had lived in earlier reigns and remembered his predecessors and had known their former actions, wondered very greatly and said in amazement: 'It is indeed a very great miracle of God that all things in his royal dominion are thus prosperously subjected to this youthful king; his predecessors, who were mature in age and very prudent and far-seeing in wisdom and hard to overcome in any strife, never could maintain this dominion [*anweald*] in so great peace and tranquility, neither by battle nor by tribute.']

The use of reported speech to present a point of view recalls the Alfredian preface to the *Pastoral Care*, which may well be a consciously used source. This is a fairly complex style, sometimes spiced with unusual vocabulary such as the compound *cild-geong* 'child-young' for 'youthful', and adorned with alliterative phrases such as *on swa micelre sibbe smyltnesse*, literally 'in such great smoothness of peace', a phrase that anticipates the 'smoooth-faced peace' of Richmond's final speech in Act V, Scene 5, of Shakespeare's *Richard III*:

> And let their heirs, God, if thy will be so,
> Enrich the time to come with smooth-faced peace,
> With smiling plenty and fair prosperous days!

In terms of theme, the highlights of this passage are unity, dominion and peace, all keynotes in the polity of Edgar's England.

As for Æthelwold's Latin, there is evidence of a clear practical style in the book called the *Monastic Agreement*, Latin title *Regularis Concordia*, which was an attempt to regulate the practices in all the English monasteries. It is by no means a literary work, but it expresses well the ideology of its time. The devotion to the Psalms as a text for meditation as well as for the daily liturgy of the church services is noteworthy, as is the provision for prayers for the king and queen, and the emphasis once again on unity of practice in a unified nation. One additional attraction for historians is the information it provides on monastic customs, and there are many minor details that illustrate the life of the time, showing glimpses of how the monks who produced all this art and literature actually lived and worked. Here for example is the passage on the 'warming room', showing at once Æthelwold's concern for his students, and illustrating at the same time the style of his Latin:

> In huius quoque hiemis tempore propter nimiam imbrium asperitatem locus aptus fratribus designetur, cuius cacumenae refugio hibernalis algoris et intemperiei aduersitas leuigetur; si autem temperies tranquilla fuerit claustro, uti libuerit, cum Christi benedictio utantur.
>
> [Thus in winter, when storms are harsh and bitter, a suitable room shall be set aside for the brethren wherein, by the fireside, they may take refuge from the cold and bad weather. When, however, the weather is fair, they shall be free to use the cloister with Christ's blessing.][10]

The one difficult 'Hermeneutic' word here is *cacumenae*, explained by the later Old English interlinear glossed version of this text, where this building is called a *fyr-hus*, literally a 'firehouse',[11] a special building for the use of the monks when reading and writing in winter. It must have been a kind of small hall with a hearth in the middle of the floor, and a louver in the roof, the usual building style of the period. Benedictine monasticism came originally from a warm climate, but at Winchester the requirement to read and write in the cloister would otherwise have been impossible to keep in the middle of the winter. In short, Æthelwold spared no cost to encourage fine scribes, calligraphy and visual arts, fine metalwork, sculpture and architecture, and a considerable number of identifiable writers were working in Winchester at this time.

LANTFRED OF FLEURY

All this was the general situation in Æthelwold's Winchester when Lantfred arrived there in the 960s. The name Lantfred itself is in a western Frankish spelling, and most likely he was the Frankish (i.e. French) monk from the monastery of Fleury on the Loire who signs himself 'L.' in an extant letter to the abbot of Abingdon. His mother tongue must have been French: as Lapidge points out, it occasionally gives him away when he writes Latin, for example at one point he writes *senior* for Lord as in French *seigneur*, rather than Latin *dominus*. The verb *reposer* in Old French, to give another example, means 'to rest', and Lantfred on this model coins his own Latin verb *repausare*, 'to lay at rest', used in Chapter 29 of his work.[12] But I would add to this that Lantfred also must have learned Old English: with only one exception the place-names are spelt in decent, correct Old English. Moreover, the content of the work indicates a man who knew how to communicate with the locals.

One characteristic of his work is the huge number of dialogues and conversations that he records from among the ordinary people of the city. Many of these dialogues have an authentic ring to them, as though they are a record of actual conversations, and their language is less ornate than the 'Hermeneutic' style used for the main narrative itself. It seems that Lantfred lived and worked at Winchester for a number of years, and learned Old English while he was there; probably his official role was advising the Benedictine Reformers and giving them guidance on monastic practices, but he was clearly acquainted with a large number of people in the locality. As Chapter 35 demonstrates, Lantfred knew Bishop Æthelwold and the other monks, for it is from the bishop himself that he hears the story of the nobleman on the Isle of Wight who has a vision of the saint and is cured of paralysis. But Lantfred does not stay confined to the monastic quarter. Unlike the Winchester monks, who according to the New Minster Charter of 964 were exhorted not to dine or fraternise with the citizens, Lantfred had the freedom of an investigative journalist to explore the city as he wished, and to talk to whoever he liked.

The result was his *Translatio et Miracula S. Swithuni*, which follows the usual literary models for 'translation accounts', but also adapts them to the particular task in hand.[13] As a monk of Fleury, Lantfred must have known the stories of how Benedict's body was 'translated' to Fleury from Monte Cassino in Italy during the Langobard invasions.[14] He must also have known the classic account of a 'translation': the traditional story of the finding of the relics of St Stephen, as told by Lucian the Deacon in Greek in the year 415.

This Greek account was subsequently rendered into Latin by Avitus, a priest at Braga in Spain. In that text the saint appears to the author in a dream:

> ... while I was lying awake, as in a sort of ecstasy, I saw approaching me an aged man, tall in height with a pleasant face and a long beard, dressed in shining clothes, vested in a cloak, on the top of which were woven golden crosses (and he held in his hand a golden rod), wearing shoes which were gilded on the surface.[15]

Lucian's dream vision leads to the *inventio*, i.e. the discovery of the relics and then their translation to a more fitting location. Similarly there is an *inventio* in Lantfred's account, but here it becomes a three-year period of rediscovery told in the first three chapters, in which the saint appears to various people in visions. And in each vision, a citizen from a different walk of life is involved in the finding of St Swithun: a smith, a moneyer, an owner of mules out on pasture land outside the city. It is Lantfred's choice of witnesses that make his work differ in interesting ways from the more standard writings of the genre.

Only after the events of these three chapters is Swithun's sanctity proven. Oddly, the ceremony of the translation is mentioned but not described by Lantfred. Apparently he was absent from the city at this period in the narrative. This discrepancy, like the absence of Æthelwold from most of the action, is another of the puzzling features of the text. This is a 'translation account' without a translation. Lantfred seems more interested in stories and experiences of the local citizens than he is in the grander events of his grand narrative.

The structure of the rest of the work confirms this impression. As the story continues Lantfred maintains his intense interest in the citizens of Winchester and the region. While the first three chapters relate the *inventio*, we now have thirty-seven chapters to cover the *miracula*, all the miracles that take place once Swithun is firmly established within the walls of the Old Minster. And a huge range of people are involved, at all levels of society, from the slave up to the ealdorman. They include a bell-founder, a stolen slave-girl, a lady land-owner, a servant, a merchant, the

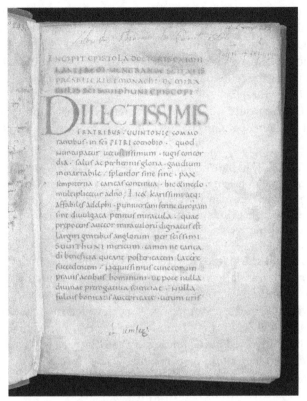

Figure 15c   Lantfred's *Translation and Miracles of St Swithun*

son of an ealdorman, the king's reeve, Bishop Æthelwold (a rare appearance of the bishop in Lantfred's story), a washerwoman, a slave; various outsiders or foreigners in the Isle of Wight, London, Rochester, Rome, France. Many of these chapters are brief reports of about a half a page in length; but about seven are substantial episodes or short stories on the same scale as the first three chapters, with description, narration and dialogue used to tell the tale to good effect. A select few examples of these stories now follow.

THE SMITH (LANTFRED, CH. 1)

In the first chapter recounting the *inventio*, i.e. the finding or discovery of the saint, there is a smith, perhaps an unusual choice, for rather than appearing immediately to the *writer*, as in Lucian's account, or to one of Lantfred's fellow monks, the man in white appears instead to an outsider figure, a *faber* or smith (p. 260, line 14), in this case Lantfred vouching for the smith's repectability, for the vision comes, he says, *cuipiam ueredico opifici*, 'to a certain trustworthy smith'. It is not clear where exactly in Winchester this particular smithy was situated, for no doubt there were many smiths active in the city. According to the survey now preserved in the Winton Domesday, a certain goldsmith or *aurifaber* was living in the reign of Edward the Confessor on Scowrtenestret ('Street of the Shoemakers', later Jewry Street), while another smith or *faber* had his residence outside the West Gate of the city.[16] These, then, are possible locations for the events of this chapter. Perhaps while he was resting in a separate sleeping chamber adjacent to his smithy, the smith was granted his vision of the man in a white robe, who charged him with an errand.

The ensuing conversation sets the tone for the work. Touching him lightly three times on his head with his staff, Swithun asks the smith:

> 'Dormisne frater, an vigilas?'
>
> ['Are you asleep, brother, or are you awake?']

(The same question will recur in Chapters 2 and 3, for Lantfred employs the phrase as a running motif in his narrative, whenever a character has a vision of the mysterious saint.) The dialogue now proceeds as follows, not without some lively humour:

> He replied, 'I was asleep, my lord, until a short time ago; but after you entered my little abode, the heavy sleep departed from my eyes'.
>
> The holy bishop said to him: 'Do you know that certain canon, who was formerly expelled from the Old Minster together with others who were living in evil ways? So that you may recognise him clearly, his name is Eadsige.'
>
> The smith replied to the blessed bishop: 'I knew him at that time father; now however, I don't know where he is.'
>
> The bishop said to him, 'He is now living at Winchcombe?'
>
> The smith said: 'Milord father, why do you ask me about him, when you know him better than I ... ?

Despite the ironies and despite the comedy of the grumpy smith woken unexpectedly out of his sleep, the message is clear – this is a waking vision granted to the smith – and he will need to takes its import seriously: Swithun, who had been buried only in the churchyard, must be granted the greater honour of a splendid tomb within the sanctity of the Old Minster itself.

The added twist in the demands made upon the smith is that another witness is to be involved; the smith is required to seek out the expelled canon Eadsige, who has managed to find some kind of living at nearby Winchcombe. Ironically, of course, Eadsige would appear to be the least obvious choice of recipient for such a message. And it is clear that Eadsige had a grudge to bear against Æthelwold, now established as bishop at the Old Minster, for this abrupt and summary dismissal. Now – in the mysterious vision – the man in white requires of the smith that he take his message to Eadsige.

The smith, who does not even know Eadsige personally, is reluctant to go to 'an important secular canon' as the narrator calls him earlier in the account, but above all the smith fears that no one will believe him. Yet the man in white who has appeared to him seems to be aware of his difficulty, for he promises him a sign. As described, the sign bears a faint resemblance to the legend of the young Arthur drawing the mysterious sword out of the stone at Canterbury Cathedral, as told in the fifteenth-century *Morte Darthur* by Thomas Malory. Eadsige is to go to Swithun's tomb in the churchyard of the Old Minster at Winchester and attempt to pull a metal ring out of the stone slab (apparently there were six iron rings fixed to the lid of the sarcophagus). If Eadsige follows these directions successfully, then he will be reassured of the authenticity of the message.

A little confusingly, events turn out differently to what was predicted. The smith now tries the test for himself, and rather unexpectedly he succeeds. So Eadsige never has a chance to try the test, for the smith passes on the message to him via a tenant farmer from Winchcombe whom he encounters making purchases on the market street in Winchester (the *forum* or market street here provides an authenticating link to the city in which these events unfold). Lantfred now hears at second hand what happened next, for the farmer is likewise hesitant, and reluctant to pass on the news:

> Much goaded by his conscience, he went to his lord, and explained to him from the beginning everything he had heard from the smith. His lord, being disgusted at the time not only with the bishop of Winchester cathedral but also with the monks living there, because of the expulsion of the canons who had been practising evil and impure customs – on account of which the venerable bishop Æthelwold, not without God's assent and with the support of glorious king Edgar, expelled them from the

aforementioned monastery and introduced holy monks in their stead –
rather than wishing to fulfil the requests of the holy father, refused to listen
to them. Later, however, when the course of nearly two years had run …
this same cleric who recently had been secular, abandoned the vanities,
prides and pleasures of this earthly life and became a devout monk much
beloved of God.

In an aside, Lantfred claims to have heard directly from the smith
himself 'that these things had happened exactly as the little book
describes'.[17] It is less clear, however, whether Lantfred ever spoke to
Eadsige, and the impression given is that he did *not*.

THE STOLEN SLAVE-GIRL (LANTFRED, CH. 20)

Eadsige has one more cameo appearance in the *Translation and Miracles
of St Swithun*, and it has to be said that he does not appear in a better
light here, despite his reconciliation with the monks, his conversion to
the monastic life and his appointment as sacristan in the Old Minster.
In this scene he appears as an authoritarian figure in a rather
disrespectful bickering dialogue that takes place at the new shrine of St
Swithun in the Old Minster. Some details of the narrative on this
occasion show that the Old Minster at this stage was still a small two-
cell building, and that the reported miracle took place before King
Edgar had had a new elaborate reliquary constructed in the years
972–4. Swithun's shrine must have been in a small precinct in the
chancel of the church and separated from the crowds in the nave by
some kind of barrier with elaborate locks.

Rather like the beginning of the History of Sunbury, which we
explored in the previous chapter, the beginning of this narrative also
concerns a stolen woman.[18] The protagonist in Lantfred's Chapter 20 is a
slave-girl (*servula* or *famula*) abducted from her master in the north of
England *ab avidis mangonibus* 'by greedy slave-traders' (as elsewhere,
Lantfred is quick to lay the blame on perpetrators of injustice) and sold
to new owners in Winchester. And as in Lantfred's story of the smith, the
High Street or market area becomes once again the scene of a chance
encounter. For it happens one day that the young woman's previous
master arrives in Winchester, for the same reason as the tenant-farmer in
the story of the smith, to make some necessary purchases, and when the
slave-girl hears of his presence she hurries to speak with him (no doubt
she wants to return to his service).

Enraged at this development, her new mistress has her legs bound in shackles, and when she goes out on business the next day leaves the young woman at home in this pitiful condition. The girl however manages to drag herself to the door of the house and prays for her release, turning towards the *templum*, as the Old Minster is here designated, which presumably was visible next to the New Minster from many points in the city. Immediately her prayer is answered: a prelate with white hair and bright garments suddenly approaches speaking kindly, takes her by the hand and transports her *in pungentis ictu*, 'in a split second', with her feet still bound, to the locked precinct in the Old Minster.

Now the sacristan Eadsige, who has just locked the door, is astonished to see the girl in the forbidden area (pp. 304–5):

> He approached the small door of the sanctuary and said to her so the people could hear: 'Tell me, woman, who put you inside this holy sanctuary, where now you are seen to stand? (*Quis te, fare, mulier, intra venerandum – quo nunc stare videris – introduxit locellum?*) On the strength of what audacity have you presumed to enter this enclosure, where Christ's bishop lies in the body? How on earth were you able to hide, since I didn't see you at all when I shut the door?'

The resourceful if rather mendacious slave girl, now sees a young cleric called Eadwold (he is later recorded as a becoming a priest at the Old Minster), who is standing outside the barrier. Much to his horror, the girl boldly declares that Eadwold brought her there:

> 'This cleric lifted me up on his shoulders – although I was struggling – and carried me to this place, and now has deposited me in front of the saint.'
>   Eadwold replied to the contrary, swearing an oath: 'I have never set eyes on you before!'
>   The woman said: 'It was indeed you who brought me here.'
>   The cleric replied: 'I would rather that the hounds of the night had torn you apart with their dreadful teeth, than that I would put so deceitful a burden on my back!'

The slave-girl now explains herself satisfactorily to Eadsige. She is believed by the crowds present 'from various parts of England' (*ex diversis partibus Anglorum*), and the miracle is proclaimed. The anecdote ends, as such anecdotes often do, with loose ends and details left unexplained. The casual reference to the crowds in Winchester and to the diversity of the English kingdom in the 970s adds a certain political edge to the story as here told.

THE MERCHANT, THE SLAVE AND THE ORDEAL (LANTFRED, CH. 25)

The presence of markets and merchants in the city has already been noted – it is a sign of the growing importance of towns and trade in the later tenth century. In his Chapter 25, Lantfred introduces one such *negotiator* or merchant by the name of *Flodoald*, which is a distinctly un-English name, as has been pointed out.[19] Flodoald, who pointedly is *in rebus prudens secularibus, plurimis habundans optibus*, 'wise in worldly affairs and very rich', has a slave, whom he holds in some affection, and who becomes in this case a similarly oppressed individual to the slave girl in the previous anecdote. And in this instance, the slave falls foul not only to the age-old requirements of the Anglo-Saxon ordeal (a distinctly magical way of dealing with proof of guilt or innocence) but also of the new harsh laws that royal government at this time was imposing on the populace:

> Is pro quodam facinore comprehensus a regis preside – qui solito vocabatur Eadric æt Calne – iussus est a regalibus custodiri clientibus donec eius veniret dominus, et ignitum carbonibus ferrum nudis minibus idem portaret protinus. Et si foret inculpabilis, relinqueretur incolomis; sin culpabilis inveniretur, capite plecteretur.[20]

> [This slave was apprehended by the king's reeve (who was called Eadric of Calne) because of a certain misdeed, and was ordered to be detained by royal thegns until his lord could come and until the slave would carry in his hand, without hesitation, an iron bar made red-hot by coals.]

The procedure for the ordeal here described can be elaborated from other accounts. The slave will probably have to fast for three days on bread, water and vegetables, hearing mass every day from a priest. On the day of the ordeal itself he will swear an oath that he is innocent of the charge made against him, hear mass, drink and sprinkle his hand with holy water.[21] He will then carry the red hot bar for a stipulated distance of nine feet. After that his hand is bound and three days later inspected by the supervisers; if it is healed he can go free, if not, he will be declared guilty. Again the details of the narrative lend some authenticity to the narrative; this is not all fiction, for Lantfred's data can be corroborated from other sources.

A few background features of this story may be noted in passing. First there is the name of the king's reeve who has arrested the slave: it is given in Old English as *Eadric æt Calne*, and as Lapidge shows, the name is found elsewhere. Probably he is the Eadric who witnesses royal charters for the year 966 to 970. Calne itself is significant, for the documents record it as a royal estate, and the Anglo-Saxon Chronicle (versions D and E) records a singularly disastrous meeting of the *witan* there in 978, when the upper story of the building tragically collapsed during the meeting of the assembly (the fact there was an upper storey is more evidence of the new building technology of the period). Dunstan himself was present, but survived unhurt because he was standing on one of the cross-beams. Whether Eadric was present is not actually known, but it is clear from Lantfred's account that Eadric in the 970s was an important royal agent, who was unwilling to be liberal or lenient. The capital punishment awaiting the slave if found guilty is the other very large point to be made as the story unfolds. This is an example of Edgar's law of great severity in action.

In particular, returning to the details of the plot, we may notice again, as in other chapters of his work, Lantfred's leniency, the fact that he omits to mention what crime the slave is accused of, stating merely that it is 'some misdeed' (*quodam facinore*). Instead, Lantfred's opprobrium falls on the machinery of the law: he criticises the detention of the slave 'in chains under cruel custody', he deplores the character of the royal reeve himself: both his pride 'exulting overmuch in his secular authority' and his stubbornness in persisting with the unjust charge and the judicial action, despite the merchant's promises to pay compensation for the alleged crime.[22] There also seems to be some kind of honour at stake in this confrontation between foreign merchant and English royal official, with Flodoald offering 'a pound of pure silver' and begging Eadric to drop the charges 'since he could not suffer the embarrassment of so great a disgrace, namely, that his slave should be executed for a trivial crime and offence' (p. 311). No direct speech or dialogue exchanges are given in this particular chapter, but Lantfred neverthelesss dwells on the anguished emotions of the accused party and his supporters.

In the end a miracle takes place, and Lantfred alludes to Psalm 29: 12, *convertisti planctum meum in gaudium*, 'thou hast turned my sorrow to joy', to express the relief of Flodoald and his friends. Surprisingly, despite the visible swellings on the slave's hand when the bandage is removed on the third day, the oblivious Eadric and his retinue fail to see them and declare the slave guiltless of the charges. In return for this unexpected result, and honouring the prayer to Swithun that he had prayed, Flodoald gives his beloved slave into the service of St Swithun at the Old Minster. Which is presumably how the account of the case eventually reached the ears of Lantfred.

LANTFRED AS SOCIAL CRITIC

From a political perspective there is a major discrepancy in the miracle stories which now ensue. Eight of the anecdotes concern miracles in which Swithun helps criminals, even convicted criminals. This may reflect the tradition of Frankish hagiography in which Lantfred has been schooled. Nevertheless it seems that Swithun the saint is a more kindly figure than the agents of royal justice, more willing to forgive, or to put right miscarriages of justice.

In some of the stories, the person cured is not sick but injured by judicial punishments, by the ordeal, or by mutilation and torture. King Edgar was called Edgar the Peacemaker, but there is an element of severity in some of the laws and punishments attributed to him. He kept the peace by terrifying his subjects with the threat of judicial violence. As both Lantfred and Wulfstan affirm, the king's purpose was a deterrent. But, as well as his story of the ordeal, Lantfred relates a case of unjust arrest and mutilation (ch. 26) and a verdict of capital punishment for a minor crime of accepting some wheat from the king's reapers (ch. 27). In both cases Lantfred is openly critical of the king's men and he is clearly on the side of those who suffer appalling punishments at their hands.

Now Lantfred is a foreigner from the monastery of Fleury, and we do not know his personal views on the draconian manner in which the Reform was first carried out – the expulsion of the clerics. It raises questions. Did Lantfred approve of monastic bishops? Did Lantfred perhaps help to effect the reconciliation between the reformers and some of the clerics? And what about unjustly tortured citizens? Did Lantfred disapprove of these measures of royal justice? Or was he reflecting the popular views and feelings of the people of Winchester? The other point is the choice of Swithun as the new patron saint. Was it really a choice? It looks like the reformers did not have any say as to who their new patron saint was going to be. Hagiography, like other kinds of literature, is a difficult genre to place under political control – it is elusive and evasive, and it offers other views on the politics and culture of the period.

LOOKING BACK WITH HINDSIGHT ON LANTFRED'S STORY

There is a coda to this story. Lantfred wrote his *Translatio et Miraculi* in the 970s, at the height of Edgar's reign. Then, in the 990s, two Winchester writers rewrote the story, both looking back with some nostalgia. Ælfric, a monk and priest of the abbey at Cerne Abbas, who had trained at Winchester, wrote an Old English version intended for oral delivery as a homily or sermon; his piece is much shorter, and he selects judicially from the writings of Lantfred, who he calls *se ofersœwisca*, 'the man from overseas'.[23] Notably, Ælfric omits mention of any miracles experienced by condemned criminals. At about the same time, Ælfric's contemporary Wulfstan Cantor also took up his pen and wrote *Narratio Metrica de S. Swithuno*, a poetic version of the same narrative.[24] It is clear from the changes he makes to Lantfred's message that Wulfstan is of the same persuasion in his praise of King Edgar's harsh deterrents to preserve law and order.

The point becomes obvious if one looks at the relevant passages in the story of the innocent man accused of theft and condemned to judicial mutilation. It will be seen that where Lantfred criticises the 'law of great severity' and castigates the king's men as criminals for this miscarriage of justice (ch. 26), Wulfstan, by contrast, sees the general benefits of this 'law' (there is no pejorative adjective attached to it) for the preservation of peace and the prevention of crime:[25]

> And terror seized all hearts with trepidation: the loathsome congress of thieves was eradicated so that, in the end, a mother could go by the winding by-roads with her children in peace of mind, without any danger, from the bounds of the eastern sea until she reached the shores of the western coast.

There is an echo of Bede here, of his account of law and order in the reign of Edwin of Northumbria, one of the seven overlords, or *bretwaldas*, discussed in Chapter 5 above. Wulfstan Cantor implies that Edgar is also a 'wide ruler', who has learnt a beneficial lesson from the history of the nation.

INTERLUDE V

The Poem *The Coronation of Edgar*

Her Eadgar wæs,   Engla waldend,
corðre micelre   to cyninge gehalgod
on ðære ealdan byrig,   Acemannesceastre;
eac hi igbuend   oðre worde
beornas Baðan nemnaþ.   Þær wæs blis micel
on þam eadgan dæge   eallum geworden,
þonne niða bearn   nemnað and cigað
Pentecostenes dæg.   Þær wæs preosta heap,
micel muneca ðreat,   mine gefrege,
gleawra gegaderod.   And ða agangen wæs
tyn hund wintra   geteled rimes
fram gebyrdtide   bremes cyninges,
leohta hyrdes,   buton ðær to lafe þa agan
wæs wintergeteles,   þæs ðe gewritu secgað,
seofon and twentig;   swa neah wæs sigora frean
ðusend aurnen,   ða þa ðis gelamp.
And him Eadmundes   eafora hæfde
nigon and twentig,   niðweorca heard,
wintra on worulde,   þa þis geworden wæs,
and þa on ðam þritigoðan wæs   ðeoden gehalgod.

[Here Edgar, ruler of the English,
In a great company was consecrated as king
in the ancient city of Akemanchester –
which the island-dwellers, the warriors,
also call by the other word Baths. There great joy
had come about for all people on that blessed day,
which children of men name and call
Pentecost Day. A crowd of priests was there,

a great multitude of monks, as I have heard,
of learned men gathered together. And by then had elapsed
ten hundred winters, as reckoned by counting,
since the time of the birth of the illustrious King,
the Keeper of the Lights, except that there still remained –
by counting the winters, as books declare –
seven and twenty. Thus for the Lord of Victories
nearly a thousand years had gone by when this event took place.
And the son of Edmund, fierce in deeds of war,
had lived nine-and-twenty winters in the world when this came about,
and then in the thirtieth was consecrated king.]

Figure 16a   The crowning of Edgar by Dunstan, in window of Bath Abbey

Epilogue

Edgar's second coronation in the year 973 at the old Roman city of Bath – at the time called either *Baðan* (literally 'Baths') or *Acemannesceastre* (Akemanchester) in the commemorative and celebratory poem – marks the theological and political highpoint of the tenth century (see Interlude V). Theologically, the consecration emphasised the sacerdotal role that kingship had assumed in recent decades as the English kingdom, in conjunction with the monastic reform movement, was strengthened and consolidated.[1] Politically, the crowning at Bath was the great display of imperial power for the south, for the heartland of the new England that had now come into being. The ceremony was matched by a similar if lesser ritual at the equivalent city in the north. Not York, as perhaps might have been expected, but Chester, on the borders with Wales. According to the Anglo-Saxon Chronicle, Edgar in the same year proceeded to Chester, where the Welsh kings, his allies on sea and land, rowed him along the broad waters of the Dee river and estuary as an act of homage. The northern versions of the Chronicle do not cite the panegyric poem about Bath, but they certainly note Edgar's presence in both regions of the country:

> Her wæs Eadgar æþeling gehalgod to cyninge on Pentecostenes mæssedæg on. v. Idus Maias, þy. xiii. geare þe he on rice feng, æt Hatabaþum, and he wæs þa ane wana. xxx. wintre. and sona æfter þam se cyning gelædde ealle his scipfyrde to Leiceastre, and þær him comon ongean. vi. cyningas, and ealle wið hine getreowsodon þæt hi woldon efenwyrhtan beon on sæ and on lande.[2]

> [Here Prince Edgar was consecrated as king on the Feast of Pentecost on the fifth of the Ides of May in the thirteenth year since he succeeded to the

kingdom, *æt Hatabaþum* 'at the Hot Baths'. And he was just thirty winters. And immediately thereafter he led his fleet to Chester and there six kings came to him, and they all pledged him that they would be his allies by sea and by land.]

The messages conveyed by Chronicle poem and Chronicle prose are clear. Edgar was an overlord of Britain, and a peacemaker, akin to those former kings celebrated by Bede in his *Ecclesiastical History*. Edgar was a lawmaker, and few it seemed dared to criticise his policies. Edgar was a patron of the arts, friend of Æthelwold and Dunstan, the leading intellectual figures of the age. Edgar was a monastic reformer, who encouraged the building of some forty monasteries across southern England in Wessex, parts of Mercia and East Anglia.

The choice of Bath for the coronation was appropriate as a former Roman city, known for its hot springs, comparable to Charlemagne's Roman-inspired capital at Aachen, broadly placed in the middle of the kingdom. Bath is mentioned in the *Life of St Dunstan* (34.2) as a monastic foundation, and its links to Flanders are possibly connected with Dunstan's stay in Ghent during his time of exile.[3] It is the scene of one of Dunstan's visions of heaven and the afterlife; here Dunstan's biographer B. breaks into English to give the form *Bathum* (cf. Baðan above), 'at the Baths', the popular vernacular name for the city:

> Erat namque uir uenerandus in amore Dei, ut diximus, semper accensus, et propterea loca sacrorum coenobiorum ob animarum aedificationem circuibat sollicitus. Venit etiam ex hac salubri consuetudine ad locum thermarum, ubi calida limpha de abissi latibulis guttatim uaporando ebullit, quem incolae locum sub paterna lingua Bathum soliti sunt appellare.

> [The venerable man, was, as I have said, always on fire with the love of God, and accordingly used to tour his holy monasteries sedulously for the edification of souls. Keeping up this excellent custom, he one day came to a place where there are hot springs, and hot water bubbles up steaming in droplets from the recesses of a chasm. The locals' name for this in their native tongue is Bath [*Bathum*, literally 'Baths'].]

Famously, the same city is celebrated in a vision of the glorious past at the end of the old poem *The Ruin*, in the Exeter Book; despite the fragmentary state of the manuscript, the key words stand out prominently on the page, including *þa baþu*, i.e. *tha bathu*, 'the baths':[4]

Stanhofu stodan, stream hate wearp
widan wylme; weal eall befeng

beorhtan bosme, þær þa baþu wæron,
hat on hreþre: þæt wæs hyðelic.
Leton þonne geotan
ofer harne stan hate streamas
un ...

... þþæt hringmere hate
þær þa baþu wæron.
þonne is
... re; þæt is cynelic þing,
huse ... burg...

[Stone buildings were standing; the flowing water threw out heat,
a wide surge, the wall entirely encompassed it
within its bright breast, where the baths [*tha bathu*] were,
hot to the core: that was convenient.
They let out the ...
hot stream then to gush over the grey stone
Un ...
... until the hot circular pool ...
... where the baths were.
Then it is ...
... ; that is a splendid thing
how the ... stronghold ...][5]

The last two ideas in the poem as it now stands are 'splendid thing', also
translatable as 'royal thing', and the by now familiar word *burg*,
'stronghold, fortification, borough, city'.

But this Exeter Book poem, likely a much older text than the
Chronicle poem *The Coronation of Edgar*, is not only a celebration of a
city; it is also an elegy that laments the passing of a former age:

Wondrous is this wall stone; disastrous events have shattered it;
The fortified cities have broken apart, the work of giants decays.
Roofs have fallen, towers are ruinous,
the ring gate is destroyed, frost is on the mortar,
the gaping protectors against storms are rent, have collapsed,
undermined by age.[6]

Almost certainly, however, by the time the scribe copied this old poem
into the Exeter Book in the 970s, the description of the ruins barely
corresponded to the actual appearance of the reconstructed city.

Figure 16b The Entry into Jerusalem, from the Benedictional of
St Æthelwold

The natural response of the monastic reformers to decayed splendour
had been to revive and rebuild it. Appropriately, the opening piece in the
Exeter Book picks up on this theme as it meditates on the theme of
advent and revival:

> You are the wall stone which long ago the workers rejected from the work.
> It is entirely fitting for you to be the head of the glorious hall and to join

together firmly the wide walls, indestructible flint stone, so that throughout the cities on earth all, with the sight of their eyes, may marvel forever. Lord of glory, steadfast in truth, victoriously radiant, skilfully reveal now your own work, and at once let wall join with wall.[7]

This text, usually called *Christ I*, though better known nowadays as the *Advent Lyrics*, is an Old English meditation on the Latin chants or antiphons sung in church after the Psalms in the liturgy for Advent. It is the most evidently monastic of the poems collected in the Exeter Book, and perhaps the most 'modern' and contemporary to the time when it was copied. As such, the *Advent Lyrics* make a suitable companion-piece to *The Coronation of Edgar*. Bath was a Benedictine foundation and literary community that would retain a defiant sense of its Englishness for another century or so until its dispersal at the time of the Norman Conquest.[8] It was a symbol of the new England, a city that had been rebuilt and reconstructed in the tenth century. Read together, the poems *The Coronation of Edgar*, *The Ruin* and *Advent Lyrics* make a fitting celebration of that achievement.

APPENDIX I

A dispute over land

The following edition provides a readable version of the text of 'The History of Sunbury' discussed in Chapter 14, with modern layout and punctuation. For the sake of clarity, the text is divided into sections and paragraphs, with explanatory sub-headings. The translation is sometimes free, in order to render the meaning, rather than always to give word-for-word translations of the legal terminology. Since all translation is interpretation, it is recommended that close attention is paid to the wording of the original Old English.

The beginning of the case

Se fruma wæs þæt mon forstæl ænne wimman æt Ieceslea Ælfsige Byrhsiges suna, Þurwif hatte se wimman. Þa befeng Ælfsige þone mann æt Wulfstane, Wulfgares fæder. Þa tymde Wulfstan hine to Æþelstane æt Sunnanbyrg, þa cende he tem, and let þone forberstan, and forbeh þone andagan.

[It all began with the theft of a woman, at Ixley, from Ælfsige, son of Byrhtsige; the woman's name was Thurwif. Then Ælfsige discovered his woman-servant in the possession of Wulfstan, Wulfgar's father. So Wulfstan declared the name of the previous owner to be Æthelstan of Sunbury, who accepted the declaration, but let it slide, and missed the day appointed for the oath of warranty.]

The compensation

Æfter þam bæd Ælfsige ægiftes his mannes, and he hine agef and forgeald him mid twam pundum, þa bæd Byrhferð ealdormann Æþelstan hys wer, for þam tembyrste, þa cwæð Æðelstan þæt he næfde him to syllanne.

Þa cleopode Eadweard Æðelstanes broðor, and cwæð: ic hæbbe Sunnanburges boc ðe uncre yldran me læfdon. Læt me þæt land to handa ic agife þinne wer ðam cynge.

Þa cwæð Æðelstan þæt him leofre wære þæt hit to fyre oððe flode gewurde, þonne he hit æfre gebide.

Ða cwæð Eadweard: hit is wyrse þæt uncer naðor hit næbbe.

Þa wæs þæt swa.

And forbead Byrhferð þæt land Æðelstane, and he of ferde and gebeh under Wulfgare æt Norðhealum.

[After that Ælfsige demanded the return of his servant, and Æthelstan returned her and paid him two pounds compensation, but Ealdorman Byrhtferth demanded that Æthelstan pay his *wergild* for failing the test of warranty.

But Æthelstan said that he had nothing to give him.

Then Edward, Æthelstan's brother, spoke out and said: 'I have the land-book for Sunbury, which our parents left to me. Hand the estate over to me, and I will give your *wergild* to the king.'

Then Æthelstan said that he would rather it went to fire or flood than ever allow that to happen.

To which Edward said, 'It is worse that neither of us should have it.'

But that was what happened.

And Byrhtferth confiscated the estate from Æthelstan, and he departed and entered the service of Wulfgar at North Hales.]

The reign of Edwy

Binnan ðam wendun gewyrda, and gewat Eadræd cyng, and feng Eadwig to rice, and wende Æðelstan hine eft into Sunnanbyrg, ungebetra þinga. Þa geahsode þæt Eadwig cyng, and gesealde þæt land Byrnrice, and he feng to, and wearp Æðelstan ut.

[In the meantime events changed, and Edred departed this life, and Edwy succeeded to the kingdom, and Æthelstan returned to Sunbury without having mended the matter. When King Edwy found out, he gave the estate to Byrnric, who took possession and evicted Æthelstan.]

The election of Edgar

Gemang þam getidde þæt Myrce gecuran Eadgar to cynge, and him anweald gesealdan ealra cynerihta. Þa gesohte Æðelstan Eadgar cyng and bæd domes. Þa ætdemdon him Myrcna witan land buton he his wer

agulde þam cynge swa he oðrum ær sceolde. Þa næfde he hwanon, ne he
hit Eadwearde his breðer geðafian nolde. Þa gesealde se cyng, and gebecte
þæt land Æðelstane ealdormenn, to hæbbenne, and to syllanne for life,
and for legere þam him leofost wære.

[Meanwhile it came about that the Mercians elected Edgar as king and
gave him all royal rights and authority. So Æthelstan petitioned King
Edgar and demanded justice. But the Mercian *witan* declared his land
forfeit unless he paid his *wergild* to the king just as he should have paid it
to the previous king. But he did not have the means to pay, nor would he
allow his brother Edward to pay it for him. So the king gave the land by
royal grant to Ealdorman Æthelstan, 'to be held, and to be granted, during
his lifetime or at his death, to anyone he pleased'.]

The case of Ecgferth

Æfter þam getidde þæt Ecgferð gebohte boc and land æt Æðelstane
ealdormenn, on cynges gewitnesse, and his witena swa his gemedo
wæron, hæfde and breac oð his ende, þa betæhte Ecgferð on halre tungan,
land and boc on cynges gewitnesse Dunstane arcebisceope to mundgenne
his lafe, and his bearne. Þa he geendod wæs þa rad se bisceop to þam
cynge myngude þære munde and his gewitnesse.

Þa cwæð se cyng him to andsware mine witan habbað ætrecð Ecgferðe
ealle his are, þurh þæt swyrd þe him on hype hangode þa he adranc. Nam
þa se cyng ða are þe he ahte twentig hyda æt Sendan tiene æt
Sunnanbyrg, and forgef Ælfhege ealdormenn. Þa bead se bisceop his wer
þam cynge.

Þa cwæð se cyng, þæt mihte beon geboden him wið clænum legere, ac
ic hæbbe ealle þa spæce to Ælfhege læten.

[After that it came about that Ecgferth bought both book and land from
Ealdorman Æthelstan, with the witness of the king and his *witan*, as was
his due, and he had it and used it until his end, whereupon he granted it,
as was his right, both land and book, with the witness of the king, to
Archbishop Dunstan, who was to act as guardian for his widow and
children. When Ecgferth's life was at an end, the bishop rode to the king
and reminded him of the guardianship and his witness to it.

Then the king said to him in reply: 'My *witan* have declared forfeit all
Ecgferth's property, by the sword that hung at his hip when he drowned.'
The king then took the property that he owned – twenty hides at Send
and ten at Sunbury, and granted it to Ealdorman Ælfheah.

Then the archbishop offered the king his *wergild*.

Then the king said: 'That might be offered in exchange for his
Christian burial, but I have left the whole case to Ælfheah.]

The resolution

Ðæs on syxtan gere gebohte se arcebisceop æt Ælfhege ealdormenn, þæt land æt Sendan, mid hundnigontig pundum, and æt Sunnanbyrg mid twam hunde mancussan goldes, unbecwedene, and unforbodene wið ælcne mann to þære dægtide, and he him swa þa land geagnian derr, swa him se sealde ðe to syllenne ahte, and hi þam se cyng sealde, swa hi him his witan gerehton.

[Six years later, the archbishop purchased – from Ealdorman Ælfheah – the estate at Send for ninety pounds and the estate at Sunbury for two hundred mancusses of gold, 'unopposed and uncontested by any man up to that day'. And so he dares to take possession of the estates just as he who gave them to him had them to give and as the king gave them to him, just as his *witan* had adjudged it.]

APPENDIX II

Passages from the Vercelli Book

VERCELLI, BIBLIOTECA CAPITOLARE, MANUSCRIPT CXVII

The Vercelli Book is an anthology of texts made by one compiler, perhaps over a period of time in the decade around the year 970, selecting and copying his or her material from different sources in order to make a personal collection of texts, like a commonplace book. The following select passages, adapted from the edition by Donald Scragg and the facsimile edited by Celia Sisam, and the edition of the poems by G.P. Krapp, are chosen for their relevance to the historical, political and literary themes covered in the present book.

From Vercelli V, fol. 25r

Swa sanctus Lucas se godspellere be þan wrat ond cwæð: In þa tiid wæs mycel gemot gebannen fram Aguste þam casere þætte gewriten wære eall ymbhwyrft middangeardes. Þæt gewrit wæs ærest ongunnen fram þære mægðe gerefan þe Syria hatte þæs mannes nama wæs Cyrinus. Ond þa eodon ealle anra gehwylc on his ceastre, þætte hie onfengon þam bebode þe þa gebannen wæs þætte æghwylc mann sceolde þam casere gaful gildan. Þa ferde se eadga Ioseph fram Galilea of þære ceastre þe Nazaret hatte to Dauides ceastre sio is nemned Bethlem, forþamþe he wæs Dauides cynnes, þætte hie þær sceoldon onfon þam bebode þæs gafoles þe þa gebannen wæs, mid Marian þe him wæs to wife beweddod; ond þa wæs hio bearneacenu of þam halgan gaste. Þa hie þa to Bethlem comon, wæron þa ða dagas gefylled þæt hio bearn cennan sceolde.

[Thus Saint Luke the gospel-writer wrote concerning this and said: At that time a great assembly was summoned by the Emperor Augustus that the whole extent of the world should be described. The description was first begun by the reeve of the region called Syria whose name was Cyrinus. And then everyone travelled, each to their own town, so that they could receive the decree that had been issued that every man should pay tribute to the emperor. At that time the blessed Joseph travelled from Galilee, from the town that was called Nazareth, to David's town, which is called Bethlehem, for he was of David's line, so that he should receive the decree [to pay] tribute which had been issued, with Mary to whom he was pledged; and at that time she was with child by the Holy Spirit. When they came to Bethlehem, the days were fulfilled that she should give birth to her child.]

From Vercelli V, fol. 26r

Manegu wundor gelumpon in Agustes rice þurh þa wundor wæs getacnod Cristes cyme on middangeard. Þæt wæs sum þara wundra þa se casere com to Rome mid sigefæste gefean ond mid blisse, ða æt þære ðriddan tide þæs dæges, þæt wæs æt underne, þa wæs mannum on heofonum gesine gyldnes hringes onlicnes ymbutan þa sunnan. Ond on þam hringe wæs getacnod þæt on his rice acenned wolde bion se æðeling se is rihtlice nemned soðfæstnesse sunna, þæt is þonne ure hælend Crist, þæt he mid his fægernesse gewlitgode þa sunnan þe us nu dæghwamlice lyhteð ond hie gesceop ond mid his mihte ealne middangeard receð ond styreð.

[Many marvels occurred in Augustus's kingdom, by which marvels Christ's coming on earth is signified. This was one of the marvels: that when Caesar came to Rome with joy of victory and celebration, then, at the third hour of the day, that is around mid-morning, men saw in the heavens the appearance of a golden ring around the sun. And by that ring was signified that in his kingdom the Prince would be born who is rightly called the Sun of Righteousness, that is our saviour Christ; that with his beauty he transfigured the sun which shines daily upon us now – which he created – and he rules and moves all this middle world with his power.]

From Vercelli V, fol. 26v

Ond in Agustes dagum wearð swa mycel sybb geworden on middangearde þæt men wæpn ne wægon, forþamþe he in sybbe wel gesette middangeardes rice, ond mid wisdomes cræfte sio sibb wæs geseted geond ealne middangeard. Ond he eac sende his cempan wide geond manega mægða þætte yfle men ne dorston nanwyht to teonan don for hyra egsan. In þære myclan sybbe wæs getacnod þære soðan sybbe cyme in middangeard, þæt wæs ure hælend Crist þe us gesybbode wið englum ond us geþingode wið Godfæder ond us to sybbe gelaðode, ond he swa cwæð: *Beati pacifici quoniam filii Dei uocabuntur.* Eadige bioð þa sybsuman men forþanþe hie bioð Godes bearn genemnde.

[And in the days of Augustus so great a peace came about in the world that men carried no weapons, because he fully pacified the kingdom of the world, and with the art of wisdom that peace was established through all the world. And he also sent his warriors through many regions so that evil men did not dare do any harm for fear of them. In the great peace was signified the coming of true peace into the world, that was our saviour Christ who made peace between us and the angels and interceded for us with God the Father and summoned us to peace, and he spoke thus: '*Beati pacifici quoniam filii Dei uocabuntur.* Blessed are the men of peace for they will be called the children of God.']

Ðrim wisum ungelice wæron mannum beboden on þæs caseres dagum, þæt is þonne þæt æghwylc man sceolde gaful gildan, ond ealle men sceoldon hit gildan ge rice ge heane, ond ðam gafole mon ne onfeng æt ænegum men butan in his swæsum eðle. On þan wæs getacnod þæt we sculon in þrim wisum Gode rihtes geleafan gaful agildan, þæt is on wordum ond on geþohtum ond on dædum, ond God þam gafole ne onfehð butan on ussum swæsum eðle þæt is gehwæðer ge in þam inneran ge in þam utteran, þæt we mid inneweardre heortan ond mid eaðmodre in God gelyfen, ond þone geleafan mid godum weorcum gefyllen ond mid muþe ondettan.

[The decree was issued to men in the days of the Emperor in three different modes, that is that each man should pay tribute, and that all men both high and low should pay it, and that the tribute was received from no man except in his own native homeland. By this it was signified that we should pay God the tribute of true faith, that is in words, and in thoughts, and in deeds, and God will not receive that tribute except in our native homeland, that is both inwardly and outwardly, that we have faith in God with sincere and humble hearts, and fulfil that faith with good works and confess with our mouths.]

From Vercelli V, fol. 28v

Ac hergen we ond wuldrien urne Dryhten on clænum geðohtum ond on halgum wordum ond on soðfæstum weorcum ond on rihtum geleafan, forþanþe his miht is ufor þonne heofon ond bradre þonne eorðe ond deopre þonne sæ ond leohtre þonne heofones tungel.

[But let us praise and glorify our Lord in pure thoughts and in holy words and in faithful actions and in true beliefs, since his power is higher than heaven, wider than earth, deeper than the sea, brighter than the star in heaven.]

Andreas, lines 1–3b

Hwæt. We gefrunan   on fyrndagum
twelfe under tunglum   tireadige hæleð,
þeodnes þegnas.

[Listen. We have heard tell in distant days
of twelve gloriously blessed heroes here beneath the stars,
the Lord's thegns.]

Andreas, lines 7–11b

Þæt wæron mære   men ofer eorðan,
frome folctogan   ond fyrdhwate,
rofe rincas,   þonne rond ond hand
on herefelda   helm ealgodon,
on meotudwange.

[They were great men upon the earth,
bold leaders of the people, eager for the expedition,
brave men, when shield and hand
defended helmet at places of battle,
on the field of the ordaining Lord.]

Andreas, lines 1718–22

Is his miht ond his æht   ofer middangeard
breme gebledsod,   ond his blæd ofer eall
in heofonþrymme   halgum scineð,
wlitige on wuldre   to widan ealdre,
ece mid englum.   Þæt is æðele cyning.

[His power and possession over the world
is gloriously blessed, and his fame over all
in the heavenly host shines among the saints,
beautiful in its glory age upon age,
for ever and ever with the angels. That is a noble king.]

Dream of the Rood, lines 150–end

Se sunu wæs sigorfæst   on þam siðfate,
mihtig ond spedig,   þa he mid manigeo com,
gasta weorode,   on godes rice,
anwealda ælmihtig,   englum to blisse

ond eallum ðam halgum   þam þe on heofonum ær
wunedon on wuldre,   þa heora wealdend cwom,
ælmihtig god,   þær his eðel wæs.

[The son was victorious in that expedition
powerful and prosperous when he came with the multitude,
a troop of souls, into God's kingdom,
the one almighty Ruler, to the joy of the angels,
and of all the saints who were in heaven before,
who dwelled in glory, when their Ruler came,
almighty God, to where his native-land was.]

Notes

INTRODUCTION   HELMET AND CROWN

1. See Martin Carver, *Sutton Hoo: Burial Ground of Kings?* (London, 2000) and the full archaeological report in his *Sutton Hoo: A Seventh-Century Princely Burial Ground and its Context* (London, 2005).
2. For a critical discussion, try Roberta Frank, '*Beowulf* and Sutton Hoo: The Odd Couple', in Catherine E. Karkov, ed., *The Archaeology of Anglo-Saxon England: Basic Readings* (New York, 1999), pp. 317–38.
3. Michael Alexander, trans., *Beowulf* (Harmondsworth, 1973); for the text see George Jack, ed., *Beowulf: A Student Edition* (Oxford, 1994).
4. For an overview of the Anglo-Saxon period, see Henrietta Leyser, *A Short History of the Anglo-Saxons* (London, 2016).
5. N.P. Brooks, 'Arms and Armour', in Michael Lapidge, *et al.*, *The Wiley-Blackwell Encyclopedia of Anglo-Saxon England*, 2nd edition (Oxford, 2014).
6. For the original text see Donald Scragg, ed., *The Vercelli Homilies and Related Texts*, Early English Text Society, original series 300 (London, 1992), p. 28, lines 145–6.
7. Catherine E. Karkov, *The Ruler Portraits of Anglo-Saxon England* (Woodbridge, 2004).
8. George Garnett, 'Coronation', in Lapidge, *et al.*, *The Wiley-Blackwell Encyclopedia of Anglo-Saxon England*. Janet L. Nelson, *Politics and Ritual in Early Medieval Europe* (London, 1986).
9. Rather paradoxically, English identity is sometimes assumed to begin with the Norman Conquest; see, for example, Antony Easthope, *Englishness and National Culture* (London, 1999), p. 26. Other studies begin their story much later. Examples include Simon Featherstone, *Englishness: Twentieth-Century Popular Culture and the Forming of English Identity* (Edinburgh, 2009); for nineteenth-century ideas and their influence on English-speaking countries today, see Robert J.C. Young, *The Idea of English Ethnicity* (Malden, MA and Oxford, 2008).
10. James Campbell, 'What is not known about the reign of Edward the Elder', in N.J. Higham and D.H. Hill, eds, *Edward the Elder, 899–924* (London, 2001), pp. 12–24.
11. Nicholas Brooks, *The Early History of the Church of Canterbury: Christ Church from 597 to 1066* (Leicester, 1984), p. 244.
12. The manuscript Tiberius A.iii is a compendium of monastic writings, containing as its main text a copy of the *Regularis Concordia* or Monastic Agreement composed in the year 970; for discussion of the monastic reform, see Chapter 15 below.

CHAPTER 1 'THE ITALIAN JOURNEY'

1. The etymology and interpretation of *Beo-wulf* as 'bear' was first argued in any detail by Henry Sweet, 'Old English Etymologies', *Englische Studien*, II (1879), 312–16. This was then pursued by Walter Skeat, 'On the Signification of the Monster Grendel in the Poem of *Beowulf*: With a Discussion of Lines 2076–2100', *The Journal of Philology*, 15 (1886), 120–31. The connections between *Beowulf* and the folktale of 'The Bear's Son' was explored in Friedrich Panzer, *Studien zur germanischen Sagengeschichte, I: Beowulf* (Munich, 1910). See Andy Orchard, *Pride and Prodigies: Studies in the Monsters of the Beowulf Manuscript* (Toronto, 1995/2003), pp. 146–50. See also his *Critical Companion to Beowulf* (Toronto, 2003), pp. 120–1, n. 117, where the meaning of the name *Beowulf* is interpreted as 'the wolf of (the god) Beow'. For a critical review of the whole issue, and an argument for an etymology based on *beow*, 'barley', see R.D. Fulk, 'The Etymology and Significance of Beowulf's Name,' *Anglo-Saxon*, 1 (2007), 109–36.
2. For more examples of literary onomastics, see Fred C. Robinson, 'The Significance of Names in Old English Literature', and 'Personal Names in Medieval Narrative and the Name of Unferth in *Beowulf*', in his *The Tomb of Beowulf and Other Essays on Old English* (Cambridge, MA and Oxford, 1993), pp. 185–218 and 219–23.
3. Adelard, *Lections for the Deposition of St Dunstan*, Lection XII, in Michael Winterbottom and Michael Lapidge, eds, *The Early Lives of St Dunstan* (Oxford, 2012), pp. 142–3; William of Malmesbury, *Life of St Dunstan*, Book I, ch. 2.1 and ch. 27.5, in M. Winterbottom and R.M. Thomson, eds and trans., *William of Malmesbury: Saints' Lives* (Oxford, 2002), pp. 174–5, 228–9.
4. In actual fact, the name Æthelwold is a version of *æthel* + *weald* and means 'noble power'.
5. B.'s biography of Dunstan is edited with a parallel translation in Winterbottom and Lapidge, *The Early Lives of St Dunstan*, pp. 1–109.
6. For an example of a medical charm containing Irish in the *Lacnunga* collection, see G. Storms, ed., *Anglo-Saxon Magic* (The Hague, 1948), at p. 303.
7. Winterbottom and Lapidge, *Earliest Lives of St Dunstan*, pp. 20–5.
8. John B. Friedman, *The Monstrous Races in Medieval Art and Thought* (Syracuse, NY, 2000). The interest in monsters is very evident in the compilation of the *Beowulf* manuscript, which can be seen as a compendium of monster-related texts, including in its contents *The Wonders of the East*, a copy of which is found also in the Tiberius Miscellany, and the *Life of St Christopher*, which features a saint with a dog's head; for texts and discussion, see Orchard, *Pride and Prodigies*.
9. P. McGurk, D.N. Dumville, M.R. Godden and Ann Knock, eds, *An Eleventh-Century Anglo-Saxon Illustrated Miscellany*, British Library Cotton Tiberius B. v, Part I, Early English Manuscripts in Facsimile, 21 (Copenhagen, 1983), p. 25. The manuscript of the Tiberius Miscellany originally belonged to the antiquarian Sir Robert Cotton in the Reformation period. The shelfmarks in the Cotton collection were devised at a time when the library was filled with bookpresses serving as bookcases; the bust of a Roman emperor was located on top of each bookpress in the library: hence the name Tiberius marks the bookpress, and B. v the actual shelfmark.
10. The Tiberius *mappa mundi* can be viewed online, for instance at http://cartographi c-images.net/Cartographic_Images/210_The_Cottoniana_or_Anglo-Saxon_Map_ files/droppedImage.png. For the Hereford *mappa mundi* on display in Hereford Cathedral, see http://www.themappamundi.co.uk/.
11. Helen Appleton, 'The Northern World of the Anglo-Saxon *mappa mundi*' (forthcoming).

12. Nicole Guenther Discenza, 'A Map of the Universe: Geography and Cosmology in the Program of Alfred the Great', in Catherine Karkov and Nicholas Howe, eds, *Conversion and Colonization in Anglo-Saxon England* (Tempe, Arizona, 2006), pp. 83–108, at p. 87.
13. Nicholas Howe, *Writing the Map of Anglo-Saxon England* (New Haven and London, 2008).
14. Anglo-Saxon Chronicle, manuscript A, under the year 874. For a good translation, see Michael Swanton, *The Anglo-Saxon Chronicles* (London, 2000).
15. Wilhelm Levison, *England and the Continent in the Eighth Century* (Oxford, 1946), p. 41.
16. For the route home, see Veronica Ortenberg, 'Archbishop Sigeric's Journey to Rome', in the journal *Anglo-Saxon England*, 19 (1990), 197–246, at pp. 228–44. For the speed of the journey there are estimates in David A. Pelteret, 'Travel between England and Italy in the Early Middle Ages', in Hans Sauer and Joanna Story, eds, *Anglo-Saxon England and the Continent* (Tempe, Arizona, 2011), pp. 245–74, at p. 253.
17. The letter is printed in Steven Vanderputten, 'Canterbury and Flanders in the Late Tenth Century', *Anglo-Saxon England*, 35 (2006), 219–44.
18. Simon Keynes, 'Anglo-Saxon Entries in the *"Liber Vitae"* of Brescia', in Jane Roberts, Janet Nelson and Malcolm Godden, eds, *Alfred the Wise: Studies in Honour of Janet Bately* (Cambridge, 1997), pp. 99–119.
19. Keynes, 'Anglo-Saxon Entries', p. 114.
20. M. Halsall, 'Vercelli and the Vercelli Book', *Publications of the Modern Language Association of America*, 84 (1969), 154–7.
21. Donald Scragg, ed., *The Vercelli Homilies and Related Texts* (London, 1992). Elaine Treharne, ed., *Old and Middle English c.890–c.1450: An Anthology*, 3rd edition (Oxford, 2009); George Phillip Krapp, ed., *Vercelli Book* (New York, 1932); Samantha Zacher and Andy Orchard, eds, *New Readings in the Vercelli Book* (Toronto, 2009).
22. There is a discussion of this author's work in Andy Orchard, 'Both Style and Substance: The Case for Cynewulf', in Catherine E. Karkov and George Hardin Brown, eds, *Anglo-Saxon Styles* (Albany, NY, 2003), pp. 271–305.
23. Vercelli Homily IX, in Scragg, *Vercelli Homilies*. A whole monograph is devoted to its Hiberno-Latin sources; see Charles Wright, *The Irish Tradition in Old English Literature* (Cambridge, 1993).
24. Eamonn Ó'Carragáin, 'Rome, Ruthwell, Vercelli: "The Dream of the Rood" and the Italian Connection', in V.D. Corazza, ed., *Vercelli tra Oriente ed Occidente tra Tarda Antichità e Medioevo: atti delle Giornate di studio: Vercelli 10–11 aprile 1997, 24 novembre 1997* (Alessandria, 1997), pp. 59–99.
25. On the Kentish origins of the Vercelli Book, see Scragg, *Vercelli Homilies*, pp. lxxviii–lxxix.
26. Umberto Eco, *The Name of the Rose* (London, 1983). Eco, a specialist not only in semiotics and literary criticism but also in medieval cultural history, begins his novel with a preface where the modern-day narrator claims to have found a transcript of a medieval manuscript in which the story of murder and mystery is told by an eyewitness, a novice monk at the time of the events.
27. Oliver Bock, 'C. Maier's Use of a Reagent in the Vercelli Book', *The Library*, 16.3 (2015), 249–81.
28. L.A. Muinzer, 'Maier's Transcript and the Conclusion of Cynewulf's "Fates of the Apostles"', *Journal of English and Germanic Philology*, 56 (4) (1957), 570–87.
29. The importance of the discipline is traced in James Turner, *Philology: The Forgotten Origins of the Modern Humanities* (Princeton and Oxford, 2014). For a study of

Kemble and other philologists of Old English, see Haruko Momma, *From Philology to English Studies: Language and Culture in the Nineteenth Century* (Cambridge, 2013).

30. John Mitchell Kemble, ed., *The Poetry of the Codex Vercellensis* (London, 1843).

CHAPTER 2 'ON THE ROAD'

1. Ann Knock, 'Analysis of a Translator: The Old English *Wonders of the East*', in Jane Roberts, Janet Nelson and Malcolm Godden, eds, *Alfred the Wise: Studies in Honour of Janet Bately* (Cambridge, 1997), pp. 121–6.

2. McGurck *et al.*, *An Eleventh-Century Anglo-Saxon Illustrated Miscellany*. Nicholas Howe, *Writing the Map of Anglo-Saxon England* (New Haven and London, 2008), pp. 170–1.

3. For the text and translation of the Latin and Old English versions of *The Wonders of the East* see Andy Orchard, *Pride and Prodigies: Studies in the Monsters of the Beowulf Manuscript* (Toronto, 2003), pp. 175–203.

4. My translation. For the Latin text, and another translation, see Winterbottom and Lapidge, *Earliest Lives of St Dunstan*.

5. English pilgrims were attacked in the Alps in the year 921; see P. Lauer, *Les Annales de Flodoard* (Paris, 1905), pp. 5 and 19.

6. S.A.J. Bradley, *Anglo-Saxon Poetry* (London, 1982), p. 549.

7. Frank Barlow, ed. and trans., *The Life of King Edward who Rests at Westminster*, 2nd edition (Oxford, 1992), pp. 52–7.

8. Tostig is pronounced 'Tosti' and Godwine has three syllables, roughly 'God-winuh'. For histories of this powerful family see Emma Mason, *The House of Godwine: The History of a Dynasty* (London, 2003) and Frank Barlow, *The Godwins* (Harlow, 2002).

9. Barlow, *Life of King Edward*, pp. 52–7.

10. The age of King Offa, the builder of Offa's Dyke, is often referred to as the Mercian Supremacy or the Mercian Hegemony; see Nicholas J. Higham and Martin J. Ryan, *The Anglo-Saxon World* (New Haven and London, 2013), pp. 179–217.

11. Margaret Gelling and Ann Cole, *The Landscape of Place-names*, new edition (Donington, 2014), p. 65.

12. The estate bounds are discussed and illustrated with a map in Della Hooke, *Warwickshire Anglo-Saxon Charter Bounds* (Woodbridge, 1999). For further information on Anglo-Saxon charters and documents, see Peter Sawyer, *Anglo-Saxon Charters: An Annotated List and Bibliography* (London, 1968); Archbishop Oswald's document is no. 1350; Sawyer's *List* is now revised and updated as the Electronic Sawyer at http://www.esawyer.org.uk where the document can be located as S 1350.

13. The Roman road of Icknield Street starts at Bourton-on-the-Water in Gloucestershire and heads northwards through Bidford-on-Avon, Alcester, Studley, King's Norton, Birmingham, Lichfield, Derby and Chesterfield. The Fosse Way was even more direct, starting at Exeter in the south-west and proceeding in a notably straight line north-eastwards through Bath, Cirencester, Moreton-in-Marsh and then up to Lincoln.

14. George Jack, ed., *Beowulf: A Student Edition* (Oxford, 1994).

15. The *Beowulf* poet apparently knew a good deal about the Danish origins of the hall of Heorot in Lejre, where excavations have now uncovered a sixth-century hall. For discussion see John D. Niles and Marijane Osborn, eds, *Beowulf and Lejre* (Tempe AZ, 2007).

16. The anonymous 'Story of St Peter and St Paul', in Richard Morris, ed., *The Blickling Homilies* (London, 1880), pp. 171–93, at pp. 188–9.
17. *Andreas* is printed in G.P. Krapp, ed., *The Vercelli Book* (New York and London, 1932), pp. 3–51, and Mary Clayton, ed. and trans., *Old English Poems of Christ and his Saints* (Cambridge, MA and London, 2013), pp. 183–299.
18. Andy Orchard, *A Critical Companion to Beowulf* (Cambridge, 2003).
19. Kenneth Sisam, 'The Compilation of the *Beowulf* Manuscript', in his *Studies in the History of Old English Literature* (Oxford, 1953); Andy Orchard, *Pride and Prodigies: Studies in the Monsters of the Beowulf Manuscript* (Toronto, 1995).
20. Michael Alexander, trans., *Beowulf* (Harmondsworth, 1973), pp. 57–8; for the text see George Jack, ed., *Beowulf: A Student Edition* (Oxford, 1994).
21. J.R.R. Tolkien, trans., *Beowulf: A Translation and Commentary, together with Sellic Spell*, ed. Christopher Tolkien (London, 2014); Seamus Heaney, *Beowulf* (London, 2000).
22. The text of the story of Jonah is printed in Scragg, *Vercelli Homilies*, pp. 321–5.
23. S.A.J. Bradley, trans., *Anglo-Saxon Poetry* (London, 1982), p. 171; for the Old English text, see *Elene*, in Krapp, ed., *Vercelli Book*, lines 225–58. There is an edition with facing page translation in Robert E. Bjork, *The Old English Poems of Cynewulf* (Cambridge, MA and London, 2013), pp. 141–235.
24. These various literary texts in the Tiberius Miscellany may be found in the following editions. The Metrical calendar was edited by E. Hampson, *Medii Aevi Kalendarium I* (London, 1841), 393–420; also J. Hennig, 'A Critical Study of Hampson's Edition of the Metrical "Calendar" in Galba A. xviii', *Scriptorium*, 8 (1954), 61–74; now re-edited as P. McGurk, ed., 'The Metrical Calendar of Hampson: A New Edition', *Analecta Bollandiana*, 104 (1986), 79–125. For the Old English treatise on the seasons see Martin Blake, ed., *Ælfric's De temporibus anni* (Cambridge, 2009). Cicero's *Aratea* is edited in V. Buescu, ed., *Cicéron, Les Aratea* (Hildesheim, 1966) and the *Periegesis* in P. van de Woestinje, ed., *La Periégèse de Priscien* (Bruges, 1953).
25. For the pictures of the labours of the months see McGurck *et al.*, *An Eleventh-Century Anglo-Saxon Illustrated Miscellany*; and David Hill, 'Eleventh-Century Labours of the Months in Prose and Pictures', *Landscape History*, 20 (1998), 29–39.
26. F.G. Payne, 'The Plough in Ancient Britain', *Archaeological Journal*, 104 (1947), pp. 103–6.
27. G.N. Garmonsway, ed., *Ælfric's Colloquy* (Exeter, 1983), p. 20.
28. B. Colgrave, ed., *Eddius, Vita S. Wilfridi* (Cambridge, 1927), p. 50.
29. Pauline Stafford, 'Charles the Bald, Judith and England', in her *Gender, Family and the Legitimation of Power: England from the Ninth to Early Twelfth Century* (Aldershot, 2006), pp. 139–53, at p. 143.
30. Joanna Story, *Carolingian Connections: Anglo-Saxon England and Carolingian Francia, c. 750–850* (Aldershot: Ashgate, 2003), pp. 224–43; Sarah Foot, 'Dynastic Strategies: The West Saxon Royal Family in Europe', in David Rollason, Conrad Leyser, and Hannah Williams, eds, *England and the Continent in the Tenth Century: Studies in Honour of Wilhelm Levison (1876–1947)* (Turnhout, 2010), 237–53.
31. Janet Nelson, trans., *The Annals of St-Bertin* (Manchester, 1991), p. 83.
32. Simon Keynes and Michael Lapidge, *Alfred the Great: Asser's Life of King Alfred and Other Contemporary Sources* (Harmondsworth, 1983), p. 70.
33. There was a tradition of West Saxon kings retiring to Rome, but they did not as a rule return to take up royal office again. See Clare Stancliffe, 'Kings who Opted Out', in Patrick Wormald, ed., *Ideal and Reality in Frankish and Anglo-Saxon Society: Essays Presented to J.M. Wallace-Hadrill* (Oxford, 1983), pp. 154–76.

34. See the entry for the year 855 in Janet Bately, ed., *The Anglo-Saxon Chronicle: A Collaborative Edition Vol. 3: Manuscript A* (Cambridge, 1986).
35. For a full translation, consult the entry for the year 855 in version A of the Chronicle in Michael Swanton, trans., *The Anglo-Saxon Chronicles* (London, 2000).
36. Janet L. Nelson, 'The Problem of Alfred's Royal Anointing', *Journal of Ecclesiastical History*, 18 (1967), pp. 145–63.
37. The classic study is H.M. Chadwick, *The Origin of the English Nation* (Cambridge, 1907), pp. 252–83. More recently there is Daniel Anlezark's 'Sceaf, Japheth and the Origins of the Anglo-Saxons', *Anglo-Saxon England*, 31 (2002), pp. 13–46.

PART II   THE REIGN OF KING ALFRED

1. Cf. Michael Swanton, *The Anglo-Saxon Chronicles* (London, 2000).
2. The phrase 'they were glad of him' echoes a similar one in the story of Æthelwulf's return from Rome in the annal for 855.
3. Ryan Lavelle, 'Geographies of Power in the Anglo-Saxon Chronicle', in Alice Jorgensen, ed., *Reading the Anglo-Saxon Chronicle: Language, Literature, History* (Turnhout, 2010), pp. 187–219, at 204–5.
4. Lavelle, 'Geographies of Power', p. 208.
5. The Watlington hoard was discovered by detectorist James Mather in October 2015.
6. See J.D. Richards, *Viking Age England* (Stroud, 2004); D. Hadley and J.D. Richards, eds, *Cultures in Contact: Scandinavian Settlement in the Ninth and Tenth Centuries* (Turnhout, 2000).
7. Edward Thomas, *The South Country* (London, 1909), pp. 3–4.
8. See Alfred's charter granting North Newnton, Wiltshire, to Ealdorman Æthelhelm; Sawyer S 348; Keynes and Lapidge, *Alfred the Great*, pp. 179–81.
9. On the term *Angelcynn*, see Sarah Foot, 'The Making of Angelcynn: English Identity before the Norman Conquest', *Transactions of the Royal Historical Society*, 6th series, vi (1996), pp. 25–49; for a different view see George Molyneaux, 'The Old English Bede: English Ideology or Christian Instruction?', *English Historical Review*, 124, no. 511 (2009), pp. 1289–1323, at 1316–18.
10. Simon Keynes, 'Edward, King of the Anglo-Saxons', in N.J. Higham and D.H. Hill, eds, *Edward the Elder, 899–924* (London, 2001), pp. 40–66.

CHAPTER 3   LITERACY AND THE USE OF ENGLISH: ALFRED'S REFORMS

1. My translation. For the Old English text see Dorothy Whitelock, ed., *Sweet's Anglo-Saxon Reader in Verse and Prose*, 15th edition (Oxford, 1967), 5–6, or the full text of the *Pastoral Care* with parallel translation in Henry Sweet, ed., *King Alfred's West-Saxon Version of Gregory's Pastoral Care*, 2 vols, Early English Text Society, original series 45 and 50 (London,1871–2; reprinted London, 1958).
2. Susan Irvine, 'The Alfredian Prefaces and Epilogues', in Nicole Guenther Discenza and Paul E. Szarmach, eds, *A Companion to Alfred the Great* (Leiden and Boston, 2015), pp. 143–70, at pp. 166–7.
3. Alfred's laws are discussed by Patrick Wormald, *The Making of English Law* (Oxford, 2001), pp. 417–26. See the anthology by Simon Keynes and Michael Lapidge, *Alfred the Great* (Harmondsworth, 1983), ch. 4; Todd Preston, *King Alfred's Book of*

Laws: A Study of the Domboc and its Influence on English Identity, with a Complete Translation (Jefferson, NC, 2012).

4. Jennifer Morrish, 'King Alfred's Letter as a Source on Learning in England', in Paul Szarmach, ed., *Studies in Early Old English Prose* (Albany, 1986), pp. 87–108.

5. Ben Snook, *The Anglo-Saxon Chancery: The History, Language and Production of Anglo-Saxon Charters from Alfred to Edgar* (Woodbridge, 2015), pp. 31–43.

6. Michael Lapidge, 'Latin Learning in Ninth-Century England', in his *Anglo-Latin Literature 900–1066* (London, 1993), pp. 409–54.

7. Francis Wormald, 'The Miniatures in the Gospels of St Augustine, Corpus Christi College, Cambridge MS 286', in *Collected Writings*, I, ed. J.J.G. Alexander *et al.* (London, 1984), pp. 13–35.

8. For a reproduction of the relevant page from the Augustine Gospels, see Michelle P. Brown, *Manuscripts from the Anglo-Saxon Age* (London, 2007), p. 22, plate 4.

9. R. Emms, 'The Early History of St Augustine's Abbey', in Richard Gameson, ed., *St Augustine and the Conversion of England* (Stroud, 1999), pp. 410–27.

10. As David Dumville shows from a study of the handwriting, the ninth-century Ealhburg document was copied into the Gospels of St Augustine at a later stage, at some time in the 920s. See his 'English Square Minuscule Script: The Background and the Earliest Phases', *Anglo-Saxon England*, 16 (1987), pp. 147–79, at 169–73.

11. Ealhburg's donation appears on on f. 74v (folio 74 verso). There is a photograph in Susan E. Kelly, ed., *The Charters of St Augustine's Abbey, Canterbury, and Minster-in-Thanet* (Oxford, 1995), plate 3. Online services at some libraries provide access to the 'Parker Library on the Web', which provides full reproductions of the manuscripts from the Parker Library at Corpus Christi College, Cambridge: https://parker.stanford.edu/parker/.

12. For Anglo-Saxon charters and documents see Peter Sawyer, *Anglo-Saxon Charters: An Annotated List and Bibliography* (London, 1968); the Ealhburg document is no. 1198; see Electronic Sawyer at http://www.esawyer.org.uk where the same document can be retrieved as S 1198.

13. Sherman M. Kuhn, ed., *The Vespasian Psalter* (Ann Arbor, 1965); for a full-size facsimile, see David H. Wright, ed., *The Vespasian Psalter: British Museum Cotton Vespasian A.I* (Copenhagen, 1967). A detailed guide to this genre is M.J. Toswell, *The Anglo-Saxon Psalter* (Turnhout, 2014); or her 'Psalters', in Richard Gameson, ed., *The Cambridge History of the Book in Britain Volume I, c.400–1100* (Cambridge, 2012), pp. 468–81.

14. Ealhburg's family is discussed in Brooks, *Early History of the Church of Canterbury*, pp. 147, 150–1.

15. Susan Kelly, 'Anglo-Saxon Lay Society and the Written Word', in R. McKitterick, ed., *The Uses of Literacy in Early Medieval Europe* (Cambridge, 1990), pp. 36–62; Simon Keynes, 'The Power of the Written Word: Alfredian England 871–899', in Timothy Reuter, ed., *Alfred the Great: Papers from the Eleventh-Centenary Conferences* (Aldershot, 2003), pp. 175–97.

16. In the period 835–85, book production was drastically reduced; see Michael Lapidge, *Anglo-Latin Literature, 600–899* (London, 1996), p. 416.

17. The manuscript of the Codex Aureus is located in Stockholm, Royal Library, shelfmark A.135.

18. See the illustrations in Leslie Webster and Janet Backhouse, *The Making of England: Anglo-Saxon Art and Culture AD 600–900* (London, 1991), nos. 1 and 154.

19. For the text and bibliography see Electronic Sawyer S 1204a; Ealdorman Alfred's last will has also survived, see S 1508. For a colour reproduction of the Matthew

portrait and Old English marginal text on the facing page see Brown, *Manuscripts from the Anglo-Saxon Age*, plates 40 and 41, pp. 62–3.

20. The bee metaphor is also found in the writings of Aldhelm, the contemporary of Bede.
21. The arrival of Beowulf and his men is told in *Beowulf*, lines 229–661; for an interesting character-based study of these scenes, see Tolkien, *Beowulf: Translation and Commentary*, pp. 204–64.
22. Asser's *Life of King Alfred* is readily available in the Penguin Classics translation by Keynes and Lapidge, *Alfred the Great*.
23. Einhard, *Life of Charlemagne* in David Ganz, trans., *Einhard and Notker the Stammerer: Two Lives of Charlemagne* (London, 2008).
24. For the debate on Asser, see the arguments for a forgery in A.P. Smyth, *King Alfred the Great* (Oxford, 1995), and the response in Simon Keynes, 'On the Authenticity of Asser's Life of King Alfred', *Journal of Ecclesiastical History*, 47 (1996), pp. 529–51.
25. Abels, Richard P., *Alfred the Great: War, Kingship and Culture in Anglo-Saxon England* (London, 1998).
26. Mary J. Carruthers, *The Book of Memory: A Study of Memory in Medieval Culture*, 2nd edition (Cambridge, 2008).
27. Mark Atherton, 'King Alfred's Approach to the Study of Latin', in D. Cram, A. Linn and E. Nowak, eds, *History of Linguistics 1996 Vol. 2: From Classical to Contemporary Linguistics* (Amsterdam, 1999), pp. 15–22.
28. On Asser's whereabouts in 887, see Keynes and Lapidge, *Alfred the Great*, pp. 28, 53.
29. For what follows, see Michael Lapidge, 'Some Latin Poems as Evidence for the Reign of Athelstan', in his *Anglo-Latin Literature 900–1066* (London, 1993), pp. 49–86, at p. 67.
30. Felix Liebermann, ed., *Die Heiligen Englands* (Hanover, 1889), p. 18.

CHAPTER 4   THE RULE OF GOVERNMENT: 'THE CRAFT OF ALL CRAFTS'

1. The doubts concerning Alfred's translation of such works as the Old English *Boethius* and the *Soliloquies* of Augustine are most forcibly expressed in Malcolm R. Godden, 'The Alfredian Project and its Aftermath: Rethinking the Literary History of the Ninth and Tenth Centuries', *Proceedings of the British Academy*, 162 (2009), pp. 93–122.
2. Carolin Schreiber, '*Searoðonca hord*: Alfred's Translation of Gregory the Great's *Regula Pastoralis*', in Nicole Guenther Discenza and Paul E. Szarmach, eds, *A Companion to Alfred the Great* (Leiden and Boston, 2015), pp. 171–99.
3. For an introduction to Gregory's career and writing, see Robert Atwell, *Spiritual Classics from the Early Church* (London: Church House, 1995), pp. 179–99.
4. The Old English *Dialogues* were translated by Wærferth, bishop of Worcester; for discussion see Keynes and Lapidge, and an article by Malcolm Godden, 'Wærferth and King Alfred: The Fate of the Old English *Dialogues*', in Jane Roberts, Janet Nelson and Malcolm Godden, eds, *Alfred the Wise: Studies in Honour of Janet Bately* (Cambridge, 1997), pp. 35–52.
5. There is a discussion of the Alfred Jewel and the *æstel* in David A. Hinton, *Gold and Gilt, Pots and Pins: Possessions and People in Medieval Britain* (Oxford, 2005), pp. 129–31.
6. The metrical preface to the *Pastoral Care* has long been available in Richard F.S. Hamer, *A Choice of Anglo-Saxon Verse* (London, 2006); it is now also printed in

Susan Irvine and Malcolm Godden, eds and trans., *The Old English* Boethius. *With Verse Prologues and Epilogues Associated with King Alfred* (Cambridge, MA, 2012).

7. For Gregory's style, see Jean Leclercq, *The Love of Learning and the Desire for God: A Study of Monastic Culture* (New York, 1961), essential reading for anyone interested in the ways of thought in the early medieval monastery.
8. Compare the translations in Keynes and Lapidge, *Alfred the Great*, p. 129, and in Sweet, p. 37.
9. Keynes and Lapidge, *Alfred the Great*, p. 130.
10. As argued in her inaugural lecture at King's College, University of London: Janet M. Bately, 'The Literary Prose of Alfred's Reign: Translation or Transformation?' reprinted in Paul Szarmach, ed., *Old English Prose: Basic Readings* (New York, 2000), pp. 3–28.
11. Gregory the Great, *Regula pastoralis* in J.P. Migne, ed., *Patrologia Latina* 77, 12.
12. Text and translation in Henry Sweet, ed. and trans., *King Alfred's West-Saxon Version of Gregory's Pastoral Care*, 2 vols, Early English Text Society, original series 45 and 50 (London, 1871–2; reprinted London, 1958), p. 23, lines 16–18.
13. For more discussion of Alfred's use of concrete images in the *Pastoral Care*, see Janet M. Bately, 'Old English Prose before and during the Reign of Alfred', in the journal *Anglo-Saxon England*, 17 (1988), pp. 93–138, at p. 127.
14. *Pastoral Care*, ch. xxxviii; Sweet, *Pastoral Care*, p. 277, lines 3–10.
15. Susan Irvine, 'The Alfredian Prefaces and Epilogues', in Nicole Guenther Discenza and Paul E. Szarmach, eds, *A Companion to Alfred the Great* (Leiden and Boston, 2015), pp. 143–70, at pp. 153–60.
16. P. Rahtz and D. Bullough, 'The Parts of an Anglo-Saxon Mill', *Anglo-Saxon England*, 6 (1977), pp. 15–37.
17. S 1560 in the Electronic Sawyer; Alexander R. Rumble, ed. and trans., *Property and Piety in Early Medieval Winchester* (Oxford, 2002), document I.
18. For more discussion and further references on the idea of *se wæterscipe*, see Susan Irvine, 'The Alfredian Prefaces and Epilogues', in Nicole Guenther Discenza and Paul E. Szarmach, eds, *A Companion to Alfred the Great* (Leiden and Boston, 2015), pp. 143–70, at p. 160.
19. The full text of the *Metrical Epilogue to the Pastoral Care* is printed in Richard Hamer's *Choice of Anglo-Saxon Verse* (London, 2006), and also in Susan Irvine and Malcolm R. Godden, eds and trans., *The Old English* Boethius: *With Verse Prologues and Epilogues Associated with King Alfred* (Cambridge, MA, 2012).

CHAPTER 5   THE IMPORTANCE OF BEDE

1. Old English *Bede*, Book II, ch. 10; my translation. For the text see Thomas Miller, ed. and trans., *The Old English Version of Bede's Ecclesiastical History of the English People*, EETS, 95 (London, 1890), pp. 134–7. Bede's original Latin text is Book II, ch. 13, edited and translated by Bertram Colgrave and R.A.B. Mynors, *Bede's Ecclesiastical History of the English People* (Oxford, 1969), pp. 182–5.
2. Helen Gittos, 'Yeavering', in Michael Lapidge *et al.*, *The Wiley-Blackwell Encyclopedia of Anglo-Saxon England* (Oxford, 2014), pp. 517–18.
3. A useful translation is Bede, *The Ecclesiastical History of the English Nation*, ed. and trans. Roger Collins and Judith McClure (Oxford, 2008).
4. Bertram Colgrave and R.A.B. Mynors, eds and trans., *Bede's Ecclesiastical History of the English People* (Oxford, 1969), pp. 116–17.

5. For the statistics, see Sharon Rowley, 'Bede in Later Anglo-Saxon England', in Scott DeGregorio, ed., *The Cambridge Companion to Bede* (Cambridge, 2010), pp. 216–28, at p. 219.
6. George Molyneaux, 'The Old English Bede: Ideology or Christian Instruction?', *English Historical Review*, 124, no. 511 (2009), pp. 1289–1323. Molyneaux takes issue with the idea that the English saw themselves as a special people chosen by God, as argued by Patrick Wormald, 'The Venerable Bede and the "Church of the English"', in his *The Times of Bede: Studies in Early English Christian Society and its Historian*, ed. Stephen Baxter (Oxford, 2006), pp. 207–28.
7. Greg Waite, 'The Preface to the Old English Bede: Authorship, Transmission, and Connection with the West Saxon Genealogical Regnal List,' *Anglo-Saxon England*, 44 (2015), pp. 31–93.
8. As Waite points out in his 'Preface to the Old English Bede', pp. 36–7, earlier scholars such as Klaeber also commented on the Alfredian tone of the Old English Preface.
9. S.E. Kelly, 'Canterbury', in *Wiley-Blackwell Encyclopedia*, pp. 86–7.
10. Nicholas Brooks, *The Early History of the Church of Canterbury: Christ Church from 597 to 1066* (Leicester, 1984), pp. 15–36.
11. Bede, *Historia ecclesiastica gentis anglorum*, Bk I, ch. 25. Translation by Colgrave and Mynors, *Bede's Ecclesiastical History of the English People*, p. 75.
12. *Halsung* or *healsung* means 'supplication, beseeching, entreaty, adjuration, exorcising, exorcism, augury'; see Joseph Bosworth and T. Northcote Toller, *An Anglo-Saxon Dictionary* (Oxford, 1898), p. 506.
13. The manuscript of the Old English *Bede* that includes charms is Cambridge, Corpus Christi College, 41; for the texts see G. Storms, ed., *Anglo-Saxon Magic* (The Hague, 1948), *passim*, and Robert E. Bjork, ed., *Old English Shorter Poems, Volume II: Wisdom and Lyric* (Cambridge, MA and London, 2014).
14. For the date see Rowley, 'Bede in Later Anglo-Saxon England', p. 221, and for more discussion, G. Waite, 'Translation Style, Lexical Systems, Dialect Vocabulary, and the Manuscript Transmission of the Old English *Bede*, *Medium Aevum*, 83(1) (2014), pp. 1–48.
15. T. Miller, ed., *The Old English Version of Bede's Ecclesiastical History of the English People*, EETS os 95 and 96 (London, 1890–1), p. 123, lines 15–24.
16. Hamer, *A Choice of Anglo-Saxon Verse*, p. 175.
17. For discussion of the sparrow passage, see Janet Bately, 'The Nature of Old English Prose', in Malcolm Godden and Michael Lapidge, eds, *Cambridge Companion to Old English Literature* (Cambridge, 1991), pp. 71–87, at p. 82.
18. Peter Barry, 'The Flight of a Sparrow', in his *English in Practice: In Pursuit of English Studies* (London, 2003), pp. 2–5, at p. 4.
19. Bede, Bk II, ch. 13; translation from Colgrave and Mynors, pp. 185–7.
20. Old English *Bede*, Bk II, ch. 10; my translation.
21. Sharon Rowley, *The Old English Version of Bede's* Historia Ecclesiastica (Cambridge, 2011), pp. 120–3.
22. The poetic style of the Chronicle here was noted by the Victorian scholar Henry Sweet, who suggested that the text may be echoing a poem composed for the occasion.
23. Hengest's name appears in *Beowulf* at lines 1083, 1091, 1096 and 1127.
24. For discussion of kingship and the Chronicle, see Nicholas Brooks, 'Why is the Anglo-Saxon Chronicle about Kings?', *Anglo-Saxon England*, 39 (2010), 43–70.

PART III   THE EXPANSION OF WESSEX

1. David Hill and Alexander R. Rumble, eds, *The Defence of Wessex: The Burghal Hidage and Anglo-Saxon Fortifications* (Manchester, 1996).
2. David Hill, *An Atlas of Anglo-Saxon England* (Oxford, 1981), Fig. 149.

CHAPTER 6   THE REIGN OF EDWARD THE ELDER

1. Keynes and Lapidge, *Alfred the Great*, map 5, p. 176; Alfred's will, pp. 171–8.
2. For an introduction to 'Cynewulf and Cyneheard' with useful references, see Susan Irvine, 'The Anglo-Saxon Chronicle', in Nicole Guenther Discenza and Paul E. Szarmach, eds, *A Companion to Alfred the Great* (Leiden and Boston, 2015), pp. 344–67, at pp. 358–62.
3. In connecting the story of Æthelwold with that of 'Cynewulf and Cyneheard', I develop a suggestion made by Thomas Bredehoft in his *Textual Histories: Readings in the Anglo-Saxon Chronicle* (Toronto, 2001), p. 62; Bredehoft discusses 'Cynewulf and Cyneheard' in great detail at pp. 39–60.
4. 'The Laws of Alfred', in Richard Marsden, *The Cambridge Old English Reader* (Cambridge, 2004), pp. 52–7, at p. 55.
5. Asser, *Life of King Alfred*, ch. 75; Keynes and Lapidge, *Alfred the Great*, p. 90.
6. Alex Woolf, 'View from the West: an Irish Perspective on West Saxon Dynastic Practice', in N.J. Higham and D.H. Hill, eds, *Edward the Elder, 899–924* (London, 2001), pp. 89–101, at pp. 98–9.
7. C.E. Blunt, 'Northumbrian Coins in the Name of Alwaldus', *British Numismatic Journal*, 55, pp. 192–4.
8. Sarah Foot, *Æthelstan: The First King of England* (New Haven and London, 2011), p. 13.
9. Martin Biddle, *Winchester in the Early Middle Ages* (Oxford, 1976).
10. Cf. Michelle P. Brown, *The Book of Cerne: Prayer, Patronage, and Power in Ninth-Century England* (London, 1996).
11. Biddle, *Winchester in the Early Middle Ages*, pp. 313–14.
12. Alexander Rumble, *Property and Piety in Early Medieval Winchester* (Oxford, 2002), p. 30.
13. S 1443 in the Electronic Sawyer; Rumble, *Property and Piety*, no. ii, pp. 50–6.
14. Alexander R. Rumble, 'The Churches of Winchester and Wessex', in N.J. Higham and D.H. Hill, eds, *Edward the Elder, 899–924* (London, 2001), pp. 236–7.
15. S 1444, charter for Beddington, Surrey, dated 901 x 908. Walter de Gray Birch, ed., *Cartularium Saxonicum: A Collection of Charters Relating to Anglo-Saxon History* (London, 1885–99), vol. 2 (1887), no. 619, p. 282.
16. The manuscript is *London, British Library, Add. 15350*, ff. 96v-97r.
17. For the discussion of the scribes' dates and stints, see David Dumville, 'The Anglo-Saxon Chronicle and the Origins of English Minuscule Script', in his *Wessex and England from Alfred to Edgar: Six Essays on Political, Cultural, and Ecclesiastical Revival* (Woodbridge, 1992), pp. 55–139, at pp. 56–70.
18. Chronicle A is edited by Janet Bately, *The Anglo-Saxon Chronicle: A Collaborative Edition, Volume 3, Manuscript A* (Cambridge, 1986). There is discussion in David A. E. Pelteret, 'An Anonymous Historian of Edward the Elder's Reign', in Stephen Baxter, ed., *Early Medieval Studies in Memory of Patrick Wormald* (Farnham, 2009), pp. 319–36; see also Lesley Abrams, 'Edward the Elder's Danelaw', in Higham and Hill, pp. 128–43, at pp. 138–40.

19. Scott Thompson Smith, 'Marking Boundaries: Charters and the Anglo-Saxon Chronicle', in Alice Jorgensen, ed., *Reading the Anglo-Saxon Chronicle: Language, Literature, History* (Turnhout, 2010), pp. 167–85, at pp. 171–5.
20. Pauline Stafford, '"The Annals of Æthelflæd": Annals, History and Politics in Early Tenth-Century England', in Andrew Wareham and Julia Barrow, eds, *Myth, Rulership, Church and Charters: Essays in Honour of Nicholas Brooks* (Aldershot, 2008), pp. 101–16.
21. Simon Taylor, ed., *The Anglo-Saxon Chronicle. A Collaborative Edition, Volume 4, Manuscript B* (Cambridge, 1983); for the Mercian Register, see pp. 49–51.

CHAPTER 7   THE LESSONS OF HISTORY: 'EDWARDIAN' LITERATURE

1. Nick Higham, 'Edward the Elder's Reputation', in N.J. Higham and D.H. Hill, eds, *Edward the Elder, 899–924* (London, 2001), pp. 1–11, at p. 2.
2. Simon Keynes, 'Edward, King of the Anglo-Saxons', in Higham and Hill, *Edward the Elder*, pp. 40–66, at pp. 50–6.
3. Simon Keynes, 'Plegmund, Archbishop of Canterbury (890–923)', in Lapidge, *Wiley-Blackwell Encyclopedia*, 2nd edition, pp. 378–9.
4. The charters are: S1288 issued by Plegmund in 905 and S1203, a reissue of an older grant of land. See the Electronic Sawyer for further details.
5. Jane Roberts, 'Some Anglo-Saxon Psalters and their Glosses', in Tamara Atkins and Francis Leneghan, eds, *The Psalms and Medieval English Literature* (Woodbridge, forthcoming).
6. Jane Toswell, *The Anglo-Saxon Psalter* (Turnhout, 2014).
7. Mechthild Gretsch, 'The Junius Psalter Gloss: Tradition and Innovation', in Higham and Hill, *Edward the Elder*, pp. 280–91; for the Alfredian text, see Patrick P. O'Neill, ed. and trans., *Old English Psalms* (Cambridge, MA, 2016).
8. S 1445 in Sawyer's Catalogue. There is a text, translation and detailed commentary in Simon Keynes, 'The Fonthill Letter', in Michael Korhammer, ed., *Words, Texts and Manuscripts: Studies in Anglo-Saxon Culture Presented to Helmut Gneuss* (Cambridge, 1992), pp. 53–97; the problem of the author/narrator's identity is taken up by Mark Boynton and Susan Reynolds, 'The Author of the Fonthill Letter', in *Anglo-Saxon England*, 25 (1996), pp. 91–5; see also Nicholas Brooks, 'The Fonthill Letter, Ealdorman Ordlaf and Anglo-Saxon Law in Practice', in Stephen Baxter *et al.*, eds, *Early Medieval Studies in Memory of Patrick Wormald* (Farnham, 2009), pp. 301–17.
9. Declarations and other documents are discussed by Scott T. Smith, *Land and Book: Literature and Land Tenure in Anglo-Saxon England* (Toronto, 2012). On disputes generally, see Ann Williams, 'Land Tenure', in Lapidge, *Wiley-Blackwell Encyclopedia of Anglo-Saxon England*, pp. 282–3.
10. Illustrations of the Æthelwulf ring or the Alfred Jewel are reproduced in Leslie Webster and Janet Backhouse, eds, *The Making of England: Anglo-Saxon Art and Culture AD 600–900* (London, 1991), nos. 244 and 260.
11. The text of the Fonthill Letter and a useful summary are readily available in Richard Marsden, *The Cambridge Old English Reader* (Cambridge, 2004), pp. 96–102. For text, translation and commentary, see Simon Keynes, 'The Fonthill Letter', in Michael Korhammer, ed., *Words, Texts and Manuscripts: Studies in Anglo-Saxon Culture Presented to Helmut Gneuss on the Occasion of his Sixty-Fifth Birthday* (Cambridge, 1992), pp. 53–97.
12. For a survey of the Old English text and its sources, see Janet M. Bately, 'The Old English *Orosius*', in Nicole Guenther Discenza and Paul E. Szarmach, eds, *A Companion to Alfred the Great* (Leiden and Boston, 2015), pp. 313–43.

13. Malcolm R. Godden, 'The Old English *Orosius* and its Sources', *Anglia*, 129 (2011), pp. 297–320.

14. The manuscript is now London, British Library, Add. 47967. D.H. Turner, 'The Tollemache *Orosius*', in Janet Backhouse *et al.*, *The Golden Age of Anglo-Saxon Art 966–1066* (London, 1984); the facsimile is edited by Alistair Campbell, *The Tollemache Orosius*, EEMF 3 (Copenhagen, 1953).

15. Janet Bately, ed., *The Old English* Orosius, EETS SS 6 (London, 1980), p. xxiii; for full discussion of the scribal hands, see David N. Dumville, 'The Anglo-Saxon Chronicle and the Origins of English Square Minuscule Script', in David Dumville, *Wessex and England from Alfred to Edgar: Six Essays on Political, Cultural and Ecclesiastical Revival* (Woodbridge, 1992), pp. 55–99.

16. Rolf R. Bremmer, Jr, 'Anglo-Saxon England and the Germanic World', in Clare A. Lees, ed., *Early Medieval English Literature* (Cambridge, 2013), pp. 185–208, at p. 195.

17. Michael Müller-Wille, 'Hedeby in Ohthere's Time', in Janet Bately and Anton Englert, eds, *Ohthere's Voyages: A Late 9th-century Account of Voyages along the Coasts of Norway and Denmark and its Cultural Context* (Roskilde, 2007), pp. 157–67.

18. For text and translation of the travels of Ohthere and Wulfstan see Elaine M. Treharne, *Old and Middle English: An Anthology* and Bately, *Old English* Orosius.

19. William A. Kretzschmar, Jr, 'Adaptation and *anweald* in the Old English *Orosius*', *Anglo-Saxon England*, 16 (1987), pp. 127–45.

20. Francis Leneghan, '*Translatio imperii*: The Old English *Orosius* and the Rise of Wessex', *Anglia*, 133.4 (2015), pp. 656–705.

21. The last two lines of *Beowulf* are frequently discussed by the critics; for a flavour, see the rich discussion by John M. Hill, *The Narrative Pulse of Beowulf: Arrivals and Departures* (Toronto, 2008), pp. 89–90.

22. Malcolm R. Godden, 'The Anglo-Saxons and the Goths: Rewriting the Sack of Rome', *Anglo-Saxon England*, 31 (2002), pp. 47–68.

23. On the prose and verse see Malcolm R. Godden and Susan Irvine, eds and trans., *The Old English Boethius*, 2 vols (Oxford, 2009), esp. I, pp. 45–6; for more general discussion of authorship see Malcolm R. Godden, 'Did King Alfred Write Anything?', *Medium Aevum*, 76.1 (2007), pp. 1–23.

24. As Mark Griffith shows in his contribution to Godden and Irvine, *Old English Boethius*, it is likely that the Old English prose was used as a basis for these new versifications; perhaps the Metres were composed at a later date than the original project to translate Boethius's work.

25. For a close study of the rich imagery of the OE Metres of Boethius, see Karmen Lenz, *Ræd and Frofer: Christian Poetics in the Old English Froferboc Meters* (Amsterdam and New York, 2012).

26. This is the B Text version; see Godden and Irvine, *Old English Boethius*, text in vol. I, pp. 271–7, and translation in vol. II, pp. 22–6.

27. *Old English* Boethius, text in vol. I, pp. 277–8, and translation in vol. II, pp. 26–7.

28. Translation by Elaine Treharne in her *Old and Middle English: An Anthology*; the concept itself is discussed by T.E. Powell, 'The Three Orders of Society in Anglo-Saxon England', in the journal *Anglo-Saxon England*, 23 (1994), pp. 103–32.

29. Scott T. Smith, *Land and Book: Literature and Land Tenure in Anglo-Saxon England* (Toronto, 2012), pp. 3–4.

30. Alfred P. Smyth, *King Alfred the Great* (Oxford, 1995), p. 585; Godden and Irvine, *Old English* Boethius, II, p. 316.

31. The OE text also refers to the *pearroc* as a *cafertun*, meaning a 'courtyard'; see Godden and Irvine, II, p. 321. The word *pearroc* survives in modern English as *parrock*, 'an enclosed area of ground', a word which, according to the Oxford English Dictionary, is of disputed origin but may relate to Latin *parricus* and medieval French *park*, a much larger enclosed area.

32. Godden and Irvine, *Old English Boethius*, II, p. 326.

PART IV   WAR, POETRY, AND BOOK-COLLECTING

1. Lapidge, 'Three Poems'. His translation reads as follows:

> You, prince, are called by the name of 'sovereign stone'.
> Look happily on the prophecy for your age;
> You shall be the 'noble rock' of Samuel the Seer,
> [Standing] with mighty strength against devilish demons.
> Often an abundant cornfield foretells a great harvest; in   5
> Peaceful days your stony mass is to be softened.
> You are more abundantly endowed with the holy eminence of learning.
> I pray that you may seek, and the Glorious One may grant, the [fulfilment implied in your] noble names.

2. The name Æthel-wold means 'noble power'; Wulfstan's interpretation of the name is found in his *Life of St Æthelwold*, ed. Lapidge and Winterbottom, ch. 9, pp. 14–15.

3. The historical context of this manuscript is discussed by Mechthild Gretsch, *Intellectual Foundations of the English Benedictine Reform* (Cambridge, 1999), pp. 343–7.

4. Sarah Foot, *Æthelstan: The First King of England* (New Haven and London, 2011), pp. 110–12; Gernot Wieland, 'A New Look at the Poem "Archalis clamare triumuir"', in Gernot Wieland *et al.*, ed., *Insignis Sophiae Arcator: Essays in Honour of Michael W. Herren on his 65th Birthday* (Turnhout, 2006), pp. 178–92.

CHAPTER 8   'KING ÆTHELSTAN THE PIOUS, FAMED THROUGHOUT THE WIDE WORLD'

1. Simon Keynes, 'King Athelstan's Books', in Michael Lapidge and Helmut Gneuss, eds, *Learning and Literature in Anglo-Saxon England: Studies Presented to Peter Clemoes* (Cambridge, 1985), pp. 143–201.

2. Simon Keynes, 'King Athelstan's Books', p. 196.

3. Sarah Foot, *Æthelstan: The First King of England* (New Haven and London, 2011), pp. 17, 38–40.

4. Janet Nelson, 'The First Use of the Second Anglo-Saxon *Ordo*', in Julia Barrow and Andrew Wareham, eds, *Myth, Rulership, Church and Charters* (Aldershot, 2008), pp. 117–26.

5. Vercelli I, lines 143–6; Scragg, *Vercelli Homilies*, p. 28.

6. For an illustration of the plain style of the initials used in this gospel book, see the exhibition catalogue by Leslie Webster and Janet Backhouse, *The Making of England: Anglo-Saxon Art and Culture AD 600–900* (London, 1991), no. 84.

7. London, British Library, manuscript Royal I B.vii, folio 15v. A facsimile of the page and the inscription is reproduced in Michelle P. Brown, *Manuscripts from the Anglo-Saxon Age* (London, 2007), plate 35.

8. The Leofric gospel book is kept in Oxford, Bodleian Library, at shelfmark Auct. D. 2. 16; the list of relics given to Exeter is printed in Max Förster, *Zur Geschichte des Reliquienkultus in Altengland* (Munich, 1943), pp. 63–114 and translated by Michael Swanton, *Anglo-Saxon Prose* (London, 1975), pp. 15–19.

9. For the passage from *De Gestis Regum*, see Dorothy Whitelock, trans., *English Historical Documents c.500–1042* (London, 1979), no. 8; also Keynes, 'King Athelstan's Books', p. 143; and L.H. Loomis, 'The Holy Relics of Charlemagne and King Athelstan: The Lances of Longinus and St Mauricius', *Speculum*, 25 (1950), 437–56.

10. S 396 in Sawyer's catalogue.

11. Scott T. Smith, *Land and Book: Literature and Land Tenure in Anglo-Saxon England* (Toronto, 2012), pp. 37–46.

12. This book is now located in Durham, Cathedral Library, shelfmark A. II. 17; the inscribed poem is found on folio 31v; see Christopher D. Verey *et al.*, ed., *The Durham Gospels*, Early English Manuscripts in Facsimile, 20 (Copenhagen, 1980).

13. For more details of the poem 'Carta dirige gressus', with a reconstructed text and a translation, see Michael Lapidge, 'Some Latin Poems as Evidence for the Reign of Athelstan', *Anglo-Saxon England*, 9 (1981), 61–98; reprinted in his *Anglo-Latin Literature 900–1066*, pp. 49–86.

14. Bede, *Life of St Cuthbert*, in D.H. Farmer, ed., and J.F. Webb, trans., *The Age of Bede* (London, 1998).

15. Brown, *Manuscripts from the Anglo-Saxon Age*, pl. 79; discussed by Catherine E. Karkov, *The Ruler Portraits of Anglo-Saxon England* (Woodbridge, 2004), pp. 55–63.

16. Ted Johnson Smith, ed., *The History of St Cuthbert* (Cambridge, 2002), pp. 54–9.

17. Gerald of Wales, *The History and Topography of Ireland*, trans. John O'Meara (London, 1983).

18. Michelle P. Brown, *The Lindisfarne Gospels: Society, Spirituality and the Scribe* (London, 2003).

19. These two images are reproduced respectively in Brown, *Lindisfarne Gospels*, pl. 8 and Janet Backhouse *et al.*, *The Golden Age of Anglo-Saxon Art 966–1066* (London, 1984), pl. 48.

20. For the work of this tenth-century scribe see Neil R. Ker, 'Aldred the Scribe', *Essays and Studies*, 28 (1943 for 1942), 7–12; A.S.C. Ross and E.G. Stanley, eds, 'The Anglo-Saxon Gloss', in T.D. Kendrick *et al.*, ed., *Codex Lindisfarnensis*, 2 vols (Olten and Lausanne, 1960), ii, pp. 25–33; W.J.P. Boyd, *Aldred's Marginalia* (Exeter, 1975); Sarah M. Pons Sanz, *Analysis of the Scandinavian Loanwords in the Aldredian Glosses to the Lindisfarne Gospels* (Valencia, 2002); Jane Roberts, 'Aldred Signs Off from Glossing the Lindisfarne Gospels', in Alexander R. Rumble, ed., *Writing and Texts in Anglo-Saxon England* (Cambridge, 2006), pp. 28–43.

21. Michelle Brown, *The Lindisfarne Gospels*, p. 90. Aldred's comment appears on folio 84r of Durham, Cathedral Library, manuscript A.iv.19; see T.J. Brown, ed., *The Durham Ritual*, Early English Manuscripts in Facsimile, 16 (Copenhagen, 1969).

CHAPTER 9 THE 'GREAT WAR' AND MEDIEVAL MEMORY

1. Alistair Campbell, ed., *The Chronicle of Æthelweard* (London, 1962), p. 54.

2. Michael Livingston, ed., *The Battle of Brunanburh: A Casebook* (Exeter, 2011).

3. Foot, *Æthelstan: The First King of England*, p. 5.

4. Sarah Foot, 'William of Malmesbury and a Lost Life of King Æthelstan', in her *Æthelstan*, Appendix I, pp. 251–8.

5. For the poem *Athelston*, see Elaine Treharne, ed., *Old and Middle English c.890–c.1450: An Anthology*, 3rd edition (Oxford, 2009).
6. See the article by John Hines, 'Egill's Hǫfuðlausn in Time and Place', in the journal *Saga-Book of the Viking Society*, 24 (1995), pp. 83–104, at 100.
7. For text and translation see the passage from *Egil's Saga*, trans. A. Keith Kelly, in Michael Livingston, ed., *The Battle of Brunanburh: A Casebook* (Exeter, 2011), pp. 69–81, at pp. 80–1.
8. Peter Baker, *Honour, Exchange and Violence in* Beowulf (Cambridge, 2013), pp. 18–22.
9. Hermann Pálsson and Paul Edwards, trans., *Egil's Saga* (Harmondsworth, 1976), pp. 128–9.
10. David M. Wilson, *The Bayeux Tapestry* (London, 2004), plate 23 and p. 180.
11. The text of the *Hildebrandslied* is available in anthologies of Old High German, e.g. Wilhelm Braune and Ernst A. Ebbinghaus, eds, *Althochdeutsches Lesebuch* (Tübingen, 1969), pp. 84–5; for discussion, see J. Knight Bostock, *A Handbook on Old High German Literature* (Oxford, 1976).
12. David R. Slavitt, 'The Battle of Maldon', in Greg Delanty and Michael Matto, eds, *The Word Exchange: Anglo-Saxon Poems in Translation* (New York and London, 2011), p. 95.
13. For the full text, and a translation of *Rex pius Æthelstan*, see Michael Lapidge, 'Some Latin Poems as Evidence for the Reign of Æthelstan', *Anglo-Saxon England*, 9 (1981), pp. 61–98, at pp. 95–7.
14. Pauline Stafford, *Unification and Conquest: A Political and Social History of the England in the Tenth and Eleventh Centuries* (London, 1989), p. 6.
15. Megan E. Hartman, 'The Limits of Conservative Composition in Old English Poetry', in Leonard Neidorf, ed., *The Dating of* Beowulf (Cambridge, 2014), pp. 79–96, at p. 85.
16. Hallam Tennyson, 'The Song of Brunanburh', *The Contemporary Review*, 28 (November, 1876), pp. 920–2, at p. 920.
17. For discussion of Tennyson's version see Edward B. Irving, Jr, 'The Charge of the Saxon Brigade: Tennyson's *Battle of Brunanburh*', in Donald Scragg and Carole Weinberg, eds, *Literary Appropriations of the Anglo-Saxons from the Thirteenth to the Twentieth Century* (Cambridge, 2000), pp. 174–93; Michael P. Kuczinski, 'Translation and Adaptation in Tennyson's *Battle of Brunanburh*', *Philological Quarterly*, 86 (2007), pp. 415–31.
18. Matthew Townend, 'Pre-Cnut Praise-Poetry in Viking Age England', *The Review of English Studies*, 51 (2000), pp. 349–70, at pp. 366–7.
19. For an introduction to *The Capture of the Five Boroughs*, see Jayne Carroll, 'Viking Wars and the Anglo-Saxon Chronicle', in Richard North and Joe Allard, eds, *Beowulf and Other Stories: A New Introduction to Old English, Old Icelandic and Anglo-Norman Literatures*, 2nd edition (London, 2012), pp. 329–50, at pp. 363–4. *The Advent Lyrics*, otherwise known as *Christ I*, or *Advent*, are printed in Mary Clayton, ed. and trans., *Old English Poems of Christ and His Saints* (Cambridge, MA, 2013), pp. 1–31.
20. Smith, 'Marking Boundaries', pp. 183–4.
21. A. Mawer, 'The Redemption of the Five Boroughs', *English Historical Review*, 38 (1923), pp. 551–7.
22. For a date of around 950 for these Chronicle poems, see Donald Scragg, 'A Reading of *Brunanburh*', in Mark C. Amodio and Katherine O'Brian O'Keeffe, eds, *Unlocking the Wordhoard: Anglo-Saxon Stuides in Memory of Edward B. Irving, Jr.* (Toronto, 2003), pp. 109–22.
23. Townend, 'Pre-Cnut Praise-Poetry', pp. 352–3.

24. The earliest manuscript to contain this prosimetric version of the Old English Boethius is London, British Library, Cotton Otho A.vi, compiled about 950. For a convenient text and translation see the Dumbarton Oaks Medieval Library edition by Susan Irvine and Malcolm R. Godden, *The Old English Boethius* (Cambridge, MA and London, 2012).

25. See Emily V. Thornbury, *Becoming a Poet in Anglo-Saxon England* (Cambridge, 2014), pp. 233–5.

26. Bill Griffiths, ed., *Alfred's Metres of Boethius* (Pinner, Middlesex, 1991), p. 45. For the latest edition, with extensive introduction and discussion of Alfredian authorship, see Malcolm Godden, Susan Irvine and Mark Griffith, eds, *The Old English Boethius. An Edition of the Old English Versions of Boethiuss Consolation of Philosophy*, 2 vols (Oxford, 2009).

27. I follow here the C text and line numbers in Godden and Irvine, *The Old English Boethius*.

28. For Dunstan's reputation as an uncompromising holy man, see also Catherine Cubitt, 'Archbishop Dunstan; A Prophet in Politics?' in Julia Barrow and Andrew Wareham, eds, *Myth, Rulership, Church and Charters: Essays in Honour of Nicholas Brooks* (Aldershot and Burlington VT, 2008), pp. 145–66.

CHAPTER 10 'PROPHET IN HIS OWN COUNTRY':
THE EARLY LIFE OF ST DUNSTAN

1. N.P. Brooks, 'The Career of St Dunstan', in Nigel Ramsey, Margaret Sparks and Tim Tatton-Brown, eds, *St Dunstan: His Life, Times and Cult* (Woodbridge, 1992), pp. 1–23.

2. For the biographer B.'s career, the most detailed study is Michael Lapidge and Michael Winterbottom, eds, *The Early Lives of St Dunstan* (Oxford, 2012), pp. lxiv–lxxviii.

3. B., *Life of St Dunstan*, in Lapidge and Winterbottom, *Early Lives of St Dunstan*, pp. 1–109. For the editors' comments on B.'s embellished language, see Introduction pp. xcviii–cxxi, and on his poetic style see pp. 15, 17, and the Introduction at pp. cxxi–cxxii.

4. On the Old Church, see Philip Rahtz and Lorna Watts, *Glastonbury: Myth and Archaeology* (Stroud, 2009), pp. 90–4.

5. *Life of St Dunstan*, in Lapidge and Winterbottom, *Early Lives*, pp. 16–17.

6. Evagrius's *Life of Antony* based on the Greek of Athanasius is translated by Caroline White, *Early Christian Lives* (London, 1998), pp. 1–70; for the demons as animals see ch. 9, p. 15.

7. *Life of St Dunstan*, pp. 14–17.

8. For B.'s use of Jerome as a source, see Lapidge and Winterbottom, *Early Lives*, p. 23, n. 67.

9. Catherine Cubitt, 'Archbishop Dunstan; A Prophet in Politics?' in Julia Barrow and Andrew Wareham, eds, *Myth, Rulership, Church and Charters: Essays in Honour of Nicholas Brooks* (Aldershot and Burlington VT, 2008), pp. 145–66.

10. By overseer, Latin *preuisor*, B. probably means a *burþegn*, literally a 'bower-thegn' or royal 'chamberlain'; cf. Lapidge and Winterbottom, *Life of St Dunstan*, p. 35, n. 96.

11. Translation here based on Lapidge and Winterbottom, *Life of St Dunstan*, p. 37.

12. A typical word for a feast in Old English is *gebeorscipe*, a 'drinking of beer'. As Hugh Magennis shows in his *Images of Community in Old English Poetry* (Cambridge, 2006), there is no mention of food in the various feast scenes in *Beowulf*.

13. Samuel Taylor Coleridge, 'The Eolian Harp' (first composed 1895); Percy Bysshe Shelley, 'Ode to the West Wind' (1819).
14. C.R. Dodwell, *Anglo-Saxon Art: A New Perspective* (Manchester, 1982).
15. Philip Rahtz, *The Saxon and Medieval Palaces at Cheddar* (Oxford, 1979).
16. Old English and Latin from E. Brenner, ed., *Der altenglische Junius-Psalter* (Heidelberg, 1908); modern English from the Douay-Rheims translation, based on the Vulgate.
17. Koert van der Horst *et al.*, ed., *The Utrecht Psalter in Medieval Art. Picturing the Psalms of David* (Utrecht, 1996).
18. Utrecht Psalter, Psalm 42.1; the facsimile edition is Koert van der Hort and J.H.A. Engelbrecht, eds, *The Utrecht Psalter* (Graz, 1982); for a facsimile online see 'Utrecht Psalter Annotated'. The Anglo-Saxon copy of the Utrecht Psalter is discussed in depth by William Noel, *The Harley Psalter* (Cambridge, 1995).
19. For a discussion of parallels between Blickling Homily XVI and Grendel's Mere in *Beowulf*, see Charles D. Wright, *The Irish Tradition in Old English Literature* (Cambridge, 1993), pp. 116-21.
20. Frederick Klaeber, ed., *Beowulf and the Fight at Finnsburg*, 3rd edition (Lexington, MA, 1950).
21. The *Life of St Eustace* (a saint also known as Placidas) is one of four works by anonymous authors copied into London, British Library, Cotton Julius E. vii, a manuscript of Old English saints' lives by Ælfric. See Walter W. Skeat, ed., *Ælfric's Saints Lives*, 2 vols, Early English Text Society, original series 76, 82 (London, 1881; repr. 1966), II, 190-219. The *Life of St Eustace* was known in England in Latin versions, discussed by Michael Lapidge, 'Æthelwold and the *Vita S. Eustachii*', in his *Anglo-Latin Literature 900-1066* (London and Rio Grande, 1993), pp. 212-23.
22. N.P. Brooks, 'The Career of St Dunstan', in Nigel Ramsey, Margaret Sparks and Tim Tatton-Brown, *St Dunstan: His Life, Times and Cult* (Woodbridge, 1992), pp. 1-23.

CHAPTER 11 'BY SKILL MUST LOVE BE GUIDED': THE SCHOOL OF GLASTONBURY

1. For the history of its landholdings, see Lesley Abrams, *Anglo-Saxon Glastonbury: Church and Endowment* (Woodbridge, 1996).
2. B., *Life of St Dunstan*, ch. 15.2-15.3, in Michael Winterbottom and Michael Lapidge, ed. and trans., *The Early Lives of St Dunstan* (Oxford, 2012), p. 53.
3. Philip Rahtz and Lorna Watts, *Glastonbury: Myth and Archaeology* (Stroud, 2009), p. 115; late Anglo-Saxon finds from the Abbey are surveyed at pp. 116-18.
4. In the eleventh century a famous Glastonbury alumnus was Archbishop Ælfheah, known today in the Church of England as St Alphege, who was consecrated archbishop in 1006 and died a martyr's death at the hands of the Vikings in 1012; later still, during the reign of King Cnut, there was Æthelnoth, perhaps a descendant of Æthelweard the Chronicler, who served as archbishop from 1020 to 1038.
5. Wulfstan Cantor, *Life of St Æthelwold*, ed. and trans. Michael Lapidge (Oxford), pp. 14-15.
6. Winterbottom and Lapidge, *Early Lives of St Dunstan*, p. lviii; the Caesarius commentary on the Apocalypse is Oxford, Bodleian Library, Hatton 30.
7. The manuscript context of Rawlinson C. 697 is discussed by Mechthild Gretsch, *Intellectual Foundations of the English Benedictine Reform* (Cambridge, 1999), pp. 343-7. The dispersal of Æthelstan's books after his death is discussed by

Michael Wood, 'The Story of a Book', in his *In Search of England: Journeys into the English Past* (London, 1999), pp. 169–85.

8. T.A.M. Bishop, 'An Early Example of Insular Caroline', *Transactions of the Cambridge Bibliographical Society*, 5.5 (1968), pp. 396–400; see also the same author's *English Caroline Minuscule* (Oxford, 1971), at pp. 1–2.

9. My discussion of Hand D and Dunstan's books is indebted to the work of Lapidge and Winterbottom, *Early Lives of St Dunstan*, pp. lii–lxiii.

10. The manuscript is held at Oxford, Bodleian Library, shelfmark Auct. F. 4. 32; the whole is printed in facsimile by R.W. Hunt; there is a very detailed description of the make-up of the book by Mildred Budny, 'St Dunstan's Classbook and its Frontispiece: Dunstan's Portrait and Autograph', in Nigel Ramsay *et al.*, *St Dunstan: His Life, Times and Cult* (Woodbridge, 1992), pp. 103–42.

11. The text is printed by H. Keil, *Grammatici Latini, V: Artium Scriptores Minores* (Leipzig, 1868), pp. 447–88, at pp. 447–60.

12. For a description of *The Book of Commoneus*, see Budny, 'St Dunstan's Classbook', pp. 120–2.

13. *Uenite filii, audite me, timorem Domini docebo uobis*; Psalm 33: 12 in the Vulgate; Justin McCann, ed. and trans., *The Rule of St Benedict* (London, 1952). For the picture, see Janet Backhouse *et al.*, *The Golden Age of Anglo-Saxon Art, 1966–1066* (London, 1984), p. 53, pl. 31; and for a colour reproduction see Michelle P. Brown, *Manuscripts from the Anglo-Saxon Age* London, 2007), pl. 82. Images of the manuscript are available online by searching for the shelfmark 'Auct. F. 4. 32'.

14. Helmut Gneuss, 'Dunstan und Hrabanus Maurus. Zur Handschrift Bodleian Auctarium F.4.32', *Anglia*, 96 (1978), pp. 136–48, at pp. 146–8.

15. The Trinity Hrabanus Maurus manuscript is shelfmark Cambridge, Trinity College, B. 16. 3. Winterbottom and Lapidge, *Early Lives of St Dunstan*, pp. liv–lvi.

16. Statius, *Thebaid*, trans. J.H. Mozeley, II, pp. 32–44. As shown by Andy Orchard, *The Poetic Art of Aldhelm* (Cambridge, 1994), Statius was widely read in Anglo-Saxon England.

17. Translation based on Michael Lapidge, in 'St Dunstan's Latin Poetry', in *Anglia*, 98 (1980), pp. 101–6; reprinted in Michael Lapidge, *Anglo-Latin Literature 900–1066* (London, 1993), pp. 151–6.

18. For the 'protective function' of poems and picture see Catherine Karkov, 'Art and Writing: Voice, Image, Object', in Clare Lees, ed., *The Cambridge History of Early Medieval English Literature* (Cambridge, 2013), pp. 73–98, at pp. 76–8.

19. Budny, 'St Dunstan's Classbook', p. 113.

20. Genesis 22, 16–17; translation based on Douay-Rheims, altered according to the Old Latin variants found in the text of Dunstan's Classbook.

21. For example, see the arguments on national identity in Nicholas Howe, *Migration and Mythmaking in Anglo-Saxon England* (Notre Dame, Ind., 2001).

22. Budny, 'St Dunstan's Classbook', p. 121.

23. The text and translation is adapted from Ovid, *The Art of Love and Other Poems*, trans. J.H. Mozley (London, 1979), pp. 12–13.

24. Andy Orchard, 'Enigma Variations: The Anglo-Saxon Riddle Tradition', in Katherine O'Brien O'Keeffe and Andy Orchard, eds, *Latin Learning and English Lore: Studies in Anglo-Saxon Literature for Michael Lapidge*, 2 vols (Toronto, 2005), vol. I, pp. 284–304.

25. Katherine O'Brien O'Keeffe, 'The Text of Aldhelm's *Enigma* no. c in Oxford, Bodleian Library, Rawlinson C. 697 and Exeter Riddle 40', *Anglo-Saxon England*, 14 (1985), pp. 61–73.

26. Richard Gameson, 'The Origin of the Exeter Book of Old English Poetry', *Anglo-Saxon England*, 25 (1996), pp. 135–85.

27. Daniel Anlezark, ed. and trans., *The Old English Dialogues of Solomon and Saturn* (Woodbridge, 2009), pp. 49–57.

28. Text and translation in Anlezark, *Old English Dialogues*, pp. 66–7; for the alternative translation see the edition of *Solomon and Saturn* in Robert E. Bjork, *Old English Shorter Poems, Volume II: Wisdom and Lyric* (Cambridge, MA and London, 2014), pp. 134–73.

29. Charles Wright, *The Irish Tradition in Old English Literature* (Cambridge, 1993).

INTERLUDE IV   PASSAGES FROM 'ST DUNSTAN'S CLASSBOOK'

1. Unusual readings in D's text include *superat* (line 747), which could mean 'remains' and echoes the *superat* of line 771 at the end of the passage. Other readings are *iacturas* (line 747), *supet* (line 748), *in orbe* (line 759), *tenuabat* (line 761), as well as some different or unusual tenses in the verbs. For the standard readings of the final section of Ovid's *Art of Love*, Book I, see the critical text of lines 747–72, and the notes on lines 747, 759, 761, in S.A. Hollis, ed., *Ovid: Ars Amatoria Book I* (Oxford, 1977), pp. 29–30, 147–9. For a text with translation see J.H. Mozley, *Ovid, II, The Art of Love and Other Poems* (Cambridge, MA and London, 1979).

PART V   BUILDING THE NATION

1. Karen Saupe, ed., *Middle English Marian Lyrics* (Kalamazoo, MI, 1997).

2. 'Historiography and Literary Patronage in Late Anglo-Saxon England: the Evidence of Æthelweard's *Chronicon*', *Anglo-Saxon England*, 41 (2013), pp. 205–48.

3. Alistair Campbell, ed., *The Chronicle of Æthelweard* (London, 1962), p. 39.

CHAPTER 12   THE REIGN OF KING EDRED: DEALING WITH THE NORTHUMBRIANS, THE QUEEN MOTHER, AND THE ARCHBISHOP

1. Eilert Ekwall, *The Concise Oxford Dictionary of Place-names*, 4th edition (Oxford, 1959), p. 544.

2. R.A. Hall, 'York', Michael Lapidge *et al.*, *Wiley-Blackwell Encyclopedia of Anglo-Saxon England* (Oxford, 2014); and R.A. Hall *et al.*, *Aspects of Anglo-Scandinavian York* (York, 2004).

3. There is a lively account of the reign of Eric at York in Michael Wood, *In Search of the Dark Ages* (London, 1981), ch. 7.

4. Peter Sawyer, 'The Last Scandinavian Kings of York', *Northern History*, 31 (1995), pp. 39–44.

5. For details on Wulfstan's charter attestations, see Simon Keynes, 'Wulfstan I, archbishop of York (931–56)', in Lapidge *et al.*, *Wiley-Blackwell Encyclopedia*.

6. Nicholas Brooks, *The Early History of the Church of Canterbury: Christ Church from 597 to 1066* (Leicester, 1984), p. 229.

7. Pauline Stafford, 'Eadgifu', in Lapidge, *Wiley-Blackwell Encyclopedia of Anglo-Saxon England*; Foot, *Æthelstan*, pp. 56–8.

8. For the Latin text, see S 509 in the Electronic Sawyer.

9. For more discussion, see Abrams, *Glastonbury*, pp. 28, 34, 35, 38, 97, 181–4, 237, 271, 307, 324.
10. See the text and discussion of this charter in Susan E. Kelly, ed., *Charters of Glastonbury Abbey* (Oxford, 2012), pp. 413–19, at p. 415.
11. S 546. Discussed by Susan Kelly, 'Reculver Minster and its Early Charters', in Julia Barrow and Andrew Wareham, eds, *Myth, Rulership, Church and Charters* (Aldershot, 2008), pp. 67–82, at pp. 81–2. The full text and translation of charter S 546 is given in the Electronic Sawyer; and there is a translation in Dorothy Whitelock, *English Historical Documents, Vol. 1 c. 500–1042*, 2nd edition (London, 1979), p. 378. For a facsimile reproduction of the handwriting see Nigel Ramsay, Margaret Sparks, and Tim Tatton-Brown, eds, *St Dunstan: His Life, Times and Cult* (Woodbridge: Boydell and Brewer, 1992), frontispiece.
12. For the text of Alcuin's letter to Arno/Aquila, see Colin Chase, ed., *Two Alcuin Letter Books* (Toronto, 1975), pp. 29–30. There is a discussion with bibliography by Andy Orchard, in his 'Monasteries and Courts: Alcuin and Offa', in Richard North and Joe Allard, eds, *Beowulf and Other Stories: A New Introduction to Old English, Old Icelandic and Anglo-Norman Literatures* (Harlow, 2012), pp. 219–45, at pp. 227–9.
13. The charter is discussed by Brooks, *Early History of the Church of Canterbury*, pp. 232–6, and Nicholas Brooks and Susan Kelly, eds, *Charters of Christ Church Canterbury Part 2* (Oxford, 2013), pp. 940–2.
14. Charters associated with Dunstan are listed in Brooks, 'The Career of St Dunstan', pp. 17–18, note 58, and discussed by Simon Keynes, 'The "Dunstan B" Charters', *Anglo-Saxon England*, 23 (1994), pp. 165–93.
15. Brooks, 'The Career of St Dunstan', p. 14.
16. For the text of the will, see S 1515 in the electronic Sawyer; translation in Whitelock, *English Historical Documents*, no. 107, pp. 554–6; general discussion in Linda Tollerton, *Wills and Will-making in Anglo-Saxon England* (York, 2011).
17. C.R. Dodwell, *Anglo-Saxon Art: A New Perspective* (Manchester, 1982), pp. 210–13.
18. For text and translation see Mary Clayton, ed., *Old English Poems of Christ and his Saints* (London, 2013), pp. 160–73.
19. The eleventh-century manuscript containing the portrait of Cnut is the New Minster *Liber Vitae*, now London, British Library Stowe 944. The same book was a repository of tradition, containing regnal lists of the tenth-century kings, and a copy of the will of King Alfred. For a reproduction of the royal portrait, see Backhouse *et al.*, *Golden Age of Anglo-Saxon Art*, no. 62, or Michelle P. Brown, *Manuscripts of the Anglo-Saxon Age* (London, 2007), plate 126, p. 160.

CHAPTER 13   POLITICS, MONASTERIES, AND THE RISE OF BISHOP ÆTHELWOLD

1. Brooks, 'Career of St Dunstan', p. 15.
2. Dominik Wassenhoven, 'The Role of Bishops in Anglo-Saxon Succession Struggles, 955 x 978', in Alexander R. Rumble, *Leaders of the Anglo-Saxon Church from Bede to Stigand* (Woodbridge, 2012), pp. 97–107, at pp. 98–102.
3. Ovid, *The Art of Love*, Book I, lines 753–4. See also Interlude IV in this volume.
4. The evidence of mutual support between Abbot Æthelwold and King Edwy is found in two documents in Old English: a memorandum from Abingdon about an exchange of lands with Wells, witnessed by the royal court (Sawyer 1292) and a bequest to Æthelwold in Queen Ælfgifu's will; see Dorothy Whitelock, ed.,

Anglo-Saxon Wills (Cambridge, 1930), no. VIII, pp. 20–1. The matter is discussed by Barbara Yorke, 'Æthelwold and the Politics of the Tenth Century', in Barbara Yorke, *Bishop Æthelwold: His Career and Influence* (Woodbridge, 1997), pp. 65–88, at p. 80.

5. Vergil, *Georgics*, 4, 467–8; Statius, *Thebaid* 2, 32–4. One scholar connected the prayer directly with Dunstan's voyage into exile: Fritz Saxl, 'Illuminated Science Manuscripts in England', in his *Lectures*, 2 vols (London 1957), I, pp. 96–110, at p. 98.

6. Winterbottom and Lapidge, *Early Lives of St Dunstan*, p. 73, n. 211.

7. Philip Grierson, 'The Relations between England and Flanders before the Norman Conquest', *Transactions of the Royal Historical Society*, 4th series, 23 (1941), pp. 71–112, at pp. 88–9; Nicholas P. Brooks, 'The Career of St Dunstan', in Nigel Ramsay, Margaret Sparks, and Tim Tatton-Brown, eds, *St Dunstan: His Life, Times and Cult* (Woodbridge: Boydell and Brewer, 1992), pp. 1–23, at pp. 14–18.

8. Adelard of Ghent, *Lections for the Deposition of St Dunstan*, in Winterbottom and Lapidge, *Early Lives of St Dunstan*, pp. 126–9.

9. Steven Vanderputten, 'Flemish Monasticism, Comital Power, and the Archbishops of Canterbury: A Written Legacy from the Late Tenth Century', in David Rollason, Conrad Leyser, and Hannah Williams, eds, *England and the Continent in the Tenth Century. Studies in Honour of Wilhelm Levison (1876–1947)* (Turnhout, 2010), pp. 67–86, at pp. 76–9.

10. T. Symons, ed. and trans., *Regularis Concordia* (London, 1953); Michael Lapidge, *The Cult of St Swithun*, p. 12, n. 27 and p. 222.

11. Lapidge and Winterbottom, *Life of St Æthelwold*, pp. 16–17.

12. Alan Thacker, 'Æthelwold and Abingdon', in Barbara Yorke, ed., *Bishop Æthelwold: His Career and Influence* (Woodbridge, 1997), pp. 43–64.

13. Donald Bullough, 'St Oswald: Monk, Bishop and Archbishop', and John Nightingale, 'Oswald, Fleury and Continental Reform', in Nicholas Brooks and Catherine Cubitt, eds, *Oswald of Worcester: Life and Influence* (Leicester, 1996), pp. 1–22, 23–45.

14. David Dumville, 'The Dissemination of Anglo-Caroline Minuscule', in his *English Caroline Script and Monastic History: Studies in Benedictinism, A.D. 950–1030* (Woodbridge, 1993), pp. 7–85, at p. 57.

15. Smaragdus, *Expositio in Regulam S. Benedicti*; in a mid-tenth-century manuscript, now Cambridge, University Library, Ee. 2.4 and Oxford, Bodleian Library, Lat. Theol. c. 3, ff. 1–2.

16. Terrence Kardong, 'Smaragdus and his Work', in Smaragdus of Saint-Mihiel, *Commentary on the Rule of Saint Benedict*, trans. David Barry (Kalamazoo, MI, 2007), pp. 1–7.

17. Cf. Lapidge and Winterbottom, *Life of St Æthelwold*, ch. 14, pp. 26–9.

18. The details of the practice are explained in David Rollason, 'Ordeal', in Michael Lapidge et al., *The Wiley Blackwell Encyclopedia of Anglo-Saxon England*, 2nd edition (Oxford, 2014).

19. There is a sympathetic discussion of the philosophy of obedience that lies behind the Ælfstan incident in Katherine O'Brien O'Keeffe, *Stealing Obedience: Narratives of Agency and Identity in Later Anglo-Saxon England* (Toronto, 2012), pp. 2–6, 46–53.

20. As Thacker points out in his 'Æthelwold and Abingdon', p. 56, Æthelwold's 'rigor and discipline' also contrast with earlier Anglo-Saxon stories told of St Cuthbert.

21. The extra drink is discussed by Thacker in his 'Æthelwold and Abingdon', p. 56.

22. Cyril Hart, 'Athelstan "Half King" and his Family', *Anglo-Saxon England*, 2 (1973), pp. 115–44, reprinted in Hart, *The Danelaw* (London, 1992), pp. 569–604.
23. William of Malmesbury, *Life of St Dunstan*, in Michael Winterbottom and R.M. Thomson, eds and trans., *William of Malmesbury Saints' Lives* (Oxford, 2002), Book II, 2.1–2, pp. 238–9.

CHAPTER 14 LAWSUITS, LAW-BOOKS AND SERMONS: ARCHBISHOP DUNSTAN AND KING EDGAR

1. For the different emphases of the sources see Brooks, 'Career of St Dunstan', in Ramsey *et al.*, *St Dunstan: His Life, Times and Cult*, pp. 18–21.
2. The writer B. is employing a poetic term first used by Ovid in his *Fasti*, v. 260; see Winterbottom and Lapidge, *Early Lives of St Dunstan*, p. 80, note 238.
3. Brooks, *Early History of the Church of Canterbury*, p. 244.
4. Sawyer, *Catalogue*, no. S 1211. Text and translation in F.E. Harmer, *Select English Historical Documents of the Ninth and Tenth Centuries* (Cambridge, 1914), no. 23, pp. 37–8, 66–8.
5. On the use of oaths see Patrick Wormald, 'Charters, Law and the Settlement of Disputes in Anglo-Saxon England', in his *Legal Culture in the Early Medieval West. Law as Text, Image and Experience* (London, 1999), pp. 289–311, at p. 301.
6. My translation; for a different wording see Harmer, *Select English Historical Documents*.
7. Charles Insley, 'Rhetoric and Ritual in Late Anglo-Saxon Charters', in Marco Mostert and P.S. Barnwell, eds, *Medieval Legal Process: Physical, Spoken and Written Performance in the Middle Ages* (Turnhout, 2011), pp. 109–21, at pp. 109–16.
8. Sawyer S 1447. My translation. The text and translation are printed in Appendix I. A standard edition of the text, with a translation, is A.J. Robertson, *Anglo-Saxon Charters* (Cambridge, 1939), no. XLIV, pp. 90–3.
9. A.J. Robertson, *Anglo-Saxon Charters*, p. 337, note to lines 9 ff.
10. For Scott T. Smith's interpretation, also with a translation, see his *Land and Book: Literature and Land Tenure in Anglo-Saxon England* (Toronto, 2012), pp. 79–94.
11. The translation is by A.J. Robertson, *Anglo-Saxon Charters*, p. 91.
12. Nicholas Brooks, *The Early History of the Church of Canterbury: Christ Church from 597 to 1066* (Leicester, 1984), pp. 252, 377.
13. III Edmund, para 1, in A.J. Robertson, ed. and trans., *The Laws of the Kings of England from Edmund to Henry I* (Cambridge, 1925), pp. 12–13.
14. T.B. Lambert, 'Theft, Homicide and Crime in Late Anglo-Saxon Law', *Past and Present*, 214 (2012), 3–43, at p. 9.
15. R.J. Faith, *The English Peasantry and the Growth of Lordship* (London, 1997), pp. 109–52.
16. That Edgar's reign is crucial is the main argument of George Molyneaux's *The Formation of the English Kingdom in the Tenth Century* (Oxford, 2015).
17. The 'Hundred Ordinance' is printed as the first of Edgar's lawcodes, that is, 'I Edgar', in Robertson, *Laws of the Kings of England*, pp. 16–19. For discussion see Henry Loyn, 'The Hundred in England in the Tenth and Early Eleventh Centuries', in his *Society and Peoples: Studies in the History of England and Wales, c. 600–1200* (London, 1992), pp. 111–34.
18. Simon Keynes, 'Edgar, *rex admirabilis*', in Donald Scragg, ed., *Edgar, King of the English, 959–975* (Woodbridge, 2008), pp. 3–58, at p. 11. See also Patrick Wormald, *The Making of English Law: King Alfred to the Twelfth Century* (Oxford, 2001), pp. 313–17.

19. Wormald, *Making of English Law*, pp. 441-2.
20. For a survey of the various approaches to the compilation of the Vercelli Book, with useful further references, see Francis Leneghan, 'Teaching the Teachers: The Vercelli Book and the Mixed Life', *English Studies*, 94 (6) (2013), pp. 627-58.
21. Donald G. Scragg, 'An Old English Homilist of Archbishop Dunstan's Day', in Michael Korhammer, ed., *Words, Texts and Manuscripts: Studies in Anglo-Saxon Culture Presented to Helmut Gneuss* (Cambridge, 1992), pp. 181-92.
22. J.E. Cross, ed., *Cambridge Pembroke College 25: A Carolingian Sermonary Used by Anglo-Saxon Preachers* (London, 1987).
23. Vercelli Homily V, ed. Scragg, lines 10-22.

CHAPTER 15   WINCHESTER, CHIEF CITY OF EDGAR'S ENGLAND

1. Lantfred's 'The Translation and Miracles of St Swithun' and Wulfstan's 'The Metrical Narrative of St Swithun' are both edited with notes and commentary by Michael Lapidge, in his *The Cult of St Swithun*, Winchester Studies, 4.ii (Oxford, 2003).
2. M. Atherton, '"Sudden Wonder": Urban Perspectives in Late Anglo-Saxon Literature', in Gale R. Owen-Crocker and Susan D. Thompson, eds, *Towns and Topography: Essays in Memory of David Hill* (Oxford, 2014), pp. 74-82.
3. The Old English word *ceap* meaning 'purchase' (and pronounced roughly as 'chep') is preserved in place-names such as Chipping Norton and Chepstow.
4. For the charter, recorded in the *Codex Wintoniensis*, see Electronic Sawyer, S 1449. The text is edited and translated by Alexander Rumble, *Property and Piety in Early Medieval Winchester* (Oxford, 2002), no. VII.
5. The Golden Charter is now in London, British Library, at shelfmark Vespasian A. viii; the frontispiece is on folio 2v; Michelle P. Brown, *Manuscripts from the Anglo-Saxon Age* (London, 2007), plate 84. There is discussion of the image in Catherine E. Karkov, *The Ruler Portraits of Anglo-Saxon England* (Woodbridge, 2004), pp. 85-93.
6. Michael Lapidge, 'A Metrical *Vita S. Iudoci* from Tenth-Century Winchester', *Journal of Medieval Latin*, 10 (2000), pp. 255-306.
7. Walter Hofstetter, 'Winchester and the Standardization of Old English Vocabulary', *Anglo-Saxon England*, 17 (1988), pp. 139-61. Mechthild Gretsch, 'Late Old English (899-1066)', in Haruko Momma and Michael Matto, eds, *A Companion to the History of the English Language* (Oxford, 2008), pp. 165-71.
8. A classic study of Æthelwold's work on the glossing of the psalter and other literary projects is Mechthild Gretsch, *The Intellectual Foundations of the English Benedictine Reform* (Cambridge, 1999).
9. Dorothy Whitelock, ed. and trans., 'King Edgar's Establishment of Monasteries', in D. Whitelock *et al.*, *Councils and Synods, I (AD 871-1204)* (Oxford, 1981), no. 33, pp. 142-54.
10. Thomas Symons, ed. and trans., *Regularis Concordia Anglicae Nationis Monachorum Sanctimonialiumque: The Monastic Agreement of the Monks and Nuns of the English Nation* (London, 1953), ch.2, section 28, p. 26.
11. Old English *þæs fyrhuses hlywing* seems to mean 'the protection of the firehouse' or punningly 'the warmth of the firehouse'. See the edition of the Old English interlinear version in Lucia Kornexl, ed., *Die Regularis Concordia und ihre altenglische Interlinearversion. Edition mit Einleitung und Kommentar* (Munich, 1993).
12. Lapidge and Winterbottom, *Life of St Æthelwold*, pp. 220-1.

13. M. Heinzelmann, *Translationsberichte und andere Quellen des Reliquienkultes*, Typologie des sources du moyen âge occidental, xxxiii (Turnhout, 1979).
14. Thomas Head, *Hagiography and the Cult of the Saints: the Diocese of Orléans 800–1200* (Cambridge, 1990).
15. See Lapidge in his *Cult of St Swithun*, pp. 13–14, 252–4.
16. Martin Biddle, *et al.*, *Winchester in the Early Middle Ages. An Edition and Discussion of the Winton Domesday*, Winchester Studies, I (Oxford, 1976), pp. 234 and 429.
17. Lapidge, *Cult of St Swithun*, pp. 264–5, lines 69–82.
18. For this unpleasant, if limited, feature of society at the time see David A.E. Pelteret, *Slavery in Early Mediaeval England from the Reign of Alfred until the Twelfth Century* (Woodbridge, 1995).
19. In his note on the name *Flodoald*, Olof von Feilitzen suggests that this is a Norman or Picard name based on the Old French name borrowed into English from Old German Hlodwald. See Biddle, *Winchester in the Early Middle Ages*, p. 557.
20. Lapidge, *Cult of St Swithun*, pp. 308–9.
21. II Athelstan 23; see Whitelock, trans., *English Historical Documents c.500–1042*, 2nd edition (London, 1979), p. 421. Lapidge, *Cult of St Swithun*, pp. 308–309, note 231 gives details and further references.
22. The complexities of the case are analysed by Dorothy Whitelock, 'Wulfstan Cantor and Anglo-Saxon law', in A.H. Orrick, ed., *Nordica et Anglica: Studies in Honor of Stefan Einarsson* (The Hague, 1968), pp. 83–92, repr, in her *History, Law and Literature in 10th–11th Century England* (London, 1981), no. V.
23. On Ælfric's hagiography there is a detailed discussion in Mechthild Gretsch, *Ælfric and the Cult of the Saints in Late Anglo-Saxon England* (Cambridge, 2009).
24. On Wulfstan Cantor as a poet and author, see Emily V. Thornbury, *Becoming a Poet in Anglo-Saxon England* (Cambridge, 2014), pp. 209–23.
25. For Wulfstan Cantor's view of Edgar's severe law, see Lapidge, *Cult of St Swithun*, p. 514, lines 453–65.

EPILOGUE

1. Mercedes Salvador-Bello, 'The Edgar Panegyrics in the *Anglo-Saxon Chronicle*', in Donald Scragg, ed., *Edgar, King of the English, 959–975* (Woodbridge, 2008), pp. 252–72.
2. G. P. Cubbin, ed., *The Anglo-Saxon Chronicle, 6: MS D* (Woodbridge, and Rochester, NY, 1996).
3. Winterbottom and Lapidge, *Early Lives of St Dunstan*, p. 96, note 280.
4. Grammatically *þa baþu* 'the baths' is the nominative plural, while *baðan* and *bathum* 'at the baths' are alternative forms of the dative plural of the same word, listed in dictionaries as singular *bæð* 'bath'.
5. Text and translation in Treharne, *Old and Middle English: An Anthology*.
6. 'The Ruin', lines 1–5, in Robert E. Bjork, *Old English Shorter Poems, Volume II*: *Wisdom and Lyric* (Cambridge, MA and London, 2014), p. 119.
7. Mary Clayton, ed. and trans., *Old English Poems of Christ and His Saints* (Cambridge, MA and London, 2013), p. 3.
8. For the history of Anglo-Saxon Bath and its reformed Abbey see the discussion and references in John Blair, 'Bath', in Lapidge *et al.*, *Wiley Blackwell Encyclopedia of Anglo-Saxon England*.

Select Bibliography

The bibliography provides references to primary works, arranged by author or by editor, and to secondary literature selected for relevance to the themes of this book.

EDITIONS, FACSIMILES AND TRANSLATIONS OF PRIMARY WORKS

Æthelstan's Gift of Relics to Exeter Cathedral, in Max Förster, *Zur Geschichte des Reliquienkultus in Altengland* (Munich, 1943), pp. 63–114; trans. Swanton, *Anglo-Saxon Prose*, pp. 15–19.

Æthelweard the Chronicler, *The Chronicle of Æthelweard*, ed. and trans. Alistair Campbell (London, 1962).

Æthelwold, 'King Edgar's Establishment of the Monasteries', in Dorothy Whitelock, ed. and trans., *Councils and Synods with Other Documents Relating to the English Church AD 871–1204* (Oxford, 1981), pp. 142–54.

Aldhelm, *The Prose Works*, trans. Michael Lapidge and Michael Herren (Cambridge, 1979/2009).

———, *The Poetic Works*, trans. Michael Lapidge and James Rosier (Cambridge, 1985/2009).

Alexander, Michael, trans., *Beowulf* (Harmondsworth, 1973).

Andrew of Fleury, *Vita Gauzlini abbatis Floriacensis monasterii*, [Life of Gauzlin, Abbot of Fleury], ed. and trans. Robert-Henri Bautier and Gillette Labory (Paris, 1969).

Anlezark, Daniel, ed. and trans., *The Old English Dialogues of Solomon and Saturn* (Woodbridge, 2009).

B., *Vita S. Dunstani* [*Life of St Dunstan*], in Winterbottom and Lapidge, *Earliest Lives of St Dunstan*, pp. 1–109.

Barlow, Frank, ed. and trans., *The Life of King Edward who Rests at Westminster*, 2nd edition (Oxford, 1992).

Bately, Janet, ed., *The Old English Orosius*, Early English Text Society, supplementary series 6 (London, 1980).

———, ed., *The Anglo-Saxon Chronicle: A Collaborative Edition, Volume 3, Manuscript A* (Cambridge, 1986).

Bede, *Venerabilis Bedae opera historica*, ed. Charles Plummer, 2 vols (Oxford, 1896; reprinted 1969).

——, *Bede's Ecclesiastical History of the English People*, ed. and trans. Bertram Colgrave and R.A.B. Mynors (Oxford, 1969).

——, *Life of St Cuthbert*, in D.H. Farmer, ed., and J.F. Webb, trans., *The Age of Bede* (London, 1998).

——, *The Reckoning of Time*, trans. Faith Wallis (Liverpool, 1999).

——, *The Ecclesiastical History of the English Nation*, trans. Roger Collins and Judith McClure (Oxford, 2008).

Bjork, Robert E., ed., *The Old English Poems of Cynewulf* (Cambridge, MA and London, 2013).

——, *Old English Shorter Poems, Volume II: Wisdom and Lyric* (Cambridge, MA and London, 2014).

Birch, Walter de Gray, ed., *Cartularium Saxonicum: A Collection of Charters Relating to Anglo-Saxon History* (London, 1885–99).

Bishop, T.A.M., *English Caroline Minuscule* (Oxford, 1971).

Bradley, S.A.J., trans., *Anglo-Saxon Poetry* (London, 1982).

Braune, Wilhelm, and Ernst A. Ebbinghaus, eds, *Althochdeutsches Lesebuch* (Tübingen, 1969).

Brown, Michelle P., *Manuscripts from the Anglo-Saxon Age* (London, 2007).

Brown, T.J., ed., *The Durham Ritual*, Early English Manuscripts in Facsimile, 16 (Copenhagen, 1969).

Buescu, V., ed., *Cicéron, Les Aratea [Cicero, Aratea]* (Hildesheim, 1966).

Campbell, Alistair, ed., *The Tollemache Orosius*, Early English Manuscripts in Facsimile, 3 (Copenhagen, 1953).

——, ed., *The Chronicle of Æthelweard* (London, 1962).

Clayton, Mary, ed. and trans., *Old English Poems of Christ and his Saints* (Cambridge, MA and London, 2013).

Cross, J.E., ed., *Cambridge Pembroke College 25: A Carolingian Sermonary Used by Anglo-Saxon Preachers* (London, 1987).

Cubbin, G.P., ed., *The Anglo-Saxon Chronicle, 6: MS D* (Woodbridge and Rochester, NY, 1996).

Delanty, Greg and Michael Matto, eds, *The Word Exchange: Anglo-Saxon Poems in Translation* (New York and London, 2011).

Einhard, *Life of Charlemagne* in David Ganz, trans., *Two Lives of Charlemagne* (Harmondsworth, 2008).

Fulk, R.D., Robert E. Bjork, and John D. Niles, eds, *Klaeber's Beowulf and the Fight at Finnsburg* (Toronto, 2008).

Gerald of Wales, *The History and Topography of Ireland*, trans. John O'Meara (London, 1983).

Godden, Malcom, and Susan Irvine, eds, *The Old English Boethius: An Edition of the Old English Versions of Boethius's De Consolatione Philosophae*, 2 vols (Oxford, 2009).

Gregory the Great, *Regula pastoralis [Pastoral Rule]* in J.P. Migne, ed., *Patrologia Latina* 77, 12.

Griffiths, Bill, ed., *Alfred's Metres of Boethius* (Pinner, Middlesex, 1991).

Hamer, Richard F.S., ed. and trans., *A Choice of Anglo-Saxon Verse* (London, 2006).

Harmer, F.E., ed., *Select English Historical Documents of the Ninth and Tenth Centuries* (Cambridge, 1914).

Heaney, Seamus, trans., *Beowulf* (London, 2000).

Hollis, A.S., ed., *Ovid: Ars Amatoria Book I* (Oxford, 1977).

Hooke, Della, ed., *Warwickshire Anglo-Saxon Charter Bounds* (Woodbridge, 1999).

Irvine, Susan and Malcolm R. Godden, eds and trans., *The Old English Boethius: With Verse Prologues and Epilogues Associated with King Alfred* (Cambridge, MA and London, 2012).

Jack, George, ed., *Beowulf: A Student Edition* (Oxford, 1994).

Jones, Christopher, *Old English Shorter Poems, Volume I: Religious and Didactic* (Cambridge, MA and London, 2013).

Keil, Heinrich, ed., *Grammatici Latini, V: Artium Scriptores Minores* (Leipzig, 1868).

Keynes, Simon, 'The Fonthill Letter', in Michael Korhammer, ed., *Words, Texts and Manuscripts: Studies in Anglo-Saxon Culture Presented to Helmut Gneuss* (Cambridge, 1992), pp. 53–97.

Keynes, Simon, and Michael Lapidge, trans., *Alfred the Great: Asser's Life of King Alfred and Other Contemporary Sources* (Harmondsworth, 1983).

Klaeber, Frederick, ed., *Beowulf and the Fight at Finnsburg*, 3rd edition (Lexington, MA, 1950).

Kornexl, Lucia, ed., *Die regularis concordia und ihre altenglische Interlinearversion* (Munich, 1993).

Krapp, George Phillip, ed., *Vercelli Book*, Anglo-Saxon Poetic Records, 2 (New York, 1932).

Krapp, George Philip and Elliot Van Kirk Dobbie, eds, *The Exeter Book*, Anglo-Saxon Poetic Records, 3 (New York, 1936).

Kuhn, Sherman M., ed., *The Vespasian Psalter* (Ann Arbor, 1965).

Lantfred of Winchester, *Translatio et miracula S. Swithuni*, in Lapidge, ed., *Cult of St Swithun*, pp. 217–333.

Lapidge, Michael, ed., 'Some Latin Poems as Evidence for the Reign of Athelstan', *Anglo-Saxon England*, 9 (1981), pp. 61–98; reprinted in his *Anglo-Latin Literature 900–1066*, pp. 49–86.

———, ed., 'A Metrical *Vita S. Iudoci* from Tenth-Century Winchester', *Journal of Medieval Latin*, 10 (2000), 255–306.

———, ed., *The Cult of St Swithun*, Winchester Studies, 4.ii (Oxford, 2003).

Lapidge, Michael, and Michael Winterbottom, eds and trans., *Wulfstan of Winchester: The Life of St Æthelwold* (Oxford, 1991).

Liebermann, Felix, ed., *Die Heiligen Englands* (Hanover, 1889).

Livingston, Michael, ed., *The Battle of Brunanburh: A Casebook* (Exeter, 2011).

Marsden, Richard, ed., *The Cambridge Old English Reader* (Cambridge, 2004).

McCann, Justin, ed. and trans., *The Rule of St Benedict* (London, 1952).

McGurck, P., D.N. Dumville, M.R. Godden and Ann Knock, eds, *An Eleventh-Century Anglo-Saxon Illustrated Miscellany*, British Library, Cotton Tiberius B.v, part I, Early English Manuscripts in Facsimile, 21 (Copenhagen, 1983).

Miller, T., ed., *The Old English Version of Bede's Ecclesiastical History of the English People*, Early English Text Society, original series 95–6, 110–11 (London, 1890–8).

Morris, Richard, ed., *The Blickling Homilies* (London, 1880).

Muir, Bernard J., ed., *The Exeter Anthology of Old English Poetry: An Edition of Exeter Dean and Chapter MS 3501*, 2nd edition (Exeter, 2000).

Nelson, Janet, trans., *The Annals of St-Bertin* (Manchester, 1991).

O'Neill, Patrick P., ed., *King Alfred's Old English Translation of the First Fifty Psalms* (Cambridge, MA, 2001).

Orchard, Andy, ed. and trans., *The Wonders of the East*, in his *Pride and Prodigies*, pp. 175–203.

Orosius, *Seven Books of History against the Pagans*, trans. A.T. Fear (Liverpool, 2010).

Ovid, *The Art of Love*, in J.H. Mozley, ed. and trans., *Ovid, II, The Art of Love and Other Poems* (Cambridge, MA and London, 1979).

Pálsson, Hermann, and Paul Edwards, trans., *Egil's Saga* (Harmondsworth, 1976).

Preston, Todd, ed. and trans., *King Alfred's Book of Laws: A Study of the Domboc and its Influence on English Identity* (Jefferson, NC, 2012).

Priscian, *Periegesis*, in Paul van de Woestinje, ed., *La Périégèse de Priscien: Édition Critique* (Bruges, 1953).

Robertson, A.J., ed. and trans., *The Laws of the Kings of England from Edmund to Henry I. Part One. Edmund to Canute* (Cambridge, 1925).

——, *Anglo-Saxon Charters* (Cambridge, 1939).

Rumble, Alexander R., ed. and trans., *Property and Piety in Early Medieval Winchester* (Oxford, 2002).

Saupe, Karen, ed., *Middle English Marian Lyrics* (Kalamazoo, MI, 1997).

Scragg, Donald, ed., *The Vercelli Homilies and Related Texts*, Early English Text Society, original series 300 (London, 1992).

Sherley-Price, Leo, trans., *Bede: A History of the English Church and People* (London, 1968).

Sisam, Celia, ed., *The Vercelli Book*, Early English Manuscripts in Facsimile, 19 (Copenhagen, 1976).

Slavitt, David R., trans., 'The Battle of Maldon', in Greg Delanty and Michael Matto, eds, *The Word Exchange: Anglo-Saxon Poems in Translation* (New York and London, 2011), pp. 92–111.

Smaragdus of Saint-Mihiel, *Commentary on the Rule of Saint Benedict*, trans. David Barry (Kalamazoo, MI, 2007).

Smith, Ted Johnson, ed., *The History of St Cuthbert* (Cambridge, 2002).

Storms, G., ed. and trans., *Anglo-Saxon Magic* (The Hague, 1948).

Swanton, Michael, trans., *Anglo-Saxon Prose* (London, 1975).

——, trans., *The Anglo-Saxon Chronicles* (London, 2000).

Sweet, Henry, ed. and trans., *King Alfred's West-Saxon Version of Gregory's Pastoral Care*, 2 vols, Early English Text Society, original series 45 and 50 (London, 1871–2; reprinted London, 1958).

Symons, Thomas, ed. and trans., *Regularis Concordia Anglicae Nationis Monachorum Sanctimonaliumque: The Monastic Agreement of the Monks and Nuns of the English Nation* (London, 1953).

Taylor, Simon, ed., *The Anglo-Saxon Chronicle: A Collaborative Edition, Volume 4, Manuscript B* (Cambridge, 1983).

Tennyson, Hallam, 'The Song of Brunanburh', *The Contemporary Review*, 28 (November 1876), 920–2.

Tolkien, J.R.R., *Beowulf: A Translation and Commentary, together with Sellic Spell*, ed. Christopher Tolkien (London, 2014).

Treharne, Elaine, ed. and trans., *Old and Middle English c.890–c.1450: An Anthology*, 3rd edition (Oxford, 2009).

van der Horst, Koert *et al.*, eds, *The Utrecht Psalter in Medieval Art: Picturing the Psalms of David* (Utrecht, 1996).

Verey, Christopher D. *et al.*, eds, *The Durham Gospels*, Early English Manuscripts in Facsimile, 20 (Copenhagen, 1980).

Webster, Leslie, and Janet Backhouse, eds, *The Making of England: Anglo-Saxon Art and Culture AD 600–900* (London, 1991).

Whitelock, Dorothy, ed., *Anglo-Saxon Wills* (Cambridge, 1930).

——, ed., *Sweet's Anglo-Saxon Reader in Verse and Prose*, 15th edition (Oxford, 1967).

——, trans., *English Historical Documents c.500–1042*, 2nd edition (London, 1979).

——, ed. and trans., 'King Edgar's Establishment of Monasteries', in D. Whitelock, M. Brett and C.N.L. Brooke, eds, *Councils and Synods, I (AD 871–1204)* (Oxford, 1981).

William of Malmesbury, *Life of St Dunstan*, in Michael Winterbottom and R.M. Thomson, eds and trans., *William of Malmesbury Saints' Lives* (Oxford, 2002).

Wilson, David M., ed., *The Bayeux Tapestry* (London, 2004).

Winterbottom, Michael, and Michael Lapidge, eds and trans., *The Earliest Lives of St Dunstan* (Oxford, 2012).

Wright, David H., ed., *The Vespasian Psalter: British Museum Cotton Vespasian A.I* (Copenhagen, 1967).

SELECT BIBLIOGRAPHY OF SECONDARY WORKS

Abels, Richard P., *Alfred the Great: War, Kingship and Culture in Anglo-Saxon England* (London, 1998).

Abrams, Lesley, *Anglo-Saxon Glastonbury: Church and Endowment* (Woodbridge, 1996).

———, 'Edward the Elder's Danelaw', in Nicholas J. Higham and David H. Hill, eds, *Edward the Elder, 899–924* (London, 2001), pp. 128–43.

Atherton, Mark, 'King Alfred's Approach to the Study of Latin', in D. Cram, A. Linn and E. Nowak, eds, *History of Linguistics 1996 Vol. 2: From Classical to Contemporary Linguistics* (Amsterdam, 1999), pp. 15–22.

———, 'Coins, Merchants and the Reeve: Royal Authority in the Old English Legend of the Seven Sleepers of Ephesus', in Gale Owen-Crocker and Brian W. Schneider, eds, *Royal Authority in Anglo-Saxon England* (Oxford, 2013).

———, 'Sudden Wonder': Urban Perspectives in Late Anglo-Saxon Literature', in Gale R. Owen-Crocker and Susan D. Thompson, eds, *Towns and Topography: Essays in Memory of David Hill* (Oxford, 2014), pp. 74–82.

Backhouse, Janet *et al.*, *The Golden Age of Anglo-Saxon Art 966–1066* (London, 1984).

Baker, Peter, *Honour, Exchange and Violence in Beowulf* (Cambridge, 2013).

Barrow, Julia, and Andrew Wareham, eds, *Myth, Rulership, Church and Charters* (Aldershot, 2008).

Bately, Janet M., 'Old English Prose before and during the Reign of Alfred', *Anglo-Saxon England*, 17 (1988), 93–138.

———, 'The Literary Prose of Alfred's Reign: Translation or Transformation?', Inaugural Lecture in the Chair of English Language and Medieval Literature delivered at King's College, London, on 4 March 1980; reprinted in Paul Szarmach, ed., *Old English Prose: Basic Readings* (New York, 2000), pp. 3–28.

———, 'The Old English *Orosius*', in Nicole Guenther Discenza and Paul E. Szarmach, eds, *A Companion to Alfred the Great* (Leiden and Boston, 2015), pp. 313–43.

Bately, Janet, and Anton Englert, eds, *Ohthere's Voyages: A Late 9th-century Account of Voyages along the Coasts of Norway and Denmark and its Cultural Context* (Roskilde, 2007).

Biddle, Martin *et al.*, *Winchester in the Early Middle Ages: An Edition and Discussion of the Winton Domesday*, Winchester Studies, I (Oxford, 1976).

Blunt, C.E., 'Northumbrian Coins in the Name of Alwaldus', *British Numismatic Journal*, 55, 192–4.

Bock, Oliver, 'C. Maier's Use of a Reagent in the Vercelli Book', *The Library*, 16.3 (2015), 249–81.

Bonner, Gerald, David Rollason and Clare Stancliffe, eds, *St Cuthbert, his Cult and Community* (Woodbridge, 1989).

Bostock, J. Knight, *A Handbook on Old High German Literature* (Oxford, 1976).

Bosworth, Joseph, and T. Northcote Toller, *An Anglo-Saxon Dictionary* (Oxford, 1898).

Boynton, Mark, and Susan Reynolds, 'The Author of the Fonthill Letter', in *Anglo-Saxon England*, 25 (1996), 91–5.

Bredehoft, Thomas, *Textual Histories: Readings in the Anglo-Saxon Chronicle* (Toronto, 2001).

Bremmer, Jr, Rolf R., 'Anglo-Saxon England and the Germanic World', in Clare A. Lees, ed., *Early Medieval English Literature* (Cambridge, 2013), pp. 185–208.

Brooks, Nicholas, *The Early History of the Church of Canterbury: Christ Church from 597 to 1066* (Leicester, 1984).

———, 'The Career of St Dunstan', in Nigel Ramsey, Margaret Sparks and Tim Tatton-Brown, *St Dunstan: His Life, Times and Cult* (Woodbridge, 1992), pp. 1–23.

—————, 'The Fonthill Letter, Ealdorman Ordlaf and Anglo-Saxon Law in Practice', in Stephen Baxter *et al.*, ed., *Early Medieval Studies in Memory of Patrick Wormald* (Farnham, 2009), pp. 301–17.

—————, 'Why is the Anglo-Saxon Chronicle about Kings?', *Anglo-Saxon England*, 39 (2010), 43–70.

Brooks, Nicholas, and Catherine Cubitt, eds, *Oswald of Worcester: Life and Influence* (Leicester, 1996).

Brown, Michelle P., *The Book of Cerne: Prayer, Patronage, and Power in Ninth-Century England* (London, 1996).

—————, *The Lindisfarne Gospels: Society, Spirituality and the Scribe* (London, 2003).

Brown, Michelle P., and Carol A. Farr, *Mercia: An Anglo-Saxon Kingdom in Europe* (London, 2001).

Budny, Mildred, 'St Dunstan's Classbook and its Frontispiece: Dunstan's Portrait and Autograph', in Nigel Ramsay *et al.*, *St Dunstan: His Life, Times and Cult* (Woodbridge, 1992), pp. 103–42.

Bullough, Donald, 'St Oswald: Monk, Bishop and Archbishop', in Brooks and Cubitt, *Oswald of Worcester: Life and Influence*, pp. 1–22.

Campbell, James, 'What is not Known about the Reign of Edward the Elder', in N.J. Higham and D.H. Hill, eds, *Edward the Elder, 899–924* (London, 2001), pp. 12–24.

Carroll, Jayne, 'Viking Wars and the *Anglo-Saxon Chronicle*', in Richard North and Joe Allard, eds, *Beowulf and Other Stories: A New Introduction to Old English, Old Icelandic and Anglo-Norman Literatures*, 2nd edition (London, 2012), pp. 329–50, at pp. 363–4.

Carruthers, Mary J., *The Book of Memory: A Study of Memory in Medieval Culture*, 2nd edition (Cambridge, 2008).

Carver, Martin, *Sutton Hoo: Burial Ground of Kings?* (London, 2000).

—————, *Sutton Hoo: A Seventh-Century Princely Burial Ground and its Context* (London, 2005).

Conner, Patrick W., *Anglo-Saxon Exeter: A Tenth-Century Cultural History* (Woodbridge, 1993).

Cubitt, Catherine, 'The Tenth-Century Benedictine Reform', *Early Medieval Europe*, 6 (1997), 77–94.

—————, 'Archbishop Dunstan; A Prophet in Politics?' in Julia Barrow and Andrew Wareham, *Myth, Rulership, Church and Charters: Essays in Honour of Nicholas Brooks* (Aldershot and Burlington VT, 2008), pp. 145–66.

Cumberledge, Nicola, 'Reading between the Lines: The Place of Mercia within an Expanding Wessex', *Midland History*, 27 (2002), 1–15.

Discenza, Nicole Guenther, *The King's English: Strategies of Translation in the Old English Boethius* (Albany, 2005).

—————, 'A Map of the Universe: Geography and Cosmology in the Program of Alfred the Great', in Catherine Karkov and Nicholas Howe, eds, *Conversion and Colonization in Anglo-Saxon England* (Tempe, AZ, 2006), pp. 83–108.

Discenza, Nicole Guenther, and Paul E. Szarmach, eds, *A Companion to Alfred the Great* (Leiden and Boston, 2015).

Dodwell, C.R., *Anglo-Saxon Art: A New Perspective* (Manchester, 1982).

Drout, Michael D.C., *How Tradition Works; A Meme-based Cultural Poetics of the Anglo-Saxon Tenth Century* (Tempe, Arizona, 2006).

Dumville, David, *Wessex and England from Alfred to Edgar: Six Essays on Political, Cultural and Ecclesiastical Revival* (Woodbridge, 1992).

—————, *English Caroline Script and Monastic History: Studies in Benedictinism, A.D. 950–1030* (Woodbridge, 1993).

Ekwall, Eilert, *The Concise Oxford Dictionary of English Place-names*, 4th edition (Oxford, 1960).

Faith, R.J., *The English Peasantry and the Growth of Lordship* (London, 1997).

Featherstone, Simon, *Englishness: Twentieth-Century Popular Culture and the Forming of English Identity* (Edinburgh, 2009).

Foot, Sarah, 'The Making of Angelcynn: English Identity before the Norman Conquest', *Transactions of the Royal Historical Society*, 6th series, vi (1996), 25–49.

——, *Æthelstan: The First King of England* (New Haven and London, 2011).

Gameson, Richard, 'The Origin of the Exeter Book of Old English Poetry', *Anglo-Saxon England*, 25 (1996), 135–85.

Gelling, Margaret, and Ann Cole, *The Landscape of Place-names*, new edition (Donington, 2014).

Godden, Malcolm, 'Wærferth and King Alfred: The Fate of the Old English *Dialogues*', in J. Roberts, J. Nelson and M. Godden, eds, *Alfred the Wise: Studies in Honour of Janet Bately* (Cambridge, 1997), pp. 35–52.

——, 'The Anglo-Saxons and the Goths: Rewriting the Sack of Rome', *Anglo-Saxon England*, 31 (2002), 47–68.

——, 'Did King Alfred Write Anything?' *Medium Aevum* 76.1 (2007), 1–23.

——, 'The Alfredian Project and its Aftermath: Rethinking the Literary History of the Ninth and Tenth Centuries', *Proceedings of the British Academy*, 162 (2009), 93–122.

——, 'The Old English Orosius and its Sources', *Anglia*, 129 (2011), 297–320.

Gretsch, Mechthild, *The Intellectual Foundations of the English Benedictine Reform* (Cambridge, 1999).

——, 'The Junius Psalter Gloss: Tradition and Innovation', in Higham and Hill, *Edward the Elder*, pp. 280–91.

——, 'Late Old English (899–1066)', in Haruko Momma and Michael Matto, eds, *A Companion to the History of the English Language* (Oxford, 2008), pp. 165–71.

——, *Ælfric and the Cult of the Saints in Late Anglo-Saxon England* (Cambridge, 2009).

——, 'Historiography and Literary Patronage in Late Anglo-Saxon England: the Evidence of Æthelweard's *Chronicon*', *Anglo-Saxon England*, 41 (2013), 205–48.

Grierson, Philip, 'The Relations between England and Flanders before the Norman Conquest', *Transactions of the Royal Historical Society*, 4th series, 23 (1941), 71–112.

Hadley, D., and J.D. Richards, eds, *Cultures in Contact: Scandinavian Settlement in the Ninth and Tenth Centuries* (Turnhout, 2000).

Hall, R.A. *et al.*, *Aspects of Anglo-Scandinavian York* (York, 2004).

Hart, Cyril, 'Athelstan "Half King" and his Family', *Anglo-Saxon England*, 2 (1973), 115–44, reprinted in Hart, *The Danelaw*, pp. 569–604.

——, *The Danelaw* (London, 1992).

Hartman, Megan E., 'The Limits of Conservative Composition in Old English Poetry', in Leonard Neidorf, ed., *The Dating of Beowulf* (Cambridge, 2014), pp. 79–96.

Head, Thomas, *Hagiography and the Cult of the Saints: the Diocese of Orléans 800–1200* (Cambridge, 1990).

Higham, Nicholas J., 'Edward the Elder's Reputation', in Higham and Hill, *Edward the Elder*, pp. 1–11.

Higham, Nicholas J. and David H. Hill, eds, *Edward the Elder, 899–924* (London, 2001).

Higham, Nicholas J., and Martin J. Ryan, *The Anglo-Saxon World* (New Haven and London, 2013).

Hill, David, 'Eleventh-Century Labours of the Months in Prose and Pictures', *Landscape History*, 20 (1998), 29–39.

Hill, John M., *The Narrative Pulse of Beowulf: Arrivals and Departures* (Toronto, 2008).

Hines, John, 'Egill's Hofuðlausn in Time and Place', *Saga-Book of the Viking Society*, 24 (1995), 83–104.

Hinton, David A., *Gold and Gilt, Pots and Pins: Possessions and People in Medieval Britain* (Oxford, 2005).

Hofstetter, Walter, 'Winchester and the Standardization of Old English Vocabulary', *Anglo-Saxon England*, 17 (1988), 139–61.

Howe, Nicholas, *Writing the Map of Anglo-Saxon England* (New Haven and London, 2008).

Insley, Charles, 'Rhetoric and Ritual in Late Anglo-Saxon Charters', in Marco Mostert and P.S. Barnwell, eds, *Medieval Legal Process: Physical, Spoken and Written Performance in the Middle Ages* (Turnhout, 2011), pp. 109–21.

Irvine, Susan, 'The Alfredian Prefaces and Epilogues', in Nicole Guenther Discenza and Paul E. Szarmach, eds, *A Companion to Alfred the Great* (Leiden and Boston, 2015), pp. 143–70.

Irving, Edward B., *Rereading Beowulf* (Philadelphia, 1992).

Janowitz, Anne, *England's Ruins: Poetic Purpose and the National Landscape* (Oxford, 1990).

Jayakumar, Sashi, 'Eadwig and Edgar: Politics, Propaganda, Faction', in Donald Scragg, ed., *Edgar, King of the English, 959–975* (Woodbridge, 2008), pp. 83–103.

Jorgensen, Alice, ed., *Reading the Anglo-Saxon Chronicle: Language, Literature, History* (Turnhout, 2010).

Karkov, Catherine E., *The Ruler Portraits of Anglo-Saxon England* (Woodbridge, 2004).

——, 'Art and Writing: Voice, Image, Object', in Clare Lees, ed., *The Cambridge History of Early Medieval English Literature* (Cambridge, 2013), pp. 73–98.

Karkov, Catherine E., and Nicholas Howe, eds, *Conversion and Colonization in Anglo-Saxon England* (Tempe, Arizona, 2006).

Kelly, Susan, 'Anglo-Saxon Lay Society and the Written Word', in R. McKitterick, ed., *The Uses of Literacy in Early Medieval Europe* (Cambridge, 1990), pp. 36–62.

Ker, Neil R. *Catalogue of Manuscripts Containing Anglo-Saxon* (Oxford, 1957).

Keynes, Simon, 'King Athelstan's Books', in Michael Lapidge and Helmut Gneuss, eds, *Learning and Literature in Anglo-Saxon England: Studies Presented to Peter Clemoes* (Cambridge, 1985), pp. 143–201.

——, 'The "Dunstan B" Charters', *Anglo-Saxon England*, 23 (1994), 165–93.

——, 'On the Authenticity of Asser's Life of King Alfred', *Journal of Ecclesiastical History*, 47 (1996), 529–51.

——, 'Anglo-Saxon Entries in the "Liber Vitae" of Brescia', in J. Roberts, J. Nelson and M. Godden, eds, *Alfred the Wise: Studies in Honour of Janet Bately* (Cambridge, 1997), pp. 99–119.

——, 'Edward, King of the Anglo-Saxons', in Higham and Hill, *Edward the Elder*, pp. 40–66.

——, 'The Power of the Written Word: Alfredian England 871–899', in Timothy Reuter, ed., *Alfred the Great: Papers from the Eleventh-Centenary Conferences* (Aldershot, 2003), pp. 175–97.

——, 'Edgar, *rex admirabilis*', in Donald Scragg, ed., *Edgar, King of the English, 959–975* (Woodbridge, 2008), pp. 3–58.

Knock, Ann, 'Analysis of a Translator: The Old English *Wonders of the East*', in J. Roberts, J. Nelson and M. Godden, eds, *Alfred the Wise: Studies in Honour of Janet Bately* (Cambridge, 1997), pp. 121–6.

Korhammer, Michael, ed., *Words, Texts and Manuscripts: Studies in Anglo-Saxon Culture Presented to Helmut Gneuss* (Cambridge, 1992).

Kretzschmar, William A. Jr, 'Adaptation and *anweald* in the Old English Orosius', *Anglo-Saxon England*, 16 (1987), 127–45.

Lambert, T.B. 'Theft, Homicide and Crime in Late Anglo-Saxon Law', *Past and Present*, 214 (2012), 3–43.

Lapidge, Michael, 'Æthelwold as Scholar and Teacher', in *Bishop Æthelwold: His Career and Influence*, ed. B. Yorke (Woodbridge, 1988), pp. 89–117.

———, *Anglo-Latin Literature 900–1066* (London, 1993).

———, 'Stoic Cosmology and the Source of the First Old English Riddle', *Anglia*, 112 (1994), 1–25.

———, *Anglo-Latin Literature, 600–899* (London, 1996).

———, *The Anglo-Saxon Library* (Oxford, 2006).

Lapidge, Michael, John Blair, Simon Keynes and Donald Scragg, eds, *The Wiley Blackwell Encyclopedia of Anglo-Saxon England*, 2nd edition (Oxford, 2014).

Leclercq, Jean, *The Love of Learning and the Desire for God: A Study of Monastic Culture* (New York, 1961).

Lees, Clare A., ed., *Early Medieval English Literature* (Cambridge, 2013).

Leneghan, Francis, 'Teaching the Teachers: The Vercelli Book and the Mixed Life', *English Studies*, 94 (6) (2013), 627–58.

———, '*Translatio imperii*: The Old English *Orosius* and the Rise of Wessex', *Anglia*, 133 (4) (2015), 656–705.

Lenz, Karmen, *Ræd and Frofer: Christian Poetics in the Old English Froferboc Meters* (Amsterdam and New York, 2012).

Levison, Wilhelm, *England and the Continent in the Eighth Century* (Oxford, 1946).

Leyser, Henrietta, *A Short History of the Anglo-Saxons* (London, 2016).

Loyn, Henry, 'The Hundred in England in the Tenth and Early Eleventh Centuries', in his *Society and Peoples: Studies in the History of England and Wales, c.600–1200* (London, 1992), pp. 111–34.

Lucas, John, *England and Englishness: Ideas of Nationhood in English Poetry 1688–1900* (London, 1990).

Magennis, Hugh, *Images of Community in Old English Poetry* (Cambridge, 2006).

Mawer, A., 'The Redemption of the Five Boroughs', *English Historical Review*, 38 (1923), 551–7.

McKitterick, Rosamond, ed., *The Uses of Literacy in Early Medieval Europe* (Cambridge, 1990).

Molyneaux, George, 'The Old English Bede: Ideology or Christian Instruction?', *English Historical Review*, 124, no. 511 (2009), 1289–1323.

———, *The Formation of the English Kingdom in the Tenth Century* (Oxford, 2015).

Momma, Haruko, *From Philology to English Studies: Language and Culture in the Nineteenth Century* (Cambridge, 2013).

Momma, Haruko, and Michael Matto, eds, *A Companion to the History of the English Language* (Oxford, 2008).

Morrish, Jennifer, 'King Alfred's Letter as a Source on Learning in England', in Paul Szarmach, ed., *Studies in Early Old English Prose* (Albany, 1986), pp. 87–108.

Mostert, Marco and P.S. Barnwell, eds, *Medieval Legal Process: Physical, Spoken and Written Performance in the Middle Ages* (Turnhout, 2011).

Muinzer, L.A., 'Maier's Transcript and the Conclusion of Cynewulf's "Fates of the Apostles"', *Journal of English and Germanic Philology*, 56 (4) (1957), 570–87.

Neidorf, Leonard, ed., *The Dating of Beowulf: A Reassessment* (Cambridge, 2014).

Nelson, Janet, 'The First Use of the Second Anglo-Saxon *Ordo*', in Julia Barrow and Andrew Wareham, eds, *Myth, Rulership, Church and Charters* (Aldershot, 2008), pp. 117–26.

Nightingale, John, 'Oswald, Fleury and Continental Reform', in Nicholas Brooks and Catherine Cubitt, eds, *Oswald of Worcester: Life and Influence* (Leicester, 1996), pp. 23–45.

O'Brien O'Keeffe, Katherine, 'The Text of Aldhelm's Enigma no. c in Oxford, Bodleian Library, Rawlinson C. 697 and Exeter Riddle 40', *Anglo-Saxon England*, 14 (1985), 61–73.

———, 'Body and Law in Late Anglo-Saxon England', *Anglo-Saxon England*, 27 (1998), 209–32.

———, *Stealing Obedience: Narratives of Agency and Identity in Later Anglo-Saxon England* (Toronto, 2012).

Ó'Carragáin, Eamonn, 'Rome, Ruthwell, Vercelli: "The Dream of the Rood" and the Italian Connection', in V.D. Corazza, ed., *Vercelli tra Oriente ed Occidente tra Tarda Antichità e Medioevo: atti delle Giornate di studio: Vercelli 10–11 aprile 1997, 24 novembre 1997* (Alessandria, 1997), pp. 59–99.

Orchard, Andy, 'Artful Alliteration in Anglo-Saxon Song and Story', *Anglia*, 113 (1995), 429–63.

———, *Pride and Prodigies: Studies in the Monsters of the* Beowulf *Manuscript* (Toronto, 1995/2003).

———, *A Critical Companion to* Beowulf (Cambridge, 2003).

———, 'Both Style and Substance: The Case for Cynewulf', in Catherine E. Karkov and George Hardin Brown, eds, *Anglo-Saxon Styles* (Albany, NY, 2003), pp. 271–305.

———, 'Enigma Variations: The Anglo-Saxon Riddle Tradition', in K. O'Brien O'Keeffe and A. Orchard, eds, *Latin Learning and English Lore: Studies in Anglo-Saxon Literature for Michael Lapidge*, 2 vols (Toronto, 2005), vol. I, pp. 284–304.

Ortenberg, Veronica, 'Archbishop Sigeric's Journey to Rome', *Anglo-Saxon England*, 19 (1990), 197–246.

———, *The English Church and the Continent in the Tenth and Eleventh Centuries: Cultural, Spiritual, and Artistic Exchanges* (Oxford, 1992).

Pelteret, David A., *Slavery in Early Mediaeval England from the Reign of Alfred until the Twelfth Century* (Woodbridge, 1995).

———, 'Travel between England and Italy in the Early Middle Ages', in Hans Sauer and Joanna Story, eds, *Anglo-Saxon England and the Continent* (Tempe, AZ, 2011), pp. 245–74.

———, 'An Anonymous Historian of Edward the Elder's Reign', in Stephen Baxter, ed., *Early Medieval Studies in Memory of Patrick Wormald* (Farnham, 2009), pp. 319–36.

Powell, T.E., 'The Three Orders of Society in Anglo-Saxon England', *Anglo-Saxon England*, 23 (1994), 103–32.

Pratt, David, 'The Voice of the King in "King Edgar's Establishment of the Monasteries"', *Anglo-Saxon England*, 41 (2013), 145–204.

Rahtz, Philip, and Donald Bullough, 'The Parts of an Anglo-Saxon Mill', *Anglo-Saxon England*, 6 (1977), 15–37.

Rahtz, Philip, and Lorna Watts, *Glastonbury: Myth and Archaeology* (Stroud, 2009).

Ramsay, Nigel, Margaret Sparks, and Tim Tatton-Brown, eds, *St Dunstan: His Life, Times and Cult* (Woodbridge, 1992).

Reuter, Timothy, ed., *Alfred the Great: Papers from the Eleventh-Centenary Conferences* (Aldershot, 2003).

Richards, J.D., *Viking Age England* (Stroud, 2004).

Roberts, Jane, Janet Nelson and Malcolm Godden, eds, *Alfred the Wise: Studies in Honour of Janet Bately* (Cambridge, 1997).

Robertson, Nicola, 'Dunstan and Monastic Reform: Tenth-century Fact or Twelfth-century Fiction?' *Anglo-Norman Studies*, 28 (2006), 153–67.

Robinson, Fred C., 'The Significance of Names in Old English Literature', in his *The Tomb of Beowulf and Other Essays*, pp. 185–218.

———, *The Tomb of Beowulf and Other Essays on Old English* (Cambridge, MA and Oxford, 1993).

Rollason, David, Conrad Leyser and Hannah Williams, eds, *England and the Continent in the Tenth Century: Studies in Honour of Wilhelm Levison (1876–1947)* (Turnhout, 2010).

Rowley, Sharon, 'Bede in Later Anglo-Saxon England', in Scott DeGregorio, ed., *The Cambridge Companion to Bede* (Cambridge, 2010), pp. 216–28.

———, *The Old English Version of Bede's Historia Ecclesiastica* (Cambridge, 2011).

Rumble, Alexander R., 'The Churches of Winchester and Wessex', in N.J. Higham and D.H. Hill, eds, *Edward the Elder, 899–924* (London, 2001), pp. 236–7.

———, ed., *Writing and Texts in Anglo-Saxon England* (Cambridge, 2006).

———, ed., *Leaders of the Anglo-Saxon Church from Bede to Stigand* (Woodbridge, 2012).

Salvador-Bello, Mercedes, 'The Edgar Panegyrics in the *Anglo-Saxon Chronicle*', in Donald Scragg, ed., *Edgar, King of the English, 959–975* (Woodbridge, 2008), pp. 252–72.

Sawyer, Peter, *Anglo-Saxon Charters: An Annotated List and Bibliography* (London, 1968).

———, 'The Last Scandinavian Kings of York', *Northern History*, 31 (1995), 39–44.

Schreiber, Carolin, 'Searoðonca hord: Alfred's Translation of Gregory the Great's *Regula Pastoralis*', in Nicole Guenther Discenza and Paul E. Szarmach, eds, *A Companion to Alfred the Great* (Leiden and Boston, 2015), pp. 171–99.

Scragg, Donald, 'An Old English Homilist of Archbishop Dunstan's Day', in Michael Korhammer, ed., *Words, Texts and Manuscripts: Studies in Anglo-Saxon Culture Presented to Helmut Gneuss* (Cambridge, 1992), pp. 181–92.

———, ed., *Edgar, King of the English, 959–975* (Woodbridge, 2008).

Scragg, Donald, and Carole Weinberg, eds, *Literary Appropriations of the Anglo-Saxons from the Thirteenth to the Twentieth Century* (Cambridge, 2000).

Sisam, Kenneth, *Studies in the History of Old English Literature* (Oxford, 1953).

Smith, Scott T., 'Marking Boundaries: Charters and the Anglo-Saxon Chronicle', in Alice Jorgensen, ed., *Reading the Anglo-Saxon Chronicle: Language, Literature, History* (Turnhout, 2010), pp. 167–85.

———, *Land and Book: Literature and Land Tenure in Anglo-Saxon England* (Toronto, 2012).

Smyth, A.P., *King Alfred the Great* (Oxford, 1995).

Snook, Ben, *The Anglo-Saxon Chancery: The History, Language and Production of Anglo-Saxon Charters from Alfred to Edgar* (Woodbridge, 2015).

Stafford, Pauline, 'Charles the Bald, Judith and England', in Margaret T. Gibson and Janet L. Nelson, eds, *Charles the Bald: Court and Kingdom* (Oxford 1981, rpt Aldershot, 1990); reprinted in Stafford, *Gender, Family and the Legitimation of Power*, pp. 139–53.

———, *Unification and Conquest: A Political and Social History of England in the Tenth and Eleventh Centuries* (London, 1989).

———, *Gender, Family and the Legitimation of Power: England from the Ninth to Early Twelfth Century* (Aldershot, 2006).

———, 'The Anglo-Saxon Chronicles: Identity and the Making of England', *Haskins Society Journal*, 19 (2007), 28–50.

———, '"The Annals of Æthelflæd": Annals, History and Politics in Early Tenth-Century England', in Andrew Wareham and Julia Barrow, eds, *Myth, Rulership, Church and Charters: Essays in Honour of Nicholas Brooks* (Aldershot, 2008), pp. 101–16.

———, ed., *A Companion to the Early Middle Ages: Britain and Ireland c.500–c.1100* (Oxford, 2013).

Stephenson, Rebecca, 'Scapegoating the Secular Clergy: The Hermeneutic Style as a Form of Monastic Self-definition', *Anglo-Saxon England*, 38 (2010), 101–35.

Stodnick, Jacqueline A., 'The Interests of Compounding: Angelcynn to Engla land in the Anglo-Saxon Chronicle', in H. Magennis and J. Wilcox, eds, *The Power of Words:*

Anglo-Saxon Studies Presented to Donald G. Scragg on his Seventieth Birthday (Morgantown, WV, 2006), pp. 337–67.

Story, Joanna, *Carolingian Connections: Anglo-Saxon England and Carolingian Francia, c. 750–850* (Aldershot, 2003).

Szarmach, Paul, ed., *Studies in Early Old English Prose* (Albany, 1986).

——, ed., *Old English Prose: Basic Readings* (New York, 2000)

Thacker, Alan, 'Æthelwold and Abingdon', in Barbara Yorke, ed., *Bishop Æthelwold: His Career and Influence* (Woodbridge, 1997), pp. 43–64.

Thomas, Edward, *The South Country* (London, 1909).

Thornbury, Emily V., *Becoming a Poet in Anglo-Saxon England* (Cambridge, 2014).

Tollerton, Linda, *Wills and Will-making in Anglo-Saxon England* (York, 2011).

Toswell, M.J., 'Psalters', in Richard Gameson, ed., *The Cambridge History of the Book in Britain Volume I, c.400–1100* (Cambridge, 2012), pp. 468–81.

——, *The Anglo-Saxon Psalter* (Turnhout, 2014).

Townend, Matthew, 'Pre-Cnut Praise-Poetry in Viking Age England', *The Review of English Studies*, 51 (2000), pp. 349–70.

Turner, James, *Philology: The Forgotten Origins of the Modern Humanities* (Princeton and Oxford, 2014).

Vanderputten, Steven, 'Canterbury and Flanders in the Late Tenth Century', *Anglo-Saxon England*, 35 (2006), 219–44.

——, Steven Vanderputten, 'Flemish Monasticism, Comital Power, and the Archbishops of Canterbury: A Written Legacy from the Late Tenth Century', in David Rollason *et al.*, eds, *England and the Continent in the Tenth Century. Studies in Honour of Wilhelm Levison (1876–1947)* (Turnhout, 2010), pp. 67–86.

Waite, Greg, 'Translation Style, Lexical Systems, Dialect Vocabulary, and the Manuscript Transmission of the Old English Bede, *Medium Aevum*, 83 (1) (2014), 1–48.

——, 'The Preface to the Old English Bede: Authorship, Transmission, and Connection with the West Saxon Genealogical Regnal List,' *Anglo-Saxon England*, 44 (2015), 31–93.

Webster, Leslie, and Janet Backhouse, *The Making of England: Anglo-Saxon Art and Culture AD 600–900* (London, 1991).

Whitelock, Dorothy, 'Wulfstan Cantor and Anglo-Saxon Law', in A.H. Orrick, ed., *Nordica et Anglica: Studies in Honor of Stefán Einarsson* (The Hague, 1968), pp. 83–92; reprinted in her *History, Law and Literature in 10th–11th Century England* (London, 1981), no. V.

Wieland, Gernot, 'A New Look at the Poem "Archalis clamare triumuir"', in Gernot Wieland, C. Ruff and R.G. Arthur, eds, *Insignis Sophiae Arcator: Essays in Honour of Michael W. Herren on his 65th Birthday* (Turnhout, 2006), pp. 178–92.

Winterbottom, Michael, 'The Style of Æthelweard', *Medium Ævum*, 36 (1967), pp. 109–18.

Wood, Michael, *In Search of the Dark Ages* (London, 1981).

Woolf, Alex, 'View from the West: an Irish Perspective on West Saxon Dynastic Practice', in N.J. Higham and D.H. Hill, eds, *Edward the Elder, 899–924* (London, 2001), pp. 89–101.

——, *From Pictland to Alba, 789–1070* (Edinburgh, 2008).

Wormald, Francis, *Collected Writings I, Studies in Medieval Art from the Sixth to the Twelfth Centuries*, ed. J.J.G. Alexander (London, 1984).

Wormald, Patrick, 'Charters, Law and the Settlement of Disputes in Anglo-Saxon England', in Wendy Davies and Paul Fouracre, eds, *The Settlement of Disputes in Early Medieval Europe* (Cambridge, 1986), pp. 149–68; reprinted in his *Legal Culture in the Early Medieval West*, pp. 289–311.

330   THE MAKING OF ENGLAND

——, 'Handlist of Lawsuits', *Anglo-Saxon England*, 17 (1988), 247–81.

——, *Legal Culture in the Early Medieval West: Law as Text, Image and Experience* (London, 1999).

——, *The Making of English Law: King Alfred to the Twelfth Century* (Oxford, 2001).

——, *The Times of Bede: Studies in Early English Christian Society and its Historian*, ed. Stephen Baxter (Oxford, 2006).

Wright, Charles, *The Irish Tradition in Old English Literature* (Cambridge, 1993).

Yorke, Barbara, ed., *Bishop Æthelwold. His Career and Influence* (Cambridge, 1988).

Young, Robert J.C., *The Idea of English Ethnicity* (Malden, MA and Oxford, 2008).

Zacher, Samantha, *Preaching the Converted: The Style and Rhetoric of the Vercelli Book Homilies* (Toronto, 2009).

Zacher, Samantha, and Andy Orchard, eds, *New Readings in the Vercelli Book* (Toronto, 2009).

Index

Words in languages other than modern English are shown in bold, and etymologies and specialised modern English words and concepts are given in inverted commas. Page references to images are given in italics. The letter A is followed by Æ, then B, and so on through the normal order of the alphabet.

Hugh, Duke of the Francs, 146
hundred, 250–1
hunting, 186–90, *187*
'Hwæt!', 'listen, attend', 172, 291

Iceland, 19, 125, 160–1
Icknield Way, 36, 38, 55
'Iohannes', name, 74–5, 139, 141, 149
Irish scholars, 16, 25, 27, 72, 75, 202
Irvine, Susan, 134
Itchen, River, 83, 256, 258
itineraries, 9–10, 21–4, 32

James, deacon at York, 101
Jerusalem, 19, *20*, 282, *282*
John the Old Saxon, 55, 72–5, 114,
    140–1, 235
John of Worcester, 213
Jorvik Viking Centre, 214
journey, theme of, 9–11, 13–14, 21–5,
    30–48
journey charm, Old English, 33–4
Judith, queen of Wessex and Kent,
    daughter of Charles the Bald,
    47–8, 115, 129
Judoc, St, Life of, 261

Kent, 19, 36, 48, 90–3, 116, 218, 241
    libraries, 29–30, 42, 251
    literacy in, 60, 65, 67, 75
kingship, 27–8, 90, 101–4, 253–4, 279
    succession crises, 111–16, 144–5,
        148, 226
Kingston-on-Thames, 144

'labours of the months', 44–6, *46*
'ladder', as image, 81
land-holding, 37–8, 107, 122, 133, 145,
    149, 250–1
    (*see also* bocland; charters;
        declarations; will)
Lantfred, Frankish author, 177, 256,
    266–71, 274–5
Lapidge, Michael, 74, 140, 266
Latin language, 11, 24, 87, 177
    Anglo-Latin, 2, 149, 216
    'Book-Latin', 155
    grammar, 44–5
    'Hermeneutic' Latin, 149, 175, 265
    Hiberno-Latin, 16, 27, 202,
        295 n.23
Laurentius, archbishop of Canterbury, 88

laws, 30, 59–60, 124, 240, 248–51
    (*see also* declarations)
Leicester, 107, 131
    (*see also* Five Boroughs)
Lejre, Denmark, 39, 296 n.15
Leneghan, Francis, 129
Liber Vitae, 'Book of Life', 24, 45, 228
Lilla, Northumbrian thegn, 95, 97
Lindisfarne, 152, *156*
Lindisfarne Gospels, *see* gospel books
Liofa, thief, 213
lion, as image, 14, 32, 61, 180, 200
literacy, 53, 57, 59–76, 122–3, 127, 143
Lombards, 23–4, 77
London, 55–6, 88, 257–8
Longinus, spear of, 146
lordship, 1, 45, 75, 86, 116, 118–19, 159,
    165, 171, 232, 251
    (*see also* **hlaford**)
loyalty, 35, 96–7, 119, 215–16, 250

Maier, Johann Caspar, 30–1
Maldon, The Battle of, Old English poem,
    86, 113, 159, 165, 222
Malmesbury, 75, 140, 144
mancus, a measure of gold, 79, 148,
    248, 262
manual labour, monastic virtue, 229,
    233–4
manumissions of slaves, 146
maps, 18–20, *20*, 32–3, 38
Marcward, abbot of Prüm, 24
Marinus, Pope, 22
markets, 56, 116, 258, 270–1, 273
    (*see also* **ceapstræt**)
marriage, 46–7, 55, 70, 107, 114–15, 146,
    208, 242
Matilda, abbess of Essen, 208–9
memory, 37, 71, 158–71, 213
Mercia, 21, 25, 36, 53, 55, 101–2, 104,
    107, 119–20
Mercian Register, 120–1
metalworking, 45, 62, 125, 201–2
Metres of Boethius, Old English poem,
    137–8, 142, 171–3
Midwinter (Christmas), 47, 102, 253–4
Molyneaux, George, 89
monks, 76, 92, 175–6
monsters, 17, 19, 40, 163, 181, 188

New Minster, Winchester, 117, 144,
    223, 228, 258, 261–2

CPSIA information can be obtained
at www.ICGtesting.com
Printed in the USA
LVHW010130010821
694234LV00018B/1264